THE LEVIATHAN
OF WEALTH

THE LEVIATHAN
OF WEALTH

The Sutherland Fortune in the Industrial Revolution

Eric Richards

School of Social Sciences
The Flinders University of South Australia

Foreword by Professor S. G. Checkland

LONDON: Routledge & Kegan Paul
TORONTO: University of Toronto Press

First published 1973 in Great Britain by
Routledge & Kegan Paul Limited
and in Canada and the United States of America by
University of Toronto Press
Toronto and Buffalo
Printed in Great Britain by
Ebenezer Baylis and Son Ltd
The Trinity Press, Worcester, and London

RKP ISBN 0 7100 7455 7
UTP ISBN 0 8020 1956 0
UTP Microfiche ISBN 0 8020 0300 1

To Jessie, Marian,
Jane, Cindy, Louise and Sally

Contents

	Page
Foreword by S. G. Checkland	ix
Preface	xix
Abbreviations	xx

Part One   Leviathan of Wealth

I	The House of Sutherland	3
II	James Loch, 'The Sutherland Metternich'	19

Part Two   The House of Sutherland and the Coming of the Railways

III	The Problematical Inheritance	37
IV	The Challenge and the Response	49
V	The Way of Compromise	56
VI	A Position of Influence	73
VII	The Edge of the Precipice	85
VIII	A Golden Opportunity	94
IX	Transport Capitalism in the Early 1830s	106
X	Uneasy Co-existence	118
XI	Into and Out of the Vortex	135

Part Three   The Sutherland Clearances

XII	Sutherland and the Highland Problem	151
XIII	William Young and Patrick Sellar	169
XIV	The Reaffirmation of the Sutherland Policy	196
XV	Capital, Labour and Prices in the New Economy	220
XVI	Progress, Poverty and Criticism	243
XVII	Famine and the Final Years	262

Part Four   Perspectives

XVIII   The Uses of an Aristocratic Fortune   283

    Bibliography   299
    Index   309

Illustrations

Facing page

1a   Elizabeth Gordon, 1765–1839 (by courtesy of the
     Scottish National Portrait Gallery, Edinburgh)   140
1b   George Granville Leveson-Gower, 1758–1833 (by cour-
     tesy of the Scottish National Portrait Gallery, Edinburgh)   140
2   Harriet Elizabeth Georgiana Leveson-Gower, 1806–68
     (by courtesy of the Scottish National Portrait Gallery,
     Edinburgh)   141
3   James Loch, 1780–1855 (by courtesy of the National
     Portrait Gallery, London)   172
4   Patrick Sellar, 1780–1851 (reproduced by kind permission
     of the Trustees of the National Library of Scotland)   173

Maps

Page

1   Connections between Liverpool and Manchester, 1830
    (after G. O. Holt, *A Short History of the Liverpool and
    Manchester Railway*, 1965)   38
2   Old and new routes connecting Lancashire and the
    Midlands   40
3   The distribution of ownership in Sutherland in 1810 and
    the new sheep farm of Patrick Sellar in Strathnaver in
    1814 (after Thomas Sellar, *The Sutherland Evictions of
    1814*, 1883)   152
4   Sutherland in 1820, showing some of the consequences
    of the clearances (after James Loch, *An Account of the
    Improvements on the Estates of the Marquess of Stafford*,
    1820)   154

Foreword

The immensely wealthy aristocratic family of Sutherland and their remarkable agent, James Loch, were much concerned in two of the great changes of the first half of the nineteenth century in Britain. These were the supercession of the canals by the railways and the conversion of Highland agriculture to pastoralism. Each of these two themes in its own way challenges the analytical capacity of historians and evokes strong human feeling. The one represents the greatest burst of promotional activity of the nineteenth century, and the other was one of the most tragic and emotive incidents in the long death of traditional peasant society in Britain.

To James Loch both were elements in the complex and changing situation that confronted him as one of the great estate managers of the day. Loch was a Scotsman, a member of that brilliant generation of young men at the University of Edinburgh during the Napoleonic Wars who created the *Edinburgh Review*. With his friend Henry Brougham the young Loch shared an intense interest in the Enlightenment and the hopes for human improvement that were built upon it. But his life was to be led not, as with Brougham, in the public eye, but as the man of business of a great family. The House of Sutherland was wealthy and powerful in both England and Scotland. The management of its estates, continuously bled by extraordinary family extravagance at a time of racking economic and social change, demanded much skill.

In Dr Richards's study there is an interplay of great interest between Loch as an individual, his ducal employers, and their enormous collection of assets. His book tells us of Loch and his problems as a leading aristocratic factotum: through him it gives new perspectives on the birth of railways, the management of widespread landed estates, and the Highland clearances. Faced with what was accessible of the vast muniments of the Sutherland family, these are the themes Richards has chosen.

First, then, there is Loch as an individual, and as an outstanding exemplar of that important class of men upon whom aristocratic landed society so much depended, the stewards of great estates. Loch required to understand estate management in both England and Scotland in the practical sense of how to get things done: the same was true of railway promotion. But, in addition, in explaining his policies and actions to himself and others he required a philosophy of economics, politics and society. For a Scot of his background, operating so intimately on the lives of others, was bound to seek a rationale. To begin with, in spite of youthful Whiggism he could be no radical, for his life was devoted to the interests of an aristocratic family. His code as the Duke's 'doer' was one of conservative amelioration: 'The object of all improvement', he wrote, is 'the increase of the comforts of life to the lower ranks and the elegances of life to the higher.' He continually reminded his master the Duke that political and social influence rested upon the possession of land; he sought to restrain his master from disposing of land, especially in Scotland, as the income derived from it fell and the public criticism of the family's dealings with the peasantry increased. Land was also, in Loch's view, the best long-term form in which to hold wealth. It may be, as Dr Richards suggests is possible, that Loch's attitudes in this respect owed something to the ideas of contemporary political economy, especially the emphasis placed by Ricardo and others on the increase in rentals that was bound to come with rising population. On other matters, certainly, Loch was a hard-minded economist and believed his ideas to be confirmed by his experience. In carrying out the clearance policy in Sutherland he resisted any alleviation of pressure on the Highlanders for fear that, given the slightest chance, they would not make the necessary move to a new place and a new way of life. Even when famine threatened Loch was unwilling to provide meal at less than the market price (or indeed to allow the government to do so), because he was afraid that if the state interfered in the supply and demand situation the market would become deranged. This brought him into conflict with the Duke. For Loch, as for the authors of the Poor Law Report of 1834, there was always a danger that mistaken

charity would 'paralyse the exertions of the industrious and encourage the less active'. Loch was, moreover, a Malthusian; it was
perhaps not surprising that he feared man's capacity to procreate
beyond his productivity.

The eclipse of the canals by the railways now seems one of the great
inevitabilities of the age. It did not seem so at the time. The men
involved, as is always the case, did not perceive obsolescence so
quickly or so clearly as do those who look back over telescoped
time. Loch's responsibility was to advise the Stafford–Sutherland
family on the part they should play in this great transition.

Stafford held very large estates in Shropshire, north-west of
Birmingham. These not only comprised one of the biggest and most
productive landed holdings in England; they were also in an area of
rapid industrialization, so that the family inevitably became involved in the regional communications system, especially its canals.
In 1803 the family had inherited the celebrated and highly profitable
Bridgewater Canal, the most important artery in south Lancashire,
joining the two great centres of commerce and industry, Liverpool
and Manchester. The Sutherlands were, therefore, heavily committed
in the two great areas of nascent English industry, and in the country-
side between. The inevitable implication was that they would be
involved in linking the two. It is perhaps not too much to say that
the Liverpool–Manchester nexus was the primary cradle of the
transport revolution, involving the unification of a region, and that
the connection between Lancashire and Birmingham and the
Midlands was the secondary one, involving the linking of two
regions, and eventually contributing to the larger trunk system
joining London, Birmingham, Liverpool and Manchester. The
attitude of so great a landed family, so situated, could have repercussions upon railway and canal promotion that went far beyond
the ventures in which the family had a direct interest. For Parliament
(consisting largely of landowners) had to be persuaded to accept
railway and canal Acts. Moreover, capitalists could be greatly reassured if the landed interest were prepared to share the financial risk.

When Loch became Stafford's factor in 1812 the Bridgewater
Canal was doing well. There was no real thought of a challenge to it,
much less of any attempt to form a major connection with Birmingham. The management of the canal was in the hands of R. H. Bradshaw, who had become an intolerable autocrat, levying as much as

he could on goods between Liverpool and Manchester. In 1822 the much aggrieved business community of Liverpool saw the prospect of relief; it proposed to build a railway to supersede the canal. So began phase one of Loch's problem in transport economics. His first reaction was that the canal management should anticipate the challenge. He urged upon Bradshaw a more reasonable rating policy so that the support for the railway could be diminished below the level of effective action. Bradshaw in his arrogance refused. The formation of the Liverpool and Manchester Railway Company in 1824 was the result. On its second attempt it secured its Act of Parliament in 1826 against the hostile manœuvres of the canal interest. But its commercial success was by no means certain. Three great questions hung over it: was the technical potential of the steam locomotive adequate, how costly would the capital works be, and, finally, could sufficient capital be raised? In a sense, the last was the crucial question for the Directors of the Company.

It was so for Loch and his masters also. The Directors of the Railway looked to the Sutherland family: the family found itself in the position of having to decide between railway and canal. Moreover, the decision to invest had to come before the technical question could be answered and before the full cost could be known. In the end the Marquis of Stafford, on Loch's advice, sank £100,000 in the Railway, acquiring about one fifth of the shares. The family had decided to hedge its bets: Dr Richards's account of this critical step, including the part played by Huskisson as the mediator on the part of the government between canal and railway interests, is of great interest.

But now an even larger question was looming. Loch knew very well that with a railway, as well as a canal, running east-west across South Lancashire, further projects to join with Birmingham and the Midlands were inevitable. He knew also that great though the unknowns had been with the Liverpool–Manchester link, that with Birmingham would involve much larger ones. For who was to say whether the railways would succeed as rivals for the heavier loads— agricultural produce, industrial raw materials and coal?

In Loch's view neither railway nor canal potential had yet been really tested. So far as canals were concerned, Loch believed that given efficient management, capital improvements (possibly steam-powered barges), and a reasonable schedule of rates, they might well keep the heavier loads. But they would do so only if the canal men

responded in a positive and constructive way. Loch urged them not
to repeat the failure that had helped to provoke the Liverpool and
Manchester Railway into being. To give them time he used delaying
tactics, blocking several schemes for a Liverpool/Manchester to
Birmingham railway.

Among the initiators of such schemes were the Directors of the
Liverpool–Manchester Railway (in which the Duke was the major
shareholder), who naturally wished to repeat their success on a
large scale. They wished Stafford to support the new venture as he
had done the old. He seems to have come near to doing so in 1830,
but now hesitated.

Indeed, the Marquis and Loch had already committed themselves
to the canal as the best link. The Birmingham and Liverpool Junction Canal was begun by Telford in 1827, with large financial support
from Stafford. Telford ran into great difficulties, his costs rose in a
frightening way, and the period of construction lengthened. But it
was useless to look for a canal response. With men like Bradshaw
so prominent it is not surprising that the canal men failed to act
effectively.

At this critical stage Loch suddenly found his responsibility much
reduced. His master, who had acted in a positive, not to say dramatic,
way in supporting the Liverpool–Manchester Railway, now, after
coming close to committing himself to the new line, suddenly withdrew into neutrality. He would neither support nor oppose the
Birmingham railway link. Here again Richards ponders his reasons.
Among them was the commitment to Telford's canal with its shocking costs, and an unwillingness to face the bitterness of public
arguments. No doubt, too, there was the fact that the Grand
Junction represented railway investment on an altogether new and
more frightening scale.

The Grand Junction Railway Company was formed in 1833 to
undertake the great venture. The Liverpool–Manchester Directorate,
who had hoped to be the sponsors of a Birmingham link, were split
as to their future policy. For now it was necessary to come to terms
with the Grand Junction lest it should build its own Liverpool–
Manchester line or sponsor another company to do so. In this
matter Loch came into play once more. This time his role was that
of reconciling the interests of the Liverpool–Manchester Railway,
the Bridgewater Canal and the Grand Junction Railway. At the
same time he had to act so as to protect Stafford's large holding,

now greatly increased in value, in the Liverpool–Manchester Railway. He negotiated a difficult and uneasy Carriers' Agreement. But merger was the inevitable outcome: it came in 1845. In the following year a much larger concern, the London and North-Western Railway, embraced the new company.

Professors Fogel and Fishlow have given a new dimension to discussion of the historical relationship between railways and canals, using the development of transport in the American West as the basis of their thinking. Richards, in studying the situation confronting Loch, has had to deal with one in which both railways and canals were present, in actual or potential competition. As he demonstrates, Loch tried to find a basis for judgment by deferring decision as long as possible, at the same time encouraging the canal men to demonstrate, by performance, their true capacity. The manner and the timing of the coming of the railway system, and the shape it assumed, were much affected by such considerations. Moreover, there is a fascination in projecting oneself back into the position of men like Loch who had to live through the birth of the railways as preoccupied and worried decision takers.

But the worry over canals and railways was never so disturbing to Loch as that over the Highland estates. The territorial principality of the Sutherlands in Scotland was a kind of Highland *latifundia*. It was of enormous extent but of very low value per acre, with a density of population that had outrun any prospect of reasonable livelihood, let alone social progress. It consisted of the greater part of a peninsula of hill and mountain. It was orientated upon its eastern coast to which its river systems mainly drained. In dramatic contrast with the English estates it was utterly remote from the changes being wrought by the industrial revolution and the spread of high farming.

The population lived largely where they had always done, in the glens in 'the high interior', relying on an inefficient system of cattle raising and upon the oats that could be grown in the cultivable parts of the valley bottoms or were imported with the proceeds of cattle sales. These elements, together with the potato, were the slender and precarious basis of the life of the glens. The population was permanently at subsistence level and was highly vulnerable to famine.

The people spoke the Gaelic; their physical isolation was reinforced by the barrier of language and culture. They knew nothing of towns; indeed their settlements were hardly villages. They certainly did not work hard for there was no incentive to do so. Nor were other factors of production available to which their labour could be applied. Yet they had always paid rents, though on a modest scale.

To a Lowlander like Loch, and *a fortiori* to his ducal masters, this was a population of primitives, full of sloth and indolence, immune to the notions of thrift, sobriety and disciplined effort, and prompt to prey upon more progressive people through theft, chiefly of sheep. Moreover, they had always exposed themselves, through their demographic behaviour, to the danger of famine; this could only get worse. Loch with his background in Scottish moral philosophy had fleeting moods in which a kind of cultural relativism passed through his mind: 'All mankind', he remarked, 'must be allowed to a certain extent to be happy in their own way'. But he put it no higher than this: neither he nor anyone he knew had any sense that the Highlander had a language and a culture worthy of preservation. Indeed, the contrary was the case. Loch's natural reaction to what he saw in the Highlands was to seek to change it. But he knew that change had to be introduced carefully. 'The ancient customs of a people are not to be rashly innovated upon', he wrote; it was necessary that their minds be gradually prepared for change.

Well before Loch's time it had become apparent that there was an alternative formula for Highland estates. Clearances on a considerable scale had been carried out on the Sutherland estates and elsewhere since the later eighteenth century. It was Loch's task to design and execute a much wider strategy: in effect a development plan. Its elements were: to remove the population from the interior, bringing them down to the coastal areas, and to some extent to aid emigration. The vacated straths and glens would then be given over to sheep pasturage, thus providing the main element in estate income. But some part of this income (all of it indeed in the earlier decades) was to be used to create new employment opportunities. The chief of these was the development of fisheries, together with harbours, houses and ancillary trades. The kelp industry too could yield some employment and income. There was to be industry also, as with the coal and salt workings at Brora, together with a brewery and brick and tile works. The people were settled on lots which allowed them to raise food on a family basis. All this was to be reinforced by improvements in communications, especially by the building of roads. So the attempt was made to create a viable regional economy in Sutherland.

In this programme, through thick and thin, Loch never lost confidence. In one sense there was grounds for it. Such an experiment called for the provision of capital on a large scale from outside. This was forthcoming from the more fertile acres of the English estates, reinforced by railway and canal revenues.

But there were two great difficulties. One was the removal of the population from the hills to the coast, with the irreparable rupture of all the old ties. Inevitably, coercion and violence took place. In its worst form it came not from the Duke's factors or servants, but from one of his tenants. It was Patrick Sellar, a sheep farmer in Kildonan Strath who, anxious to get on with his sheep rearing, used the clearance methods that so distressed Loch and the Duke and which have provided the lasting basis of the charge of inhumanity, joining Sellar and Captain Boycott in infamy.

The other problem, more difficult in practice though not emotionally, was: could the coastal economy, so heavily dependent upon the fisheries, be made capable of supporting the population? It would seem that neither Loch nor anyone else attempted to quantify the challenge thus presented. No calculation of the numbers to be moved from the glens and their allocation to the various coastal settlements was made. It would seem as though the elements of the programme, clearance and reception, were often out of step, causing hardship to the 'lotters' when they arrived at the coast. Much less was there an effort to assess the number of jobs to be created by the new investment. There seems to have been no drawing upon the experience of others who had tried, at least in part, this kind of programme, for example, the Dukes of Argyll. Only on the basis of direct experience did Loch learn that the sheep farms did not need to be so large as was originally planned, nor did they need to abandon self-support entirely. For a certain amount of arable cultivation, including that of turnips for the sheep, could provide useful diversification.

Loch's attitude was that the condition of the Highlander could not be left as it was, for it was bad and would get worse. There was no alternative but to carry out the programme.

Yet there were constraints. One arose from the continued public criticism of clearances, led by *The Times* correspondent. The other was the unwillingness of the Duke to continue to subsidize the

Scottish from the English estates. Loch and the Duke had tried to act as a kind of Highland Board, treating Sutherland as a planning region, 'borrowing' capital from elsewhere, setting the sheep rents against deficits on the coastal employments, and hoping, over time, to create some slight surplus. But economic viability escaped them. More and more Loch and the Duke came to accept the hard conclusion that the necessary self-supporting employment could not be created and that there was no alternative to emigration. There was no formula indeed upon which the Sutherland families could be put in a position to support themselves, even when they had borne the painful change of leaving the glens.

The contrast between the two situations within which Loch had to think, decide and administer is striking. In the railway–canal case it was not possible to impose an overall solution. It was necessary for the respective potentials of the two modes of carriage to be tested, and to reconcile the two in terms of an investment programme. The Stafford–Sutherland family, wealthy and powerful though it was, had to operate within a situation with enormous implications, over which it had very partial control. There was never any sign of Loch or his master assuming any sort of masterful attitude in the railway world, as did George Hudson later. In the case of the Sutherland estates, on the other hand, control was almost total. In an isolated, self-contained situation, the family could do as it saw fit. But it was unable to find a satisfactory solution.

Did Loch have the estate agent's bias towards land? Could he have achieved a better economic return for his masters had he taken a wider view of investment opportunities in the first half of the nineteenth century? It might well be argued, so far as the Sutherland estates were concerned, that the Duke would have been financially better off to have simply left the Highlanders to themselves, abandoning his rights as landlord, and investing the surplus from his English assets elsewhere. But the outlook of a territorial magnate and especially that of his steward could be compulsive, for it was a case of role fulfilment, compounded of habit, tradition, paternalism and the somewhat mystical belief that the land and its tenants properly administered were the best investment.

What this man of immense business capacity thought of the family he served is not clear. His conviction that the Duke and his kind were essential to the stability and well-being of the nation is plain enough (though it is of course much less plain how far this view of

social organization grew upon him as his years of service to territorial grandees lengthened). In the more immediate sense his feelings towards his masters would presumably have two main facets,
depending upon the support they gave their agent in promoting
sound policies in the management of the estates, and, secondly, on
their behaviour as spenders. On the former Loch and men of his
kind could often have a profound influence. Indeed, they might
well take policy effectively into their own hands. But, on the spending side, matters were much more delicate. Loch could and did urge
the family to reduce its outlays, pointing out the revenue limitations
on the estates. But when it came to criticizing the lavish hospitality,
the palace building and other extravagances of the family, Loch
had always to beware of intruding. His career was lived out under
the shadow of spending so heavy as to impair the provision of new
capital required to improve or even to maintain long-term income.
Loch, as a middle-class professional man whose life was given over
to conserving his master's assets and maximizing their earning power,
had to do so under a nobleman whose spending was not far from
feckless. (Did it ever occur to Loch that the Highlander with his
rejection of thrift and his inability to think in terms of longer-term
planning shared these characteristics with his ducal master?)

In a sense Loch's career, for all the skill and devotion he showed,
was a failure, for the long story of declining family income and
falling capital values dominated the last quarter-century of his life,
and indeed continued after his death. That he was subject to great
stress appears from his recurrent anxiety dream as his end approached:
he imagined himself in Sutherland 'always striving to reach Tongue
as the place in which he hopes to find quiet and repose'.

Whether on more general grounds Loch's life was of a kind in
which he and his family might justifiably take pride is for the reader
of Dr Richards's book to decide. This question is of course related
to one that is broader still: how do we cast up the balance sheet for
the landed aristocracy and their agents in England and Scotland
between the Napoleonic Wars and the Great Exhibition?

S. G. Checkland

Preface

This book is about one of the largest inherited fortunes in modern British history. It is concerned mainly with the deployment of the great Sutherland wealth in two areas of the industrializing economy of the early nineteenth century—in transport innovation in Lancashire, and in the promotion of economic change in the Scottish Highlands. The structure of the book is dominated by these geographically-separate areas of enterprise connected with the Sutherland family. They are linked by ownership, by the career of James Loch who did so much to guide the family's interests in both spheres, and by the notion that both were characteristic but contrasting responses to the unique expansion of the national economy during the Industrial Revolution.

Some of this work began under the supervision of the late Professor J. D. Chambers at the University of Nottingham. This particular draft was virtually completed in July 1969. I have received a great deal of help from Professor S. G. Checkland who not only provided the Foreword, but read through the entire manuscript and made many useful suggestions. Mrs Monica Clough gave me invaluable help by introducing me to parts of the Highlands previously unknown to me. Mrs R. M. Mitchison saved me from several errors. But all the remaining imperfections of style, structure, fact and interpretation are mine alone. Over several years Mr F. B. Stitt and his colleagues gave me much assistance in my searches at Stafford County Record Office. The universities of Adelaide and Stirling gave financial assistance towards the research that underlies this book, for which I thank them. Not least is my gratitude to Miss Betty Neech and Mrs Brenda Wilson for cheerfully typing successive versions of the manuscript.

Bridge of Allan

Abbreviations

AR	*Annual Register*
BAP	Blair Adam Papers
DNB	*Dictionary of National Biography*
EBC	Ellesmere–Brackley Correspondence
EcHR	*Economic History Review*
JEH	*Journal of Economic History*
OSA	*Old Statistical Account of Scotland, 1790–8*
NLS	National Library of Scotland
NSA	*New Statistical Account, 1835–45*
PP	*Parliamentary Papers*
SC	Sutherland Collection, Stafford CRO. All references are to Estate Correspondence (D593K) unless otherwise stated
SHR	*Scottish Historical Review*
SJPE	*Scottish Journal of Political Economy*
TGSI	*Transactions of the Gaelic Society of Inverness*
TRHS	*Transactions of the Royal Historical Society*

Part One

Leviathan of Wealth

I

The House of Sutherland

The Sutherland fortune was an unrivalled concentration of aristo-cratic wealth in the 'Age of Improvement'. It had been caught up in that unpredicted expansion of the national economy that we now know as the Industrial Revolution. This great and complex process, at once dramatic, cumulative and virtually unprecedented, generated new tensions and pressures in every corner of British life. Rapid economic growth is always a disturbing and often a dislocating experience. Any society undergoing it is committed to continuous change and adjustment. In Britain there was no example to follow, no planners to guide the process, and no specific machinery of government to influence the course of the change. Yet somehow the revolution of the economy was contained, the social framework did not break asunder. Somehow the dislocation of traditional social relationships was minimized.

It is perhaps symptomatic of the gradual nature of social change that, in vital areas of national life, Britain remained an aristocratic country throughout the nineteenth century. Although the relative position of the aristocracy had been undermined by the transforma-tion of the economy, its capacity for survival in an increasingly alien world is a curious historical phenomenon. At the beginning of the twentieth century the landed aristocracy still retained a surprisingly large share of economic resources, political importance and, of course, social esteem. The diminution of landed authority was peaceful, gradual, without revolution.

In the first half of the nineteenth century the Great Governing Families of England[1] lived in a world characterized by unprecedented

[1] J. L. Sanford and M. Townsend, (1865) *The Great Governing Families of England.*

3

change and by irksome political questions. One of the greatest of such families, the richest, the most powerful, and the most disliked, was the House of Sutherland—an Anglo-Scottish alliance of aristocratic connections then reaching the zenith of its wealth and power. Of all the tall poppies of British society—including the Dukes of Devonshire, Bedford and Northumberland, the Egremonts and the Rockinghams—the Sutherland family was probably the tallest in terms of both income and acres.

The affairs of the House of Sutherland were inevitably involved in the general metamorphosis of the nation. In contemporary eyes the Sutherland family was mainly associated with three facets of its activities. First, and most conspicuously, the family had become a leader of fashionable society life in London—at Stafford House, the largest and most gorgeous of London's private palaces. The diaries and memoirs of the early nineteenth century speak long and admiringly of the splendid entertainments offered by the Duchesses of Sutherland at Stafford House. As intended, they attracted envious attention. Second, the House of Sutherland endured a rising tide of public wrath and obloquy provoked by the economic policies undertaken on its estates in the extreme north of Scotland. These policies were part of a general movement known as the Highland clearances. The depopulation of the Scottish Highlands generated a substantial body of pamphleteering and polemical literature both then and since; it remains a controversial subject and is likely to continue so. Third, the name of Sutherland was associated with a formidable accumulation of property—territorial and financial. Its wealth was renowned, exaggerated and awed. The 1st Duke of Sutherland was variously described as the richest man in Europe, the richest in England, the most wealthy member of the aristocracy— almost invariably, he has received the sobriquet of 'Leviathan of Wealth'.

The historical significance of the Sutherland family derives almost entirely from the wealth which gave it power and initiative in many areas of national life. Apart from their inherited privileges the Sutherlands are not especially interesting—they tended to conform to the accepted norms of aristocratic behaviour, they were intellectually rather limited and their political attitudes were largely unexceptional. Yet the history of the family in the early nineteenth century illuminates the economic and social changes of the time, and the response of the aristocracy to these changes. The Sutherland

4

interest involved many aspects of British existence: canals and railways, iron and coal, agricultural improvement and the resettlement of population, political influence and electioneering, social conflict and the role of paternalism in the new society, even literature and fine art.

Most of all, the Sutherland fortune allowed the family to pursue two great and contrasting experiments in the early nineteenth-century economy. One was set in the heart of industrial Britain—the promotion of railway technology in its pioneering phase. The other was located on the periphery, in a distinctly pre-industrial context—it was an attempt to transmit rapid economic growth to a traditional peasant economy in the Highlands.

What were the antecedents of the Sutherland wealth? Vicissitudes of marriage and descent largely determined the course of the familial fortune. Disraeli remarked, without much exaggeration, that the family had made good by its talent for 'absorbing heiresses'. The most spectacular example of this occurred in 1785 when George Granville Leveson-Gower married Elizabeth Gordon, Countess of Sutherland. It was the prelude to the effective convergence of two ancient families, one English, the other Scottish, and it laid the foundation for the family's social ascendancy in the nineteenth century.

On the English side were the Leveson-Gowers, their wealth and position the product of earlier alliances. The Gower element had been settled at Stittenham, Yorkshire, since the time of the Norman Conquest. They remained relatively obscure country squires until the seventeenth century; in 1620 Thomas Gower obtained a baronetcy from James I. He married the daughter and co-heiress of Sir John Leveson—and eventually, in 1689, the properties of the Levesons were joined with those of the Gowers, in the hands of Sir William Leveson-Gower.

The Levesons were a Staffordshire family. They had 'acquired great riches' in the sixteenth-century wool trade and invested heavily in land in the Midlands—particularly in land thrown on the market during the reign of Henry VIII. Trentham, which was to be the main landed seat of the family, had been an Augustinian priory before the dissolution. A Royalist family, the Levesons suffered during the Civil War, but recovered sufficiently by the end of the seventeenth century to rebuild their house at Trentham.[2]

---

[2] Sanford and Townsend, op. cit., I, 266–75. James Loch, 'Memoir of George Granville, late Duke of Sutherland' (1834, not published).

At the beginning of the eighteenth century the family possessed three landed estates—in Yorkshire (Stittenham), Salop (Lilleshall), and Staffordshire (Trentham). The rise of the Leveson-Gowers had begun. In 1865 they were described as 'the luckiest of the great English families. They have risen within 250 years from simple country baronets into the greatest . . . territorialists in Great Britain.' The same authorities commented that 'the source of their dignity has been a succession of lucky alliances . . . The pedigree, though curiously uncertain, is by no means a bad one as English nobles go.'[3]

The accretion of wealth and dignity proceeded during the eighteenth century. Sir John Leveson-Gower (1675–1709) became a peer in 1702. He was ennobled when Queen Anne needed a Tory majority in the Lords to impeach the Duke of Portland. He became Baron Gower of Stittenham. His wife was the daughter of the Duke of Rutland, who furnished a portion of £15,000. Their son began his political life as a Jacobite, but changed his allegiance to the Hanoverians. In 1746 he was created Viscount Trentham and Earl Gower, his reward for loyalty in raising a regiment to confront the Jacobite Rebellion. He died in 1754, considerably richer than his father had been.

Thus far his family had achieved an earldom, good connections with other aristocratic families, a consolidated position in Staffordshire politics, and a respectable territorial establishment. The foundations of a great Whig family were being laid. The luck of the Leveson-Gowers was not confined to felicitous marriages and political adroitness. In 1720 Lord Gower was involved in the select circle of men who perpetrated the South Sea Bubble affair. Gower apparently made one of the largest gains—he sold out before the Bubble burst and took a reported profit of £64,000. He had certainly bought £20,000 worth of stock and it is probable that he sold it at a profit of 300 per cent.[4]

In 1754 Granville Leveson-Gower (1721–1803) succeeded as the 2nd Earl Gower. In political history he was the most celebrated and important of the Leveson-Gowers. In a turbulent and rather erratic political career he was for many years Lord Privy Seal and President of the Council. In the early part of the reign of George III he was a member of the 'Bedford Group'—he was connected by marriage to the Dukes of Bedford and Bridgewater, and the Earls of Galloway

---

[3] Sanford and Townsend, op. cit., 266.
[4] SC, D593P/16/2/4/14. J. Carswell, *The South Sea Bubble* (1960), 116, 267.

THE HOUSE OF SUTHERLAND

and Carlisle. He was described as 'a boon companion, with the best cook in London, a man whose sweetness of nature made him a power in the Cabinet'. In 1768 the Bedfords felt that Gower ought to be prime minister,[5] and in 1771, after the death of Bedford, Gower took over the leadership of the remnants of the Bedford group.

The 'Gower Party' was an influential grouping and was held together largely by family connections. In October 1778 Gower resigned from North's government; he told the king that there was 'a want of activity, decision, or subordination in every department', particularly in the administration of the American War and of Irish affairs. Only a coalition, he declared, could avoid the 'impending ruin'—'no man of conscience could any longer' sit in the Cabinet. He remained at the centre of political affairs, but his ambitions were limited. He was willing to form the centre of a union of political interests, but had little desire for leadership. It is said that he 'had sufficient resolution' to refuse the post of prime minister on the fall of Shelburne in 1783, but he joined Pitt's Cabinet in the following year. In 1786 he became 1st Marquis of Stafford—another reward for political services.[6]

In the latter part of his life Stafford withdrew from political affairs, although he maintained a very considerable electoral influence. His wife said of him, 'he loves his own place in the country, is a great farmer, likes his ease, is in very good circumstances, and happy at home.' He was thrice married. His second marriage was immensely important for the future advance of the family fortunes. In 1748 he married Lady Louisa Egerton, the eldest daughter of Scroop, and favourite sister of the heirless Duke of Bridgewater. He began the connection with the Canal Duke which later developed into a major involvement in the evolution of the transport sector of the British economy. Stafford fathered four children by this marriage. When the Duke of Bridgewater died in 1803 he left the profits of his famous canal to Stafford's first son. It was a most lucrative inheritance. The 1st Marquis of Stafford died in the same year.

The recipient of the canal profits was George Granville Leveson-Gower (1758–1833), Lord Trentham, Earl Gower, and (in 1803)

[5] K. G. Feiling, *The Second Tory Party, 1714–1832* (1959), 107, 128.

[6] Feiling, op. cit., 133. A. Aspinall, *Later Correspondence of George III* (1962), I, 8. E. Fitzmaurice, *The Life of Lord Granville* (1905), I, 1–2. I. R. Christie, *The End of North's Ministry* (1958), 206. L. Namier and J. Brooke, *History of Parliament: The House of Commons, 1754–1790* (1964), I.

2nd Marquis of Stafford. He was created 1st Duke of Sutherland in the year of his death. He was 'a dull, nervous man with a large, beaky nose and a prim mouth', a man generally thought to have been dominated by his brilliant wife. Educated at Westminster and Oxford, he cultivated his taste for classical scholarship, philology, botany and chemistry. As a young man he was noted for his shyness and lack of interest in politics. On Burke's advice he was sent to learn French at Auxerre and he travelled abroad for two years. In 1778 he entered the Commons where he represented Staffordshire seats until he went to the House of Lords in 1798.[7]

In 1790, at the age of thirty-two, and without previous diplomatic experience, he became ambassador to Paris, only quitting with the hurried withdrawal of the embassy in 1792. During that distraught period his wife became a close friend of Marie Antoinette, to whom she sent clothes when the Queen was imprisoned. Their eldest son was a playmate of the Dauphin. On his return to England Gower was offered the position of Lord Steward, and the Lieutenancy of Ireland, both of which he refused—mainly because of failing eyesight. Instead he accepted the office of Joint Postmaster-General, which he held from 1799 to 1810.[8]

While not as prominent as his father, Gower was by no means a passive figure in political life. He gave loyal support to the Pitt administration, but in 1804 'he felt the Addington administration to be inadequate, and took a leading part in the formation of a strong government.' In 1807 he moved a resolution condemning the King's conduct on the Roman Catholic question, which was defeated. Failing eyesight and, perhaps, growing hypochondria led him to retire from politics in 1812, and he 'devoted himself to the improvement of his estates and the patronage of the arts'. Very much the improving landlord of the early nineteenth century, he possessed a fortune which allowed him to indulge his tastes for progressive ideas in agriculture. But increasingly the initiative slipped into the hands of his son, his wife, and his agents. His health was a source of mounting anxiety in the 1820s. But he was still head of a large political influence—in 1819, Creevey observed that 'old Stafford uttered an opinion that is worth ten votes at least in the House of Commons'. The influence suffered a diminution in the 1820s, and Stafford

[7] Namier and Brooke, op. cit., III. Loch, op. cit. G. Huxley, *Lady Elizabeth and the Grosvenors* (1965), 15.
[8] R. Gower, *My Reminiscences* (1883), 78.

gained the reputation of being a liberal in his political views, supporting Catholic emancipation, Huskisson's commercial policies, and the Reform Bill—in November 1830 the family were described as 'violent reformists'.[9]

When it was suggested that Stafford had supported Reform in order to obtain a dukedom, his second son, Lord Francis, commented that 'the poor old man had no such thoughts, but was frightened at the idea of losing the present title and estates and supported the Reform Ministry out of mere cowardice and dotage.' Lord Francis relinquished the representation of Sutherland in 1831—probably because he refused to join the rest of the family in their support of the Reform Bill.[10]

Lord Stafford had first visited Scotland in 1780. 'He performed this tour on horseback, availing himself of the hospitality of the inhabitants, and he became thoroughly acquainted with the disposition of the people.' Five years later he married the Countess of Sutherland—another lucky alliance since 'Elizabeth Sutherland brought her husband at her wedding the whole county of Sutherland [a slight exaggeration] in her *corbeille de mariage*, a province for a *dot*!' This was the Scottish strand of the family.[11]

Elizabeth, Countess of Sutherland and Baroness of Strathnaver, (1765–1839) was the only surviving child of William Gordon, 17th Earl of Sutherland—a title which had 'a length of succession unparalleled in the peerage of this country'. The parents of the Countess died of putrid fever at Bath in 1766 when their daughter was one year of age. 'In the five and a half centuries of the family's existence no Earl of Sutherland had died without a male heir.' There was a good deal of dispute concerning the succession of the infant Countess, and it was only after considerable litigation that the succession was secured in 1771. The inheritance was worth fighting for. Situated in one of the most remote areas of the British Isles, the Sutherland estates comprised between 800,000 and one million acres. It was a wild northern empire insulated by its remoteness from the main current of affairs in the south.[12]

[9] Loch, op. cit. H. Maxwell (ed.), *The Creevey Papers* (1904), I, 336. F. Leveson-Gower (ed.), *Letters of Harriet, Countess Granville, 1810–1845* (1894), II, 62.

[10] Huxley, op. cit., 81. SC, Loch to Gunn, 16–3–1831, 30–5–1831.

[11] Loch, op. cit. Duke of Sutherland, *The Story of Stafford House* (1935), 39.

[12] D. Stewart, *Sketches of the Character, Manners and Present State of the Highlanders of Scotland* (1822), I, 166n. Sutherland, op. cit., 39. AR (1771), XIV, 84.

The infant heiress was placed in the care of Lady Alva, her maternal grandmother in Edinburgh. This was later said to have been the origin of her alleged alienation from the people of her Sutherland estates—she was educated by her ambitious grandmother in the south, 'far removed from the influence of those general sympathies with the people of her clan for which her ancestors had been so remarkable, and in the faith of a church not theirs'. During her minority, the affairs of the Countess were arranged by a number of tutors whose directives were executed by a General Commissioner of the estates.[13]

The teenage Countess was taken to London in 1779, not returning to Scotland until 1782 when she visited her ancestral home at Dunrobin Castle on the east coast of Sutherland. 'From this date the Countess took an active interest in her estates, and from time to time made representations to her tutors regarding them.' But she lived mainly in London and Edinburgh. After her marriage in 1785 Dunrobin was fitted out at great expense.[14]

At the age of twenty-seven she accompanied her husband to Paris. Her passport described her as 'five feet in height, hair and eye-brows light chestnut, eyes dark chestnut, nose well formed, mouth small, chin round, forehead low, face somewhat long'. When young she was regarded as a woman of great beauty: her admirers included Pitt, Huskisson, Canning, Sir Walter Scott, and Talleyrand. When she was forty-eight, Byron wrote of her, 'She is handsome, and must have been beautiful, and her manners are princessly.' She was also the object of a good deal of scurrilous gossip. Sylvester Douglas retails several allegations of her *liaisons dangereuses*. He records that the physician treating Lord Stafford's failing eyesight recommended that 'he must strictly abstain from all conjugal intercourse with his wife.' However, during the period of abstinence 'unluckily her Ladyship proved with child'—Lord Francis. The father, it was said, was Lord Carlisle, Stafford's brother-in-law. The rumours were widely believed but totally unverifiable. When she was seventy Creevey thought the Countess had 'all the appearance of a wicked old woman'. During the early decades of the nineteenth century her charm and wealth were put on exhibition at the extravagant centre of aristocratic life in London. She was a leading hostess

---

[13] *The Times*, 26-5-1845. R. J. Adam (ed.), *John Home's Survey of Assynt* (1960), xix ff.

[14] W. Fraser, *The Sutherland Book* (1892), I, 466-8.

of her day. More privately she spent her time raising four children, sketching, corresponding with Sir Walter Scott, and consuming snuff.[15]

Although the Countess and her husband lived mainly in England they were directly involved in the administration of their northern realm. They visited it annually in the summer season. By southern standards the income of the Sutherland estates was by no means commensurate with the acreage. It is likely that the estates were in financial difficulties before the Countess married into the Leveson-Gowers, and this may have been an inducement for the alliance. Nevertheless, after the conjunction of the two families, the empire was extended. Adjoining estates of impecunious lairds were added to the main body, especially in the 1820s. The family regarded the land purchases as promoting the reunification of their ancient Sutherland properties which had been dispersed in previous centuries. The *Quarterly Review* observed that the Sutherland territory amounted to almost $1\frac{1}{2}$ m. acres, 'a single estate certainly not in these days equalled in the British Empire, and in the same hands of the same peer who enjoyed also the English estates of the Gowers and the Levesons with the canal property of the Bridgewaters'.[16]

The 'great lady of Sutherland' achieved a considerable degree of notoriety during her lifetime. This was largely the result of the Sutherland clearance policies which were undertaken in her name, though they were financed by her husband. Until his death in 1833 the English and Scottish estates were administered as though they were one property. But from 1833 to her death in 1839, the northern estates were treated quite separately for the benefit of the dowager Duchess/Countess of Sutherland (as she was then known).

The northern estates then reverted to her son—the 2nd Duke of Sutherland (1786–1861) who, in 1833, had succeeded to the rest of the family property—with the crucial exception of the Bridgewater Canal.[17] The estate of the 1st Duke in the province of Canterbury

[15] Fraser, op. cit., I, 466–8, 478. D. Marshall, *The Rise of George Canning* (1938), 152–7. P. J. V. Rollo, *George Canning* (1965), 33–4. C. R. Fay, *Huskisson and his Age* (1951), *passim.* Maxwell, op. cit., II, 306. N. L. Smith (ed.), *Letters of Sydney Smith* (1952), II, 615. F. Bickley (ed.), *The Diaries of Sylvester Douglas* (1928), II, 27–8.

[16] Fraser, op. cit., I, 306, 480–1. J. Loch, 'Dates and Documents relating to the Family and Property of Sutherland' (1859, not published). *Quarterly Review*, LXIX, 421.

[17] Under the terms of the complex Bridgewater Will of 1803, the income of the Bridgewater Trust (on the death of the 1st Duke of Sutherland) went to the second son—Lord Francis Leveson-Gower (later Egerton), 1st Earl of Ellesmere.

alone was valued in excess of £1 m. Greville exclaimed that 'he·was a leviathan of wealth; I believe the richest individual who ever died.'[18] There were notable offshoots of the House of Sutherland—for example, the Egertons and the Granvilles—and their aristocratic relations were impeccable.

The 2nd Duke was forty-seven when he succeeded his father. A rather sensitive man, he played a less energetic role in political life than his two predecessors. In 1820 he withdrew ignominiously from a vital Staffordshire election contest; thereafter he took no great interest in politics. A descendant described him as 'one of the most excellent of men', but 'so deaf that he withdrew himself early from affairs, and attended only to the management of his estates . . . he was very liberal in his political views.' Parliament held little attraction for him: 'I know of little other advantage to be gained from it', he wrote in 1808, 'but that of being able to frank letters, and I am not sufficiently in debt to make it desirable on that account; and I can hear the debates now whenever I wish. And as to speaking—not much chance of that.' Election campaigns were a torture to him. He was sometimes bored with society life in London. In 1809 he wrote to his friend Sharpe from Dunrobin: 'You may take it for granted that I feel quite happy to be breathing the pure air of the Highlands, and that I was really beginning to be tired of the endless dissipation of London, which can amuse any sensible person, such as we are, only for a very short time—the same thing over and over and over, without variety.'[19] Yet, in later years, he was to add his own overflowing measure to metropolitan dissipation.

He remained a bachelor until he was thirty-seven, by which time most people had given up hope for him. His reluctance to marry was ascribed to his enduring and frustrated love of Queen Louise of Prussia. In 1813 he emphatically asserted his determination not to marry. Ten years later he relented and married the seventeen-year-old Harriet, third daughter of George Howard, 6th Earl of Carlisle. Like his father, he took a wife socially more brilliant than himself. She 'was built, mind and body, on a large scale and overflowing with *joie de vivre*'. She luxuriated in splendour and extravagance and

[18] H. Reeve (ed.), *Greville Memoirs* (1888), III, 20. For a sympathetic portrait of the family circle, see Huxley, op. cit.

[19] Sutherland, op. cit., 30. A. Allardyce (ed.), *Letters from and to Charles Kirkpatrick Sharpe* (1888), I, 330–2, 378; II, 34. F. Leveson-Gower, op. cit., I, 96. Dowager Duchess of Argyll (ed.), *George Douglas, 8th Duke of Argyll, Autobiography and Memoirs* (1906), I, 223–4.

undoubtedly dominated her deaf husband: 'they lived whirling lives, combining a devastating social life with a great deal of travelling and the raising of a family of eight children.' Their lives centred around Stafford House and their several country residences. At the same time, however, the 2nd Duke was intimately concerned with the administration of his many properties; and, despite his retiring nature, he was more active than his father in dealing with the mundane affairs of his estates. He felt a direct responsibility for the welfare of his tenants: in 1846–8 he suffered real emotional stress while grappling with the appalling rigours of the potato famine in Sutherland. He died in 1861.[20]

Bateman, in 1883, estimated the wealth of Britain's landowners. In acreage Sutherland headed the list, with *c.* 1,300,000 acres in Scotland and *c.* 32,000 acres in England. In terms of rental income Sutherland came fifth, with £141,000 per annum. These figures referred to the property of the 3rd Duke who acceded in 1861. It was claimed that he was 'distinguished only for his interest in suppressing fires—a useful but eccentric taste'. But this is probably a rather unkind verdict on a man who took an active and expensive interest in the agriculture of the Highlands and who sponsored the construction of the Highland Railway to the extent of almost £$\frac{1}{4}$ m. In the twentieth century the estates of the House of Sutherland have gradually slipped out of the hands of the family. 'The direct descendants have been as a race respectable and even useful', wrote Sanford and Townsend tartly, 'but their fortunes have been beyond their deserts.'[21]

In the first half of the nineteenth century the House of Sutherland was at the height of its expansionary phase—when its influence on the economy and society was at its greatest. The financial basis of this influence was virtually unshakeable. It derived from the rental income of landed estates in Scotland and England; from the expanding profits of the Bridgewater Trust; from dividends of shareholdings in canal and railway companies, and from government and private stock. In the latter years of his life the 1st Duke received a gross annual income of almost £200,000.

[20] Sutherland, op. cit., 9. Allardyce, op. cit., II, 68. Lady Leconfield and J. Gore (eds.), *Three Howard Sisters* (1955), II. J. Cornforth, 'Trentham, Staffordshire', *Country Life*, 25–1–1958, 179.

[21] J. Bateman, *Great Landowners of Great Britain* (1883), 431. Sanford and Townsend, op. cit., 275. F. M. L. Thompson, *English Landed Society in the Nineteenth Century* (1963), 322, 329.

The demands upon an aristocratic fortune were manifold. Heavy outlays were devoted to the improvement of the estates through long-term schemes of agricultural investment. There was a stream of purchases of land and miscellaneous property. The Dukes of Sutherland were great builders: all their residences were either reconstructed or altered at enormous expense. Large sums were invested in railway and canal shares and in other stock. Money was spent on the preservation of political influence, particularly in the early part of the period. There were certain fixed items of expenditure —maintenance, repairs, expenses of management and so on. Finally, there were the family expenses—portions, pin-money, living expenses, travel, entertainment—a style of living which, in the 1830s, cost about £40,000 per year at Stafford House alone.[22]

It would not be difficult to convey an impression of the opulence and conspicuous consumption of the Sutherlands. They were not ascetic. Fellow aristocrats and others found their wealth strangely disturbing. The family maintained substantial country houses at Lilleshall, Trentham and Dunrobin. On the death of the Duke of Bridgewater in 1803, Cleveland (late Bridgewater) House in London passed to Lord Stafford together with its libraries and galleries, to which Stafford added his own remarkable collection of pictures. The Stafford Collection, valued at £150,000, was one of the finest in Europe and was well worthy of its surroundings. In 1806 Lady Beaumont was moved to remark of Bridgewater House: 'the long succession of rooms, their spaciousness and loftiness had such an effect that people in [them] look like Lilliputians, which produced one good effect, all awe of people was done away for no one seemed of consequence enough to make any particular impression.' She added that the style of living of the Marquis of Stafford 'exceeded everything in this country, no one could vie with it'. Such was the London house of the Sutherland family: derived from and supported by the profits of the increasingly lucrative Bridgewater Canal.[23]

The country seats were also impressive and provided seasonal relief from the *longueurs* of London life. There is a description of Lilleshall in Shropshire written by Stafford's sister-in-law in 1810. So idyllic was Lilleshall that she began

to wish for something or some place to dislike, as I think my eternal raptures much sicken all my friends and acquaintances . . . Lord Stafford

[22] SC, Jackson to Loch, 9–3–1840.
[23] Huxley, op. cit., 60. J. Grieg (ed.), *Farington Diaries* (1923), III, 189, 236.

... is abominably rich, and there is so little to make one feel that his immense wealth is well lodged in his hand ... when I see his canals, and his coals, and his timbers, and in short all his properties, I feel as I suppose Whittington's Cat did when she travelled over the Marquis of Carrabas's territory.

Lilleshall was extensively reconstructed by Wyatville in the 1820s in order to provide a suitable home for the heir of the family.[24]

Less cosy, but much grander than Lilleshall, was Trentham Hall in Staffordshire. It was an immense Italianate palace set amid ornate gardens, pleasure grounds, broad terraces and woods and an elaborately planned lake. It was a sanctum of the most refined version of aristocratic ease but it contrasted uncomfortably with the less elegant environs of the Potteries situated not far from its gates.

The family lavished vast supplies of income and energy in an effort to make Trentham perfect in every way. They employed the best architects, the finest materials, the most tasteful decorations, the best available craftsmen and gardeners. As Lord Ronald Gower put it in 1883, 'Nothing can be less suggestive of beauty than that district of ... the Potteries. There it seems always muddy and miserable, squalid and unclean. Yet within a couple of miles of Stoke lies this wonderful garden of Trentham, gay with hanging woods mirrored in its still lake.' The extravagant incongruity of Trentham came to symbolize one half of the 'Two Nations'—an effect sharpened by the withdrawal of the family from local affairs in the 1820s. Trentham Hall was the most obvious target for popular political agitation in Staffordshire in the 1820s and 1830s.[25]

A similar response was evoked by Dunrobin Castle in Sutherland. Creevey referred to it as ' "Cock Robin" Castle at the other extremity of Scotland'. Modernized and improved, rebuilt and refurnished, Dunrobin attracted a growing seasonal migration of friends and relatives of the family—they were keen to establish a fashion for the glories of the Highland summer. Grouse shooting, salmon and trout fishing and deer stalking became major attractions. Each visit was 'a source of eagerly anticipated pleasure'. Indeed, the Sutherland family was fully immersed in the cult of medievalism and the 'tartan frenzy', which did so much to distort the realities of Highland life in the nineteenth century. But the veneer of Highland

---

[24] Castalia, Countess Granville (ed.), *Lord Granville Leveson-Gower, Private Correspondence, 1781–1821* (1917), II, 363.

[25] F. Leveson-Gower, op. cit., I, 29–34.

romanticism did little to insulate the family from sneers against 'the tyranny and intrigues of English proprietors and holiday Celtic chiefs'.[26]

The rank of the family in metropolitan society life was much enhanced in 1827 when Stafford acquired York House, thereafter known as Stafford House. The construction of this palace had begun in 1825 by the heir-presumptive, the Duke of York, who had resolved to raise 'an edifice not unworthy of Vicenza in its best days, though on a far more extensive style than any pile that city boasts'. However, York died in 1827, irretrievably in debt, with the building incomplete. It seems that he had borrowed £60,000 from Lord Stafford for its building costs: this was never repaid. In rather peculiar circumstances, the Government purchased York House for nearly £82,000 and then leased it to Stafford for £72,000 with an annual rent of £758. But this was only the beginning of the financial liability attaching to Stafford House. Within thirteen years the family spent a further £150,197 on completing and extending the building, and £53,357 on decoration and furniture—it was 'the last of the great houses decorated with all the pomp and magnificence of the days of Louis XIV's reign'.[27]

Nor were the country seats neglected. Lilleshall Hall was largely rebuilt between 1826 and 1834 at a cost in excess of £80,000. Building at Trentham in the 1830s cost £123,000. Alterations at Dunrobin Castle between 1844 and 1848 amounted to about £60,000. Cliveden House in Buckinghamshire was in 1849 bought for about £30,000, but soon after was destroyed by fire and rebuilt.[28]

In his novel *Lothair*, Disraeli captured the spirit of Stafford House (i.e. Creçy House)—where fabulous entertainments were graced by 'Princes of the Blood and grandees of the Golden Fleece ... The palace, resonant with fantastic music, blazed amid illuminated gardens'. Another novelist, Harriet Beecher Stowe, was fascinated by the retinue of stately Highlanders and 'what seemed to be an innumerable multitude of servants in livery, with powdered wigs, repeating our names through the long corridors, one to another.'[29]

[26] Huxley, op. cit., 50. See H. J. Hanham, 'Mid-century Scottish Nationalism', in R. Robson (ed.), *Ideas and Institutions of Victorian Britain* (1967).
[27] Gower, op. cit., 7. Earl of Ilchester (ed.), *Lady Holland and her Son* (1946), 66. SC, Loch to Duncannon, 6–5–1841; Loch to Mackenzie, 30–6–1827.
[28] SC, Hughes to Loch, 8–1–1834; Loch to Sutherland, 27–8–1849.
[29] O. F. Christie, *The Transition from Aristocracy* (1927), 19–20. H. B. Stowe, *Sunny Memories of Foreign Lands* (1854), I, 289.

Queen Victoria, visiting Stafford House, is reported to have said to her hostess, 'I have come from my house to your palace.' Charles Greville (in 1835) noted in his diary that he had attended 'a great concert on the staircase of Stafford House, the most magnificent assembly I ever saw, and such as I think no crowned head in Europe could display, so grand and picturesque ... The splendour, the profusion and the perfect ease of it all were really admirable.' Greville also reported that Queen Victoria (in 1839) had been reluctant to confer the Garter on the Duke of Sutherland—'partly because she disliked the Duchess of Sutherland and partly because she fancied the Duke was already too great with his riches and magnificence and she did not wish to aggrandize him'. The 2nd Duchess, indeed, frankly acknowledged her happy position: 'We are so well off that there can be no cause of uneasiness in any respect with regards to any of our worldly goods, of which there is such a plentiful abundance for us.'[30]

The 2nd Duchess 'made her assemblies the most sought after in London'. Somehow, she managed to combine the most luxurious and extravagant entertainments with a soothing patronage of charity and freedom: her causes included the conditions of life of prisoners, paupers, coal-miners, Poles, Italians, and slaves. Shaftesbury described her as 'my dear and steady friend, most zealous, serviceable and high-minded'. A specific measure of her social influence occurred in 1859 when the depressed silk-weavers of Spitalfields begged the Duchess to accept a roll of newly-coloured magenta silk to be made into a dress to make it fashionable: fashionable it became and the Spitalfields looms were working night and day within a few weeks.[31]

In the middle of the century the prestige of Stafford House was refreshed by

a succession of illustrious guests who were welcomed within its walls ... Italian patriots, Poerio and his heroic band of patriots, fellow sufferers of Bourbon tyranny, recently in Neopolitan dungeons, Garibaldi the Deliverer, clad in his famous red shirt and grey cloak, Livingstone, Mrs Stowe, Charles Sumner, and scores of American abolitionists, besides a host of princes, potentates and magnates from the Shah of Persia to the Queen of Honolulu.

[30] H. Reeve (ed.), *The Greville Memoirs* (1888), III, 285. R. Gower (ed.), *Stafford House Letters* (1891), 184. B. Falk, *The Bridgewater Millions* (1942), 150.
[31] Sutherland, op. cit., 9, 30.

John Bright had been present at the reception of Garibaldi in 1864 and was struck with the incongruity of the scene. [32]

> It was a singular spectacle to see the most renowned soldier of Democracy cared for as by a loving daughter by a Lady who is Countess and Duchess, at the head of the aristocracy of England. Lord Stanley said to me a day or so ago, I wonder if it ever occurs to the Duke that if Garibaldi had his way there would be no Dukes of Sutherland.

Students of élites, it has been remarked, should concern themselves with 'the interrelation and interaction of ... political power, economic strength and social prestige or magnetism'. [33] The conspicuous consumption of the House of Sutherland represents only one aspect of its activities—the icing on top of the cake.

It may be that the Marxian emphasis upon the conflict between bourgeoisie and proletariat in nineteenth-century Britain has diverted attention away from the role of the territorial aristocracy in the economy. [34] The Sutherland 'Leviathan of Wealth' is probably the most remarkable demonstration of the uses of an aristocratic fortune in an age of economic revolution. The following chapters explore the character of their involvement in this broader process.

---

[32] Gower, *Reminiscences*, 3. R. A. J. Walling (ed.), *The Diaries of John Bright* (1930), 275.

[33] H. J. Perkin, quoted in D. Spring, 'English landed society in the eighteenth and nineteenth centuries', *EcHR*, August 1964, 150.

[34] See O. R. McGregor, 'Research possibilities for family study', *British Journal of Sociology*, 1961.

II

James Loch, 'The Sutherland Metternich'

In August of the year 1812 it was reported, somewhat peevishly, that 'The Staffords seem to have turned their thoughts entirely to economy and the society of Scotch agents.'[1] At approximately that date James Loch entered the service of the House of Sutherland. Thenceforward, until his death in 1855, Loch was the major instrument in the direction and execution of the economic policies of the family. An Edinburgh intellectual, lawyer, economist, financial expert, M.P., estates commissioner, political agent, apologist, family historian and antiquarian, as well as trusted friend, Loch was a dominant influence in the life of the family. He as much as anyone determined the uses of the Sutherland fortune.

Loch was born at Drylaw near Edinburgh in 1780. He was a lowland Scot—a point which his Highland critics never allowed themselves, or others, to forget. He came from the ranks of the fallen Jacobite gentry. The Loch family had acquired the estate of Drylaw in 1641, having accumulated 'great wealth' apparently in the sixteenth-century Baltic trade. During the seventeenth and early eighteenth centuries the Lochs busied themselves in 'civic and wider affairs' and had built up considerable landed wealth. But the upward progress of the family was not to continue. In 1769 George Loch succeeded to the estates; thereafter began the deterioration of the Loch fortunes. There were several reasons. The estate was burdened with a heavy debt. Part of it derived from the prodigality of his predecessors. Part of it followed the decision of the family to help sponsor the Stewart Court at Rome; £10,000 is said to have been

---

[1] F. Leveson-Gower (ed.), *Letters of Harriet*, I, 39.

placed at the disposal of James VII and his descendants. It was an expensive loyalty with few rewards. George Loch decided to live in Italy—'in a retired manner, both for the sake of his health and also in order to reduce the burden of debt which had been imposed on the estate.' Moreover, in his absence the estate at Drylaw was mismanaged. The inevitable upshot was the sale of the Loch estates in 1786, and the ignominious retreat of George Loch to an impecunious existence in England. In 1788 he died—'of a broken heart'.[2]

With the finances of the family similarly broken, James Loch, the eldest son, was brought back to Scotland from England. He lived with his uncle, William Adam, at his Blair Adam estate near Kinross. The Adams were an immensely talented family and still justly renowned for their contribution to eighteenth-century architecture. William Adam was a lawyer and politician of considerable influence; he occupied a central role in national politics; he was counsel to the East India Company and in 1816 became Lord Chief Commissioner of the Scottish Jury Court. Loch was fortunate to spend his formative years with the Adam family. It was an instructive training for his future career. In addition to his other accomplishments William Adam was an 'improving landlord'—the family transformed a wild, desolate moor into an estate 'which was surpassed by few in the country'. This result was achieved by drainage, afforestation, landscape gardening and sixty miles of roads and paths. James Loch thus became well-versed in the practices and details of estate supervision.[3]

In 1797 Loch was studying law at Edinburgh University. Here he entered a charmed circle of extremely able young men—including Francis Horner, Sydney Smith, Jeffrey, Lord Henry Petty, Charles Grant, Cockburn, John Murray and Henry Brougham. It was the world of the Speculative Society in 'perhaps the most brilliant period in the Society's history'—with a membership (limited to thirty) which 'inspired a high tone of virtue'. This remarkable confluence of youthful talent produced its permanent memorial in the *Edinburgh Review*. Indeed, Loch's intellectual background has been characterized as 'the rationalist milieu of the *Edinburgh* reviewers'. His time

[2] Gordon Loch, *The Family of Loch* (1934), 236 ff. J. P. Wood, *The Ancient and Modern State of the Parish of Cramond* (1794), 28–9.

[3] T.M.T., *Distinguished Men of the County, or Biographical Annals of Kinross-shire* (1932). D. E. Ginter, 'The financing of the Whig party organisation, 1783–1793', *American Historical Review*, LXXI. G. Loch, op. cit., 242–3.

at Edinburgh also coincided with the revival of Smithian political economy under the aegis of Dugald Stewart with whose guidance Loch studied.[4]

Formed 'for improvement in Literary Composition and Public Speaking', the Speculative Society attracted to its membership 'all the distinguished youth of Scotland' as well as foreign medical students. At the age of eighteen Loch delivered a 'democratical essay' to the Society which his uncle considered mildly daring 'in a place where Dundas reigns so despotically'. On another occasion soon afterwards Loch presented an essay 'having for its object the Refutation of the doctrine of the Trinity', which apparently met with the disapprobation of some of the members. Loch's essays, supported by Brougham and Horner, achieved a certain degree of notoriety. 'The utmost pains were taken', he recollected, 'to vilify our characters as young men from whom no good was to be expected, and I know . . . that many people in Edinburgh forbid their children from having any communication with Brougham, Horner or me, as persons who were too bad to be admitted into company.' However, Loch remained in favour with the Society—he was president in 1799–1800, and an extraordinary member in 1801. He followed the path of his uncle who had filled similar positions in the 1770s.[5]

The interests of the young student ranged from the esoteric to the prosaic. His correspondence dwelt on the origins and progress of language, natural history, botany, theories of history, chemistry and the drainage of farmland. His discussions revealed a fascination with the political life of the nation which, in the company of Henry Brougham, was inevitable. In these years at the turn of the century Bougham held Loch in high esteem. Their correspondence is full of exuberant, often effusive, friendship. Several times Brougham implored Loch to join him on a tour of the north of Scotland, and then of Germany. In 1801 he wrote to Loch: 'how infinitely better I like you than anyone else, man, woman or child, and like you better everyday I know you.' As Brougham's literary output began to swell Loch remained his closest informant and Brougham told him, 'you

[4] W. Watson, *The History of the Speculative Society, 1764–1904* (1905), 11. F. Hawes, *Henry Brougham, A Nineteenth-Century Portrait* (1957), 21. D. Spring, *The English Landed Estate in the Nineteenth Century* (1963), 89. Edinburgh University Matriculation Rolls, Arts, Law, Divinity, II, 580. I owe the last reference to Dr A. C. Chitnis.

[5] R. H. M. Buddle Atkinson and G. A. Jackson, *Brougham and his Early Friends, Letters to James Loch, 1798–1809* (1908), I, 11, 51. BAP, 1804.

B*

are the only person I can unbosom myself to.' Even after a disagreement (in 1804) Brougham was able to write, 'perhaps nine-tenths of
all the kindness of my nature centres in yourself.' He sought Loch's
assistance with his literary endeavours—for news, information,
advice and criticism. Their mutual interests, their study of the law
and their uncertainty concerning future careers brought them closer
together. They even considered a joint literary production.[6]

Loch was admitted to the Faculty of Advocates in Scotland in 1801.
While Brougham and Horner took the road to London, Loch delayed his departure. His uncle asked him to supervise a number of
renovations on the Blair Adam estate—roads to be built, fences to
be erected, drains to be laid, and trees to be planted. There was much
stress on the need for economy. They must 'leave things to bring the
profit possible, for every farthing of rent must now be collected to
pay after interest.'[7]

Loch accepted and enjoyed these responsibilities. 'It would be a
great deal too much to expect', wrote Brougham, 'that you could
for any enticement tear yourself away from a single second's worth
of rural felicity.' Loch hoped to bring his 'rural propensities' into
harmony with his legal training. From 1802 to 1806 he seems to have
commuted between Blair Adam, Edinburgh, and London, where he
pursued his studies at Lincoln's Inn. He continued his 'croneyship'
with Brougham and other members of the Edinburgh circle. From
both capitals he communicated political observations and reported
the reception of the early issues of the *Edinburgh Review*. He is said
to have engaged the complete confidence of the Whigs in all things,
and in their cause 'he was a most vigorous and at the same time a
silent and effectual worker.'[8] Nor did his intellectual intensity
diminish.

In 1802 he described to Francis Horner the wretchedness of the
lower orders in England, and Horner agreed with him that despite
'all our talk of the grandeur and prosperity of the country, it would
appear that there is yet an immense field for improvement, even in
the rudiments and fundamentals of political happiness.' But Horner
reproached Loch as a 'philosopher', for 'imputing profound emo-
tions to the most insignificant actions of great people'.[9] Involved so

[6] Atkinson and Jackson, op. cit., I, 205, 285, 299, 343, 366; II, 4, 163.
[7] Ibid., I, 196, 282.
[8] Ibid., II, 95, 141, 203.
[9] L. Horner (ed.), *Memoirs and Correspondence of Francis Horner* (1843), I,
203, 425.

closely with the Whigs, Loch was faced with the problems of political manœuvring. In his youth Brougham had once upbraided Loch for attempting a *'full and complete* justification of all treachery in electioneering'. Some years later there is evidence that Loch was helping (in some way) to engineer a scheme to manipulate part of the press for Whig purposes.[10]

In July 1804, Loch made his first contribution to the *Edinburgh Review*. It was a long, anonymous review of a book concerned with the rural economy of India. It was an acid piece of criticism in which Loch reviled the author for his naked plagiarism and his equally evident *naïveté*. For an article in the *Review* the tone was not exceptional. Loch focused his attack on the operations of the East India Company; his assurance was clearly founded on the eternal truths of the *Wealth of Nations*. With laboured emphasis he condemned what he termed 'the force of established habits' in India.

This piece of work had unwelcome repercussions for Loch. Brougham found it distasteful and ill-considered and he gave Loch his candid opinion:

Tho I approve of it critically speaking, I most entirely differ from the whole doctrine and tendency, and can't help wishing that you had been more cautious and circumspect in bringing forward your opinions . . . I think your Pol. Economy more than questionable, and your politics decidedly wrong. Not that you have advanced an erroneous theory, far from it, but that you have committed to paper . . . a number of *plain blunders*. Above all [Brougham went on] you have argued a practical conclusion from one insulated, trivial, economical theoretical speculative, political view of the whole question.

Brougham's strictures were similar in kind to criticisms which, in later years, were levelled at Loch's thinking on the clearance policies on the Sutherland estates. The *Review* article had infuriated the East India Company and Loch felt that he should divulge his authorship. Brougham sensibly dissuaded him from this course and glossed over their disagreement: 'Everyone to their taste as the woman said when she hugged her sow.'[11]

Loch was called to the English Bar in 1806 and apparently practised as a conveyancing counsel for some years. He was also employed as private secretary to George Tierney at the India Board. In 1808

---

[10] Atkinson and Jackson, op. cit., I, 313; III, 278–81. See, however, A. Aspinall, *Politics and the Press, 1780–1850* (1949), 291, 298.

[11] *Edinburgh Review*, IV, 303 ff. Atkinson and Jackson, op. cit., II, 141 ff.

Loch was told of Lord Grenville's need for 'some person on whose secrecy, integrity and capacity and knowledge of the state of things, whom he could depend on, who could communicate with the confidential Editors of Newspapers his ideas on leading points.' Tierney had recommended Loch, and it promised to lead to 'a situation of permanent provision'. It has been suggested that Loch refused this 'entrée into public life', choosing to 'avoid a career in the public eye'. However, there is evidence that he was already engaged in political activity and that he did not lack contacts with the higher echelons of London society. Between 1806 and 1812 Loch continued his studies, probably worked for both Tierney and Grenville, and maintained his conveyancing practice. Though rather overshadowed by his more brilliant Edinburgh contemporaries, Loch remained close to the centre of the political power of the Whig opposition.[12]

Until 1812 Loch's career remained unsettled. In 1806, for instance, he considered the prospects of colonial service in 'the new conquests in South America, and as all must be equally ignorant of the people and their ways, a person tolerably well-grounded in . . . political economy might by some industry make himself useful.' For several years he postponed any permanent choice of career. Loch may have been waiting for an opportunity in politics—his uncle, William Adam, recorded that 'if the Regent had called Lord Grey to his Council . . . . he was determined to have made Mr. Loch an under-Secretary of State.' However, at the age of thirty Loch declared that 'To look upon politics (as they are in fact) is out of the question.' The prospects of a legal career were equally dismal, and he decided to concentrate his mind on agriculture and property law, 'and having adopted this course to hold myself out as a Candidate in time for the auditorship of any estate'.[13]

Two years later, according to the family historian, Loch attended a dinner party in the company of the Marquis of Stafford. Stafford was heard to express the belief that it was not possible for a gentleman to administer estates with success. Loch was roused to contradict this, and was so indignant that he offered to administer the estates of the Marquis. As a result, according to the tale, Loch became commissioner to the Staffords in the same year. In reality, the appointment had been negotiated by William Adam on behalf of his nephew. Stafford's wife, the Countess of Sutherland, specified

[12] Ibid., II, 295–6, 323–31. G. Loch, op. cit., 242–3. Spring, op. cit., 90.
[13] BAP, William Adam Boxes, 1806, 1810, 1812.

the qualifications she required. To this Adam replied, 'Your lady-ship's description excludes (very fitly) a pure unadulterated native of Scotland, but admits a Scotchman English bred and belonging to the law of England as a Barrister.' James Loch was not excessively Scotch and was perfectly qualified. He accepted the superintendence of Lord Stafford's English estates in September 1812, with a salary of £1,000. The connection was to last for forty-three years. Thomas Coutts congratulated Adam—it was 'a most splendid thing for so young a man, and gives him promise of great success in life with the talents he has to bring into action'. The administration of the largest fortune in Britain offered a challenge appropriate to the political, economic and social education of James Loch, and to his tempera-ment.[14]

A managerial revolution changed the face of aristocratic rural economy in the early nineteenth century. This James Loch epitomized. He was one of those 'competent, efficient, zealous and versatile agents, whose concern to preserve estates and enhance their value could well exceed that of their employers'.[15] Loch was the manager of the largest aristocratic fortune in Britain and he wielded power and influenced decisions fundamental to the prosperity and good name of a great family. In the affairs of the House of Sutherland he found ample opportunity to exercise his wide-ranging talents.

'His Lordship's territories', Loch wrote in 1814, 'are a Kingdom and ought to be considered in this light by those he employs'. He quickly cut away the dead wood from the estate bureaucracy— 'in another year', he declared, 'we shall have everybody understand-ing each other and carrying on things in a regular and systematic order.' Of Lord Stafford's affairs, he wrote 'the interest I feel in their success and propriety is as if they were my own, indeed more if possible . . . and nothing but an error of judgement, I should hope, can ever make me go wrong.'[16]

Loch held clear opinions on the nature of his commission. In a manifesto-like letter written in 1816 he asserted that the 'property of a great English Nobleman must be managed on the same principle

[14] G. Loch, op. cit., 242. BAP, William Adam Boxes, 1812. See also S. H. Romilly, *Letters to 'Ivy' from the 1st Earl of Dudley* (1906), 85–6.

[15] See Thompson, op. cit., 158.

[16] SC, Loch to Stafford, 11–7–1813, 29–9–1813; Loch to Lady Stafford, 29–9–1814.

as a little kingdom, not like the affairs of a little Merchant. The future and lasting interest and honour of the family as well as their immediate income must be kept in view—while a merchant thinks only of his daily profits and his own immediate life interest.' Lord Stafford, as recipient of the Bridgewater profits, enjoyed 'the greatest free income of any English nobleman'. His direct descendants would not be so fortunately placed. His estates in Scotland were extensive, remote, and undeveloped. These circumstances, Loch contended, implied a particular principle of management. It was incumbent upon Lord Stafford to finance the basic capital requirements of his estates, using gains from the more prosperous in order to develop the less. 'The great sinews of improvement should be Lord Stafford's object.' This was the crux of the economic policy of the House of Sutherland. It was designed as a long-term programme of concerted improvement which depended, for its finance, on Stafford's peculiar inheritance. Loch instructed his sub-agents in the following way: 'You must look forward fifty years that you may make the most of the present.'[17]

It was Loch's responsibility not merely to guard the financial viability of the House of Sutherland but to promote the welfare of its many tenants. Loch emphasized 'how much the fate of about 20,000 people are connected with and dependent on' Lord Stafford. It is undeniable that a real measure of autocratic control was exercised by the family over the lower strata of society within its estates. Loch once tried to explain the rationality of the established mode of social and economic relationships in England to a Frenchman—a M. Silvestre, of the French Agricultural Society. 'The utility of the Gentlemen of England', he wrote, was that they were 'managing by themselves all the local affairs of their district, such as roads, bridges, drainage, etc. To this we think is owing in a great degree the prosperity of our nation, as it gives the management of these matters to those both the most capable and the most interested in their being well and economically executed and always kept in repair'. Loch felt very strongly on this point and repeatedly defined the landlord's role. Rent was the reward of the landlord's invested capital—and the landlord should 'confine his attention, in the application of his capital, to the removal of the physical difficulties of the country, leaving everything else to be done by those who find

[17] SC, Loch to Grant, 1–7–1816; Loch to Suther, 11–10–1816. Cf. J. Loch, *Account of the Improvements on the Estates of the Marquess of Stafford* (1820), 168.

it their interest to settle in it'. The invisible hand of classical economics played a large part in Loch's thinking.[18]

To Loch, the aristocracy was equally indispensable in national as well as in local affairs. In a constitutional monarchy he believed that 'a hereditary and wealthy aristocracy must form a branch and that fully as much for the safety of the people as the safeguard of the throne.' Horrified by events in contemporary Europe, he sensed and feared the danger of turbulence in England. After a devastating electoral defeat of the Stafford family in Staffordshire in 1820, Loch complained bitterly of the changing political climate. He exclaimed that the yeomanry and the manufacturing districts had arrogantly cast off their dependence on the higher ranks and that such action presaged catastrophe. 'The fact is the revolution is begun, how and when it is to end God knows, but can anyone shut his eyes to the state of the country and observe the progress of the Spanish Revolution which must be followed by similar event in France and Germany and doubt our turn next? At least I cannot.' Loch, of course, lived through the relatively peaceful transformation of British society in the following decades—and indeed he supported the *via media*, which entailed the extremely gradual diminution of aristocratic influence. But in 1820 the hope of assimilating the new radicalism into the body politic required a high degree of optimism. Even the democratization of education was fraught with danger. Loch remarked that the consequences of education spreading to the masses would be the issuing 'forth of a vast body of cultivated talents which has no knowledge or feeling for the older Establishments of England and indeed feels towards them a spirit of rivalry and hostility.'[19]

But Loch was no reactionary. In the early 1820s he gave keen support to measures of parliamentary reform: he advocated an extension of the franchise to the new manufacturing areas and the educated classes, and the reduction of placemen. He remained true to the cause of moderate, conciliatory reform. Indeed, Loch regarded himself as an architect of the Reform Bill. In March 1831 he stated that he 'had drawn up Lord John Russell's Bill for disfranchising Grampound and then was employed to draw up that

[18] SC, Loch to Lady Gower, 6–7–1823; Loch to Silvestre, 22–11–1820; Loch to Sellar, 20–5–1832.
[19] SC, Loch to Stafford, 9–11–1819, 16–2–1820; Loch to Adam, 16–3–1820; Loch to Sutherland, 16–2–1848; Loch to Fenton, 16–3–1820.

more general plan of reform which he afterwards propounded to Parliament—and which in some respects is the foundation of parts of the present measure.' Loch told a doubting Scotsman that 'In regard to the very difficult and important question of Parliamentary Reform, I assure you it is impossible to avoid it . . . It may be guided, it cannot be stopped and the sooner that it is conceded the less will be required'. In 1831, though suffering considerable pain from a broken collarbone, Loch, as M.P. for the Wick Burghs, managed to attend the crucial Reform debate in the Commons, and paired off with an opponent—which, he claimed, decided the outcome of the vote. One consequence of Loch's stand was his dismissal as auditor to Lord Dudley—though this was widely attributed to Dudley's insanity.[20]

Loch gave full support to Huskisson's programme of commercial liberalism and strongly favoured the reduction of agricultural protection. Referring to the agricultural distress of 1822 he told Sir John Sinclair, 'It does not appear to me that Parliament can do anything to grant the relief required and I am sure it ought not to attempt it. If it does it may postpone the evil, it cannot cure it, it may put off the crisis, but only to make it the worse.' He advocated the reduction of Corn Law protection in the 1820s, but insisted that gradualism was essential 'to keep the squires in good humour'. Among his many activities Loch was a member of Brougham's Society for the Propagation of Useful Knowledge, the 'Steam Intellect Society', and also made great efforts to promote the establishment of the University of London: 'I assure you', he told Huskisson, 'it is most worthy of the support of all liberal men.'[21]

In the period following the Napoleonic War many of the English aristocracy felt themselves confronted by new threats to their status. 'Good intention and good acts', wrote Loch in 1820, 'by no means secures approbation, especially in these times when everything done by the upper classes is the subject of reflection and abuse.' To an unprecedented extent the aristocracy needed to justify its

[20] SC, Loch to Russell, October 1821, 1–5–1822, 14–3–1831; Loch to Dempster, 25–12–1830; Loch to Innes, 25–3–1831; Loch to Sellar, 18–3–1831; Loch to Laing, 16–3–1831; Loch to Gunn, 16–3–1831; Loch to Mackenzie, 10–11–1831; Waters to Loch, 21–2–1832; Loch to Abercromby, 20–4–1821.
[21] SC, Loch to Sinclair, 2–2–1822; Loch to Captain Loch, 8–10–1824; Loch to Huskisson, 10—9—1824. Liverpool Public Library, Letters of Huskisson. Brougham Papers, University College Library, London.

existence. Virulent public comment was made on the policy of the House of Sutherland in Scotland. Loch found himself its principal apologist. He sensed the essentially defensive attitude required on behalf of the aristocrat. This was expressed in many ways. In 1830, for instance, when it was suggested that the Sutherland estates were under-rented Loch explained the wisdom of low rents:

Lord Stafford's rents . . . have always been fixed at rather under the general average of the district. This rule has been adhered to. I mean that the tenants should feel that they hold their lands on rather easier terms than their neighbours. It is fit and proper that those who hold of a great man should do so.

He added that this was 'one sacrifice that large estates must pay and it is that which reconciled the Public to their existence'. Nothing could be more realistic—'In England his [Stafford's] rents are put at 1/– to 2/– an acre below the common average of the country . . . and as the attachment of mankind is secured more through their interest than any other way, it is an object to be attended to.'[22]

It is unlikely that the members of the Sutherland family itself gave much thought to the justification of private property in land, despite the fact that the extent of their territory, and the policies they adopted, provided the Swiss economist, Sismondi, in the 1830s, with a perfect target for his castigation of landed monopoly. The very idea of justification was alien to the Sutherlands' attitude to society, though they believed that unless they could perform the recognized functions of an improving landlord they should sell out their property. Contemporary critics frequently denounced landlords for their abuse of the rights of property. But until Sismondi they rarely (with a few notable exceptions such as Thomas Spence) denounced the institution of property itself. After 1840 the criticisms tended to become more fundamental—and thereby more worrying to the Sutherland family and James Loch.

While engaged as *homme d'affaires* to Lord Stafford, Loch also acted in the management of the estates of Lord Francis Egerton, the Earl of Carlisle, the Bridgewater Trust, and the trust estates of the Earl of Dudley and Viscount Keith. Lord Wharncliffe was told that a few minutes in conversation with Loch 'would be worth guineas of manuscripts.' There was no better or more able adviser on financial matters. Certainly Loch had a voracious appetite for work. From 1827 to 1852 he was a Member of Parliament, holding seats which

[22] SC, Loch to Lewis, 22–8–1820; Loch to Horsburgh, 17–11–1830.

were in the gift of the Sutherlands. He sat unopposed for the Wick Burghs from 1830 until his defeat in 1852. Never a mere cypher, Loch's opinions were sought by men of first rank, including Peel, Grey and Huskisson. He continued to correspond with Henry Brougham. Apparently, he declined the Under-secretaryship of State for the Colonies, but he contributed to several important committees.[23]

In his political opinions Loch was generally liberal and non-doctrinaire, except in economic matters in which he was a devout free-trader. He could see only folly in directly resisting public opinion and believed that all extremes should be channelled into compromise by active governments dedicated to the maintenance of law and order. In 1844 he complained that 'Both the great parties of the state no longer rest upon the wisdom of their measures, as being the reason for adopting them, but they call in the feelings, prejudices, passions and ignorance of the lower orders, as the arbiters, who shall decide.' After the Chartist débâcle at Kennington Common in 1848 he rejoiced in the

preservation of the Constitution of this country and the social happiness of the world ... the result of the devoted combination of the Upper and Middle classes of Society—which it is the duty of both to foster and cement. I confess it is a matter of regret to me ... that this course is something departed from—and that a line is drawn between the middle and working classes through the instrumentality of the Upper, which will be attended by disastrous consequences if persevered with.

In the last years of his life ill-health led him to withdraw from the political world, but his opinion on public policy remained firm. In 1851 he chastised the Whigs for 'their total ignorance of the opinion of the country and their incapacity to meet practically any combination of persons'. He predicted 'that we shall lose the benefit of Peel's great measures and ... we shall spend the rest of our lives under a reactionary government which will be succeeded by a more democratic ministry than has ever existed under the English Monarch.'[24]

In many ways Loch was a pragmatist, his opinions changing and developing to meet contingencies. He was sometimes guilty of mouthing the required platitudes of improving landlordism, but there was always an undertone of worldly realism in his thinking.

[23] Spring, op. cit., 89; G. Loch, op. cit., 247. *PP*, 1828, VII.
[24] SC, Loch to Sutherland, 23-3-1844, 25-3-1844, 16-4-1848, 25-2-1851.

He was thoroughly, but not uncritically, versed in the works of the political economists—Smith, Ricardo, Horner, MacCulloch, Chalmers and especially Malthus. 'The natural tendency of population', Loch wrote in 1820, 'is to increase more quickly than the means of subsistence.' He believed that this was so in the Scottish Highlands. It stemmed from early marriage, the selfish gratification of passion and, pre-eminently, the subdivision of lots.[25] To Loch the problem of population and poverty required a very firm hand and strong radical solutions. This, more than anything else, made this man of unquestionable compassion seem guilty of rank harshness and cruelty.

Loch has been criticized as a slave of political economy, a man who rigidly and indiscriminately acted upon the received tenets of a body of doctrine which were never universally applicable. It is true that Loch regarded his legal and economic training as an excellent guide to action, but it is equally true that he was explicitly aware of the hazards of trying to implement what he termed 'the strict rules of Political Economy'. He expressly warned against such a course in the Highlands where, he pointed out, the people were not prepared to turn their full labours to fishing—even though it would maximize their economic welfare. 'We theorists', he said, must take cognizance of 'the nature of man' and the force of traditional habits.[26] Such counsel required very considerable reserves of patience, often more than Loch possessed. His urgent desire for improvement and progress sometimes led him into precipitate decisions. He made mistakes, and he admitted them—but never publicly.

Loch controlled an elaborate structure of management and authority. Thomas Mulock, a hostile critic of the Sutherland policies, described Loch as 'the Duke's Premier' and 'The Sutherland Metternich'—conducting a 'despotic experiment' with the aid of his Scottish factors, 'the Duke's cabinet ministers'. The Scottish Herald held similar views—'Sutherlandshire, that the Old Lords of Dunrobin loved so well, seemed to their daughter [the Countess], a wild, rude country, where all was wrong, where all had to be set right, a sort of Russia, to be handed over to the autocratic civilization of another Peter, in the person of Mr. Loch'. Loch himself regarded the administration of his agency as though it were composed of governmental departments. In 1830 he described it in this way: 'As in the expenses of the Country, each head of the department works his own to be

[25] Loch's *Account* (1820), 124.
[26] SC, Loch to Sellar, 20–5–1832.

the most perfect and that he can afford the least to part with any of it.' In such a way Loch delegated his responsibility to the sub-agents of the multifarious estates of the Sutherland family—each of whom was finally accountable to Loch who co-ordinated the finances and undertook the general decisions. Significantly, Loch acknowledged what he termed his 'double duty to Landlord and People'.[27]

Above all else, Loch was a practical man, remarkably competent in the affairs of the world. At least one contemporary believed him infallible, though Loch knew and admitted that he was less than that. To Loch efficiency and improvement were a gospel, a moral duty. Most problems were soluble, but they had to be faced realistically. His attitude to the growing rivalry among railway promoters typified the man. 'I understand', he wrote in 1834, 'that some of our friends think God would aid us in opposing them [i.e. rival companies], how visionary such an idea'. As for his many critics, he remarked in 1837 that he had 'made it a rule through life to act according to my conscience and judgement, unaffected by what may be written or said of me in public prints'.[28]

Later critics of Loch and his policies have been both strong and diverse. I. Grimble, for instance, clearly believes that Loch was a heartless hypocrite, and has poured on him a deluge of ironic scorn. Similarly J. Prebble has presented a picture of Loch as a desk-working sycophant who used 'soothing syrup' to gloss over draconian policies. The *Dictionary of National Biography*, however, asserts that nothing has ever been proved against Loch, and maintains that the work he undertook in the Highlands averted all likelihood of a catastrophic famine comparable with that in Ireland. The family historian, George Loch, believed his forebear to have been 'courageously right' and that his policies were fully justified by the condition of the Highlands in the twentieth century: 'His whole existence is one long lesson—how simple, direct in his aims, sagacious, wise and fine!' The most recent commentator, David Spring, has testified to Loch's 'flexibility and soundness of judgement'.[29]

[27] T. Mulock, *The Western Highlands . . . of Scotland* (1850), 29–31. *The Times*, 26-5-1848. SC, Loch to Atkinson, 27-11-1830; Loch to Gower, 19-1-1831–D593/N/4/1/1d, 143.

[28] Spring, op. cit., 89. SC, Loch to Currie, 25-8-1834; Loch to Brenner, 19-1-1837.

[29] I. Grimble, *Trial of Patrick Sellar* (1962), esp. chapter 2. J. Prebble, *The Highland Clearances* (1963), *passim.* G. Loch, op. cit., 253. Spring, op. cit., 88–96.

As for Loch's contemporaries, their views were equally diverse. In 1819 Robert Southey had met Loch and his impressions were generally favourable. One year later Thomas Bakewell, keeper of a lunatic asylum in Staffordshire, published a frontal attack. He believed that Loch's agency was the prime cause of the downfall of the popularity of the House of Sutherland—he cited Loch's 'cheese-paring and candle-end economy contemptible in any household and much more so in one of the most opulent noblemen in Europe'. Loch, said Bakewell, was 'deficient in the knowledge of human nature and rural affairs, as well as domestic economy'. His manner, too, was unfortunate for he was incapable of that 'conciliatory and attractive deportment which are so necessary to obtain the confidence and goodwill of mankind'. He thought Loch's 'juvenile appearance, for one invested with so much power and consequence' operated to his disadvantage. Loch had ignored the feelings and interests of individuals and had persisted with chaotic alterations which were 'the reverse of improvements and the objects of contempt and ridicule'. [30]

Writing in the 1830s, Sismondi considered the Lochian policies in the Highlands to be morally, politically and economically indefensible. Some years later the French economist, Lavergne, defended the same policies with great vigour. Loch, he declared, had wrought a revolution in the north, a revolution which was not only inevitable but also 'beneficial, useful and well ordered'. [31]

Loch's attitude to his critics was generally dismissive. He invariably discredited their motives. In 1820, for instance, there was widespread denunciation (particularly in Edinburgh and London) of the clearance policies in Sutherland. Loch bluntly asserted that the complaints were mainly from ex-Highlanders who conceived 'it a necessary part of their patriotism to abuse loudly all alterations that are made for the improvement of the country', together with 'English philanthropists who believe any story, if it consists of lamentable details of cruelty and oppression, especially if occasioned by the better orders of society'. [32]

[30] C. H. Herford (ed.), *Robert Southey's Journal of a Tour of Scotland* (1929), **40**. T. Bakewell, *Remarks on a Publication of James Loch, Esq.* (1820), 19, 37, 101, 135. See also E. S. Richards, 'James Loch and the House of Sutherland' (Ph.D. thesis, University of Nottingham, 1967), appendix 4.

[31] S. de Sismondi, *Political Economy and the Philosophy of Government* (ed. Mignet, 1857). L. Lavergne, *The Rural Economy of England, Scotland and Ireland* (1855), chapter 22.

[32] SC, Loch to Suther, 22–1–1820.

Opposing views of the life and work of James Loch recur again and again: for example, Karl Marx, Harriet Beecher Stowe, Thomas Mulock, Charles Knight, David Stewart of Garth, T. S. Escott, and Donald Macleod, all reaching emphatic conclusions. Two points are clear. Loch is largely associated with the Highland clearances. Second, he emerges as a distinctive figure of the new industrial society of nineteenth-century Britain: he was 'a managerial entrepreneur' employed by a millionaire aristocrat, a liberal rationalist devoted to the most traditional of Britain's institutions, and an economic planner in an age of classical economics.

Upright, righteous, strong-principled, even puritanical—Loch was no man of straw. He felt a profound need to justify to himself every decision, every action. But he was not humourless, not without personal charm; the impression that he gave to some of unbending earnestness was deceptive. The burden of responsibility he carried was compensated by a sense of power. The power was real, and sometimes Loch exercised it in a naked form. At his discretion lay the future of vast domains and the lives of many people.

As for the gratitude of posterity Loch expected very little, and tried to adopt a stoic attitude towards it. In 1835 he wrote to the ageing Duchess/Countess of Sutherland: [33]

Those who succeed us, who only enjoy the result and did not know that which was to be overcome, will find fault. Someone said to me at Tongue how much the young Lord [the heir] will say of his Grandfather and Grandmother's exertions and those who executed their intentions. I said don't flatter yourself that this will be so, he will be told how much *better* these things might have been done and so ever will it be the case, and we must all submit to this.

[33] SC, Loch to Duchess/Countess of Sutherland, 12–8–1835.

Part Two

The House of Sutherland and the
Coming of the Railways

III

The Problematical Inheritance

In 1842 an anonymous writer in the *Quarterly Review* scrutinized the progress of the improvement policies of the House of Sutherland which had been in operation during the previous thirty-five years in the Northern Highlands of Scotland. He observed that 'it was in consequence of the Scotch estates being connected with a command of English capital that these northern regions have been, within living memory, advanced in productiveness beyond, we may safely say, any other example that could be pointed out in the history of British territorial expansion.'[1] He was right. The English wealth of the Leveson-Gowers was the *sine qua non* of the Sutherland clearances and improvements.

In effect, as a result of the unusual priorities entertained by the Sutherland family, there was a remarkable channelling of English capital northwards to the Scottish Highlands in the early nineteenth century. A large part of the command of English capital by the family derived from its interest in the canal and railway sector of the economy. Directly and indirectly the House of Sutherland had acted the role of aristocratic entrepreneur in the Industrial Revolution—and it had reaped substantial rewards. A considerable proportion was directed to the development of the Scottish estates. In this sense there was a diversion of capital away from the advancing industrial sector of the British economy to an economically backward area. Furthermore, this diversion was not determined, in the first instance, by any 'rational' balancing of returns to the factors of production. Less impersonal forces were at work.

[1] LXIX, p. 421.

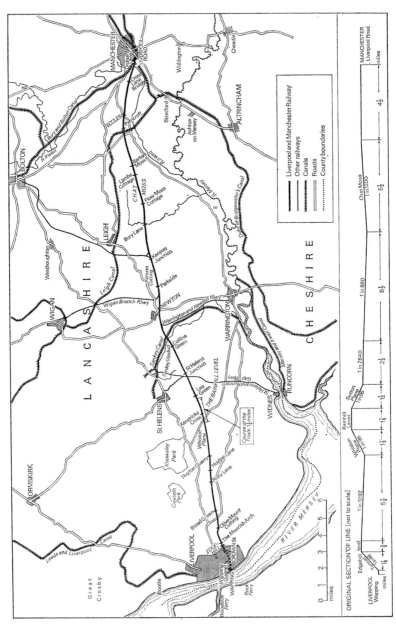

Map 1   Connections between Liverpool and Manchester, 1830

The development of inland transport in Britain experienced two structural changes between 1750 and 1850: the dramatic expansion of canal enterprise from the 1760s, and the sudden emergence of railway construction as a leading sector in the 1820s. The House of Sutherland deserves a special place in the history of these changes— its involvement was very great. It is likely, for instance, that in 1826 Lord Stafford was both the largest canal proprietor and the largest railway proprietor in the kingdom. But the role goes deeper. The family's interests were located at the very centre of the turmoil that arose in the 1820s and 1830s between the established canal faction and the aggressive railway promoters. For this reason Lord Stafford was able to exert a critical influence on the timing and character of the coming of the railways. In a dramatic moment, in December 1825, the aristocratic titan among the canal-owners decided to switch part of his allegiance and his capital to the assailant railway interests—'Thus was the great canal proprietor propitiated and thus was the way paved for success.'[2] During the next two decades the House of Sutherland continued to wield a striking (though eventually a declining) influence over relations between the canals and the railways, thus helping to widen transport services in the economy.

In recent years techniques of investigation have been pioneered[3] which have thrown entirely new light on the central problem of the contribution of railway capital to historical economic growth. It is now clear that the benefits and costs of railways must be measured against the alternative (and necessarily hypothetical) benefits and costs of other means of accomplishing comparable ends. As long ago as 1852, the railway-manager, Braithwaite Poole, using a very crude counter-factual method, calculated that the railways of Britain saved the nation £27m. per annum in transport costs. Poole's calculation refers to the gross rather than the net benefits and is, understandably, a very inexact estimation.[4]

The efforts of this Victorian precursor must eventually be superseded by more sophisticated measurements. A vital consideration in these calculations will be the response of other elements in the

[2] J. Francis, *A History of the English Railway* (1851), I, 116.

[3] Notably by A. Fishlow, *Railroads and the Transformation of the Ante-Bellum Economy* (1965), and R. W. Fogel, *Railroads and American Economic Growth: Essays in Economic History* (1964).

[4] *Minutes of Proceedings of the Institution of Civil Engineers*, XI, 452. Cf. W. Harding, 'Facts bearing on the progress of the railway system', *Journal of the Statistical Society of London*, XI, 341.

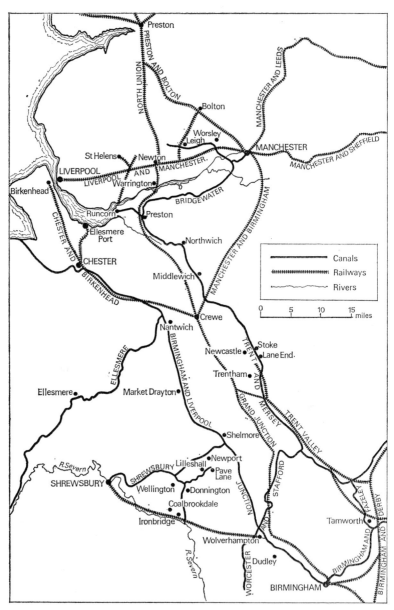

Map 2   Old and new routes connecting Lancashire and the Midlands

transport sector to the interloping railway. In many cases the railways were designed expressly to break monopolies amongst navigation interests. However, perhaps because of the degree of natural monopoly inherent in the provision of transport services, the result often appeared to be the substitution of one form of monopoly for another.

In several respects the experience of the first railway, the Liverpool and Manchester, corresponds to this pattern. The intervention of Lord Stafford in 1825 helped to perpetuate a long tradition of monopolistic collusion in transport in this quarter of England. Restrictive trade agreements survived the coming of the railway, and the impact of the new mode of transport on costs was less than it might otherwise have been. The defensive tactics of the canal interest were contrived mainly by James Loch and Lord Stafford. Had they achieved full fruition, their policies could have altered substantially the pattern of transport development. In reality, they accomplished a lesser objective in tempering the full force of competition by the consolidation of collusive arrangements with the railway. Some of the benefits of the railway were thereby withheld from the public. It was thus rather more than a minor episode in the shady history of restrictive practices.

The railway may be regarded as the introduction of a profoundly disruptive innovation into an economic environment dominated and closely regulated by deeply established counter-interests. The reception of the railway and the adjustments forced upon the defenders of the old transport order illuminate the character and structure of the regional economy. And it is in this context that the House of Sutherland played a positive, moulding influence.

In essence, the Sutherland connection with railway building is the story of an aristocratic investor caught in a turbulent episode of industrial history. Geographically, the events are set roughly in the triangle between Liverpool, Manchester and Birmingham. The Sutherland family inherited a deeply entrenched position in communications between Manchester and the Mersey—from 1803 the profits of the Bridgewater Canal were theirs. Lucrative though it was, the inheritance was fundamentally threatened in the 1820s. The railways might well injure the Bridgewater income. The problem was inescapable.

It was rendered more perplexing by two vital circumstances enforced by the Bridgewater Will. First, the Sutherland family had neither *de facto* nor *de jure* control over the policy and administration of the canal. It was in the hands of an autocratic and perverse superintendent, R. H. Bradshaw. This formidable man was a law unto himself. Second, the Will prescribed that the canal must pass into the possession of the second son of the family (Lord Francis) on the death of Lord Stafford. This dynastic problem created potentially conflicting interests within the family. James Loch made many attempts to reconcile them.

This was the complicated background of Loch's efforts to come to terms with the railways—to evolve a *modus operandi* in relations between the canals and the railways. Through his efforts the Sutherland family became a bridge between the opposed groups. Loch followed a deliberate policy designed to minimize conflict and to limit the harmful consequences on the canals which were feared from the advent of railways. His policy was an essay in compromise, involving lengthy and complicated negotiations in which patience and steady judgment were essential.

The beginnings were found in the earliest days of the 'canal age'. Earl Gower was a genuine pioneer in the transport improvements which had developed in the 1750s and thereafter. He was the eighteenth-century aristocrat/industrialist *par excellence*. In 1758, for instance, he had employed James Brindley (before his illustrious Bridgewater days) to survey a proposed canal between the Trent and the Mersey. Gower was deeply interested in the Grand Trunk and Bridgewater canals from their inceptions. The canal innovators met difficulties similar to those of the railway pioneers: resistance from landowners and from existing transport monopolies, and problems of mobilizing capital. Gower provided some of the loan-capital for the building of the Bridgewater Canal. He was a canal builder on a more local scale on his Shropshire estate where, in 1764, he formed a company in association with the Gilbert brothers (a further connection with the Duke of Bridgewater). They built a canal to exploit the mineral resources of the estate, a capital investment which helped the development of the Shropshire iron and coal industry dominated by its Quaker dynasties.

In 1803 the Duke of Bridgewater died and his canal passed into the hands of his nephew, the 2nd Marquis of Stafford. The inheritance included income from the waterway, wharves, collieries and various estates, together with a valuable art collection and Bridgewater

House. Stafford received the income derived from the fortune until his death in 1833 when it descended to his second son, Lord Francis Egerton Gower, later Earl Ellesmere. It has often been stated that the inheritance increased Stafford's income by £100,000 a year, but this is an exaggeration. In only three years, 1823–5, did the annual profits reach this figure, the average being close to £75,000 per annum. [5]

The other crucial clause of the Will specified the control of the canal. The management was placed in the hands of three trustees; the heirs to the canal were to enjoy the income but to have no part in the management of it. Robert Haldane Bradshaw, the Duke's last superintendent, was named as the man to be given 'the sole control ... without accounting to anyone'. Bradshaw had the 'most absolute dominion over the property'. Legal advice in 1803 concluded that it was an 'extraordinary will'. Bradshaw even had the power to appoint his own successor. The purpose of these clauses had been to ensure the beneficial use of the canal by the public for as long a period as possible in order to perpetuate the benevolent image of the Duke of Bridgewater. [6]

The result was perverse. By all accounts Bradshaw was the very last man to have been entrusted with such an obligation. That he was an extremely astute manager of canal business no one ever called into doubt. But Bradshaw took his efficiency to the point of rapacity. Certainly this was contrary to the wishes of the dead Duke: Bradshaw squeezed the canal users without mercy and thereby thoroughly alienated them. [7] Stafford was but the passive recipient of the profits—powerless to exert any influence over Bradshaw or the management of the canal.

Bradshaw's policy provoked its own penalty in the 1820s, in the form of the railway offensive. Looking back, the heir to the Bridgewater Canal, Lord Francis, denounced the exercise of irresponsible power by Bradshaw as the reason which 'accelerated a crisis which

[5] Bridgewater Will, 1803, at Stafford CRO. Ellesmere-Brackley Collection, EB 1461 (1); Canal Papers, Box X, 474, vol. 1, 71–2. F. Mullineux, *The Duke of Bridgewater's Canal* (1959), 28–9. SC, D593/C/23/4, Account of sums paid to the Marquis of Stafford, etc.

[6] SC, Loch to Fenton, 18–5–1822. D593/C/23/4, The opinion of Henry Atherton of Lincoln's Inn, December, 1803, on the Will of the late Duke of Bridgewater.

[7] B. Falk, *The Bridgewater Millions* (1942), 122. H. Malet, *The Canal Duke* (1961), 17. Very recently Bradshaw has been defended by F. C. Mather in *After the Canal Duke* (1970), especially chapter 1.

might for a time have been delayed'. As for the Will, Lord Francis had never seen 'a document more calculated to defeat its own great purpose of benefitting the public, or more exquisitely devised for the purpose of permanently separating power from property'.[8]

In the decade after 1815 complaints of the alleged inadequacies of the transport facilities between Liverpool and Manchester became more vocal and urgent. A virulent controversy developed. It derived from a collision of interests. On one side were the canal-owners, the conservative land-owners, the river interests, the coach proprietors, and the trustees of the turnpike roads—all entrenched in the *status quo*. On the other side were interests which stood to benefit from developments which promised to lower freight rates. Public opinion divided between those who claimed that the capital invested in existing communications should be preserved from the destruction inherent in the rise of competition, and those who complained against the monopoly of the canals and turnpikes. Bradshaw, Stafford and Loch, try as they might, could not avoid involvement in this emerging conflict.

Pressure on the supply of transport facilities was, of course, greatest during periods of trade expansion, and it was at such times that the adequacy and policy of the Bridgewater Canal were most closely questioned. The year 1818 was an exceptionally good one for Bridgewater profits. 'Mr. Bradshaw', wrote Loch in December, 'tells me that for the last three weeks there has been more trade on the canal than was ever known and this has always been the slackest time of the year.' Bradshaw exulted in the situation: 'Indeed he tells me they have not been able to meet the demand. He further tells me there are 29 new factories building in Lancashire.' Bradshaw's revelling in his profits had its dangerous counterpart in the dissatisfaction of the merchants and manufacturers of Lancashire.[9]

A basic imbalance had developed between the growth of industry and the provision of transport in Lancashire. As W. T. Jackman pointed out, 'Canal navigation had failed to meet the conditions of the expanding trade and a developing industry, and therefore the only thing to do was to obtain parliamentary authority for laying down a railway which would combine the requisites of speed,

[8] Earl of Ellesmere, *Essays on History, Biography, Geography, Engineering, etc.* (1858), 244; SC, Lord Francis to 2nd Duke of Sutherland, 20–11–1833.
[9] SC, Loch to Lady Stafford, 21–12–1818.

economy and safety.'[10] In the provision of transport between Liverpool and Manchester before 1825 there were two parties working in collusion: the Mersey and Irwell Navigation Company (known as the 'Old Quay' and mainly owned by Manchester interests) and the Bridgewater Canal Trustees. In 1810 they had found it mutually advantageous to share the monopoly: they publicly announced a joint rise in freight rates. They were already very considerably higher than they had been in 1795—'they had abused their power and controlled their customers.' Both groups profited greatly— the Old Quay taking 50 per cent profit per annum, the Bridgewater Canal sometimes approaching £80,000 a year on the investment which was originally probably about £350,000.

In the early 1820s, it was easy to believe that the railways were not a practicable alternative. Only when, in 1824, it became imperative to try to forestall growing railway initiatives, did the canals moderate their rates. Before that time 'It never seemed to occur to them that by lowering their rates they might perpetuate their business and their profits', wrote Jackman.[11]

Nor could effective rivalry come from other canal companies. All attempts to extend water transport facilities were blocked by blatant restrictions agreed among the existing companies. In 1810 Bradshaw signed an agreement with the Grand Junction Canal

[10] *The Development of Transportation in Modern England* (2nd ed. 1962), 521.

[11] Jackman, op. cit., 520–1; Francis, op. cit., 77–80; F. C. Mather, 'The Duke of Bridgewater's trustees and the coming of the railways', *TRHS*, 1964, 134–5. In his recent book, *After the Canal Duke*, F. C. Mather has tried to erase the view that Bradshaw was involved in efforts to minimize competition on the route (12–17). He notes that evidence of formal collusion after 1821 is hard to find and that freight rates fell from 1821. But the problem is illusive. By its nature collusion is usually secret and often tacit. The crux of the issue is whether or not the transport interests were operating restrictive practices to the injury of the public. As W. Fellner in *Competition Among the Few* (1949) has demonstrated, formal alliance, in certain oligopoly situations, is not necessary. The evidence that rates of the companies were not the same, and actually fell with most other prices after 1821, cannot be taken as proof that the collusion (be it Fellner's 'spontaneous co-ordination' or its variants) was moribund. Waterway rates fell when the railway came—see Booth, op. cit., 30. This very fact is a demonstration that the canal charges had previously included a substantial element of monopoly rent. The coming of the railway, by increasing competition, induced the canals to pass on to the public some of the benefits 'achieved from earlier technological advances in transportation'. See P. D. McClelland: 'Railroads, American growth and the new economic history: a critique', *JEH*, 1968, 114, n. 58. Whether the monopoly rent was derived with or without formal collusion is another question. See also Eric Richards, 'The finances of the Liverpool and Manchester Railway again', *EcHR*, May 1972.

explicitly to prevent any extension of new canals into his territory. In 1818 the Old Quay threatened to fight 'tooth and nail' any move to improve transit to Liverpool. In that year Loch could see that all canal boats were subject to 'the inconvenience of the tideway of the Mersey ... which exposes the trade both to considerable risk and much irregularity and delay'. The Mersey section was open for only three hours a day; with its winds, sands, shallows and tides it was a real danger. The canals were subject to droughts and frosts. Delays had reached a stage at which some cotton-spinners had found it necessary to revert to land-carriage; manufacturers claimed that it had often 'taken longer time to pass goods from Liverpool to Manchester, than to bring them over from America to Liverpool'. Transport irregularities compelled factory owners to carry large stocks of cotton. Without new means the position could only get worse. 'We want more cotton, and we want more everything', exclaimed one complainant in 1825.[12] Such, in general, was the situation that faced James Loch as adviser to Lord Stafford.

Loch was certainly aware of the beneficial effects of transport improvements. He spent a large part of his life pressing for a wide variety of such projects. It was an essential part of Loch's gospel of 'Improvement'. In the Sutherland economy Loch regarded the introduction of modern transport as indispensable in his plans for the accelerated development of the region. He possessed a considerable technical knowledge of the details of civil engineering; 'I have always been a great road Engineer', he once told Brougham. He was well-grounded in the developments in canal and railway construction and took an active part in the supervision of projects in all these fields.

In 1813 and 1816 he had tried to set in motion schemes for railways in Shropshire to link unconnected canals. The intention had been to aid the depressed ironmasters of the West Midlands to get their products to Birmingham and London, to widen the market for the produce of Lord Stafford's estates, to increase employment and to take advantage of low labour costs, and to increase traffic on existing canals. Loch was enthusiastic and hopeful. But his plans were not carried out. The railways he had in mind were primitive industrial lines, the immediate precursors of the Stephenson

[12] SC, Loch to Lord Francis, 24–12–1810. EBC, 1477. *PP*, 1825, Proceedings of the Committee of the House of Commons on the Liverpool and Manchester Railroad Bill.

railways. Their spread in various parts of England during the 1810s was symptomatic of the increasing problem of inland communications.

Loch's belief in 'Improvement' was affronted by the intractable, reactionary tactics of R. H. Bradshaw. But there were few signs of hostility between the two men in the early years of acquaintanceship —their correspondence is full of amiable worldliness. At times Loch sympathized with the incorrigible old man. Loch had a better understanding of Bradshaw than almost anyone else. Bradshaw was possessed by a total, blind commitment to his canal. For him the canal was the perfect means of transport. In 1828 Bradshaw recounted how 'the old Duke had made him promise 26 years ago to attend to the interest of the Canal from which day he, Mr. B., had not once dined out, if he did he must give parties and women would get into my House!!'[13] Other forms of transport were unspeakable and unthinkable. So obsessive was he that as the railways, in the end, encroached upon his canal, they encroached also upon his sanity.

Loch's other major problem in the coming conflict with the railways was the dynastic question. His loyalties were clearly to the Stafford family. But within the family his obligations were divided. Loch knew full well that on the death of Stafford, the first son (Gower) would assume the title without the revenue of the Bridgewater Trust. This would revert to the younger son (Lord Francis). Loch admitted that this perplexing situation weighed heavily upon him in his negotiations between the canals and railways. When in 1825 he advised Lord Stafford to invest £100,000 in the direct rival of the Bridgewater Canal, i.e. the Liverpool and Manchester Railway, Loch was fully aware of the ambivalence of his loyalties. On the face of things it was a rather odd piece of entrepreneurial decision-making and 'an extraordinary slice of luck' for the railway.[14] One of Loch's many tasks was that of making the decision acceptable to all members of the Stafford family.

When Lord Francis was eighteen, Loch lectured his young master on the duties that adulthood would impose. He told him that the grand object of his life 'must be to prevent the Trade of London getting to Liverpool or Manchester through any other channel than by the Grand Trunk and Bridgewater Canal'. The year was 1818

[13] SC, Moss to Loch, 23–10–1828.
[14] Falk, op. cit.

47

and Loch was thinking of rival canals. He continued, 'The most likely thing to force the public to think of any such measure is the inadequacy of the Grand Trunk to meet the demands of trade . . . This subject must become a matter of grave and serious consideration.' The problem was straightforward—to maintain its existing position, the canal system must continually prove its capacity to meet the demands of trade. If it failed in this, it would provoke a substitute and a competitor and a menace to the established interests, one of which was that of Lord Francis. The familiar posture of the monopolist, wary of attracting competition to the market, was implicit in Loch's summary, and was an almost exact premonition of the position that developed in the 1820s.[15]

In Joseph Schumpeter's vivid phrase, 'a monopoly is in general no cushion to sleep on. As it is gained, so it can be retained only by alertness and energy.' Loch knew the precariousness of monopoly. The Duke of Bridgewater had known it: 'We shall do well enough if we can keep clear of these d—d tramroads', he had said. Indeed, in 1797 and 1798 surveys had been taken for horse tramroads between Liverpool and Manchester. Bradshaw, however, greeted all change with self-assured sarcasm. In December 1821, he wrote, 'I am in ignorance of everything relating to the Steam Carriage; and have only been told that some such nonsensical Idea exists.' He believed it would soon be extinct.[16]

While the problem of the railway threat emerged and sharpened in the 1820s, Loch found his responsibilities multiplying in scale and complexity. He had already spent a decade wrestling with the grim social and economic problems of distant Sutherland. On the English estates, agricultural improvement, industrial dispute, political and social turbulence all heaped growing burdens on the man. And throughout, the health of his master, Lord Stafford, deteriorated— leaving Loch more initiative and further responsibility. To all this Loch was soon to add an active parliamentary career and more managerial work for fellow-aristocrats. The coming contest of the canals and the railways impinged increasingly on his crowded life. Yet it was on Loch's reading of the situation that the Sutherland family depended—it was the basis of their coming policies.

[15] SC, Loch to Lord Francis, 24–12–1818.
[16] J. A. Schumpeter, *Capitalism, Socialism and Democracy* (1950 ed.), 102. F. Espinasse, *Lancashire Worthies* (1874), 286. SC, Bradshaw to Loch, 25–12–1821. W. L. Steel, *The History of the London and North Western Railway* (1914), 2–3.

IV

The Challenge and the Response

The complaints against the unyielding attitude of the waterways were translated into action in 1822. One possibility was the construction of a ship canal from the Dee estuary to Manchester: a project was set in motion; it remained active until its defeat in parliament in 1825. But a much more effective plan was for a railway to link Liverpool and Manchester.

Its genesis is not entirely clear, but it seems to have been born of the seething discontent of the Liverpool and Manchester mercantile and manufacturing interests. Early in 1822 the merchants of Liverpool Corn Exchange asked Bradshaw for a reduction of freight rates, alleging that they were being over-charged. Bradshaw brushed aside the allegations. He did not feel himself justified 'in making any alleviation in the trustees' present rate of freight'. Some time later a declaration by 150 Liverpool merchants was issued to the public: for too long they had experienced difficulties in obtaining carriage of goods to Manchester. Delays were 'highly prejudicial to the trading and manufacturing interests at large' and the waterways were 'quite inadequate'. They concluded 'that a new line of conveyance had become absolutely necessary to conduct the increasing trade of the country with speed, certainty and economy.'

Beyond the immediate complaints of the merchants there were other factors propitious to railway building. Technological developments exerted a major influence: so too did the decreasing costs of railway innovation. Bar-iron and copper prices were falling in the 1820s, as also were interest rates. The costs of horse-borne transport were, apparently, rising. Moreover, the growth of the Lancashire cotton trade after 1821 provided a generally expansionary context.

49

Many men of business were persuaded that the water-carriers not only abused their monopoly situation, but that the existing facilities were absolutely inadequate, monopoly or no monopoly.[1]

In 1821 Joseph Sandars, the Liverpool corn merchant largely responsible for recruiting support for the idea of a railway, was introduced to William James, a man of fertile ideas and considerable experience in canal and railway engineering.[2] Sandars conferred in Liverpool and Manchester, set up committees and engaged James to conduct a survey for a railway. In the summer of 1822 a Provisional Committee was established. Its chairman was John Moss, a Liverpool merchant and banker with interests in shipping, sugar plantations and oil-milling. In September *The Times* told the world that a 'stupendous undertaking' to connect Liverpool, Manchester and Bolton by rail would be taken to parliament in the next session.

In spite of a good deal of local hostility James completed his survey in October 1822, but this was too late for submission to parliament. The delay extended for almost two years—the plan for a railway lay strangely dormant. The survey was not implemented, we are told, because of the fear of opposition, because the survey itself was defective and because of 'the lack of knowledge of railways and the absence of plans'.[3] But, equally, there was a lack of conspicuous and effective support. The transition from the promotion of the railway 'idea' to its execution presented formidable difficulties. Success depended upon the acceptance of the idea by socially and economically significant parties—such was the condition of parliamentary approval. Furthermore, financial backing had to be demonstrated.

It was a time of contagious rumour. It seems that a committee of Liverpool and Manchester capitalists again approached Bradshaw for a reduction of rates and an increased accommodation. Their

---

[1] James Wheeler, *Manchester, Its Political, Social and Commercial History* (1836), 279–80. Thomas Baines, *History of the Commerce and Town of Liverpool* (1852), 598. *The Times,* 11–2–1825. P. H. Cootner, 'The Role of railroads in United States economic growth', *JEH*, 1963.

[2] See L. T. C. Rolt, *George and Robert Stephenson* (1960), 87–92. Baines, op. cit., 559. R. E. Carlson, 'The Liverpool and Manchester Railway Project, 1821–1831' (University of Pittsburgh, Ph.D. thesis, 1955), 58.

[3] G. S. Veitch, *The Struggle for the Liverpool and Manchester Railway* (1930). H. Pollins, 'The finances of the Liverpool and Manchester Railway', *EcHR*, 1952. E. A. Pratt, *A History of Inland Transport and Communication in England* (1912), 235. See also E.M.P.S., *The Two James's and the Two Stephensons* (1961, ed. L. T. C. Rolt), esp. 68.

tone had been conciliatory but they were again rebuffed with a flat refusal. This strengthened their resolution to form a railway. Early in 1824 a deputation was despatched to investigate the Stockton and Darlington line. In May a subscription list for £300,000 had been started and a Company was formed; William James was abandoned in favour of George Stephenson, and the promoters were actively soliciting support. The opposing parties began to take shape and to assume extreme positions. Suggestions for other railways were also in the air, sufficient to raise panic amongst canal interests in various parts of the country.

In June 1823 there was a strong rumour of a railway project to connect the collieries of Staffordshire 'through the streets of Birmingham to the centre of the town'. The established canal parties were thrown on the defensive. Their spokesman was Thomas Eyre Lee; he wrote to James Loch 'to ascertain whether rumours industriously circulated ... have any more solid foundation as connected with the Marquis of Stafford than I have found them to be when connected with the names of other respectable Noblemen ... One would have thought the age of wild speculation had passed away'. Eyre Lee feared that such support might help 'to establish as a Parliamentary principle the propriety of running railroads parallel to old canals'. It would be the thin end of the wedge.

Loch assured Eyre Lee that there was no substance in the rumour.[4] It was, as yet, still plausible to believe that the railways could be scotched as a mere novelty. In May 1825 the *Quarterly Review* confidently dismissed as 'palpably absurd and ridiculous' the notion that locomotives would attain a speed twice that of stage-coaches. The idea had been conceived, it was being taken seriously in many minds, but it was far from being established. It had to prove itself in the face of belligerent opposition.

The hiatus in railway promotion following 1822 had ended in June 1824 when George Stephenson was engaged by the newly formed Liverpool and Manchester Railway Company. On 29 October a prospectus was issued.

This was the first overt and clear-cut challenge to the canal interests; there was a feverish bustle in Liverpool, Manchester and Birmingham. Various projects were in circulation. Already in contemplation was a railway from London to Edinburgh, using

[4] SC, Eyre Lee to Loch, 13–6–1823; Loch to Eyre Lee, 14–6–1823.

locomotive and stationary engines to convey goods and passengers at a predicted speed of 12 m.p.h. James Loch kept a wary eye on the developments, but reliable information was scarce. He asked an under-agent to investigate, privately and 'through some third party', the possibility of a railway from the Midlands to Lancashire. Loch was thinking ahead and wanted to know 'what are the advantages they hold for the public both in point of economy and saving of time? Are they such that the Canal could not meet?' Characteristically, Loch was trying to by-pass the current propaganda in order to get less partial evidence. But in 1824 no one could answer his questions, except to say that the railway projectors were taking active steps.[5]

Already a company to join Birmingham and Liverpool had been mooted. In September 1824 this group, with considerable effrontery, requested the support of Lord Francis Gower. Eyre Lee, the Birmingham canal proprietor, fully realized that the Stafford family would be an obvious object of enticement by the railway interests. In October he wrote to Loch to report again a rumour that 'the Marquis of Stafford is wavering as to whether he should or should not oppose their scheme.'

He then retailed the stock arguments of the canal party: a railway would cost as much to build as any canal; railway rates would not be any less than those of canals; 'the passage of the railroad through the country with the locomotive engines must be a great nuisance.' The railway scheme was essentially 'a Banker's manœuvre', he claimed, 'and is supported ... by few people of real importance' in Birmingham. He could not conceive of a railway carrying goods 'at a lower freight than the present carriers by water, viz. $2\frac{1}{2}d.$ per ton per mile. Locomotive engines can only move cheaply on level ground and a very slight ascent involves their owners in a heavy expense by the necessary use of additional power in stationary engines.' Most of all, Eyre Lee believed that Lord Stafford's interests and allegiance ought to be with his canal colleagues. The proposed railway would impinge upon the trade of the Bridgewater Canal and therefore Stafford must oppose it. The railway promoters promised to extend branch lines into the counties of Stafford and Salop as a carrot to wavering landowners with mineral interests (including Lord Stafford). But the scheme was premature (it made little progress before 1830) and Loch coolly answered Eyre Lee, 'I never heard

[5] SC, Loch to Fenton, 8–6–1824; Fenton to Loch, 31–8–1824.

before that Lord Stafford had altered his opinion on the subject.'[6]

Loch was a difficult man to convince and he continued uncommitted in his views. The extravagant language of enthusiasm and hostility never affected his approach to the problem. For two days the clerk of the Birmingham Canal Company had tried to persuade Loch that railways could not succeed, 'neither being a cheap or a speedy conveyance'. Loch asked the obvious question: 'I said why throw away money in opposing it', and the clerk replied, 'because many foolish people will use a new thing.'[7]

The canal interests could not base their case solely on derision. A counter attack was required. The Birmingham Canal Company hatched its own plan of positive action in late 1824—it undertook a campaign designed specifically to stop the railway promoters encroaching upon canal territory in the Midlands.[8] In essence, it was a project to undermine the case for a railway by constructing a new direct canal route from Wolverhampton to the Mersey. This had been a demonstrable necessity for some time, and plans to improve the existing tortuous route had lain idle for years. Meanwhile the original shares of the Birmingham Canal had appreciated from £140 in 1770 to £2,840 in 1824.[9] Significantly, it had required the threat of opposition to provoke the execution of the project. Loch briefed the Stafford family on the likely implications of the scheme. He was not above considering the narrow gain of his employer as the compelling criterion of his recommendations. The landed estates in the Midlands would receive only small benefits. There was also the question of compensation. 'By dissenting', wrote Loch, 'there is this advantage that in assessing damages you get the utmost value of your land by the speculation, whereas if you "assent" you are supposed by the Jury to have waived all claims beyond the actual bare value of the soil.'[10] In December 1824 there was no inkling that Stafford would even assent to the canal, still less invest in it. The Stafford interest sedulously adhered to its bland, non-committal attitude.

Concurrently, a running battle went on for the prototype railroad,

---

[6] SC, Eyre Lee to Loch, 30–10–1824; Loch to Eyre Lee, 2–11–1824. C. Gill, *History of Birmingham* (1952), I, 284. Jackman, op. cit., 535–40.

[7] SC, Loch to Gower, 14–12–1824.

[8] L. T. C. Rolt, *Thomas Telford* (1958), 161.

[9] *A Statement of the Claim of the Subscribers to the Birmingham and Liverpool Railroad to an Act of Parliament* (pamphlet, 1824), 63.

[10] SC, Loch to Gower, 14–12–1824.

the Liverpool and Manchester. The company had been floated and Stephenson had begun the new survey, but the next steps were more difficult. Apparently, the company offered the Bridgewater Trust (in effect Bradshaw) a shareholding in the railway undertaking. With arrogance, insolence, ignorance and contempt (so it is told), Bradshaw demanded 'All or none'—which was refused.[11]

From then on no holds were barred. In October 1824 Joseph Sandars issued a scathing pamphlet denouncing the waterways in general and Bradshaw in particular. He accused the Bridgewater Trustees of charging twice the amount of the authorized tolls, of buying up all the available land and warehouses along the canal in Manchester and of operating a cunning monopoly against the public interest. Inevitably Sandars exaggerated the abuses of the waterways but even the canal party admitted, privately, that the public interest had suffered.[12] 'No man', declared Sandars, 'can bring a Bill forward for a canal in any part of the Kingdom but Mr. Bradshaw interferes as a sort of Canal Neptune, directing where, how and at what price it shall run. He has tortured the trade of the country to become tributary to him in all directions.'[13] Sandars asserted that the monopoly compelled the public to pay 'in one shape or other, £100,000 more per annum than they ought to pay'.[14]

Bradshaw replied in kind. He issued his own pamphlets and attempted to sway public opinion. He gained one ally in the *Liverpool Advertiser* which, in December 1824, predicted that the railway would endanger the safety of elderly gentlemen crossing the line; it would disturb foxes and pheasants; cows would not be able to graze in peace; horses would become redundant and farmers would suffer.[15] More importantly Bradshaw was able to mobilize other canals to oppose, totally, 'and by united effort, the establishment of railroads wherever contemplated'. Nor did Bradshaw eschew direct action— he attempted to intimidate Stephenson's survey team. In October 1824 Stephenson reported:[16]

[11] Francis, op. cit., 94–5. O. J. Vignoles, *Life of Charles Blacker Vignoles* (1889), 114 n. 2. H. Booth, *An Account of the Liverpool and Manchester Railway* (1830), 24. It is doubtful whether Bradshaw had the authority to accept or refuse such offers.
[12] See F. C. Mather, op. cit., 134–5.
[13] J. Sandars, *A Letter on the Subject of the Projected Railroad between Liverpool and Manchester* (1824). Pratt, op. cit., 231–2.
[14] Sandars, op. cit., 14.
[15] Quoted in Pratt, op. cit., 247.
[16] Letters of George Stephenson, Liverpool Public Library, 385/MD9.

We have had sad work with Lord Derby, Lord Sefton and Bradshaw the Great Canal Proprietor, whose grounds we go through with the projected Railway. Their ground is blockaded on every side to prevent us getting on with the Survey. Bradshaw fired guns through his ground in the course of the night to prevent the Surveyors getting on in the dark. We are to have a grand field day next week, the Liverpool Railway Company are determined to force a Survey if possible. Lord Sefton says we will have a hundred men against us. The Company thinks the Great men have no right to stop a survey. It is the Farmers only who have a right to complain, and by charging damages for trespass is all they can do.

Bradshaw sent despatches to James Loch from the war front. In December 1824 he complained, 'It is very true that I am hurried and worried almost to death, at present, and am likely to continue so, but I hope to survive it all and outlive the battle, notwithstanding the abuse and obloquy heaped upon me in Pamphlets, Newspapers . . . by our Railroad Adversaries.' Bradshaw clearly looked on Loch as an ally. Nevertheless, a few days later he pointedly repeated to Loch—in an offhand fashion—a persistent rumour which raised doubts about the allegiance of the Marquis of Stafford. He wrote:

The mode and manner in which the war is carried on, and the extraordinary assertations made, and relied upon, would be amusing, if they were not actually believed, and repeated as facts, by the Dupes of these Schemes and speculations. For instance, I have been assured that Lord Stafford is, *au fond*, friendly to the railway from Liverpool to Manchester, and the reason is this, that if the late Duke of Bridgewater's concerns should continue to prosper as they have done, his second son [Lord Francis] might eventually have a better income than his eldest son Gower and as a few thousands a year are no object to him he had rather sacrifice that, than run the risk of such being the case.

The blunt statement of the dynastic issue seemed a plausible line of motivation and the suspicion haunted Bradshaw. He also reported that it was widely believed that Lord Stafford had invested heavily in the projected Birmingham and Liverpool Railway. The newspapers were full of it.[17]

Rumour and intrigue of this sort were distasteful to the Staffords. The *Morning Chronicle* reported that Stafford had bought railway shares. Lady Stafford was furious—it was 'a very impudent trick' and the deception must be instantly contradicted. Loch issued the denial and the battle continued towards its parliamentary climax in February 1825.[18]

[17] SC, Bradshaw to Loch, 25–12–1824; Innes to Loch, 9–1–1825. *Inverness Journal*, 1–1–1825.
[18] SC, Lady Stafford to Loch, 25–12–1824.

V

The Way of Compromise

As the railway assault was mounted in late 1824 and early 1825 'great fear and confusion of mind fell upon canal proprietors.'[1] But the canal interests closed their ranks in good time. They were ready for the parliamentary battle against the Liverpool and Manchester Railway. It came in February 1825. This was regarded as a test-case. Elaborate preparations were made to defend the interests of the canal proprietors, many of whom believed that the railways could be snuffed-out once and for all.

James Loch, however, favoured a conciliatory policy; in the last resort the public interest must prevail. The railways could be temporarily blocked by concerted resistance, but eventually some degree of compromise on the part of the canals was unavoidable. In the long run the relative technical capacities of railways and canals would determine the outcome. At the beginning of 1825 Loch believed that the canals could meet public feeling by extending their own facilities. It was the only sound basis on which to mount an opposition to the railways.

Loch reported to Bradshaw that the Birmingham Canal people felt that 'they had no case for the public against the Railways unless they held out some facilities to the public beyond that which they now possessed.' They had already commissioned Telford to survey the line of a new canal to Liverpool.

I find all my friends Railway mad [Loch continued] it is beyond conception how universal it is—and I firmly believe from what I see that though the great part of the present agitation arises from ill-favoured expectation and

[1] Ellesmere, op. cit., 244.

skilful manœuvres of persons who mean to prosper by the rage, yet I am satisfied that there is a general demand for an additional means of transport which must be met in some way or other.

Bradshaw replied that it was absurd to undertake vast expenditure 'to make out a case, merely as if it were nothing. What will Lord Stafford say to similar expenditure, on our parts, for the same object, for we certainly want a case, very much.' The railway madness was quite ridiculous, said Bradshaw; 'they all begin by running us down and abusing me, but I consider their censure praise.' In that sense he was indeed well praised.[2]

But Loch was emphatic: 'Upon so momentous a subject', he remarked, 'it is folly to blink the question and deceive oneself.' Even so, a clear line of policy was difficult since the major variable in the situation—the operational efficiency of the railway—was an unknown quantity. In January 1825 Loch obtained confidential reports on 'the power of the locomotive engine and the facilities of railways' from the Killingworth and Hetton collieries in Northumberland, and the Cromford Railway. He consulted Jessop, the engineer, as a person of 'science and practical experience and cool judgment'. 'You know', he told Jessop, 'I am interested on the other side, but it is my duty if I can to endeavour to make up my mind upon the subject by understanding the real merits of the question.' The reports were more favourable than Loch had anticipated. Loch was convinced by the evidence that the railways would have no difficulty in transporting goods at 8 m.p.h. and passengers at 12 m.p.h. At the same time it was clear that the railway 'must be kept very level with great embankments and cuttings or much deviation or by use of stationary engines'. Loch concluded 'from a very dispassionate consideration of the case, founded on information got from the most disinterested sources', that the railways could be 'a very superior mode of conveyance, if constructed on the proper principle'. Loch was not impressed by another correspondent who alleged that wet weather and continuous use would so reduce friction on the railway that 'the locomotive must be reduced to nothing and power to drag destroyed.'

Loch acknowledged that the country required and demanded additional means of communication, and that there was a strong feeling in favour of railways. It could not be ignored. Nor need such a development necessarily be catastrophic to the canals:

[2] SC, Loch to Bradshaw, 26–12–1824; Bradshaw to Loch, 30–12–1824.

There is no doubt much of what we see in the newspapers is mere speculation, but every concern includes respectable names, and much wealth is embarked in them. That they must affect both Canals and Turnpikes is true, but as they must increase the wealth and commerce of the Country prodigiously they will not do so to the extent supposed by some.

Loch did not underestimate the potential of the railways. If to the advantage of speed 'can be clearly added great economy in the transport of goods, what argument', he asked Lord Gower, 'can be urged to defeat ultimately this mode of conveyance?' Loch was well aware of the argument concerning the preservation of the existing capital invested in the canals—and, although it was an increasingly difficult notion to maintain, it continued to carry weight in the canal faction. Loch was more conscious than most of the parlous position of the canal proprietors; he believed that the only answer was to press them into the improvement of their facilities.

I only hope Bradshaw may take the same course. And as every increased facility must add to the rapidly growing trade between Manchester and Liverpool and Ireland, that Property [the Bridgewater Canal] must continue to flourish, if these improvements are adopted which the state of the times and the impatience of the public requires and it certainly might be a subject for Bradshaw's consideration whether by withdrawing opposition to this measure he might not yet without difficulty act to curb the defects in those of the Duke which now hamper him, and get powers sufficient to enable him to grapple with the new wants of the districts.

Loch thus placed conciliation at a high premium. Co-existence between canals and railways was possible—since trade multiplied itself under conditions of improved transport. Better facilities could create traffic. In other words, if the canals invested in improvements, they would be placed in a more competitive position if the railways gained parliamentary assent; such a policy might even preclude the necessity of the railways. [3]

Bradshaw was not moved, or so it appears. Perhaps he was immovable. And despite Loch's doubts the Stafford family lined its formidable parliamentary strength behind the canal interests in the contest which lasted from February to June 1825. Stephenson had completed his survey and the Bill for the Liverpool and Manchester Railway was introduced into parliament on 11 February 1825. The elaborate and expensive campaign to canvass opinion had

[3] SC, Loch to Fenton, 12-1-1825; Loch to Gower, 1-1-1825; Thomas Graham to Loch, 12-12-1825.

brought wide support for the railway promoters. 'Nothing was left undone to secure success in parliament' and 'a secret and irresponsible committee for influence' had operated.[4] Petitions of support were received from mercantile and manufacturing interests and there was a growing feeling that the railway should be judged on its merits. Thus, although the Marquis of Chandos declared outright opposition, the Duke of Athol said that he 'would not promise his support to his valued friend Lord Stafford', but would 'hear both sides'. Most importantly the railway had gained the parliamentary leadership of William Huskisson, M.P. for Liverpool. Huskisson was a shareholder in canals but he was already committed to the idea of improved facilities. 'In some shape', he had said, 'additional accommodation is wanted for the traffic . . . I feel it incumbent upon me to support any plan brought forward by my Constituents for conferring these advantages upon their trade.'[5]

In many ways Huskisson's attitude to the transport problem was similar to, though more committed than, that of James Loch. This is not surprising since Loch was a friend and great admirer of Huskisson's approach to economic questions. Huskisson sought 'only improved transport facilities of some kind and the reduction of canal tolls'. Speaking in the debate, Huskisson was able to say that 'In this project there was no appearance of a desire to further private interests. The great object seemed to be to confer a benefit on the commerce of the country.' The railway projectors appeared to have a higher objective than the mere accumulation of wealth and were not likely to obtain very high profits.[6] In fact, they had carefully cultivated this aspect of their undertaking. In order to sway public opinion they had offered extraordinary concessions in terms of their future profits and pricing policy.

On the face of things it seems that the first major railway paid heavily for the right to pioneer the railway system. There were three major concessions. First, in order to placate opposition, the shares in the company were to be divided equally between Liverpool, Manchester and the landowners on the line of the railway. Second, it was decided that no individual subscriber could hold more than ten shares—and thus Huskisson could say to parliament that 'the

[4] Baines, op. cit., 603–4.
[5] G. S. Veitch, *Huskisson and Liverpool* (1929), 46. SC, Eyre Lee to Loch, 17–2–1825. Liverpool and Manchester Railway Correspondence and Circulars, Liverpool Public Library, Ellis to Booth, 5–2–1825.
[6] Hansard, 2–3–1825.

profit could not be an object.' Third, the idea of a 10 per cent dividend limitation was accepted, though with considerable reluctance. This was tentatively agreed in February 1825 at the instigation of Huskisson, to which the London delegation of the railway hastily assented. At first the directors in Liverpool were hostile to the suggestion. They argued that it was an infringement of 'the principles of Free Trade'; any surplus beyond 10 per cent would be an embarrassment; it would deter economy in management and remove any motive for exertion; moreover, it would make the position of the canals more rather than less difficult—as Lister Ellis said, 'if we are limited to 10 p. cent the Old Quay Navigation will not produce sufficient returns to pay for repairs, the Duke's will be restricted to that part of its trade that communicates with the canals south of his line and with Worsley and for coals'—and Ellis was not disposed to advocate 'wholesale destruction of Property'.

Yet the directors did accept the limitation—it was the price of Huskisson's support. And, it was thought, the profit limitation might allow the railway to demand exclusive use of their line instead of making it a public highway. During the course of the discussion Ellis pointed out that stationary engines would probably be necessary for some time. It was impossible to say, he said, how expensive it would be to create a level line and it could take ten years to excavate Kirkby Moss. The construction expenses might have to be financed later from the working profits. But these were private admissions which the railway party did not ventilate in parliament.[7]

Each of the three concessions was modified in the course of time. Although the Liverpool and Manchester Railway was promoted to serve local ends, it drew a good deal of support from the rest of the country. It did not rely entirely on local capital. Liverpool was certainly prominent in the early sources of railway capital—the first railway was very much a Liverpool concern. Within the Liverpool contingent there was a striking Quaker involvement. The Quaker James Cropper gave his support because 'railways . . . tended to break up the reign of vested interests under which the slave-owners of the West Indies claimed they had the right to buy and sell their fellow men.'[8] But in Manchester feeling and support for the railway was much less enthusiastic. In March 1825 Hugh Birley tried to raise

[7] Liverpool and Manchester Railway Correspondence, Ellis to Booth, 5-2-1825, 9-2-1825, 13-3-1825; Rotheram to Booth, 9-2-1825.
[8] F. A. Conybeare, *Dingle Bank, A Sketch* (1925), 23.

support in Manchester for a petition to be sent to the London deputation of the railway in parliament. He carried his petition from warehouse to warehouse, but without success. 'I was surprised at the general backwardness and occasionally a decided repugnance which I could not account for.' The Manchester newspapers had claimed that the interests of their city had been neglected, and there was a general fear that the railway promoters would bring locomotives into the streets of Manchester. Birley was told that it was 'seriously in contemplation to petition from this Town against the Bill because of the contempt shewn for the feelings of Manchester'.[9] The coolness of Manchester in March 1825 cannot be attributed to a depression in the cotton trade since the peak of the boom was not reached until April.[10] By the middle of July 1825 business confidence had dissolved and thereafter the problem of raising capital was very much greater. Neither Manchester nor the affected landowners showed any alacrity in taking up the shares reserved for them—in December 1829 less than 2 per cent of the shares were held in Manchester. Similarly, the clause limiting shareholding to ten shares was not adhered to for long—though until late 1825 the principle stood.[11] The clause limiting profits to 10 per cent had a longer life but it also was subject to very wide interpretation in the later history of the company.

With the support of Huskisson and Brougham the Liverpool and Manchester Railway emerged well from the first debate in the Commons. But the real contest was in Committee. There the Bill was subjected to minute examination over a period of ten weeks. The opposition, comprised mainly of the three navigation interests together with the obstinate local aristocrats, Lords Derby and Sefton, was led in London by Atcheson on behalf of R. H. Bradshaw.[12] Sandars, the railway director, said dejectedly, 'Every man, every Corporate Body, seems spellbound the moment Mr. Bradshaw

[9] Liverpool and Manchester Railway Correspondence, Birley to the London Deputation, 3-3-1825; Potter to Booth, 16-4-1825. *PP*, 1825, Proceedings of the Committee of the House of Commons on the Liverpool and Manchester Railroad Bill, 525. SC, Currie to Loch, 9-12-1829.

[10] B. W. Clapp, *John Owens, Manchester Merchant* (1965), 47. I owe this reference to Professor T. C. Barker. Cf. Pollins, op. cit., 91.

[11] Pollins, ibid. SC, List of Shares, 9-12-1929 (the distribution of shares in 1829 was roughly Liverpool 47 per cent, London 15 per cent, Lord Stafford 19 per cent, elsewhere 18 per cent.

[12] Unfortunately the correspondence between Loch, Bradshaw and Atcheson is missing from the SC.

interposes his authority.'[13] James Loch, with the consent of the Bridgewater Trustees (including the Archbishop of York) presented one of the 150 petitions of opposition and organized Lord Stafford's influence in parliament. Eyre Lee, in London rousing opposition to railways, was bubbling with confidence. The public would not accept the railways' claims of cheapness or necessity; they could not be allowed to usurp the authority of the landowner; the 'engines and machines cannot be constructed so as to consume their own smoke'; he claimed that the railways were unable to raise the required capital except on mortgage and that they 'assume the right to dictate the price to be charged by any carrier or porter for delivery of goods from their wharfs and this is little less than an actual monopoly'. Eyre Lee, spellbound by his own optimism, contended to Loch: 'Surely it is a good public ground that the capital to be laid out in iron would be more beneficially laid out for the public in conversion of the iron into manufactured goods.'[14]

Feeling ran high; Sandars grumbled about the 'lies and misrepresentations' of his canal opponents. On the other side, Creevey condemned 'the infernal, impudent, lying jobbing' of the railway promoters.[15]

The Committee of the House of Commons listened patiently to an almost endless stream of confusing evidence. The railway promoters claimed technical superiority; they claimed that the waterways were uncertain, risky and expensive; most of all they claimed that the canal owners 'combined and confederated' to manipulate their rates and traffic to suit their own convenience. There existed a *de facto* monopoly; only a railway could provide an essential element of competition. The waterways had required a stimulus of danger to persuade them to reduce rates; if the Bill were rejected the canals would coalesce once more and raise their rates. Most of all, concluded the promoters, the railway sought to 'open the line of communication never liable to that confederacy and combination which have so long existed to the prejudice of the public'.

The canal interests denied every point of the railway case; the potential commercial advantages to the country simply did not warrant the wholesale interference in private property; the engineering

[13] Quoted in Jackman, op. cit., 523.

[14] SC, Eyre Lee to Loch, February 1825; Loch to Archbishop of York, 18-3-1825.

[15] Liverpool and Manchester Railway Correspondence, Ef. 391, Sandars to Ellis, 5-3-1825. H. Maxwell (ed.), *The Creevey Papers*, II, 88.

and locomotive problems were unsolved and probably insoluble; there was always a real degree of competition on the canals since they were open to any individual to trade, and the number of carriers had increased in proper proportion to the growth of trade; there was no virtue in excessive competition since it led automatically and painfully to wasteful destruction of fixed capital and to further monopoly; if the railways were able to carry lighter goods, the canals would have to charge more for heavier goods which would be against the public interest; the railway would in itself be a form of monopoly; it was all unnecessary since the canals had their own 'improvement in contemplation'.

But, most of all, the canal advocates concentrated upon, multiplied and magnified, the technical doubts concerning railways. In the upshot it was this which proved decisive. Errors were discovered in Stephenson's survey of the line of the railway—'opposing counsel were able to argue that less material would be taken from the cuttings than would be required for the embankments.' The Bill was lost at the Committee stage on a technicality.[16]

The day after the withdrawal of the Bill, Lord Francis Gower reported the defeat of the railway to his elder brother. He felt great personal relief. The result had not been certain until the final day when Creevey had 'objected to everything' and the railway had suddenly been 'deprived of every description of power'. He felt much exalted by the victory: 'Thank God there is another new light quenched.' Bradshaw was equally gratified and felt that the repulse would prove fatal to the loathsome interlopers.[17]

Yet the light was not quenched. Indeed, the railway promoters almost immediately retrimmed their lamps. There was 'a spontaneous and indignant manifestation of feeling' in favour of the railway. A meeting between the Liverpool and Manchester directors and twenty-one M.P.s was led by William Huskisson. He declared that nothing should prevent them from trying again.[18] There was a general rekindling of confidence and resolution. Within a month the railway promoters took steps towards a second assault. The campaign of 1825–6 was designed to remove the technical deficiencies of the survey, and to open cleavages in the previously united opposition.

[16] *PP*, 1925, Proceedings, 1–10, 117, 136–9, 305–7, 352, 520–25. Veitch, *Struggle*, 47–8.

[17] SC, D593P/22/1/5, Lord Francis to Earl Gower, 2–6–1825.

[18] Baines, op. cit., 610. Veitch, op. cit., 50.

The organization of financial amd moral support for the various companies was a rather furtive activity. Pressures and inducements were brought to bear privately, away from the public ear. Natural groupings of interests existed. 'It was impossible', we are told, 'for a man to hold any of these railway shares and still be loyal to the canal company of whose shares he had any considerable amount.'[19] This notion seemed to restrict the range of action of James Loch and Lord Stafford. The canal interests regarded Stafford as a natural ally; yet the railways were not pessimistic about the possibility of winning him over. Despite the fact that Stafford had repeatedly denied any intention of involvement, he received several approaches from railway companies. It was known that both Stafford and Loch regarded Brougham and Huskisson with friendship and admiration; it was known that Adam, counsel for the Liverpool and Manchester in the House of Commons Committee, was a relative of James Loch. There can be no doubt that both sides felt Stafford's allegiance to be vital.

Bradshaw had at last been forced into some modification of his administration of the Bridgewater Canal. The heightened hostility of public opinion had compelled him to reduce rates by 25 per cent in late 1823, a time of expanding trade. Other such tendencies were evident: by October 1825 Bradshaw had made it known that he was prepared to allow new carriers on the canal, and was ready to let or sell land for building warehouses in Manchester; but the response had been poor, perhaps due to the worsening trade conditions of late 1825. Moreover, Bradshaw eventually countenanced improvements on the canal to help appease public opinion—though in a rather sullen fashion. As soon as the parliamentary defeat of the railway was known, the canal improvements were announced. In effect, it was a public admission that the canal facilities were inadequate; at the same time it represented an attempt to conciliate public opinion—'to make out a case', as Bradshaw put it. A large part of the financing of the new works came from Lord Stafford—£58,000 in all.

It was a significant investment. By it Stafford had discharged his financial obligation to the Bridgewater Canal. As James Loch wrote later, Stafford 'took care not to neglect the interests of the Bridgewater Canal', and his gift of £58,000 would 'enable it to meet the

[19] Jackman, op. cit., 523.

competition which the other means of transit might create'. Stafford's investment of June 1825 was an essential step. It meant that he could consider, on their merits, the rival projects of canal and railway.[20]

At almost the same time, the Stafford family took 200 shares in the proposed Birmingham and Liverpool Junction Canal Company. This new canal, to be constructed by Telford at an estimated cost of £400,000, had been brought into existence by the threat of a railway. It would save 21 miles and 60 locks as compared with existing canal routes. Loch had been considering the proposal since November 1824. It was an awkward project because it impinged upon the interests of the existing canals—it would 'get to Liverpool without going by the Grand Trunk' or the Bridgewater Canal.

It threatened to bring the existing canal companies into conflict. Even in normal times the canal interests were notorious for their disputes. And as Bradshaw pointed out, the scheme was 'as old as the Duke's time, and was fought, and put an end to, (I believe) by him'. To assuage all this, the proponents of the new canal proposed to offer shares in the concern to the Bridgewater Trust, and the other affected canals, in lieu of the expected loss of trade. At first Bradshaw thought that this was 'rather too good *a joke*', but eventually he conceded that the canal could not be opposed.

Loch declared that 'it will give . . . much new trade, and the additional impulse this measure must give to the prosperity of the Country will soon fill up any vacancy it may create. It is clearly better than a railway and both cannot be opposed. The country must have some vent.' Competition would not necessarily be ruinous; the new canal might even increase the use of existing facilities. It was an enlightened thought, coming as it did from a member of the 'canal interest'.

The Birmingham and Liverpool Junction Canal has been described as 'the last victory of the canals over the railways'—and the rival railway was indeed delayed. The Stafford family pledged £20,000 to the canal; in June 1825 the shares were 'in vast request'. Loch thought it 'a very good speculation' and had actually bought shares on his own account. The Stafford family had been able to state its own terms in the agreement—the canal would have to have a connecting arm into Shropshire to benefit the family estates and there were clauses to guarantee part of the trade of the Bridgewater

[20] SC, Loch to Fenton, 2–6–1825; Captain James Bradshaw to Loch, 13–10–1825. Carlson, op. cit., 83, 95.

Canal. Loch found it necessary to act as a watchdog to safeguard the original agreement.[21]

At this stage, in June 1825, there was no intimation that Stafford would sink much greater sums into an opposing railway company. Bradshaw, apparently, had no suspicion of it.

During the middle months of 1825 James Loch became a sounding-board for ideas that might break the impasse between the railways and the canals. For instance, a certain Edris Marwade had suggested that a railway could be built alongside the canal so that an engine could pull along the canal boats 'with much greater celerity, and no damage to the canal'. This, he thought, was the perfect compromise. Lady Cork sponsored ideas of steam navigation on the canals, while Thomas Graham made elaborate calculations to prove the inherent superiority of traction on water compared with rail. Loch told Bradshaw of an idea of 'moving steam-boats by means of an artificial fishes tail' which would propel boats along the canal and thereby help to fend off competition from the railways. Loch was not ignorant in these matters. In 1825 he was supervising the construction of a mineral railway on the Naworth Castle estate of the Earl of Carlisle.[22]

It was only a matter of time before the Liverpool and Manchester Railway Company would press again for parliamentary approval. Bradshaw agreed that they were bound to try again in 1826. But a new survey, less objectionable to local landowners, had to be taken. In September 1825, Bradshaw reported sardonically to Loch:

Their acting Surveyor has just been here to shew me their Plans, and ask permission to go over our lands, to which (you will scarcely believe it) I have consented, but the man behaved so fairly and openly I really could not refuse, am I not a Liberal? Their new line is certainly less objectionable than their former . . . they profess their great object to be, the getting over our Canal . . . with the least possible injury, or inconvenience to us, Kind Souls.

[21] SC, Loch to Eyre Lee, 30–6–1825, 13–9–1825; Loch to MacDonald, 18–6–1825; R. H. Bradshaw to Loch, 30–12–1824; Gower to Loch, 5–8–1824; Eyre Lee to Loch, 8–11–1824, 13–12–1831; Loch to Stafford, 26–12–1824; Loch to Bradshaw, 26–12–1824, 10–11–1825. Rolt, *Telford*, 172. It is worth noting that virtually no Liverpool capital entered this project: see SC, Eyre Lee to Loch, 4–7–1831; List of Proprietors, etc.

[22] SC, Marwade to Stafford, 30–6–1825; Graham to Loch, 12–2–1825, 16–2–1825; Lady Cork to Loch, June 1825; Loch to Bradshaw, 28–6–1825; Loch to Gower, 9–7–1825.

Bradshaw also wrote, 'I am poorer than usual this Year, my expenses are heavy, and the Railroad fight cost me, altogether, little short of £10,000.' Bradshaw had always regarded himself as the personification of the Bridgewater Canal.[23]

Bradshaw remained unshakeably opposed to the railway. The canal interest once again rallied for united and total opposition to impending competition. In early December 1825 Lord Stafford was called upon to join with other canal owners to attempt the public suppression of the Birmingham and Liverpool Railroad.[24] Within a matter of three weeks the ranks were broken in the most dramatic fashion.

Soon after Christmas 1825 it was announced, quite suddenly, that the Marquis of Stafford had bought a thousand shares in the Liverpool and Manchester Railway—one fifth of the total. The previous limitation of ten shares per shareholder was completely overturned and Stafford's holding became easily the biggest. Immediately following the decision the Company issued a new prospectus.

The financial and moral support implied by Stafford's decision was momentous. Even in the boom of 1824–5 it had not been 'easy to dispose of scrip' for the railway.[25] In December 1825 the confidence of the business world had been drained away and the slide into panic and depression was unmistakable. Certainly it was a most unpropitious time for raising capital. Moreover, the new survey for the railway had demonstrated that the original estimates would have to be increased from £400,000 to £510,000. The investment of £100,000 by Lord Stafford was, therefore, a very timely fillip to the Company. The purchase price of shares immediately rose 50 per cent when the news was made known.[26]

Beyond the financial benefits, it is proper to stress the investment as a moral victory for the railways. It represented the enlisting of the very interest that would virtually guarantee the success of the railway in parliament. As William Currie remarked retrospectively in 1831, 'If . . . Lord S. had kept back, it would have been put down to doubts of the feasibility of the plans—to Telford's unfavourable reports etc.,—and must have been productive of the most serious consequences.'[27] For the railway it was a remarkable conversion from

[23] SC, R. H. Bradshaw to Loch, 27-9-1825; Captain Bradshaw to Loch, 13-10-1825.
[24] SC, Eyre Lee to Loch, 7-12-1825.
[25] Pollins, op. cit., 91.
[26] Baines, op. cit., 611.
[27] SC, Currie to Loch, 19-5-1831; Pollins, op. cit., 92.

within the ranks of the canal proprietors; it was the most acceptable fruit of their long labours of public persuasion.

The decision came as a startling surprise to most of England; it had all the appearance of a *volte-face*. Ostensibly, it looked as though Stafford had deserted the canal camp for the enemy after having unswervingly supported them for two years. The categorical denials of December 1824 of involvement in any railway venture, the investment in the Bridgewater Canal, followed by that in the Birmingham and Liverpool Junction Canal, together with persistent rebuffs to railway approaches—all this seemed to indicate a fixed allegiance to the canal interests.

Yet Stafford had abstained from the attempt made by the canal-owners to suppress competitive opposition. In effect Stafford had avoided being exclusively committed to either side—wisely in the outcome. Indeed, in this way, he was unique. His position allowed him to stand aside from the fray—but yet to support both sides. He alone, it seems, among canal-owners, was able to reject the notion that railway and canal investments were mutually exclusive.

James Loch, undoubtedly the most important influence in the Stafford family, had viewed the situation with concern, but also with cool-headed composure. His judgment was undisturbed by the cacophony of dispute around him and he managed to view the developments as a whole—aware of the critical position of Stafford at the centre of events. In the long months of agitation Loch had repeatedly voiced one vital notion: that increased transport facilities were likely to multiply the total quantum of traffic and would thereby benefit old and new concerns alike. Such a view gave a solid basis for a policy of compromise.[28]

[28] In view of the judgments very recently published by F. C. Mather in *After the Canal Duke*, it is probably worth re-emphasizing the basic assumptions of Loch's thinking and strategy in these years: that the canals could save themselves so long as they increased their efficiency and maximized their bargaining strength *vis-à-vis* the railways. Mr Mather has handed down interesting and highly critical judgments on James Loch—to the effect that his policies were pedestrian and unimaginative and actually hindered the adaptation of the Bridgewater Trust to the coming of the railways (e.g. 65–77). This is a view directly contrary to that offered in these chapters. Mr Mather also remarks (77–8): 'If the protectors of the Duke's Canal did not rush headlong into alliances with railways, neither did they exert themselves much to oppose the new form of transport. Where they fought, it was for limited objectives which stopped short of annihilation of the enemy.' R. H. Bradshaw at one time believed annihilation was possible, but it is extremely unlikely that Loch even considered it either a moral or a realistic possibility.

Yet it was a tortuous policy and was not the product of a single line of motivation. The final decision was not taken in a vacuum but was contingent on a whole set of circumstances. And since the decision was an acknowledged turning-point in British railway history, and therefore in a lesser way in economic history, it is worth some consideration.

One suggestion has been made that James Loch was hostile to R. H. Bradshaw and that this, in the upshot, determined the final alignment.[29] But active hostility is not easily identifiable. There was a considerable degree of frankness in the relationship between the two men; they had established a *rapport* based on a professional respect that was mutual. There was much in contention, and occasionally a degree of friction between the two men. Loch was wary of Bradshaw's tactics. He did not agree with Bradshaw's course of action and he attempted to influence it, with only a little success. Eventually, in later years, Loch moved further away from Bradshaw's reactionary tactics, perhaps in despair. Yet, despite the cantankerous nature of the canal-master, Loch managed to get on amazingly well with him—even to the point of being in his confidence. In 1825 there was little personal antipathy in evidence; far from being hostile, Loch was conciliatory.

Another suggestion is that Lord Stafford was won over to the railway by a 'bribe'—in the form of a 20 per cent control of the railway.[30] But Stafford had been tempted by bribes before and had uniformly resisted. Stafford had to be persuaded to accept the offer. The persuasion came mainly from William Huskisson and other close associates of James Loch.

Huskisson was a great friend of the Stafford family; he had started his political career under the patronage of Lord Stafford in 1791. He was described, when on his death-bed, as the 'most intimate friend of Lord Stafford'. Lady Stafford said of him, 'We had a very real esteem for Mr. Huskisson, and a real friendship for him'— indeed there were unproved allegations of intimacy between Huskisson and Stafford's wife. Certainly he was on confidential terms with James Loch—a true Huskissonian in his views—and his friendship extended to Lord Francis.[31] He was a frequent visitor of the family.

[29] Pollins, op. cit., 92. Falk, op. cit., 125.

[30] J. Hughes, *Liverpool Banks and Bankers* (1906), 197.

[31] A. Brady, *William Huskisson and Liberal Reform* (1928), 2–3. C. R. Fay, op. cit., 7, 42, 63–5, 90, 257.

It was as a family guest, in June 1825, that Huskisson spoke of the railway/canal dispute and offered advice and opinion to his hosts. Lady Stafford reported, 'I saw Huskisson who says much for *us* will depend next year, on the manners of the Canal being conciliatory and accommodating and to avoid bullying by all means.'[32] Huskisson was clearly referring to Bradshaw's notorious intransigence. Later in the year a small group of the Liverpool and Manchester Railway directors took an unauthorized initiative to seek a negotiation with Stafford with a view to circumventing Bradshaw. Adam, counsel for the railway in the 1825 contest, was induced to open talks with his friend and relative, James Loch. The negotiations were conducted 'with the utmost secrecy'.[33]

At this point Loch consulted Huskisson, whose persuasion tipped the scales. Writing to Lord Gower, whose interest would eventually be greatly affected by the decision, Loch stated that 'Huskissons' opinion was so much in favour of compromise that it was agreed to ... the terms in which Lord Stafford is to be secured for his advances, are not yet quite settled, but that is his affair, independent of the Railway ... it engages my best attention I assure you.' Loch was in close agreement with Huskisson and some years later he described himself as 'Having been the means of inducing Lord Stafford to embark so large a sum in the adventure'. Loch certainly took the responsibility for the decision.[34]

The process of winning support among the Stafford family was made clearer by Loch in a letter to the Archbishop of York. It had not been a simple matter of convincing Lord Stafford as head of the family. The multifarious, and in the long run, conflicting interests of the family had to be reconciled, or at least compromised. This applied most significantly to the affairs of Lord Francis, the heir of the Bridgewater Canal. Loch disclosed the news to the Archbishop:

The decision was come to after the most mature deliberation and after Lord Francis had seen Mr. Huskisson. Lord Stafford has become, as representing the Bridgewater Canal, the proprietor of about ⅕ of the whole concern and it is now under consideration what will be the better way of communicating to those in remainder [i.e. the future claims of

---

[32] SC, Lady Stafford to Loch, 9–6–1825.
[33] Baines, op. cit., 611. The tactics of the railway had changed. John Moss told Huskisson that 'The experience of last year has taught us that something more than a good case is necessary to secure a Bill a passing.' Liverpool Public Reference Library, Letters of William Huskisson, 26–11–1825.
[34] SC, Loch to Gower, 29–12–1825; Loch to Currie, February 1829.

Stafford's sons on the railway shares] their proper contingent interest or shares in the concern.

The question of power within the railway was vital. Loch reported 'A proportional control in the management will be reserved to the proprietors of these shares.'[35] From the outset the Staffords placed great emphasis on the aspect of control; it was an essential part of the transaction. Lord Stafford had bought not merely an investment, but also a large influence in the future conduct of the railway.

The dynastic problem was inescapable. The divergent interests within the family had been held together by the influence of Loch and by the articles of the purchase. F. C. Mather has represented the decision as a yielding to pressure 'for public rather than for private reasons', and as an example of the responsible exercise of aristocratic power in an age of organized public opinion.[36] Yet it must be said that the pressure came from within the family as well as from outside. Only a fortnight before the decision was reached Loch had reminded Lord Gower that, if he died without a son, his inheritance would descend to his younger brother, Lord Francis, and his daughters would receive none of it.[37] It could be argued that Stafford was thinking primarily of the future welfare of his first son, Lord Gower. In the outcome a balancing of financial interests in the family had been achieved, a dynastic compromise. The canal income had been buttressed by the investments in the Bridgewater Canal and the Junction Canal; on the other side, Lord Gower's future income was given better prospects with the investment in the railway adventure. To the rest of the world, with few exceptions, it had all the appearances of a statesmanlike compromise by the leading canal proprietor between the ostensibly irreconcilable interests of the railway and the canals. Thus the public talk of Stafford's self-abnegation in promoting a railway which was expressly designed to break the power of his canal. Loch himself, in a later rationalization, wrote that Stafford had been moved by a feeling of virtuous beneficence.[38]

Loch's comments on the decision lacked consistency. In 1829, for instance, he declared that Stafford had invested in the Liverpool and Manchester Railway 'in order to indemnify himself against any loss that might arise in . . . the trade carried by the Duke', spreading the

[35] SC, Loch to Archbishop of York, 29–12–1825.
[36] Mather, 'The Duke of Bridgewater's trustees', 139.
[37] SC, Loch to Gower, 6–12–1825.
[38] Loch, 'Memoir'.

risk, a genuine economic motive. Lord Francis, in a slightly different way, also regarded the decision as economically sound. He had written to his brother, Lord Gower, in December 1825:[39]

It is, of course, impossible to calculate on the ultimate result of this spirited measure, but I am sure at least that what we resign is of no value and that if any advantage should result it will be pure gain, as our opposition could not be worth a farthing to the scheme in its present state. In the meantime peace and good will upon earth is no slight immediate benefit to all but the lawyers.

The Stafford family had bought more than peace and good will. Through the agency of James Loch they were now in a better position to pursue the policy of promoting co-existence between canals and railways.

---

[39] SC, Loch to Currie, 4–11–1829; Loch to Bather, 25–10–1830; D593P/22/1/5, Lord Francis to Earl Gower, 29–12–1825, 31–12–1825. Mather, *After the Canal Duke*, 55, remarks that in 1828 'Lord Francis was still smarting under the recollection of his father's treachery in purchasing the railroad shares to the detriment of his own inheritance.' This does not seem to square with the evidence of Lord Francis's own correspondence, nor does it take into account the general strategy of the Leveson-Gower family—which, it is suggested, was not detrimental to the interests of Lord Francis.

VI

A Position of Influence

The decision of Lord Stafford to sink £100,000 in a railway came as a surprise to most people. Even Lord Gower was not told until the bargain had been concluded. Eyre Lee, the canal representative, discovered the alarming news from the newspapers. For astonished enquirers, James Loch tersely verified the reports. He gave no elaborate explanations; it was a *fait accompli* and no justification was offered. Lord Derby was not immediately told of Lord Stafford's action and took umbrage at the 'want of courtesy'. This was later given as the reason for Derby's continued opposition to the railway.[1]

Although the railway shares had been bought by Stafford, 'as representing the Bridgewater Canal', they were exclusively the property of Stafford alone. Stafford could dispose of them entirely of his own volition. Loch did suggest that Lord Francis (heir of the Bridgewater Canal) should be given the option of buying the shares on the death of his father, but the idea was never taken up. It is clear that the shares were intended for Lord Gower who had no place in the Bridgewater concern. The position of Lord Francis was invidious and Loch found it necessary to dispel any doubts about the allegiance of the younger son. Lord Francis gave the Railway Bill his 'decided support' and, insisted Loch, he wished to avoid all idea that he had any doubt about 'the propriety of the step that has been taken'. Similarly, doubts were expressed about the allegiance of Lord Gower towards the Birmingham and Liverpool Junction Canal which was also seeking parliamentary sanction. Lord Clive, a fellow promoter of the canal, asked Gower to issue 'a decided expression of

[1] SC, Lord Belgrave to Loch, 2–1–1826; Loch to Mackenzie, 9–1–1826; Loch to Eyre Lee, 3–1–1826; Currie to Loch, 20–11–1829.

approbation . . . to prevent misunderstanding on this matter'; it was essential to 'ascertain whether his Lordship is really firm in his determination to support the Canal'.[2] The Stafford family's simultaneous assistance to both canal and railway naturally perplexed interests on both sides and the doubts were never entirely removed.

Loch insisted that Stafford should be given a share in the management commensurate with his financial holding. The demand was met and Stafford was empowered to appoint three directors, one fifth of the railway board. The choice was significant: James Loch, Captain James Bradshaw, son of R. H. Bradshaw, and James Sothern, a very close colleague of, and eventual successor to, R. H. Bradshaw. Lord Stafford had thus made a gesture in appeasement of the redoubtable Bradshaw. The question of control and influence was equally of interest to the Old Quay Navigation, the future prosperity of which had also been placed in suspense by the railway project. The Old Quay representative, Eccles, approached Loch prior to the rehearing of the Bill for the railway. 'We had a very friendly meeting', reported Loch to Stafford, 'he was very open and gentlemanlike, he said the Old River [Quay] could not appear in Parliament as their property was avoided [i.e. was not affected by the route of the railway] . . . He was very anxious we should secure as much of the management as possible.'[3]

There were also problems concerning the form of the new Railway Bill. The clause limiting the shareholding had to be removed. Lord Stafford also demanded that 'the clause limiting the amount of profits must be struck out entirely.' Huskisson's 10 per cent limitation had been used as a guarantee of the good faith of the projectors in the campaign of 1825, in order to secure its passage through parliament. In 1826 the railway promoters again tried to resist the clause, but Huskisson remained 'stiff on the subject of his clause', and forced them to accept it 'to protect the rights of the public'. However, the company successfully demanded that the previous agreed maximum tonnage rates be increased by 25 per cent. The canal interests, the landowners and the public had each gained concessions from the railway, and, notwithstanding the undiminished hostility from Lord Derby, the Liverpool and Manchester Railway received the Royal Assent on 9 May 1826. At almost the same time the Bill for the

[2] SC, Loch to Stafford, 18–1–1826, 4–3–1826, 11–3–1826; Loch to W. G. Adam, 20–1–1826; Eyre Lee to Loch, 1–3–1826, 9–3–1826.
[3] SC, Loch to Stafford, 22–1–1826; Loch to Pritt, 25–5–1826.

Birmingham and Liverpool Junction Canal was passed despite being 'frustrated by the railroaders' in its initial stages.[4]

Loch worked energetically to assert Lord Stafford's influence in the management of the railway. In a letter of May 1826 Loch made absolutely clear the Stafford strategy. He wrote to Pritt, solicitor to the railway, that 'it is . . . a matter of great importance to . . . Lord Stafford's family, as well as to himself, that the trade in the Railway should be increased as much as possible, at the least possible loss to the Duke's Canal.' But, Loch insisted, Lord Stafford's directors were determined 'to make the Railway as profitable to Lord Stafford and of course to the proprietors as possible', the more so because they concurred in the view that 'the Railway will create a Trade of its own.'[5] This was the essence of the compromise that had been achieved by Lord Stafford's decision to invest in the railway.

The opening months of the active life of the Liverpool and Manchester Railway were extremely difficult for both internal and external reasons. The financial climate had rapidly deteriorated in 1826. As early as March of that year a correspondent of Loch had said that the railway could not pay because the original estimates of its traffic were made 'on the scale of demand when speculation was at its highest'. The scale of demand had certainly diminished: profits on the Bridgewater Canal had fallen by almost 50 per cent compared with 1824. In June 1826 the railway applied for a sum of £200,000 from the Exchequer Loan Office—on the grounds that money was scarce, and that it was still a private company. Captain Bradshaw, a less truculent man than his father, but equally candid, thought the request improper. He commented:

I fear Lord Stafford's Interest will be placed in an awkward position, as in case of any failure (which is by no means unlikely from all I hear) he may be saddled with responsibilities of a very heavy and awkward nature. His Lordship is a *bona fide* subscriber and able to pay, which is more than can be said, I believe, of others, whose burthens he may be compelled to bear.

But his ominous warning was balanced by reassurance—'I shall do all in my power to promote Lord Stafford's interest both in the Canal and the Railroad.'[6]

[4] SC, Loch to Sherwood, 22-1-1826; Eyre Lee to Loch, 2-5-1826; Pritt to Loch, 1-5-1826, 10-1-1829; Moss to Loch, 22-3-1836.
[5] SC, Loch to Pritt, 25-5-1826.
[6] SC, MacPherson Grant to Loch, 17-3-1826; J. Bradshaw to Loch, 17-6-1826.

At first the Loan Office turned down the request for financial assistance. This added to the general gloom and threatened to depress share values. Trade conditions in Northern England were appalling; Captain Bradshaw declared in July 1826 that 'Nothing ever has been so wretchedly bad as the present state of trade . . . and if a very material change for the better is not soon made God only knows what will be the result.' East Lancashire and the West Riding of Yorkshire were almost at a standstill and the employment of thousands was threatened. 'The utmost distress, bankruptcy and alarming riots stare us in the face . . . violent meetings are holding in Manchester and neighbourhood, and the Military are in almost daily requisition, with little doubt but that their services will soon be brought into action.' By August the area was more tranquil but, as Bradshaw pointed out, it could not be attributed to an improvement in either trade or the disposition of the people, but to the 'overbearing military force in Manchester and neighbourhood'.[7]

It is undoubtedly true that employment provided by the construction of the railway helped to alleviate a small part of the distress of 1826. On Chat Moss alone 200 men laboured on the initial stages of the enormous drainage project. The railway had been planned in good times but, since it was a long-term capital investment, it generated employment through good times and bad. It had a very valuable contracyclical impact on the local economy. In October R. H. Bradshaw hoped to contract for work on tunnel-construction for the railway specifically 'in order to keep his Colliery Miners and other men in Employ'. As Pritt had said, one of the grounds for the loan request had been 'to better enable us to give employment to large numbers of the distressed labouring classes in this Country'. The Loan Commissioners would only reserve £100,000 for the railway on the condition that parliament sanctioned the loan. Meanwhile, calls on the shares had to be made.[8]

Within the company there developed an unseemly squabble over the choice and relative merits of the rival engineers—Rennie, Jessop, Raistrick and Stephenson. At one stage Telford had been asked, but refused, to be engineer for the line. Discussion on the Board became a 'striving for the mastery of the concern by one half

[7] SC, Loch to J. Bradshaw, 13–6–1826; J. Bradshaw to Loch, 5–7–1826, 18–7–1826, 20–8–1826.
[8] SC, J. Bradshaw to Loch, 5–7–1826, 20–8–1826; Pritt to Loch, 10–5–1826, 16–8–1826. See also G. O. Holt, *A Short History of the Liverpool and Manchester Railway* (1965), 5.

of the Directors against the other half'. Captain Bradshaw was particularly critical of the discussion, saying that 'however clever they might be in their own individual businesses . . . they were completely at sea upon the business' of running a railway. Eventually George Stephenson was chosen largely because he had experience on the Stockton and Darlington line and also because his methods promised a better economy of time and money. The Stafford interest concurred in this view, but Loch implied criticism when he strongly suggested that 'there should be a more scientific and more generally experienced Engineer over him.' Temporary supervision was arranged but eventually Stephenson gained complete command.[9]

If Loch was to exert a constructive influence on the management of the railway he had to be conversant with all the technicalities of its construction. On the basis of his agricultural experience he claimed a hearing on the problem of draining that 'waving, trembling place', Chat Moss. He felt that Stephenson's attack on Chat Moss was at fault and pursued the subject at great length and detail. In October 1826 Loch visited Lord Carlisle's railway and the Stockton–Darlington Railway and was again critical of the engineering—'it is most imperfectly executed', he said in a remarkably detailed inspection of the line. But generally he was optimistic.

Notwithstanding the defects [he wrote] I found the Railway capable of much greater things than I expected, especially as a means of carrying passengers, and look forward to this being an immense source of profit to our railway, indeed to an extent hardly contemplated . . . I am convinced we shall see the Edinburgh mail carried in this way.

Before the construction of the railway there had been no communication between Stockton and Darlington; at first the railway had provided one passenger coach which did not succeed, but when fares were reduced the passenger trade sprang into life and yielded a revenue of £800 a year. Yet the population of the two towns amounted to little more than 10,000, they had little commercial connection and 'not much enterprise', and the coaches were horse-drawn. 'How much would this amount to between Liverpool and Manchester?' asked the enthusiastic Loch. But though his views were sanguine and perspicacious, he was not over-impressed. 'I saw few locomotives at work', he continued, 'They are as yet decidedly

[9] SC, J. Bradshaw to Loch, 24–6–1826; Loch to J. Bradshaw, 30–6–1826; Booth to Loch, 29–6–1826; Loch to Booth, 7–7–1826. Vignoles, op. cit., 118. J. Mitchell, *Reminiscences of My Life in the Highlands* (1883), I, 101.

imperfect machines, large, lumbering and inconvenient and I am not quite sure they are economical—they are decidedly only in their infancy ... it may be unreasonable to have expected more than has been accomplished.' He suggested that a railway should have four lines, two for slow traffic and two for quick, otherwise delays would prevent 'railways becoming the general means of communication throughout the Country'. Loch's foresight was demonstrated in his desire that parliament legislate for a standard gauge track, so that 'all future railway companies make the breadth of their Railway to a certain width so that in the event of their becoming extensively used, one set of carriages might travel from Land's End to Johnny Groats.' Canals had always suffered the consequences of lack of uniformity of construction which had become a serious obstacle to the improvement of their service to the economy. The railways, if properly guided, could avoid such mistakes.[10]

By 1827 the construction of both the major transport projects in which Lord Stafford was involved had begun. The Junction Canal, under the direction of the ageing Telford, began in January and by November Telford was able to assure James Loch that 'the New Canal promises to be the most productive concern lately undertaken.' The railway had also made headway, and Henry Booth, the Treasurer, wrote to tell Loch that progress was good at Chat Moss, that confidence was high and share prices rising, and that the main difficulty they faced was the delay of the £100,000 loan from the Exchequer Loan Commissioners. In April 1827 the loan was at last sanctioned; and by January of the following year the Company had expended £213,000, while calls on shares totalled £154,000. It was already becoming clear that construction costs would soon exceed the estimates.[11]

In March 1828 a further loan of £100,000 was successfully requested from the Commissioners. The loans created complications over the future interpretation of the 10 per cent profit limitation clause since it was not clear whether it referred merely to the share capital alone or was to include borrowed capital. There was a feeling that the clause ought to be reconsidered. John Moss had little doubt

[10] SC, Booth to Loch, 7–11–1826; Loch to J. Bradshaw, 12–10–1826. Francis, op. cit., 108. Cf. Mather, *After the Canal Duke*, 48–9.
[11] SC, Telford to Loch, 14–11–1827; Booth to Loch, 23–4–1827, 14–9–1827, 7–1–1828.

that 'it would be made a dead letter by future committees.' It seems that Huskisson had said that the profit should be limited to 10 per cent and any surplus should 'be divided between the subscribers and the public', but it was obscure and Moss believed that the rates of tonnage should never be reduced by more than $33\frac{1}{3}$ per cent. Loch was perplexed and the question remained unclarified. Confidence was rising, and it was predicted that the railway would be open by mid-1830. Public opinion was increasingly favourable and the shares, in June 1828, were at a £40 premium. Interest was so great at the opening of the Bolton and Leigh Railway in August 1828 that the locomotives were unable to show their paces due to the pressure of the crowds.[12]

Towards the end of 1828 the Railway Board began deliberations on a planned change in its original entry and terminus in Manchester. It would require parliamentary authority and the co-operation of R. H. Bradshaw, who feared that the alteration would threaten the Yorkshire trade of the Bridgewater Canal by a possible extension of the railway beyond Manchester, or by connections with new railways. Bradshaw could either oppose the measure or thrash out an agreement with the Railway. Since Lord Stafford's decision to invest in the Company, Bradshaw had remained aloof and relations were decidedly chilly. The railway directors favoured a negotiation. John Moss believed that if Bradshaw could forget his previous opposition he might meet the railway directors and they could 'consult together upon the best mode of making the two properties productive without sacrificing the interest of either'. A meeting was eventually arranged, but Moss faced the prospect with considerable apprehension. Bradshaw wanted a security that the Railway would extend no further than the newly proposed terminus in Manchester.[13]

Soon after, in October 1828, John Moss entered the lion's cage. The meeting was, no doubt, a little strained. Bradshaw sent Loch a wry account of the confrontation. Moss arrived at Worsley to discover 'that I am not quite so terrific, and uncompromising an animal, as he supposed ... but a simple, quiet Carrier and Wharfinger.' Clearly Bradshaw had opposed Moss's plans with a flow of ill-concealed sarcasm—even though he was already privately committed

---

[12] SC, Booth to Loch, 14–9–1827, 25–7–1828, 5–8–1828; Moss to Loch, April 1828, 27–6–1828; Loch to Moss, 23–4–1828.
[13] SC, R. H. Bradshaw to Loch, 12–7–1828; Moss to Loch, 19–9–1828, 30–9–1828; Loch to Moss, 15–9–1828, 20–9–1828.

to a compromise under pressure from the Stafford family. He was bitter and cynical about the family being 'disposed to succumb to the views and objects of our competitors'. With laboured scorn he told Loch that 'In my *younger* and *stronger* days, I felt differently, or I should not have had the satisfaction of paying Lord S. nearly two Millions sterling.' Bradshaw had not forgiven Lord Stafford his *volte-face* of 1825. Moreover, had he not resisted all potential competitors for as long as he had done, Stafford would have been much the poorer for it. Did he not therefore deserve all of Stafford's gratitude?[14]

Moss was impressed by the rudeness and continued opposition of the irascible old man and the way he spoke of 'my canal'. He said the Bridgewater Canal would have nothing to do with the railway 'for 2 generations' unless the railway would limit itself to light goods, and leave the canal the heavy traffic. Further, Moss recounted, '. . . he said that he should count our wagons from his window and if we got much trade he would lower his price, that Lord S. should not gain by both.' Moss left Bradshaw, 'apparently in good humour after *3 hour's conversation*—during which time he never asked us to partake of even a sandwich'. Yet Moss also regarded Bradshaw as a man of great soundness and fairness, a very astute manager of commercial affairs. Despite the show of conflict Bradshaw accepted an informal assurance from the railway that they intended no active projects to impinge more widely on the Bridgewater trade.[15]

The proposed deviation, together with the mounting costs of construction and the creation of a carrying department, made essential yet another request for more capital. A great deal of thought was given to the subject in late 1828 and early 1829. A new Bill would be required and it was hoped that the Exchequer Loan Commissioners would lend the company £125,000; alternatively they might apply for a new capital issue equal to a quarter of the existing capital, a sum of £127,500. There was a strong feeling that the 10 per cent profit limitation would have to be repealed. The directors devised a plan to substitute for the restriction clause a permanent reduction of the maximum level of freight rates by 25 per cent—for, as Pritt told Loch, 'This we think never can hurt us, as it will leave a larger

[14] SC, R. H. Bradshaw to Loch, 8–10–1828; Loch to Bradshaw, 4–10–1828; Loch to Moss, 4–10–1828.
[15] SC, Moss to Loch, 22–10–1828, 5–9–1829; J. Bradshaw to Loch, 18–10–1828.

rate than the Company will ever think of charging.' But Huskisson remained absolutely adamant: 'Huskisson will not listen to any alteration of our 10 per cent clause', wrote Moss. The directors decided not to press the matter. Loch believed that they must wait until the public saw the 'practical absurdity of the clause', while another director agreed that 'It will, by and by, demonstrate its own clumsy inefficiency.' The Bill was not designed to subvert the restriction clause; the first priority was the pressing need for more capital. The Company simply did not believe that the 10 per cent clause could work, but their Bill would be opposed if they attempted to tamper with it. The directors were genuinely puzzled. 'Nobody seemed clearly to understand', wrote one, 'how the non-restriction of profit on the Carrying Department can be arranged in the division of profit so as to be compatible with the restriction of Tonnage profit.'[16]

Even more difficult were the negotiations concerning the loan request. Thomas Telford, the great man of internal communications before the railway age, was consultant engineer to the Exchequer Loan Commissioners. He was asked to examine the Liverpool and Manchester Railway on their behalf in order to judge the expediency of the loan. In January 1829 William Wallace Currie, Lord Stafford's new director who replaced James Sothern, reported that Telford had been supplied with all the necessary information and that 'We have no reason to expect an unfavourable report.' In fact, Telford was critical of the organization of the work and of the proposed use of stationary engines; it would require further capital in excess of £200,000 and the line could not be completed before 1830; he felt he had been treated rudely by the company who had withheld proper facilities for the examination. John Moss, in company with the majority of the directors, was livid, and abused Telford as 'the paid advocate of the Canals', and, in a fit of pique, he sold his shares in the Macclesfield Canal. 'I am more than ever confident that Railroads will be most formidable Rivals of Canals', he asserted. The directors regarded Telford's reports as maliciously inaccurate, prepared a public statement to counter his remarks, and organized a deputation to the Loan Commissioners. Currie believed the report 'unfriendly rather than unfavourable', but the effect on morale was profound. Telford's assistant, Mills, had told shareholder John Gladstone 'so unfavourable a story that he on hearing it sold out

[16] SC, Moss to Loch, 27–11–1828, 21–2–1829; Currie to Loch, 29–12–1829, 23–2–1829, 27–5–1829; Pritt to Loch, 10–1–1829; Loch to Currie, 25–2–1829.

about 20 shares. This was a very gratuitous communication proceeding from no friendly feeling to us.' A month before there were strong rumours that Cropper was selling out because Chat Moss was slipping, and in March Currie said that Chat Moss was still 'tremulous'.[17]

Loch was seriously perturbed by the report and by the ever increasing expenditure on the railway. He was relieved that Telford's report was no worse than it was but, he said, 'if such a man as Mr. Gladstone sells 20 shares on Mills' report, what may, nay, what will not happen with others.' He blamed Stephenson for failing to treat Telford with sufficient respect.[18] But they must avoid panic at all costs, he warned: 'the risk is, that if such men as Gladstone act precipitately on the representations of such men as he has been influenced by, that a panic may be created and much injury done and then depend on it the Shares would go like South Sea shares.' Characteristically, Loch counselled, 'It requires on the part of the Directors much prudence, firmness and temperate conduct.' Loch believed that, in view of Telford's bias against the railway, the report should be regarded as favourable.[19]

Imprudently, the company issued a statement attacking Telford's report—the only effect of which was to provoke Telford to an even more critical treatment of the operation of the railway. The Company could not afford to grapple with the master engineer. It seems that it agreed to mend its ways. Eventually a loan of £100,000 was authorized late in 1829. Meanwhile the Company had obtained powers to raise £127,500 in quarter shares by the Bill of 14 May 1829. Lord Stafford accepted the new issue of supplementary shares, thereby increasing his stake in the railway. Loch had to press R. H. Bradshaw for the payment of Bridgewater profits in order to pay off financial obligations of the family which included calls on the railway shares.[20]

[17] SC, Currie to Loch, 29–1–1829, 9–2–1829, 12–3–1829; Moss to Loch, 16–2–1829, 7–3–1829. Rolt, *Telford*, 157–9. Rolt, *George and Robert Stephenson* (1960), 152–7.

[18] Four months earlier Loch had been delighted with Stephenson. 'Everything that I have had an opportunity of examining, reflects the greatest credit on the intelligence, ingenuity and industry of Mr. Stephenson and no part of his conduct appears more deserving of approbation than the ready adaption of every improvement than his increased experience has suggested as he proceeded.' SC, Loch to Booth, 11–9–1828.

[19] SC, Loch to Currie, 7–1–1829, 11–2–1829, 13–2–1829; Currie to Loch, 7–2–1829, 5–3–1829.

[20] SC, Currie to Loch, 11–6–1829, 15–9–1829; Loch to Currie, 13–6–1829. Rolt, op. cit.

The four years between Lord Stafford's decision to invest in the railway in December 1825 and the Rainhill locomotive trials of October 1829 was a period in which there was a tentative acceptance of the idea of the railway. The general feeling remained predominantly sceptical. The construction of a few lines went on quietly (except for the unending rancour between the engineers), but conclusive evidence of the capacity of railways to provide a reasonable return on the very large initial capital requirements was necessarily a thing still to be proven. The unedifying dispute with Thomas Telford had done nothing to eliminate very real doubts.

The pessimism and hesitation of the early part of 1829 gave way to infectious enthusiasm in the flurry of activity and confidence that followed the Rainhill trials in October. James Loch had maintained that the use of stationary engines would make further progress very difficult. He believed that the locomotives were bound to succeed in the course of time, and that to facilitate their eventual adoption it would be preferable to use horse-power in the interim. Rainhill proved the practicability of the locomotive system.[21]

Before Rainhill the question was a matter of great debate which became heated in the January of 1829. As Pritt observed, 'occasionally the Thermometer has nearly got to blood heat'. Stephenson was strongly committed to locomotive propulsion but Walker and Raistrick reported in favour of fixed engines. Loch wanted the Company to hedge its bets: 'the world is too young in their experience of Railways as yet to justify a considerable expenditure on a permanent and fixed system of conveyance.' In April he inspected the railway with Stephenson and was very impressed, but the engine controversy was unresolved. In July Stephenson crossed Chat Moss at 12 m.p.h. on a vehicle moved by sail power, while other experiments used 'hand-power and the American's wheels ... 2 men propelled 12 others besides themselves ... some 350 yards at the rate of 12 miles an hour—and it seems very probable that this power will be applicable to ... carrying passengers'—it received 'intense attention'. These experiments rapidly became irrelevant when the preparations for the locomotive trials began. On 11 October 40 passengers in the Director's Carriage experienced a speed of 30 m.p.h. and afterwards, at the self-congratulatory dinner, Currie complimented

---

[21] SC, Loch to Bourne, 8–4–1829. See Rolt, *Stephenson*, chapter 8. J. C. Jeaffreson, *The Life of Robert Stephenson* (1884), I, 121 et seq.

Lord Stafford 'on having been long the Patron of the Fine Arts and having now embarked in the most splendid undertaking of the useful arts that this country had yet witnessed'. The trials were a foregone conclusion.[22]

After the trials, Currie declared that 'The public mind appears to be excited all over the Kingdom.' Indeed, the trials had convinced practically everyone except the elder Bradshaw. Loch was ebullient and wrote to Robert Peel, 'I have long thought that the Revolution to be effected by Steam on Land would be greater than any that Steam Navigation has hitherto produced.' To Moss he wrote in the same spirit, 'I quite go along with you as to the revolution that is likely to take place in the mode and rate of conveyance throughout the kingdom.'[23]

[22] SC, Pritt to Loch, 10–1–1829; Currie to Loch, 5–1–1829, 23–2–1829, 12–3–1829, 10–3–1829, 9–5–1829, 6–7–1829, 13–7–1829, 17–8–1829, 1–9–1829; Loch to Currie, 7–1–1829; Booth to Loch, 15–4–1829, 8–10–1829, 11–10–1829, 26–10–1829; Bourne to Loch, 6–4–1829; J. Bradshaw to Loch, 10–9–1828; Report from Mr Loch to Lord Stafford on Railway, 26–4–1829; D593/P/18/1, Loch to Lady Stafford, 23–8–1829, 13–9–1829.
[23] SC, Currie to Loch, 27–10–1829; J. Bradshaw to Loch, 3–10–1829; Loch to Peel, 15–10–1829; Loch to Moss, 26–10–1829.

VII

The Edge of the Precipice

The celebrated contest at Rainhill in October 1829 offered a prize of £500 for the best performance of steam locomotion on the new railway. The trials triumphantly vindicated Stephenson and provided the first incontrovertible evidence of the efficiency of locomotive power on rails. It was a remarkable exercise in public relations, dramatically revealing the strength of the challenge of the railways to the canals. As late as 1827 'the horse and the canal seemed safe enough.'[1] The events of late 1829 destroyed all remaining illusions of security for the canals. It seemed that they could either come to terms with the growing rival or passively accept a fate of inexorable decline. The ecstatic optimism of the railway promoters expanded into the public belief that railways must inevitably serve and unite the nation.

The more far-seeing of the independent freight carrying companies began to manœuvre for the carrying-trade of the railway. Previously they had remained almost exclusively united with the canal proprietors against the railways. In September 1829 Currie reported to Loch that a 'spontaneous proposal' had been received by the Liverpool and Manchester Railway from a major carrying concern, the New Quay Company. They had offered

to become carriers on the rail-road *the day we are ready*, and to take the whole charge of delivering the goods, guarding them and finding waggons—we only find the locomotive power—and they agree to pay us to whatever price we choose—and to show us their books etc.—to enable us to see what they have hitherto paid and charged and can afford to pay. Their example will no doubt be followed by other companies. The New Quay Company were afraid we meant to be *exclusive* carriers.

[1] J. D. Chambers, *Workshop of the World* (1961), 52.

A negotiation was begun. Currie favoured the idea because it would greatly simplify the affairs of the railway and, at the same time, 'convert a host of rivals into friends to the concern'—the carrying companies had always feared that the railway would monopolize its own traffic. Moreover, Currie pointed out, 'they are *masters* of their carrying business—we in the midst of violent opposition should have to serve an *apprenticeship* to it.' The arrangement would help to reduce some of the costs of pioneering the railway idea. Most important of all, the New Quay Company promised to quit their canal trade altogether, to sell their seventeen flats, and to 'give us 36,000 tons a year, 2/5th of which Tonnage they will secure back'. Most of the railway Board were favourably inclined towards the proposal.[2]

James Loch, however, was disturbed by the prospect and was surprised by the precipitate attitude of his co-directors. He had been under the impression that it had been agreed 'that it was for our interest to keep the public off our line and that we should be the sole carriers'. If the railway company allowed the independent carriers onto the line it would complicate the operation (and therefore the avoidance) of the 10 per cent clause. Equally important, it would, he said, 'immediately bring us into collision with the Canals'. Currie replied that everyone knew that a collision with the canals was inevitable. The carriers would switch their allegiance to the railway and it would be a painful blow to the canal companies. Bradshaw would undoubtedly disapprove but, noted Currie, they must think as railway directors first and foremost.

If the independent carriers, in competition with the Rail-road remained on the Canals, they would be unable to stand the competition, and the Canals would lose them . . . the same result arises in either case—so that it is the existence of the Railroad not our admitting carriers upon it, which will be detrimental to the Canals and this was all along foreseen.

The directors, he said, were constantly on their guard against any attempt to operate the 10 per cent clause against them. John Moss was particularly eager to have not only the New Quay carriers on the railway, but also Pickfords, the Grocers Company and the Kenworthy Company. Moss told Loch that the railway 'ought if possible to secure the tributary streams of influence, capital and good feeling which the different carrying companies have the power of dispensing'—the railway could only benefit by the arrangement and the

[2] SC, Currie to Loch, 12–9–1829.

position of the canals was irrelevant. Loch was unconvinced; he feared that it would disrupt the basis of any continuing compromise with the canals; it was therefore unacceptable to him. 'I recollect', wrote Loch, 'Sandars saying that now our business was to make the most of our concern and that it would be highly impolitic to run a race of cheapness with the canals, and that the Monopoly of our carrying was the only way to serve this advantage.' [3]

Despite the initial good feelings towards the New Quay approach the negotiations were protracted and eventually, in January 1830, the two parties decided that they could not agree on terms. 'I rather think you will not be sorry for this failure', wrote Currie to Loch. And thus one major threat to the canals had been rendered abortive; but there were other equally serious dangers. [4]

James Loch realized more than anyone the full gravity for the canal proprietors of the recent events. He wrote hard, biting and often irritated letters to his canal associates trying to move them to positive thinking. John Moss had said plainly that 'the canals have more to dread from an opposition than I formerly thought or than they now contemplate.' Loch foresaw the rapid extension of railways and the slow decay of the canals unless the challenge was met. Uppermost in Loch's mind was the latent threat that the agricultural interest would throw its support to the railways unless the canal companies improved their facilities. Communications between Ireland and Lancashire were so much better that Midland farmers feared that their best markets in Manchester and Liverpool would be 'swamped by Irish cattle', and thus they would have to look to London and Birmingham as outlets—in which case they would demand improved access from either the canals or, failing that, the railways. Loch suggested that the canal companies should adapt their carriage to include livestock—as the railways were doing. He wrote to Captain Bradshaw of the revival (resulting from the success at Rainhill and the current low price of iron) of a project for a railway between London and Manchester: 'one person suggests that it would be worthy of Mr. Bradshaw's genius to step in and make the Duke into a railway.' He also mentioned the proposition of a general

[3] SC, Currie to Loch, 12–9–1829, 15–9–1829, 22–9–1829, 21–10–1829; Moss to Loch, 5–9–1829, 21–9–1829; Loch to Currie, 13–9–1829, 20–9–1829.

[4] SC, Currie to Loch, 10–12–1829, 31–1–1830, 1–2–1830. Wheeler, op. cit., 296–7.

conversion of canals into railways, while Moss thought that the Bridgewater Canal itself would make a very useful railway 'and prevent what is now talked of another Rail Road Company from Manchester to Liverpool'. Loch believed that the canals must drastically improve their services, or submit to rival railways, or 'ourselves become a railway, as nothing else will do'. He gave Captain Bradshaw a warning, direct and unadorned:

depend on it that unless the Canals afford the Agricultural Interest some such accommodation, you will throw them entirely into the hands of the promoters of the Railways ... let your father see what I write, though he will abuse me as a liberal, yet no man knows so well how to meet the coming dangers and he has no better means of learning it than through me.

The elder Bradshaw had retreated into a surly silence.[5]

Equally trenchant were Loch's remarks to Eyre Lee, the other major canal spokesman. Loch wrote, 'It will not, I assure you, do to sleep.' The natural exertions of the ironmasters would be powerfully seconded by the agricultural interest if the canals continued to slumber. 'I wish', he continued, 'we could get our friend Telford to apply his powerful mind to this subject, but as yet he has not given his full attention to nor has he at all calculated on the amazing power of Steam applied as a moving power.' In Loch's opinion the canals were meeting the potential competition with nothing more than apathy. Only two canals had done anything at all positive—the Bridgewater Canal which had spent £60,000 on improvements, and the new Birmingham Canal which Loch commended as 'the most magnificent works imaginable'. In each case, of course, the Stafford interest had been a prime mover.[6]

Eyre Lee agreed, and felt that the southern canals should unite with Telford and construct a new canal between Birmingham and London; nothing less could prevent a railway. But, he said, the canal companies would not bury their differences; 'I am sure that Mr. Telford is fully satisfied that nothing but perfect canals can compete with the power of steam, but if he be not properly supported ... he

[5] SC, Loch to Captain Bradshaw, 29–10–1829; Lewis to Loch, 11–11–1829; Moss to Loch, 24–10–1829; Captain Bradshaw to Loch, 3–10–1829. In his recent book, *After the Canal Duke*, F. C. Mather has produced the curious verdict that James Loch and his son George consistently cast their influence against any concerted action by the canals (see especially 200). It is difficult to reconcile the evidence of this and the next chapter with Mr Mather's interpretation.

[6] SC, Loch to Eyre Lee, 28–10–1829.

cannot be blamed for injuries brought on by the blindness of others'. Lord Clive, another major canal owner, also agreed with Loch that the Rainhill trials had 'given a very different relative value to canals and rail-road property'. But he continued to doubt whether railways could transport heavy traffic competitively.[7]

In the 1820s the risks in railway investment were of course high; decisions, of necessity, were made with very little reliable information. Methods for collecting information were by modern standards primitive; so too were accounting methods. In November 1829 Loch investigated, with immense thoroughness, the whole position of canals and railways. Employing memoranda, questionnaires and correspondence from all sources, Loch attempted to dispel a good deal of worthless propaganda.[8] He expended great energy in an effort to find a solution to the problem of Lord Stafford's divided investments.

The last few months of 1829 had seen a reawakening of projects for railways to Birmingham and London and elsewhere, many of which had been lying dormant for half a decade. John Moss was already in contact with interests planning a southern railway and he asked Loch, 'Do you think Lord Stafford would assist, if the Duke, Lord Brougham and Ellesmere would co-operate? I am confident it would be a very good thing for all.' Lord Stafford, the largest holder of railway shares in England, would soon be compelled to decide whether he would participate in the extension of the system. Tactics had to be planned. Loch continued to believe, despite the jubilation following Rainhill, that the situation could be manipulated to allow some kind of acceptable co-existence between canals and railways. If a collision could be avoided, and if canals improved their accommodation, they would be able to 'serve the public for many a day yet'. Another small ray of hope came to Loch from the turnpikes on which, in July 1829, Goldsworthy Gurney had driven a steam-carriage from London to Bath and back at a reported average speed of 15 m.p.h. Resistance from the turnpikes, he thought, would help to delay the impending extension of the railway network.[9]

---

[7] SC, Eyre Lee to Loch, 30–10–1829; Clive to Loch, 6–11–1829.

[8] See especially, 'Particulars of Stockton and Darlington Railway', J. Loch, 23–11–1829, Birmingham Public Library.

[9] SC, Moss to Loch, 28–10–1829; Loch to Jardine, 19–11–1829; Loch to Moss, 31–10–1829.

The most immediate question was that of a railway link from the Liverpool and Manchester line to Birmingham. The projectors were 'stirring again' in November 1829 and sent deputations from Liverpool to canvass support among the Liverpool and Manchester directors, many of whom were keen to listen. The sensible Currie reported that a great change was operating on men's minds in favour of rapid railway extension; it was neither wild enthusiasm nor speculation; many canal proprietors were selling out and buying into railways. John Moss said that he did not want a second war with the canals nor the annihilation of their property. He was working, he said, on the idea of a co-operation between canal and railway capital.[10]

Any extension of the railway would adversely affect Lord Stafford's property in the Bridgewater Canal, the Grand Trunk and the partially-constructed Birmingham and Liverpool Junction Canal on which £400,000 had already been expended. Loch made it absolutely clear that Lord Stafford's decision of 1825 had not committed him in any way whatsoever to seek an extension of the railway system. Indeed, at the time of the promotion of the Liverpool and Manchester, it appears to have been agreed that the participants would have nothing to do with later projects—certainly Bradshaw believed this to be the case.[11]

The threat to the 'interior canal interest' was reaching a climax. Loch tried desperately to rouse the canal interest. He told E. J. Littleton that they must

so expedite and otherwise arrange their mode of conveyance as to make the extension of the Railway system into the interior unnecessary—so that time may be gained and that the full value of all these new systems may be ascertained . . . the probability being if this can be accomplished that the heavier conveyance will be retained by the canals, while the quicker will be performed by the Common Turnpike.

Loch believed that if the canals, even at that eleventh hour, were to mobilize their resources their position could be preserved. But he was scathing about the canal proprietors and managers. In general they were 'a set of antiquated persons who will sit quietly still until their concerns are swept away from under them. Their resolution seems to be most carefully to avoid looking at the precipice on

[10] SC, Currie to Loch, 2–11–1829, 7–11–1829, 11–11–1829.
[11] SC, Loch to Currie, 4–11–1829; Currie to Loch, 11–11–1829.

which they stand, to take all they can in the meantime and they will hold up their hands and exclaim who could have thought it.'[12]

Loch felt that he was alone in confronting the problem. This added to his bitterness. R. H. Bradshaw dwelt in silent intransigence. He offered no co-operation from Worsley. Loch complained to Lord Francis, 'it is ridiculous their locking themselves up there and not saying what they fear or what they don't. I don't want them to tell me any of their secrets but we should have some information as to whether the schemes are likely to be detrimental or not—because they affect Lord Stafford's various interests.' But Bradshaw merely poured scorn on the opposition. The railways, he said, would cost a 'Million of Money' and have an interest to pay of £50,000; the obnoxious engineers and attornies were at 'full play', but he, Bradshaw, would 'be able to exist, if he cannot live' with the locomotives. He added a gratuitous sneer at Telford—'We suppose Telford to be the "Practical Man" who recommends converting the Duke's Canal into a Railway. The Selling out his canal shares, and getting a job in Railway Jobs maybe no bad spec. for him as it has been remarked as extraordinary that the first Engineer of the day has hitherto had no employment in Railway Business'. There was no evidence that Telford was the man in question: Bradshaw was simply acting out his role.[13]

Loch was frustrated not only by the indolence of the canal-owners but also by the persistence of the dynastic dilemma within the Stafford family. Once more the interests of Lord Gower and Lord Francis were potentially at odds. It was the most embarrassing problem Loch had ever faced. He consulted a 'cabinet' of advisers on the position. 'In confidence', he told one colleague, 'between ourselves if I had Lord Gower only to advise, my task would be easier but when I am also expected to think of his brother's interests my task is more, nay most, difficult.' Essentially the problem was this: there was a project to construct a railway from Liverpool to London; the projectors suggested that the Birmingham and Liverpool Junction Canal be adopted as part of the line; to Loch it was 'a proposition worthy of much consideration'. It would be very advantageous to Lords Stafford and Gower and to the Liverpool and Manchester Railway—'But to the Bridgewater Canal it would eventually prove

[12] SC, Loch to Littleton, 5–11–1829; Loch to Lewis, 18–12–1829.
[13] SC, Loch to Lord Francis, 23–11–1829; J. Bradshaw to Loch, 4–11–1829.

very injurious indeed—unless it also is made a Railway which has been suggested.' The last suggestion was anathema to Bradshaw. Loch and his advisers concurred in the view that the decision of Lord Stafford to invest in the Junction Canal had been made 'one year too soon'—Telford's canal had become an embarrassment.[14]

As if to emphasize the weakness of the canals, the Liverpool and Manchester Railway shares were appreciating rapidly. In November 1829 Loch told Gower that the shares were at a £60 premium. The shares for which Lord Stafford had paid £115,000 were worth £188,750, a 'profit' of £73,750, 'and they will rise much higher'. Within ten days the shares were selling at a premium of £78 10s. 0d. All this added to the conviction that the railways were bound to come—there was 'a want of employment of capital in the country', while the low price of iron and the level of unemployment also favoured the railway promoters. But, Loch told Gower, they were encouraged even more by the 'feebleness of the canal opposition' which gave them a free hand. He was filled with anxiety about his ability to advise Lord Stafford.[15]

Bradshaw was no help whatsoever. Letters from Worsley, probably dictated by the canal-master, were rarely coherent, often contradictory, and always contemptuous.

It is true [began one such letter] we are . . . in the thick of Railway projects, which appear to threaten the Canal with almost total annihilation, but we live in hope, that the practice of railroads will not be found to be overpowering, as its friends so sanguinely anticipate. That they may cause a very material alteration in the mode and rate of conveyance of Goods on canals, and materially lessen the profits hitherto gained, is very probable, and I fear will before very long, be seriously felt in the Annual Wind-up of this concern.

Bradshaw, while admitting the likely strength of the competition, insisted that the case for the railway had not been proven, therefore he would continue to oppose all railways. Negative thinking of this sort had prompted Loch to declare that canal managers were 'an antiquated set of persons'. Loch denounced Bradshaw's 'cavalier' attitude and also castigated the current mismanagement of the Grand

---

[14] SC, Loch to Lord Francis, 23–11–1829; Loch to Gower, 14–11–1829; Loch to Currie, 8–11–1829.
[15] SC, Loch to Gower, 14–11–1829, 21–11–1829; Currie to Loch, 26–11–1829. BM Add. 38758, Loch to Huskisson, 31–12–1829. A. Gibb, *The Story of Telford* (1935), 240.

Trunk Canal: 'they continue to creep while the rest of the world Gallop', he told Lord Gower.[16]

At this critical time, in late 1829, Lord Stafford, through the energetic agency of James Loch, remained the main bridge between the railway and canal factions. Loch was in close contact with both sides. He was playing for time in which the canals might salvage their position. Despite the seemingly defeatist or indifferent attitudes of the canal-owners, Stafford was not ready to abandon his dual alliance—even though his railway shares were rising as rapidly as his canal shares were falling. Stafford continued to intervene on behalf of the canals—as Currie put it:

They will see that if his Lordship did, in joining the Liverpool and Manchester Railroad, take a step apparently so hostile to their interests as a body, looking at the consequences immediate and remote he is at least desirous to give them the opportunity, where Railroads are likely to come into collision with Canals, of having the advantage of time and experience to enable them ... to prevent their property from being altogether ruined.

The plan, it seems, was to canvass the idea that the existing canals should have the first option of building a railway. In that way the £30 million invested in canals might be legitimately saved from 'utter destruction'. Above all else, time was necessary to prevent a chaotic expansion of facilities being sanctioned, and time for the canal companies to define their own course. Loch directed his energies to this end.[17]

---

[16] SC, J. Bradshaw to Loch, 6–12–1829; Loch to Gower, 4–12–1829.
[17] SC, Currie to Loch, 1–12–1829, 9–12–1829.

VIII

A Golden Opportunity

A specific purpose of Lord Stafford's initial investment in the Liverpool and Manchester Railway had been to exert a direct influence over the future development of railways in the region so that the canal interest would not be entirely neglected. Such an essentially conciliatory policy depended in large measure on the persuasive power of James Loch. His intelligent and cogent presentation of the case for delay in 1829 was an important factor in gaining a breathing space for the canals. In this Loch was aided by the very size of the surge of confidence in railways that had followed the Rainhill Trials. The rapid proliferation of projects raised doubts about their wisdom; it produced a conservative reaction. In addition, it was becoming increasingly evident that the interest of the Liverpool and Manchester was not best served by an unbridled extension of railway lines. The directors were aware that they had created a monopoly of a specialized market in transport services between the two towns. An orderly development would not only avoid duplication, but would also discourage any attempt at direct competition.

While the motives of the railway promoters were far from altruistic, nevertheless, in the period from October 1829 to October 1830, they went to extraordinary lengths in seeking a way of co-operation with the canal interests. Urged on by James Loch and by a wish to avoid a second war with the canals, they instigated a series of plans which promised an astonishing degree of compensation to the canals. The Liverpool railway promoters accepted Loch's assumption that canal capital ought not to be annihilated and that 'indemnification' and co-operation were the most expedient policies. Prompted by Loch, the initiative came almost exclusively from the side of the railways. But the canals resisted the blandishments as though they were insults. It was an extraordinary episode in transport history, the second critical moment in the development of railways.

The linking of south Lancashire and the Midlands had become inevitable. The Liverpool and Manchester directors hoped to retain the lion's share of the undertaking for themselves. They particularly sought to persuade the new concern to make a connection directly on to their own rails. New promoters in Birmingham were also involved and were even more anxious to set the project in motion. But it was only one of 'the thousand and one schemes . . . springing up' in November 1829—including a line from Liverpool to London.[1]

Moss and Pritt were the main initiators of the project for a railway to Birmingham. They had already suggested that the affected canals be converted into railways for the project. As Currie reported, Moss deprecated a 'second war with the Canals—he would not annihilate their property, but render it available in this joint mode of communication.' The directors all understood the difficulty of Lord Stafford's position and were inclined to accept Loch's request for a delay while the canals were consulted. Pritt said that the government should be asked to oppose '*any* new Rail Road scheme next year until the public has had the experience of the one great work—the Liverpool and Manchester—that, in a national point of view it would be undesirable for Parliament to sanction other Rail Roads till the present enthusiasm has either subsided into rational feeling or is justified by our Rail Road.' Moss concurred, but pointed out that it would be difficult to keep Birmingham quiet for a whole year. At the same time Loch extracted a pledge from the Company that it would not support a proposed junction railway through Stockport, and that it would not take its Birmingham railway plans to parliament in the forthcoming session 'without the approbation of the Marquis of Stafford'. The Company put pressure on its engineers to prevent them assisting the Stockport Railway. Currie congratulated Loch: 'I think you will see that your ideas are completely met. The parties

[1] SC, Currie to Loch, 2–11–1829. The accumulation of expertise and prestige in the hands of the Liverpool and Manchester directorate gave them an enviable position in the subsequent extension of railway capital. It was one major benefit to be set against the many disadvantages they incurred in pioneering British railway developments.

engage to take no step that may preclude negotiation or arrangement with Lord Stafford and Lord Clive—and no person, unwilling to give an engagement, will be permitted to be a party.' The railway board was virtually unanimous in the opinion that the canals should have time to see the practical operation of railways. If the railway fulfilled the current expectation the canals would be ruined; therefore, reported Currie, they should have 'the power of saving our property, as far as we can, by adapting our Canals to Rail Roads, rather than others, whose vital existence is not at stake, should step in prematurely and occupy the ground to our utter destruction'. It was hoped that the government would concur in this view of the position even though it savoured of interference with private capital.[2]

Moss wrote to Huskisson to lay the issues before him. Everyone, he said, wanted a railway, but the public should be protected from private adventurers. The Liverpool and Manchester Company intended to conciliate all parties and therefore had made their pledges to Lord Stafford. The railways, Moss urged, were inevitable, but they should be constructed so as 'to injure as little as possible and to protect as much as lies in our power the canal interests'. The best plan would be to persuade Lord Francis and Bradshaw to convert the Bridgewater Canal into a railway, together with a similar conversion of the partially completed Birmingham and Liverpool Canal. Above all else, they wanted to prevent a re-enactment of the parliamentary warfare of 1825–6.[3]

Loch also wrote to Huskisson. Many of the new projects, he said, were ill-imagined, too hasty, impatient, irrational, and promoted by scheming engineers. They would injure the promoters themselves, the landowners and the canals. The Rainhill Trials were wonderful but had not conclusively established that railways could carry heavy and bulky goods more economically than canals. Even if the railways were unsuccessful they would adversely affect canal profits. All this gave good reason for a delay, during which more information could be obtained, and judgments made about the necessity of sacrificing the capital vested in the canals. Loch had received from Moss's friends a proposal that the interested canal and railway

[2] SC, Currie to Loch, 7–11–1829, 11–11–1829, 26–11–1829, 1–12–1829, 9–12–1829; Moss to Loch, 7–11–1829, 21–11–1829, 19–12–1829; Pritt to Loch, 19–12–1829; Loch to J. Bradshaw, 9–1–1830.
[3] SC, Moss to Huskisson, 14–12–1829.

parties might unite in order to accommodate the needs of the public, and, at the same time, permit the canal-owners an opportunity of saving part of their capital. Loch had replied that it was impossible to decide on such a complicated question in a hurry, and they had agreed to a conditional delay. Loch asked Huskisson if the government might also postpone all projects for one session—so that the commercial operation of the Liverpool and Manchester could be judged. Loch fully accepted the proposition that the railways must come: 'What we asked for is no preference—no interference with the employment of private capital—but simply delay.' The force of Loch's argument was that 'it can never be advantageous to a country that much of its capital should be unnecessarily annihilated and a vast number of persons dependent on that capital reduced to poverty, except such a sacrifice is demanded on the clearest public necessity, founded on incontrovertible general principles.' Neither the principles nor the necessity had yet been established. [4]

Loch wrote to Robert Peel in similar terms with a statement on behalf of the canals asking for a chance of indemnification and the avoidance of the reckless speculation of 1825. Now, however, Loch went further and suggested that the government should intervene in railway investment and establish some form of Railway Board through which the government could exercise some control over the railway situation. This was a surprising suggestion, at least ten years before its time. Loch pointed out to Peel that the railways were a 'new and most important system of communication which must call for the expenditure of many Millions'. It was inevitable that the ordinary processes of private investment would produce a system ill co-ordinated and wasteful. Piecemeal investment (as with the earlier canals) necessarily created 'circuitous and inconvenient routes'. It was therefore advisable to establish 'a formal board . . . to say that they think the plan is well suited to the purpose'—in effect, a supervising body watching over the national interest. Moreover, Loch claimed it would not 'be an interference with private or individual speculation' since parliamentary authority was already required in the case of railway investment. Peel, however, was sceptical of Loch's suggestion for 'a permanent Body taking a comprehensive view of various projects of internal improvements'. Parliament, Peel suggested, would feel 'exceedingly jealous of any establishment, under whatever name or with whatever object, which

[4] BM Add. 38758, Loch to Huskisson, 25–12–1829.

should have the appearance of intermediate agency between the People and Parliament'. It was not politically feasible.[5]

Yet Loch, on behalf of Lord Stafford and the general canal interest, had achieved part of his aim. The Liverpool and Manchester Railway had pledged themselves not to press forward with the Birmingham extension until the next session of parliament. They had agreed in principle to collaborate with the canals in future development. Stafford was able to act as mediator primarily due to his large stake in the Liverpool and Manchester. His support was important for any extension of the operations of the company. To James Loch it appeared as a golden opportunity of indemnification. But time was short.

Loch tried desperately to put the respite to good use. This entailed mobilizing the affected canal groups in such a way that their interests might be most effectively protected. There were formidable difficulties. The canal interests, though happy with the delay in railway promotion, were extremely suspicious of any compromise. Bradshaw in particular felt little inclination to co-operate. On the other side there was mounting impatience with any delay in the further construction of railways. Moreover, Lord Stafford's holdings were distributed in such a way that, at almost every turn, he received both advantage and disadvantage. 'You see how variously and differently we are affected', Loch told Huskisson.[6]

Among the canal men, Eyre Lee remained unconvinced of the power of the railway to carry heavy goods; the rails and pistons were simply not strong enough, he claimed. Bradshaw declared that speed was a minor consideration in this traffic. Lord Clive believed that the operating costs on canals and railways would be about equal, but that the construction costs of railways were almost twice those of canals, making the eclipse of the canals most unlikely. As for Telford, he had refused to toast the success of the Liverpool and Manchester Railway. This, Loch angrily declared, 'betokens fears on behalf of the Canals and a blindness as to enquiry which I have always seen attend the losing party'. If they did not wake up the opportunity would be lost.[7]

[5] SC, Loch to Peel, 14–12–1829; Loch to Currie, 28–12–1829; Peel to Loch, 11–1–1830.
[6] BM Add. 38758, Loch to Huskisson, 31–12–1829.
[7] SC, Loch to J. Bradshaw, 19–11–1829; J. Bradshaw to Loch, 6–12–1829; Loch to Eyre Lee, 14–12–1829; Loch to Clive, 26–1–1830; Eyre Lee to Loch, 3–12–1829, 6–12–1829; Clive to Loch, 20–1–1830.

Loch's hopes that the canals would come to terms with the railway began to evaporate in the early months of 1830. The idea of converting the waterways into railways—'the transmutation of an element into another', as Currie put it—failed to appeal to any of the canal parties. They remained adamant and, despite Loch's assurance that the Liverpool railway party was composed of 'fair, open and honourable' men, there was a solid wall of resistance from the canals. One thing was abundantly clear to Loch. A railway to Birmingham would come into existence with or without the support of the canals. In mid-1830 the engineers were surveying various lines.[8]

Even so, the chance of co-operation was still open. In April the Birmingham and Liverpool railway promoters offered to reserve 'a large number' of their shares for the canals.[9] While this idea was under consideration Loch raised another compromise proposal. He told Lord Francis that a railway would be built from Liverpool to Birmingham by the shortest possible route, crossing the Mersey somewhere near the Runcorn Gap. He wrote that 'to oppose such a measure would be worse than fruitless, it would be against all principles, as well as all chance of success.' The railway would be very damaging to the Bridgewater Canal. Nevertheless, there was still a chance that the existing interest could be 'indemnified or partly so, at the expense of the projectors' by a scheme which would gain both public and governmental support. Loch's new proposal was that the Bridgewater Trustees construct a railway bridge over the Mersey at Runcorn Gap with the power to levy a toll on goods crossing the bridge. Loch had contacted Sir Robert Peel and the Duke of Wellington and his own associates and they had agreed that it was a reasonable method of dividing the losses by permitting the existing interest 'to share the benefits of the New Concern on fair and reasonable terms'.[10]

Loch's efforts to provide indemnification for the canals were sometimes misconstrued by the railway board as signs of opposition to the railway *in toto*. Loch vehemently denied such suggestions and reaffirmed his desire for an arrangement, possibly arbitrated by William Huskisson. Loch seems for a time to have persuaded both the railway projectors and Bradshaw of the plausibility of the bridge

[8] SC, Loch to Clive, 4–4–1830; Currie to Loch, 9–12–1829.

[9] SC, Loch to Currie, 23–3–1830; Loch to J. Bradshaw, 19–4–1830; Loch to Lawrence, 28–3–1830; Loch to Clive, 23–3–1830, 4–4–1830; Clive to Loch, 12–5–1830; Currie to Loch, 3–5–1830.

[10] SC, Loch to Lord Francis, 25–5–1830; Loch to Currie, 3–2–1830.

idea. In June 1830 Loch addressed the railway board (with Bradshaw in attendance). Quite unexpectedly Bradshaw decided to oppose Loch's suggestion. Loch reported, 'This scheme I thought had been adopted by Bradshaw—he has however rejected it in his character of Trustee, and I am at a non-plus for a moment.'[11]

Time was running out. Pritt complained that the railway projectors were being paralysed by the inertia of the canals; they could not wait on Bradshaw for much longer. The canals had been offered the most favourable treatment, he said; their opposition would be worthless; 'if the Canal Proprietors choose to remain blind when all the rest of the world can see, and refuse advantages offered to them because they think it is in their interest to do so, what claim will they have to conciliate after the game is played out.' John Moss warned that the canals had 'no idea of the importance to them of an alliance with us—I do not hesitate to state that unless they join us they will be ruined if we get our Act.'[12]

Bradshaw was clearly the main obstacle to any agreement. Loch had become increasingly angry with his intransigence. Currie commented that the late Duke of Bridgewater would never have acted in such a manner. He asked 'when did you ever know a very old man (like Bradshaw) relinquish his habitual views and fall in *voluntarily* with the progress of new ideas, or even new improvements, the result of those ideas?' It was generally believed that Bradshaw was making a mockery of Lord Stafford's best interests.[13]

While James Loch continued his desperate search for compromise, Lord Stafford's support was being solicited for other railway projects. In July 1830, for instance, Stafford was offered a one-half interest in a projected railway from Birmingham to Coventry and London. It was given a civil refusal. Stafford was also asked to take a larger stake in the Birmingham and Liverpool Junction Canal by Eyre Lee. He hoped Stafford would 'permit about £50 or £60,000 of his wealth to flow in aid of this undertaking'. But even before 1830 Loch was already regretting the original investment in this concern—

[11] SC, Loch to Moss, 21–6–1830; Moss to Loch, 15–5–1830; Loch to Currie, 23–6–1830, 25–6–1830, 28–6–1830; R. H. Bradshaw to Loch, 31–5–1830; Loch to Lawrence, 8–4–1830; Loch to R. H. Bradshaw, 25–5–1830, 13–5–1830; Loch to Lord Francis, 25–5–1830; Loch to Huskisson, 14–7–1830. Jeaffreson, op. cit., 151–2. Vignoles, op. cit., 139.

[12] SC, Pritt to Loch, 10–6–1830, 22–6–1830; Moss to Loch, 8–5–1830, 9–6–1830, 19–6–1830; Moss to Pritt, 14–5–1830.

[13] SC, Currie to Loch, 23–6–1830, 30–6–1830; Loch to Currie, 25–6–1830; Loch to Moss, 13–6–1830, 21–6–1830.

before engineering problems had inflated the costs far beyond the original estimates. Stafford did not invest more in the canal and Loch chided Eyre Lee for his failure to come to terms with the railways. Eyre Lee retorted that he was by no means indifferent to the railway system, that he knew full well that it must come. He said the railway would seriously affect turnpike traffic, but he continued to doubt 'that any sort of railroad can rival a well co-ordinated and well-managed canal'. Loch's pessimism, he asserted, was misjudged; if the canal was 'not a good security for a loan woe betide the original shareholders who will have expended £400,000 to no good purpose'. He implied that Lord Stafford had an obligation to provide a good part of the £200,000 still required. Loch dissented.[14]

The canal interests had, in effect, spurned a series of 'extraordinary inducements and privileges' for co-operation with the projected railways—the shares had been refused, Bradshaw did not want the Mersey bridge, no one would think of conversion. Shares were in great demand and everyone knew that after the opening of the Liverpool and Manchester the chance of 'indemnification' would be lost. Lord Stafford remained uncommitted. Only nine days before the opening of the railway, John Moss made yet another effort to persuade Stafford to support the line to Birmingham regardless of the other canal proprietors. His proposal was that 'The Stafford Canal Interest' should take one fifth of the total shares in the Liverpool and Birmingham Railway, with a proportional share in the management. It was a seductive offer—even though it would cost Stafford £150,000 and did not entirely meet his requirements on the questions of route or of the bridge over the Mersey. The offer was the more attractive in view of the rising market price of railway shares, a point which Moss emphasized. Loch made no immediate reply to the offer.[15]

Loch had regarded William Huskisson as a possible mediator in his protracted negotiations between the railways and the canals. Huskisson had already played a major role in the first five years of railway development. More than anyone else, his views were respected by each side, he was above the conflict and his influence had been tried and trusted. On 15 September 1830 the Liverpool and Manchester

[14] SC, Loch to Stafford, 9–7–1830; Benson to Loch, 26–6–1830; Eyre Lee to Loch, 3–9–1830, 27–9–1830.
[15] SC, Moss to Loch, 6–9–1830; Loch to Moss, 5–7–1830, 8–7–1830. Jackman, op. cit., 541.

Railway was opened and Huskisson was killed. Currie was there. He wrote, 'Poor Huskisson was conveyed from the spot at the astonishing speed of 33¾ miles an hour, so great was the anxiety of the physicians to get him to the place where amputation (the only chance) could be performed. It was dreadful. Think that out of the hundreds of thousands assembled in the densest masses, he alone should be the sufferer! How Melancholy!'[16]

Although the opening was marked by great tragedy it proved to be another major fillip to the optimism of the railway interests. Even Lord Derby was moved to congratulate the railway company he had once so bitterly opposed. It was all accurately reflected in the price of the Liverpool and Manchester shares—in August £190 each, at the end of September £210. 'Here is £100,000 at one hit' to Lord Stafford, enthused one agent, meaning a net profit on his original shares if he sold. Joseph Sandars reported, 'I see *another* Birmingham and Liverpool Road advertised, the whole country will go Rail Road Mad and it will require prompt and decisive conduct on the part of Parliament to prevent the Country looking like a Gridiron.'[17]

Bradshaw was predictably less impressed. His thoughts were communicated to James Loch:[18]

it appears the Lawyers and Surveyors are likely to furnish their nests tolerably well in next session, as for the subscribers the Lord have mercy upon them for I am sure neither Lawyers, or Surveyors will! As for the Canal, it is doing tolerably well, as times go, picking up the Wee Things that the Wind Scatters abroad and would continue to do well if it were not for the 'envy, hatred, malice and all uncharitableness' of its enemies.

Lord Stafford's support continued to be courted by the promoters of the railway to Birmingham. The canal proprietors could still buy shares if they wished; Moss dreaded the opposition of Lord Stafford's interests and repeatedly offered the one-fifth share in the railway which Stafford could take up at any time 'without giving any explanation'. But it was not so much Stafford's capital as his moral support that was required; they would have no difficulty raising the money so long as the country was at peace.[19]

By October 1830 the canal proprietors began to realize that the

[16] SC, Currie to Loch, 16–9–1830.
[17] SC, Young to Loch, 24–9–1830; Sandars to Loch, 30–9–1830; Derby to Moss, 12–8–1830. See also G. Loch, op. cit., 249.
[18] SC, J. Bradshaw to Loch, 11–10–1830.
[19] SC, Moss to Loch, 5–7–1830, 21–8–1830, 31–8–1830, 6–9–1830, 22–9–1830, 29–9–1830.

railway could not be opposed. Lord Clive admitted that the 'temper of the times' made opposition futile. The landowners were now unlikely to object. Having belatedly reached this conclusion the leading proprietors of the Birmingham and Liverpool Canal began to consider seriously the idea of the conversion of their canal into part of the new railway. Suddenly they changed their tune and asked Loch to pursue his dual role with renewed vigour. 'You must consider yourself to be *Webb footed* when with our Company', said Clive, 'and a *Railer* whenever you choose elsewhere.' But it was now too late; the prospect of conversion was no longer feasible. And the other canal parties would not buy shares.[20]

It became painfully clear to Loch that he had failed to mobilize the canals into a position in which they could temper the full force of the impending railway competition. The canals had lost the opportunities repeatedly held out to them of taking a prominent share in the expanding railway system. They were not prepared to follow Lord Stafford's precedent of 1825. Loch resignedly accepted that his plan for conversion had failed—Telford had opposed it in early 1830 and that had been enough. Loch admitted that 'it would have been at all times a matter of difficulty, without doing the same with all the canals connecting with it, and over which he had no control.' The plan for a bridge had also lapsed. With all these hopes of compromise laid aside, Loch was prepared to relieve Lord Stafford of the burden of acting as guardian of the canal interest in general.[21]

In October 1830 Loch appears to have tentatively accepted the proposals made to Lord Stafford by John Moss on behalf of the Liverpool and Birmingham Railway. They had treated the Stafford interest fairly:

The Liverpool gentlemen [he said], after putting off coming to Parliament during last session at the desire of Lord Stafford in whose hands they placed themselves this year, found themselves this year compelled to proceed this session without waiting for the determination of the canals, in order to preserve the ground which otherwise would have been usurped by others.

The railway was now utterly inevitable and it would create for itself a new and valuable trade, and would 'add to the general

---

[20] SC, Clive to Loch, 18–9–1830, 30–10–1830; Loch to Bather, 25–10–1830; Loch to Lowndes, 25–10–1830; Loch to Pritt, 3–11–1830; Moss to Loch, 29–9–1830.
[21] Ibid.

intercourse of the country and thereby increase the trade of the Canals'. Loch declared that he did not regret his advice to Lord Stafford in 1825 which had led to his investment in the Liverpool and Manchester. The other decision to invest in the rival canal had been made in the hope of checking 'any attempt at a Railway between Liverpool and Birmingham for at least a time'. The hope had been deceived, and future opposition was worthless. Therefore, he continued, 'I am determined to accept the offer made to the Canal Proprietors and become a shareholder in the Rail Road.' The shares were reserved for Lord Stafford though a final decision had not been made.[22]

It appears that Lord Stafford was virtually committed to the new railway—but within two months the decision was reversed. Lord Stafford declared his 'neutrality'—Loch explained, 'he is brought chiefly to this conclusion by his advanced time of life, he takes no share in its progress, either for or against.' This second major decision implied that Lord Stafford would take no further part in the extension of the railway network. Having been a pioneer railway proprietor in 1825, he now retreated.[23]

It is perfectly feasible that Stafford's age—he was seventy-two— and nerve were incapable of withstanding further acrimonious negotiation. It was not the first time that Stafford had tried to evade the rancour of public dispute. If he entered the second stage of railway development it would upset the delicately poised balance of interest in his own family which had been created in 1825. Both Loch and Stafford were uneasy about the growing possibility of the Birmingham Railway supporting a railway in direct opposition to the Liverpool and Manchester Company. Nor did they wish to be unjustly accused of a breach of faith with their canal colleagues. Neutrality avoided all such unpleasant repercussions. While he did not escape involvement in the following months, Stafford certainly lessened his trouble by claiming neutrality.

Loch represented the decision to withdraw as a typical act of a self-denying aristocrat, thinking only of the good of the country. To some extent this rings true, but Loch had already acknowledged that opposition would be futile. Moss had no longer to dread

[22] Ibid.
[23] SC, Loch to Currie, 13–12–1830; Loch to Stafford, 2–1–1831; Loch to Moss, 20–11–1830; Pritt to Loch, 5–12–1830, 11–12–1830.

Stafford's opposition. Instead of investing further in railways Lord Stafford continued to buy up large tracts of the Scottish Highlands—in May 1830 he bought a 100,000-acre estate because, as Loch explained, 'there was £30,000 lying doing nothing.'[24]

By claiming neutrality Stafford's position at once became clearer and simpler. His transport involvement after 1831 was confined to three concerns—the Liverpool and Manchester Railway, the Bridgewater Canal (still in the control of Bradshaw), and the Birmingham and Liverpool Canal (in process of construction by Telford). They represented three overlapping concerns—and Loch remained in the thick of the unending manœuvring that was the essence of the history of transport improvements in the 1830s.

Had Loch's responsibilities been confined to the world of railway and canal negotiations he would have remained an unusually busy man. But he was, of course, concurrently involved in many other consuming activities. For instance, at the time of Lord Stafford's decision for 'neutrality', Loch was almost literally chasing suspected rick-burners across rural Salop and Staffordshire. His annual trip to the northerly extremities of Scotland ate into his time: so also did his daily auditing duties which entailed the examination of virtually all the details of the administration of no less than five landed estates. In addition, he was becoming deeply immersed in the growing excitement of the Reform Bill question—from which even a broken shoulder in May 1831 would not deter him. His own family—itself developing into a dynasty—was also an enlarging element in his life. In 1830 he was fifty years old, at the height of his powers: a man who had made himself indispensable in several spheres.

[24] SC, Loch to Mackenzie, 26-5-1830. J. Loch, 'Memoir'.

IX

$\bullet\!\!\!\leftrightarrow\!\!\!\bullet\!\!\!\leftrightarrow\!\!\!\bullet\!\!\!\leftrightarrow\!\!\!\bullet\!\!\!\leftrightarrow\!\!\!\bullet\!\!\!\leftrightarrow\!\!\!\bullet\!\!\!\leftrightarrow\!\!\!\bullet$

Transport Capitalism in the Early 1830s

$\bullet\!\!\!\leftrightarrow\!\!\!\bullet\!\!\!\leftrightarrow\!\!\!\bullet\!\!\!\leftrightarrow\!\!\!\bullet\!\!\!\leftrightarrow\!\!\!\bullet\!\!\!\leftrightarrow\!\!\!\bullet\!\!\!\leftrightarrow\!\!\!\bullet$

The coming of the railways in Britain in the 1820s had disrupted the relatively settled pattern of transport and had created a seemingly limitless opportunity for entrepreneurial energy. Yet it was a piece-meal and jerky development, often hesitant, frequently subject to mindless optimism or partisan pessimism, but never guided by the direction of a central authority. No one could predict the overall outcome of the expansion of railway investment; decisions were necessarily made in isolation and the government remained extremely diffident, even hostile, towards the idea of intervention. It was in this environment that the railways were pioneered. The early railway promoters improvised solutions to a bewildering series of problems, paid for their mistakes, and bought their own compromises with their opponents, the public and the government. Varying measures of competition and collusion moulded the character of the evolving transport system in the 1830s.

In this unplanned, almost blind, growth of railway capital, the Stafford interest necessarily exerted a relatively diminishing influence. As a result of Lord Stafford's withdrawal from the prospective expansion of the railway network and of the failure of the canals to accept the opportunities offered to them, the role of James Loch as mediator was much reduced. But it remained considerable—as Currie told him in 1831, 'I often think of your incessant occupation with regret for your own sake and that of Mrs. Loch.'[1]

[1] SC, Currie to Loch, 12-3-1831.

The certainty of railway competition had thrown into doubt the future of the unfinished Birmingham and Liverpool Junction Canal. Loch, though concerned, remained mildly optimistic. At the time of Stafford's original investment, he recalled, 'it was the best speculation of its sort in England'. It remained true to say that the new canal would produce 'new and unlooked for sources of trade', especially from the West Midlands and North Wales to Manchester. It would no longer be necessary to send goods down the Severn and around Wales by sea. He admitted that the railway would undoubtedly take the light goods but, he insisted, 'the bulk of the weighty trade must continue to go by Canals as the most economical.'[2]

The financial position of the canal deteriorated rapidly in 1831. Loch was alarmed at the state of the works, the estimates were being exceeded, and a loan had become essential. Faith in Telford was dwindling. No less than £400,000 had already been expended, but another £160,000 was required. Eyre Lee was panic-stricken. Without a loan, 2,000 unpaid labourers would have to be dismissed at a moment's notice—it would 'create a riot and no one can foresee all the consequences', he warned. The proprietors sought a loan from the government; without it contracts would be broken, the construction stopped and many men thrown on to an already unfavourable labour market. While the government delayed, the proprietors were compelled to raise a private stop-gap loan on the personal guarantee of the Committee of Management; Loch explained 'it was quite necessary to take this step in order to prevent the men being turned upon the Country ... and the contracts vitiated.' Telford was convinced that the extra expenditure would reap a sufficient return.[3]

Telford had forecast completion by Michaelmas 1832, but the course of construction took a savage turn for the worse. Telford, his aides and his navigators, fought treacherous conditions during a succession of intensely frustrating months when 'one of the finest and most costly lines of canal ever built in England was cut into two useless halves by the morass at Shelmore' in Staffordshire. Even before the full gravity of the situation at Shelmore became apparent, Loch had expressed doubts about the management, construction,

[2] SC, Loch to Marjoribanks, 6–6–1831; Loch to Stafford, 26–11–1831.
[3] SC, Marjoribanks to Loch, 3–6–1831; Eyre Lee to Loch, 3–9–1830, 27–6–1831; Loch to Gower, 20–7–1831; Loch to Spring-Rice, 30–6–1831; Telford to Loch, 21–7–1831; Loch to W. G. Adam, 19–7–1831; Loch to Clive, 3–6–1831.

and leadership of the canal. He told Lord Clive, 'I cannot conceal from myself as I have it from other sources as well as from my own observations that Telford is not the man he was, and that he trusts exceedingly in those in whom he has confidence, which in some instances I rather think has been abused.' In the following months Loch became a more active voice in the affairs of the canal.[4]

Morale fell very low. Eyre Lee moaned to Loch: 'It requires I assure you some nerve as well as a little sanguine temperament to bear the brunt of all the complaints of ruin, injury and injustice which are continually uttered to me.' Even with government help Eyre Lee was calculating on resources which Loch did not believe were available. The unfinished canal was in a bankrupt condition. Loch told him: 'you must really impress upon Telford that we have need of every 6d. of our money—it will be time enough to talk of wharfs when we have any prospect of trade. I assure you I am doubtful exceedingly of the result.'[5]

The crisis deepened and Loch began to complain bitterly of Telford's incompetence. The struggle over the crossing of the Shelmore Embankment dragged on. In early 1833 no solution was in sight. Loch wavered between resentful desperation and hopeless resignation. At one stage he thought the only escape from the difficulty was to re-route the canal away from Shelmore. The embankment was necessary because Lord Anson had refused to allow the canal through his game reserves at Norbury Park—as Mr Rolt has noted, 'Through this wood the canal could have been driven on a level, but so that his Lordship's pheasants might not be disturbed Telford was forced to swing his line westwards in a great arc . . . to be carried on an embankment a mile long and sixty feet wide.' Loch tried to persuade Anson to relent and allow the original line to be followed—pheasants or no pheasants. 'How much money might have been saved had this been adopted at an earlier stage', he exclaimed. Anson remained unmoved. The Canal Committee had no alternative but to resume the apparently hopeless battle at Shelmore. In February 1833 Loch was told that 'it keeps sinking and bulging out, and I really think more than ever.'[6]

[4] SC, Loch to Clive, 30–11–1831. See also Gibb, op. cit., 238, and Rolt, *Telford*, 178–86.

[5] SC, Eyre Lee to Loch, 15–5–1832; Loch to Eyre Lee, 13–2–1832; Loch to Clive, 13–2–1832.

[6] SC, Loch to J. Bradshaw, 16–10–1832; Eyre Lee to Loch, 24–1–1833; Lewis to Loch, 6–2–1833. Rolt, op. cit., 179.

Loch was deeply depressed. 'No part of the Canal is likely to pay well', he predicted. With this in mind, Loch was more than ever anxious to open up the Shropshire (Newport) branch of the incomplete canal. This at least would benefit Stafford's estate in that county. Loch saw little point in delaying this section simply because the main line remained in two unconnected pieces. He bluntly told Telford that he had received 'the very worst possible accounts of the Shelmore Embankment ... that the money therefore which is now being laid out on it, is entirely thrown away.' He demanded, 'in the most strenuous manner', that their remaining capital be spent on the Newport branch—'it affords, moreover, the only chance we have, which I confess is not a very bright one, of obtaining Money sufficient to complete the work.' Loch's will prevailed and the Newport branch was opened in July 1833. He had made the best of a bad job. The Shelmore Embankment, under Telford's supervision, remained unconquered for a further twenty-four months.[7]

By the way of contrast, the Liverpool and Manchester Railway continued on its wave of confidence. Within three months it had carried 61,500 passengers. In January 1831 George Stephenson told Loch that the railway was 'beginning to carry goods, and in a short while shall be able to carry all the goods that are required to be taken between the Towns of Liverpool and Manchester'. Winter weather had had no effect on the efficiency of the locomotives, he reported: 'In my opinion the Canals cannot compete with the Railway in the carriage even of heavy goods.' But the main impact was on passenger traffic—by the middle of May only one coach continued to operate on the turnpike between the two towns. Before the railway the total daily capacity of the road coaches had been 700 passengers; in June 1831, 1,500 passengers were daily using the new railway. Even the promoters were astonished.[8]

The major doubt left in the minds of the railway directors was the threat of competition from newly projected railways between Liverpool and Manchester, notably the North Line. Consideration was given to various plans of defence. Cropper had suggested that the railway should make over to the government half of its net profit beyond 10 per cent as a form of taxation—in order to induce

[7] SC, Loch to Stafford, 24–1–1833; Loch to Telford, 15–2–1833.
[8] SC, G. Stephenson to Loch, 22–1–1831; Currie to Loch, 13–12–1830, 19–5–1831.

E

the government not to sanction a rival. The idea was rejected because it smacked too obviously of bribery. Pritt argued that if the North Line were sanctioned the Liverpool and Manchester would 'have an undeniable right to ask for a repeal' of the 10 per cent limitation clause. Pritt also revealed that Huskisson, just before his death, had changed his mind on the subject: 'the poor fellow said that he thought the restriction wise at the time—that he had since entertained doubts on the subject', and that he would offer no further opposition to its repeal. On the whole the Board was against the idea of spending a likely £12,000 in parliamentary opposition; but they were prepared to wring the utmost concessions from the government if competition were allowed.[9]

In May 1831 the Liverpool and Manchester proposed to issue more shares in order to construct warehouses and to pay off previous loans. The question arose of 'how far it will be for Lord Stafford's interest to increase his capital in the Rail Road?' William Currie made a reappraisal of the state of the railway. He was most anxious about the potential rise of competition—he felt that the threat of a rival line should be the major consideration in Stafford's decision. For as long as the Liverpool and Manchester was the only line, he said, 'we shall have a profitable game ... The natural effect of a new line will be to diminish our receipts, and rates must fall.' It was almost an exact echo of the fears of the canals some five years earlier. Currie pointed out that the railway had borne the irretrievable costs of being the pioneer in the field—'ours has been made at great expense ... the experience gained will benefit others—and ... future roads will be constructed much cheaper than ours had been.' None the less Currie favoured the purchase of the new share-issue since it would not much affect the market price and since there was no longer doubt about the feasibility of the railway.[10]

The motives of the Liverpool and Manchester directors in issuing more shares have often been questioned. The Act of 1826 had placed, in effect, a ceiling of 10 per cent on dividends. Few other companies were restricted in this fashion. It had been suggested that, instead of reducing tolls and rates and thereby keeping profits down to 10 per cent, the company issued more shares—to circumvent the Act. The directors were certainly hostile to the clause, but the historians

[9] SC, Pritt to Loch, 18–9–1830, 9–12–1830, 11–12–1830; Currie to Loch, 4–1–1831, 7–1–1831; Loch to Currie, 6–1–1831; Lawrence to Loch, 26–1–1831.
[10] SC, Currie to Loch, 24–5–1831, 30–5–1831, 14–6–1831.

Jackman and Pollins[11] agree that 'The increase of the capital of the Company in the early 1830s was the legitimate and normal addition to the physical equipment expected by an expanding public utility.' This is probably true of the 1831 share issue. Currie explicitly told Loch that he did not believe 'our trading upon our receipts would be a sufficient fund to defray the new works we may require.' The motives became less innocent in later years.

When the shares fell from £196 to £180 in August 1831, Loch welcomed the fall: 'I have no objection to this because I think it may have the effect of stopping wild goose schemes.' Currie believed that each share would be worth £100 more, but for the continued threat of the North Line. Loch was more concerned about the level of the running expenses of the railway and suggested that the number of men employed could be reduced by a 'judicious application of steam power'. However, within a few months the price of shares rose again and Loch calculated that Lord Stafford's investment of £155,000 was now worth £303,000—a 'profit' of £148,000, 'and the canal trade flourishing', he added with satisfaction.[12]

The following year, 1832, was unsettled and difficult in many respects, but activity in the railway world continued buoyant. Two major lines were projected—connecting Liverpool with Birmingham and the latter city with London. It appears that the early wrangling about the route of the first line had subsided and that opinion had consolidated in favour of a connection from the Liverpool and Manchester at Newton, and south via Warrington to Birmingham. It was called the Grand Junction Railway. True to his declaration of neutrality, Lord Stafford refused to oppose either this or the London line, despite keen representation from the canal interest.[13]

In January 1833 there was a firmly held rumour that the Liverpool and Manchester Railway was in dire difficulties, that it could pay dividends only by robbing its capital, that the locomotives had entirely failed,[14] and that the company was to revert to the use of

[11] Pollins, op. cit., 94–6. Jackman, op. cit., 530.

[12] SC, Loch to Booth, 6–8–1831; Loch to Gower, 27–10–1831; Currie to Loch, 26–10–1831, 25–7–1831.

[13] SC, J. Bradshaw to Loch, 22–10–1832; Loch to Clarke, 27–2–1832. Jackman, op. cit., 541–2.

[14] This rumour was incorrect but not completely groundless. In 1829 the independent report of Walker and Rastrick estimated that the cost of locomotive power for the conveyance of merchandise on the Liverpool and Manchester

horses. Much of the impression was produced by well-directed adverse propaganda, but genuine scepticism came from men like J. R. McCulloch, the economist. It was also true that the number of passengers had fallen, but in spite of this, the company announced a £4 4s. per cent dividend for the half-year, and Currie exclaimed 'we are a prosperous concern'. Within two months the price of shares rose and the clouds of doubt disappeared. [15]

It seems likely that in April 1833 there was a crisis, perhaps a split, in the Board of Directors. It was probably connected with the perpetually thorny question of the policy of the railway towards canal competition and rates of freight; that is, the most sensitive zone of Loch's responsibilities. From its earliest instigation the railway had piously declared that its very *raison d'être* was the introduction of competition into the provision of transport between Liverpool and Manchester. Yet even before it began operating it had negotiated collusive freight agreements with the canals. In January 1830 John Moss had engineered a loose arrangement with R. H. Bradshaw to avoid mutually destructive rate reductions—Moss reported, 'I never conversed with a gentleman I was more satisfied with and I do most sincerely wish that we had such a one on our Railroad—worth all our Committee put together.' In May 1831 the railway, the Bridgewater Canal, and the Old Quay Company met 'with a view to an arrangement to charge all alike.' If so, reported Currie, 'these 3 concerns will in time do all the business. The Carrying Companies will give up.' A tripartite agreement was arranged; 'the old Squire at Worsley' saw the necessity of acting in concert and, notwithstanding 'some jealousies and difficulties', a feeling of 'good fellowship' had been created. [16]

The warm cordiality seems to have broken down in 1833. Within the railway, the original directors, especially Moss, were subject to

---

Railway would be 0.278 of a penny per ton per mile. Their findings were regarded by the Company as unduly pessimistic. In March 1834 the Sub-Committee of Directors on the Cost of Locomotive Power stated that 'In the year 1833 . . . the actual cost was 0.625 of a penny per ton per mile, or considerably more than double the anticipated rate.' SC, Currie to Loch, 26–3–1834.

[15] SC, Currie to Loch, 21–1–1833, 23–3–1833. J. Simmons, *The Railways of Britain* (1961), 7.

[16] SC, Currie to Loch, 30–1–1830, 18–1–1830, 30–5–1831; Moss to Loch, 26–1–1830; G. Winter to Loch, 4–6–1831. The principal sources of difficulty in the renewed collusion were (a) the fluctuating levels of general economic activity, (b) the fact that the services provided by the transport interests were not identical, and (c) the recurring clashes of personality.

pressure from newer, more aggressive members. Feeling ran high and the upshot was a *fait accompli* reduction of the voting strength of Lord Stafford, now 1st Duke of Sutherland, and also the threatened resignation of John Moss. 'I daresay', commented Loch, 'if the now prevailing interests get the sway that they may reduce expense and increase income, they are a money making race, and will cut down everything to the lowest—the crying evil of the day, for talent will soon be without reward and wherever it is better paid there it will go.' Loch had to accept the new position, but he continued to exert a moderating influence in the affairs of the railway. This role began with the first investment of 1825, and part of its purpose was to avoid internecine trouble between the canal and the railway. Loch feared, most of all, successive rounds of rate-warfare. Moss believed action against the Duke of Sutherland to be virtually intolerable. 'You will have to exercise the very clear head you have', he told Loch, 'whether it is advisable to dispose of the Duke of Sutherland's shares.' Such a drastic abdication did not occur, and Moss was persuaded not to resign. But Loch was clearly shaken by the events. The 'ancient confidence and cordiality' of the company, he said, had been lost. The ascendant group of the company was 'an incessantly active set of people ... whose influence may be more affected by guiding it than by opposing it'. This line of policy—the quintessence of Loch's general policy—was accepted by Sutherland and Moss. The railway itself in 1833 was flourishing.[17]

At this time of 'great superabundance of money and want of profitable employment for it', two issues dominated the affairs of the railway. First, there was a proposal to unite the Liverpool and Manchester with the Grand Junction Railway. Second, the so-called North Line, a rival between Liverpool and Manchester, was mounting its attack. Around these two issues, particularly the latter, developed an acrimonious struggle which surpassed in bitterness all previous dissension. The two issues were inextricably linked. An alliance with the Grand Junction had long been canvassed but there were many problems concerning the conditions of such an arrangement. If the Grand Junction was to use the Liverpool and Manchester rails, both sides had to be satisfied. Without an agreement the Junction could look elsewhere, possibly to a rival. Currie reported, 'Let it be permanently settled and we shall have nothing from the

[17] SC, Loch to Currie, 2–4–1833, 10–5–1833; Moss to Loch, 1–4–1833; Currie to Loch, 10–6–1833.

North Line to fear.' An alliance would obviate the problem of the North Line.[18]

The untimely and increasingly unpredictable intervention of Bradshaw rapidly made the North Line a much more ominous threat. It was reported that Bradshaw had taken a thousand shares in the rival line and that he had declared a freight-rate war, instructing the Bridgewater agents 'to take goods . . . on any terms, so as to pay'. It was also believed that the Stafford family had bought a further five hundred shares. It seemed that Bradshaw had taken a stand to embarrass the Liverpool and Manchester Railway. Currie was astonished and Loch was unusually apprehensive—'I expect nothing but discomfort from Bradshaw', he said. An official denial from the Stafford family was urgently requested and eventually given, and the rumours were condemned as impertinent falsehoods.[19]

Negotiations for the alliance with the Grand Junction Railway advanced more smoothly than had been anticipated and the directors began to talk in terms of an actual merger 'into one great concern'. Moss, however, was hesitant: 'We ought to recollect that powerful as we are—these are not times to execute Monopoly with too tight a Hand.' Currie was also apprised of the danger: 'Parliament would I think exclaim against such a huge monopoly.' Though the government showed little sign of intervention in railway development the promoters felt they knew the limits beyond which they could not go. By the end of October 1837 a working arrangement for a junction between the two railways had been drawn up. The Sutherland camp was gratified and Loch was full of confidence. 'There should be some Grand Alliance', he said, meaning a thoroughgoing union of the two concerns. It was a far cry from the neutrality policy of 1830. There seemed to be every reason for confidence, particularly as Currie reported, 'I believe the North Line project is really on the point of dying a natural death.' The case against the North Line had been based primarily on the claim that it would be an unnecessary duplication of transport facilities—the identical argument that had been employed only eight years earlier by the navigation interests in their case against the Liverpool and Manchester Railway.[20]

[18] SC, Currie to Loch, 23–3–1833, 22–8–1833.
[19] SC, Currie to Loch, 28–8–1833, 3–9–1833, 18–9–1833, 24–9–1833.
[20] SC, Loch to Sutherland, 15–9–1833; Currie to Loch, 12–9–1833, 20–11–1833, 21–10–1833, 5–10–1833, 12–10–1833, 29–10–1833, 16–12–1833; Loch to Currie, 3–11–1833, 23–10–1833; Moss to Loch, 12–9–1833.

Relations between Loch and Bradshaw became increasingly strained in the years after 1830. Bradshaw's behaviour, never very reliable, had become more and more erratic. In March 1831 his son resigned from the Board of the Liverpool and Manchester Railway and was replaced by his father's close Manchester friend, Gilbert Winter. Without doubt the younger Bradshaw had been unhappy in the position and embarrassed in presenting to the world his father's edicts. He had rarely attended. The elder Bradshaw continuously put in jeopardy Loch's policy of moderation.[21]

In November 1831 the seventy-three-year-old Bradshaw fell ill with an attack of paralysis. He was not expected to recover. Loch was unable to resist the temptation of passing premature judgment on the ailing man. Loch told Lord Clive, 'his position has been a painful one—the world has passed him by—he has so withdrawn himself from it, that he has separated from its sympathies and regards and I regret exceedingly that he should have had the impression last year that I neglected him. I had no such intention.' Loch gave a graphic description of a visit to the aged invalid. Bradshaw had been drinking, refused to be bled, and was 'uncontrollable in obtaining what he fancies, such as wine, brandy, etc.' Loch went on, 'I think he is desirous to recover and that his determination to have what he wishes proceeds from the habit of constant animal indulgence to which he has given way for so many years.'[22]

But Bradshaw did not die. In January 1832 he rejected Loch's advice on the rating policy of the Bridgewater Canal. Several months were necessary to persuade Bradshaw to agree to lower his rates. Loch welcomed the change saying that the amount of business would increase, though the rate of profit on the concern would never again reach former heights.[23]

The railway certainly did not destroy the trade on the Bridgewater Canal and, in the expanding commerce of 1833, traffic greatly increased. But, claimed Bradshaw, they 'had no means of meeting it'. He complained that warehouse facilities on the canal were totally inadequate. 'It is absolutely necessary if the concern is to be carried

[21] SC, Loch to Stafford, 22–2–1831, 8–3–1831; Currie to Loch, 10–9–1831, 16–12–1831; Loch to Currie, 30–9–1831. Mather, op. cit., 141–2.

[22] Bradshaw was indeed in a semi-dotage aggravated by alcohol, his conversation increasingly diffuse and incomprehensible. SC, Loch to Clive, 22–11–1831; Loch to Stafford, 26–11–1831.

[23] SC, Loch to J. Bradshaw, 5–1–1832, 20–6–1832; J. Bradshaw to Loch, 1–4–1832.

on at a profit, that means should be found to make the requisite conveniences and afford facilities to our trade ... our trade is very good and doing a great deal of business, but *no profit*.' £85,000 was required. Bradshaw felt that the Duke of Sutherland, as recipient of the canal profits, should provide the finance.[24]

Loch was not convinced. Within five years, he predicted, Liverpool and London would be joined by a railway. The Liverpool and Manchester Company was thriving. He continued, 'it may be naturally asked, what is the Canal doing? The answer is a vast deal—but trade of a different sort.' The Bridgewater Canal was, he said, using 'Market boats' which could exploit the trade in lime-carrying, the Irish trade, and the coal trade. 'I am certain', he wrote, 'that in a few years it will be more lucrative than ever—which is owing to the Duke of Sutherland having expended £40,000 at Runcorn when he became an owner of the railway.' It was a triumphant vindication of the policy Loch had pursued for eight years—to guide the activities of the rival canal and railway along a course which would benefit the directly opposed interests of the heirs of the House of Sutherland. The railway was demonstrably a successful investment. The Bridgewater Canal retained a large proportion of its old trade; it had adapted to changed conditions, and its profits were again rising.[25]

One problem remained—the perverse and almost senile Bradshaw. In August 1833 Lord Francis wrote to his brother, who had just succeeded as 2nd Duke of Sutherland, to ask if he could obtain part of Loch's time to replace Bradshaw in the running of the Bridgewater Canal. But it was a delicate business. In the last week of September 1833 the younger Bradshaw committed suicide. Loch spoke of 'the affecting account of Capt. Bradshaw having made away with himself ... if it had been unfortunately the old one I should have been less surprised'. Loch described the suicide as 'one of the results of the old gentleman's conduct'. Within a fortnight Bradshaw resigned from the position of Superintendent of the Bridgewater Canal which he had held for more than thirty years.[26]

There were no sad farewells. Currie wrote, 'I rejoice with you my dear Loch, most heartily at the fortunate termination of all your Bradshaw anxieties.' Getting rid of Bradshaw had been a mortifying

[24] SC, J. Bradshaw to Loch, 13–3–1833, 27–2–1833, 22–6–1833.

[25] SC, Loch to Greville, 10–6–1833.

[26] SC, D593P/22/1/5, Lord Francis to 2nd Duke, 12–8–1833; Loch to Currie, 27–9–1833, 29–9–1833; Loch to Lewis, 7–10–1833.

and degrading business but the canal had been saved from ruin.[27]

The resignation had been dearly bought. Bradshaw was retired on his full salary and received £47,000 for various properties he had bought on his own account near the canal.[28] The Duke of Sutherland helped in the purchase of Bradshaw's retirement. Costly though Bradshaw's retirement was, it was a notable service by Loch to the Sutherland family.[29]

Loch at once investigated the management of the canal. One informant thought the management required much revision. But others were less critical—one said he 'had no reason whatever to complain', another that the management was very good and very civil. Such opinions, together with the continuing prosperity of the canal, are in clear opposition to the allegations made by Loch, Currie and Moss, that Bradshaw was bringing ruin to the canal. When he died in 1835 Moss remarked, 'Old Bradshaw has by his will made, I trust, some atonement for his injustice to his Family.'[30]

Bradshaw made one final departing gesture of defiance to the Sutherland family. To the astonishment and boiling frustration of Lord Francis, Bradshaw, using the right given him by the Bridgewater Will of 1803, appointed his own successor—in open contradiction of the express wishes of the family. He named James Sothern. Lord Francis, who had not even read the Will until he heard the news, was very angry. Loch considered Sothern 'the most unfit person to be kept and Lord Francis will not on any account think of him'. Lord Francis exploded: 'I am eager for battle, and by the blessing of God will spare neither time, trouble nor expense to make a clean sweep of these villains'. He made preparations to take Bradshaw to the Court of Chancery or even parliament. But it soon became clear that Bradshaw was within his rights. Sothern remained as his successor. Lord Francis had no alternative but to console himself that he had now only 'to deal with a man who is at least sane and likely to consult his own real interests which must be perilled by any undue opposition to my views or claims.'[31]

[27] SC, Currie to Loch, 21–10–1833; Loch to Moss, 28–10–1833.

[28] According to Falk, op. cit., 126.

[29] SC, Moss to Loch, 28–10–1833, 30–10–1833; D593P/22/1/5, Lord Francis to 2nd Duke, 1–11–1833.

[30] SC, Loch to Currie, 31–10–1833; Currie to Loch, 5–11–1833; Sandars to Loch, 5–11–1833; Moss to Loch, 5–2–1835. See also Picton Autographs, VI, 151–2, Picton Library, Liverpool.

[31] SC, Gatty to Loch, 14–11–1833; Loch to Lewis, 19–11–1833; Loch to Sutherland, 27–11–1833; D593/22/1/5, Letters of November, December, 1833.

X

•••

Uneasy Co-existence

•••

In the last thirty years of his life, the 1st Duke of Sutherland (who was Lord Stafford until 1833) had received a total income of £2,243,017 from the Bridgewater Trust. On his death in 1833 the income of the Bridgewater Trust had been detached from the main body of the Sutherland inheritance. It became the property of Lord Francis Egerton. His brother, the 2nd Duke, inherited the shares in the Liverpool and Manchester Railway in addition to the rest of the Sutherland fortune. Throughout the following years the ties of kinship and the skilful agency of James Loch reduced some of the tension implicit in the troublous world of rail and canal. The influence of the two brothers continued to operate in alliance even though their interests were ostensibly in opposition. In fact, it was in their mutual interest to prolong and foster the oligopolistic arrangement that spanned the coming of the railway. Not everyone regarded the influence as beneficial, and in 1842 James Loch and 'this hermaphrodite connexion' were publicly denounced as opponents of the railways.[1]

For the year 1833 the fruits of the dual inheritance were fairly evenly divided. It was a particularly poor year for the Bridgewater Canal and Lord Francis received only £17,473 in navigation profits, but this was several thousand pounds more than Sutherland received from his railway shares. However, the railway shares had rapidly appreciated, so that in February 1834 Sutherland's saleable holding was worth £321,250—more than twice the amount his father had paid for it. In 1830 a doubting canal spokesman had asked

[1] SC, D593/C/23/4; Loch and Laws, *Correspondence between James Loch, Esq., M.P., and Captain Laws, R.N.* (1842), xviii-xix.

if the railway could make a true profit, 'not by premiums on their shares which is mere gambling and the result of temporary excitement in favour of an elegant and splendid invention but by regular income'.[2]

In fact, the Liverpool and Manchester Railway, during its independent existence, rarely declared a dividend of less than 9 per cent; it was a clear financial success. This, however, did not lead to the destruction of the rival canal companies. Unexpectedly, the largest source of railway income came from passenger traffic while the freight department remained for long a financial disappointment. In its first year it carried only one third of the predicted level of freight. In 1839 the Bridgewater Canal carried twice as much as the rival railway. As F. C. Mather has remarked, 'despite the growing strength of railways, the canal entered, in 1833, upon a period of revival which lasted until the late 1840s.' Indeed, the canal continued to do good business until it was absorbed by the Manchester Ship Canal in 1887. J. H. Clapham long ago pointed out the survival-capacity of many canals in the face of railway competition and the fact that 'no British railway ever made very large profits'. The decline of the canals was generally very slow. Nevertheless, there were casualties, even on the most lucrative routes, and the railways, by injecting a new degree of competition, certainly had a major impact in reducing freight-rates. For instance, as soon as the Liverpool and Manchester Railway began operations, the canals were compelled to reduce rates on general freight from 15s. to 10s. per ton. In 1836 canal rates were approximately 40 per cent lower than the average for the years between 1812 and 1826. The quality of the service provided by the waterways almost certainly improved in these years: for instance, the average time of passage was more than halved between 1824 and 1836. Tonnage carried by the Bridgewater Canal doubled between 1830 and 1849, but, significantly, the growth of profits failed to match this rise. On this route at least the canals were able to compete (and collude) effectively with the railway. In part, it reflected a division of monopoly rent between the old and new modes of transport—a result which had been directly promoted by Loch's policy of compromise. It was also a partial fulfilment of James Loch's early prediction that the new mode of transport would create a separate trade of its own. Just as important was the

[2] SC, Currie to Loch, 4–2–1834; Loch to Gatty, 6–2–1834; Bather to Loch, 10–12–1830.

growing quantum of trade between the two towns. In any case, as P. H. Cooter has remarked, 'Rarely does a new technology make obsolescent all existing means of achieving a given end.' Large revenues continued to flow from both the canal and the railway. [3]

In the short run the rival concerns co-existed uneasily. The operation of the minimum-rate policy between the three transport facilities —the canal, the railway and the Old Quay—was a very precarious balancing act easily upset by petty jealousies. In February 1831 the railway had found it necessary to reduce its rates on cotton, and the canals replied by reducing still further. In 1833 the Bridgewater Canal carried 43,000 tons more than it had in 1830 but its total receipts fell by £33,000. In 1832 the railway directors decided finally to charge the same rates as the Duke's Canal, but there was no permanence in such an arrangement. Two years later the railway again tried to persuade the canal concerns to moderate the element of competition. James Sothern, almost as intransigent as his predecessor, R. H. Bradshaw, was adamant, saying that it was necessary for the canal to charge lower rates than the railway since it was 'their only chance of getting a share of that business'. But he grudgingly agreed to raise some of his rates, on condition that the Old Quay was pressed into the collusion. A further temporary arrangement was agreed to in late 1834. [4]

While the trade and profits of the railway slowly expanded, renewed threats to its security appeared. The prospect of a rival North Line re-emerged. Most of the Railway Board regarded it as little more than a nuisance, but Loch was more concerned and warned them that unless they improved their facilities the North Line would become a reality. The promoters of the North Line realized that there was a chance of driving a wedge between the Bridgewater Canal and the Liverpool and Manchester Railway—Sothern's overt antagonism provided an opportunity. They offered Lord Francis favourable terms for his support. Lord Francis, to the enduring frustration of the railway camp, remained uncommitted. The North Line party

[3] L. Donaghy, 'An Operational History of the Liverpool and Manchester Railway, 1831–1845' (Ph.D. thesis, University of Pittsburgh, 1960), 85–94, 114–18, 235–6. Mather, 'The Duke of Bridgewater's trustees', 148–53. J. H. Clapham, *An Economic History of Modern Britain* (1926), I, 397–8, II, 192. Wheeler, op. cit., 282, 299. H. Fairbairn, *A Treatise on the Political Economy of Railroads* (1836), 49–50. P. H. Cootner, *The Railroad and the Space Program* (ed. B. Mazlish, 1965).

[4] SC, Currie to Loch, 8–7–1834. Mather, op. cit., 148–9. Donaghy, op. cit., 99–100.

grew in confidence—in December 1834 Currie reported that 'they have lodged their plans and talk big', and intended to approach Lord Francis again. Currie suggested to Loch that the best chance was to persuade Lord Francis that the North Line would prejudice the interest of his brother, the Duke of Sutherland. Loch, however, pointed out that although Lord Francis's fraternal sympathies were real enough, 'they can only go so far, for his own family is his first consideration'. Loch himself could not intervene since a 'direct application would be indelicate and unwise'.[5]

This episode was part of a recurring pattern. Each time an interest established a lucrative position it quickly generated a vigorous assailant. In this sense the free market economy operated effectively. Moreover, in each instance, strenuous efforts were made to divide any alliance of the established interests. The Liverpool and Manchester Railway succeeded in doing this in 1825; the North Line used similar tactics a decade later.

Loch believed the North Line 'much more likely to happen than our quiet Directors are willing to believe', and it was assisted by the general rise of railway share prices. The scheme, he said, was 'deeply laid in the interest, the prejudice, and the passions of a considerable body of men . . . and which can only ultimately be defeated by dividing its supporters'. The railway should improve its facilities particularly in the town centres. Already, in January 1834, Loch had been instrumental in persuading the railway board to set aside one tenth of its profits to form a sinking fund 'applicable to future contingencies'. But, for the most part, the board relied on parliamentary opposition and its own prospective closer union with the Grand Junction Railway to intimidate the premature challenger.[6]

The high hopes of a closer union between the Liverpool and Manchester and Grand Junction railways faded away in 1835 when negotiations steadily deteriorated. Robert Benson bitterly complained that they had 'been somewhat cavalierly laid upon the shelf . . . by the Grand Junction Committee'. The latter had bought the Warrington and Newton Railroad cheaply. John Moss gave an ominous warning that the Grand Junction subscribers were aware of

[5] SC, Loch to Currie, 27-2-1834; Benson to Loch, 3-3-1834; Currie to Loch, 8-7-1834, 3-12-1834, 8-12-1834.
[6] SC, Currie to Loch, 14-1-1834, 3-12-1834, 9-10-1834, 12-2-1835, 11-2-1835; Loch to Benson, 4-2-1835, 16-2-1835; Benson to Loch, 19-2-1835.

the disadvantages of inclines and extra mileage if they took the route along the Liverpool and Manchester. 'This is very important to us', he wrote, 'in case the L. and M. should be unreasonable hereafter.' He also added that it was a great shame that neither Lord Francis nor Sutherland had an interest in the Grand Junction—'it will be a cheap and good line and a profitable concern.'[7]

But the 2nd Duke of Sutherland was committed to a canal which lay in direct competition with the Grand Junction Railway. Telford's canal continued to be troubled by the intractable problem of Shelmore, and as the months dragged by the difficulties seemed to worsen. Loch's representative on the canal castigated the superintendence for its incompetence—'the proprietors have not a single efficient person in their employ to look strenuously after their interests. Mr. Telford has been for some time quite unfit for the task.' In September 1834 Telford died and Cubitt was elected to succeed him. More than £650,000 had already been spent. Within a few months a clear improvement began to show at Shelmore and the canal was opened for traffic in March 1835. The long-suffering Eyre Lee at last had tangible reason for optimism. In May 1835 he told Loch that trade on the canal was very good and that it would prove 'cheaper than any other way'. Fortunately the canal opened in a year of expanding economic activity and some time before the coming of its railway rival.[8]

The canal was not a great success. In 1838, for instance, there was a strong rumour that a certain Mr Price (a large property owner in Cheshire) was offering £800,000 for the canal in order to convert it into a railway. Stephenson had been consulted and was reported to have said that one day it would be converted into a railway—inevitably so, and done at 'a comparatively trifling cost'. Sir John Wrottesley voiced the general sentiments of the proprietors when he exclaimed that 'the idea of getting back all our money, when I never expected a farthing' was extremely tempting. Loch was sceptical of the truth of the report—correctly in the event—and soberly urged the proprietors to think of improving their facilities rather than of living in hope of a lucrative take-over.[9]

[7] SC, Moss to Loch, 5–2–1835; Currie to Loch, 11–5–1835.
[8] SC, Lewis to Loch, 21–10–1834; Eyre Lee to Loch, 18–7–1834, 2–5–1835; Smith to Loch, 27–9–1834, 5–6–1834; Clive to Loch, 16–9–1834; Loch to Marjoribanks, 12–3–1834.
[9] SC, G. Loch to Loch, 23–2–1838, 28–3–1838; Wrottesley to Loch, 23–2–1838. See also Loch to Sutherland, 23–7–1845.

The idea of improving existing canal capital was feasible but there was no further talk of constructing new canals. Their old deficiencies remained, as for instance in February 1838 when a long frost rendered the Trent and Mersey Canal impassable, bringing a complete stoppage of trade, especially in the Potteries. An observer commented that it would 'make many converts to a railway communication'.[10]

Railway shares were relatively quiet in the early 1830s but boomed between June 1835 and May 1836—'the first great fit of speculation' in railway finance. The frantic energy of these months strained all relationships and brought new dangers to existing interests. In J. H. Clapham's vivid phrase, 'railways were propagated blindly and wastefully like living things.'[11]

Much of the speculative energy came from the widening deployment of capital from the dynamic economy of Lancashire—there appears to have been a marked preponderance of Lancashire capital in railway promotion before 1845. In part this evidence tends to support E. J. Hobsbawm's thesis that railways were often promoted, not to fulfil the pressing economic needs of a particular locality, but because money was burning holes in subscribers' pockets. A similar interpretation could be given to the comments of Joseph Sandars in March 1836. He attributed the current railway speculation to the fact that the Liverpool and Manchester Railway had awakened 'the public mind'. Shares in honestly-projected railways were quickly taken up, thereby inflating the market prices. In an attempt to emulate this experience, new companies were set up: 'and the next best scheme that was offered immediately tempted a new set of speculators to come in; and so they have gone on from one scheme to another till, at present, if you start a railway from any point to another you are sure to get plenty of subscribers.'[12]

The Liverpool and Manchester consistently fought all potential

[10] SC, Lewis to Loch, 19–2–1838.

[11] A. D. Gayer, W. W. Rostow and A. Schwartz, *The Growth and Fluctuation of the British Economy, 1790–1850* (1953), I, 259. Clapham, op. cit., 387. Simmons, op. cit., 6. On the determinants of railway investment see R. C. O. Matthews, *A Study in Trade Cycle History* (1954), 106–13; A. G. Kenwood, 'Railway investment in Britain, 1825–1875', *Economica*, August 1965, esp. 316.

[12] S. A. Broadbridge, 'The early capital market: The Lancashire and Yorkshire Railway', *EcHR*, 1955, 210–11. E. J. Hobsbawm, *Industry and Empire* (1968), 90. *PP*, First Report from the Select Committee appointed to look into the State of Agriculture, March 1836, Q.6217.

interlopers on its prosperous trade between the two towns. Its own financial success was a lure to competitors—in May 1835 it had announced a 9 per cent dividend on its share capital of £800,000 and the payment of 4 per cent interest on its loan capital of £400,000. It served to provoke a further threat from the projected North Line. The Grand Junction directors were playing with the notion of a direct line to Manchester through the Potteries—without using the metals of the Liverpool and Manchester. John Moss, the rather excitable Chairman of the Grand Junction, went further and advised Lord Francis to convert the Bridgewater Canal into a railway and sell shares to Manchester capitalists. He spoke expansively of a connection to Glasgow.[13]

Loch was critical of the tactics used by Liverpool and Manchester in this atmosphere. In January 1836, for example, the railway board decided to raise the annual dividend. It was absurd, said Loch; it could only be interpreted as a piece of speculative manœuvring. It would 'provoke a rival scheme and it takes away all the arguments that could with any success be urged against it.' Indeed, the most cogent argument the North Line possessed was that the existing railway was reaping profits which were too high for the public interest.[14]

The question of railway competition, expansion and, incidentally, the public interest, came to a head in early 1836 when the problems came under the consideration of parliament. The attitude of the government to the early railways is usually characterized as one of doctrinaire *laissez-faire*—even though the Liverpool and Manchester Railway was saddled with restrictions.[15] But, in general, it is true that recognition of the need for a national supervising policy was very tardy. There was no machinery to operate in a supervisory fashion, and the politicians were generally extremely wary of trespassing on the sacred ground of private capital, even when, as in 1836, reckless speculation was an obvious threat to the national

[13] SC, Booth to Loch, 2–5–1835; Currie to Loch, 26–5–1835, 8–6–1835; Loch to Currie 1–5–1835; Loch to Lewis, 28–9–1835; Loch to Davidson, 8–9–1835; Moss to Loch, 10–10–1835.

[14] SC, Loch to Currie, 27–1–1836. In September 1840 the Grand Junction Railway increased its fares by 10 per cent even though it was already paying 14 per cent profit to its shareholders. G. Loch commented, 'this is scandalous, and would justify almost any interference.' G. Loch to Loch, 14–9–1840.

[15] See Simmons, op. cit., 15. G. R. Porter, *The Progress of the Nation* (1847), 336. H. Parris, *Government and the Railways* (1965), ch. 1. J. R. McCulloch, *Commercial Dictionary* (1859), 1090. F. E. Hyde, *Mr. Gladstone at the Board of Trade* (1934), 132–40.

interest. It is significant that the initiative for governmental inter-vention often came from the railway companies. In February 1836 the established railway interests attended 'a very important debate in the Commons', reported Loch, 'losing no time in bringing their views before Parliament'. Poulett Thomson, President of the Board of Trade, was told of the need for a tribunal of enquiry into the progress of railways. Loch, Moss and Lord Sandon met Sir Robert Peel to discuss a proposed petition from the existing railway interests. Loch, cynically, said that the purpose of the exercise was to elicit 'an opinion from the leading members of the House in favour of extending to them some patent right of protection . . . against rival schemes'. Peel, fully conversant with the situation, would have none of it; as Loch said, he was 'dead against us—except as regards the Liverpool and Manchester'. Both Peel and Thomson regarded the latter as a special case, which, because of the 10 per cent clause limiting its dividends, was entitled to protection. However, Peel could find no reason for protecting the Grand Junction, 'in depriving Manchester of a more direct and shorter road to London. No amount of argument had been capable of moving him on this point.' The feeling of the main movers of political influence had been made clear—the Grand Junction had suffered a setback.[16]

The next day, perhaps as a result of this turn of events, it was announced that the Grand Junction had signed the seals of agree-ment with the Liverpool and Manchester Railway. Currie was jubilant and told Loch that it was a thing 'for which you and I have both so longed—I am truly glad.' There was a great surge of con-fidence in the Liverpool and Manchester and its shares appreciated rapidly. Parliament had refused to 'recognise the principle of mono-poly' and one speaker, James Morrison, had gone further and sug-gested that the government should systematically control rates, dividends, and capital undertakings on all new railways. Morrison pointed out the natural degree of monopoly in railways and canals, and implied that this was justification enough for intervention. But he received little support in 1836 and there the matter rested.[17]

Between 1830 and 1837 the Liverpool and Manchester raised more money by way of loans and share-issues than it paid out in dividends. Hostile critics claimed the profits were paid only by robbing the

[16] SC, Loch to Booth, 13-2-1836; Loch to Currie, 15-2-1836, 1-8-1836.
[17] SC, Currie to Loch, 16-2-1836; Loch to Lawrence, 21-2-1836.

capital, but H. Pollins has demonstrated that the dividends declared reflected genuine operational profits.[18] But the question of share-issues is also linked with the 10 per cent limitation clause on profits. If more shares were issued the company had the opportunity of distributing a larger total profit within the 10 per cent limitation—thereby circumventing the clause. In the early 1830s this was probably not the reason for the share issues, but after 1835 the motives were more clouded.

In May 1835 it was proposed that the company should issue more shares to pay off its Exchequer Loan debt. This Loch greeted 'as an important object' and a cleverly conceived scheme. In 1836 the suggestion was developed more actively and it generated a bout of acrimonious discussion. There were two proposals. As things stood, the company had £800,000 in share capital, and £400,000 in loan capital. The first plan (led by Moss) was to sell 2,000 new shares on the market for £400,000—to redeem the debt—and bring the capital stock of the company to £1m. (at par). The second plan (Rathbone's) was to create 4,000 new shares 'to be offered the Projectors at Par, rateably, in proportion to the number of shares held by each respectively'. This would increase the share capital to the sum actually expended on construction and operation.

'The principal inducement to create more shares', wrote Henry Booth, 'is to *lower*, the *dividend* p. *share*.' Rathbone's plan would reduce the dividend more and therefore Booth preferred his plan to that of Moss. Moreover, said Booth,

On this latter plan, also, the present proprietor obtains a handsome Bonus if he decides to increase his stock. A holder of 20 shares would be entitled to 10 *new* ones which would yield him about £1000 as bonus, now, whilst his present shares which he retains, will probably, in a few years, again yield an income of 10 per cent per annum.

Booth hoped that Sutherland would support the Rathbone plan at the forthcoming General Meeting.[19]

Moss abominated Rathbone's plan and the day before the meeting he had been under the impression that the Sutherland directors would oppose it: 'they dare not now proceed with it', he thought. In fact, Sutherland abstained, to the great offence of Moss. He wrote bitterly to Loch that the entire Board was against him, and that he

[18] See Jackman, op. cit., 530. Pollins, op. cit., 94–5.
[19] SC, Booth to Loch, 2–5–1835, 15–3–1836; Loch to Currie, 1–5–1835; Loch to G. Loch, 17–3–1836.

could do no other than resign. He railed against the Rathbone plan—it meant no less than 'a direct bonus of £70 p. share, and defers the operation of the 10% clause', he claimed. He stated the moral implications bluntly:

You will recollect that clause was set by yourself and me in poor Huskisson's private room. I thought he left it sufficiently Liberal! ! ! It was mentioned by Poulett Thomson the other day, and after having presented a petition to Parliament, I contend you and I ought not to be parties to defeat the clause Mr Huskisson forced upon us to protect the rights of the public.

To emphasize his point, Moss added that 'if it is desirable to get out of debt, which I much doubt, the sale of 1,600 whole or 3,200 half shares at the market price of the day would extinguish it—then why raise 7,800 half shares?' The reason was cynical: the railway would receive £20,000 per year from new connecting lines which would add about 3 per cent to dividends—inflating profits to 13 per cent. It was the 'third bonus' the shareholders had received and Moss concluded that, as an honest man, 'there could be no doubt of the impropriety of my being one of those to do what I conceive an improper act.'[20]

Loch, however, disagreed with Moss's interpretation of the Huskisson clause. Indeed, much of the confusion derived from the ambiguity over the method of accounting the net profits of the railway. Loch believed the restriction referred to all the capital that had been expended on the railway, and that a share issue to that amount was perfectly legitimate. He was more anxious about the tactical wisdom of the move. The threat of the North Line continued, and one of the aims of the Rathbone plan had been to facilitate 'a more extended propriety' in Liverpool and Manchester. On the other hand Moss believed that lower freight-rates would be more effective in 'keeping off the North Line'.[21]

Somehow Loch was able to pour oil on the troubled waters and Moss renounced his intention of resigning. He paid tribute to Loch's judgment; the railway would be safe, he told him, 'as long as you continue in it . . . I wish I possessed a little more of your coolness, what seems to have no effect on you would drive me mad.'[22]

Loch was 'very much at a loss what to do about these new shares'.

[20] SC, Moss to Loch, 22–3–1836.
[21] SC, Loch to G. Loch, 24–3–1836.
[22] SC, Moss to Loch, 28–3–1836.

He considered that the Duke of Sutherland already possessed a sufficient stake in the railway—'£150,000 is large enough to embark in any one boat'. Second, there was an element of risk involved as a result of the persisting threat of competition. Third, it was no longer necessary for the Duke to give the company 'a lead name'; moreover, if his shares were sold it would 'spread more widely the benefits intended . . . an extension of connection and of interest'. Finally, Sutherland could meet the annual instalments on the shares only by diverting income from other sources; he wanted to maintain 'the same interest' rather than increase it. On the other hand Currie pointed out that a 10 per cent return per annum was a very profitable investment; it would be at least seven years before any rival could actively compete with the Liverpool and Manchester; it would be preferable to sell from the Funds to pay for the shares. 'Although the prospect of war and general tumult might affect the price of Stocks', he wrote, 'yet the Railway has become so essential to communications, that the traffic on it would in no degree be so much affected by the above prospects as would the Funds, the most sensitive of all securities. Recollect *we* [the Railroad] are made of *iron* and not so easily affected.' He added that the railway traffic was expanding 'with the prodigious increase of both towns . . . and will so in an accelerated ratio'. Having considered these diverse elements Loch eventually determined that Sutherland should sell enough of the new shares on the market to pay for the remainder. Loch commented, 'if he retains one half of the whole for nothing he does well, and he has made up his mind not to regret any loss of profit which he may suffer from adopting this line of conduct.' The capital gain was calculated at £76,100. When his co-directors expressed disapproval, Loch pointed out that, despite the sales, Sutherland was actually increasing his commitment to the railway.[23]

Two further factors influenced the decision to sell some of the share-issue. First, it reflected Sutherland's reduced financial situation in the mid-1830s. Second, there were reports that the management of the railway had become less than efficient. There had been recurrent interruptions and delays. George Loch, in 1836, said that 'the line is in a shameful state'. The reason, he thought, was that the

[23] SC, Loch to Currie, 1–5–1835, 7–5–1835, 5–8–1836, 6–8–1838, 1–8–1838, 12–8–1838, 19–9–1838, 6–10–1836, 9–10–1838, 10–10–1836; Currie to Loch, 2–5–1835, 17–3–1835, 28–6–1836, 30–6–1836, 30–7–1836, 8–8–1836, 21–9–1836; Loch to Moss, 17–3–1836; Loch to G. Loch, 23–6–1836, 15–6–1836; G. Loch to Loch, 10–8–1836.

management had 'no standard by which to compare their railroad' and were therefore unaware of its imperfections. James Loch blamed the Huskisson clause—'It strikes me that the limitation clause has, unknowingly to ourselves, the usual effect of such restriction, a degree of want of economy in expenditure.'[24] Indeed, it is conceivable that the existence of the 10 per cent profit limitation may have occasionally reduced, in some degree, the competitive urgency of the Railway in its attitude towards winning trade from the waterways. As a hostile critic observed in 1842, it deprived 'the public of any inducement to an economical transit of goods', and implanted 'a canker in the heart of the first of these modern wonders'.

It was an inopportune moment to attempt to sell shares. Optimism in the share market had declined into deep pessimism. Joseph Sandars, in March 1837, described the state of the economy as 'a commercial influenza killing right and left'—which he ascribed to 'the rottenness of paper money'. At the same time, opposition to the Liverpool and Manchester had become yet more strident.[25]

Time and again in these years the very diversity of Loch's portfolio brought him into conflict with one party or another. The world of railway promotion in the 1830s lacked order and direction. There were no established codes of business conduct to accommodate the unprecedented capital undertakings that railways now demanded. The labyrinthine complexity of the established, the threatened and the rumoured lines of railway, together with the covert interlocking directorates and alliances, confused the participants as well as the public. A chaotic proliferation of railway lines in every direction seemed imminent and, while the government remained indecisive (or indifferent), there was little hope of guidance.

Henry Booth, guardian of the Liverpool and Manchester, saw the dangers in 1837, and called on his fellow directors to put down vigorously all projected rivals and to serve 'a combined and successful opposition to new Projects of uncalled for and *competing* lines of Railway'. Every projected railway impinged upon one established interest or another—and even within the railway itself there were conflicting allegiances. When Sutherland announced that he would support a line to the Potteries he was accused of duplicity and

[24] SC, G. Loch to Loch, 15–5–1836; Loch to Currie, 18–8–1836.
[25] SC, Sandars to Loch, 10–3–1837; Loch to Sandars, 18–3–1837; Loch and Laws, op. cit., xix.

threatened with retaliation—to which Loch coldly replied that it was unwise 'to endeavour to influence the Duke of Sutherland's conduct by his fears'.[26]

Some of the Liverpool and Manchester Board thought a principle was at stake, 'the conservative principle relative to railway property' which forbade any support whatsoever for any 'distinctly, rival duplicate' line of railway—'duplicate' being a euphemism for any facility even marginally competitive with an established company. Loch was unsympathetic and would not concur in the tenor of the reaction to potential competition; he would have no part in a deputation to parliament; the principles involved were wrong. The railway directors, predictably, were angered at Loch's stand. They blamed him for the fall in their share-prices and said that he did 'not seem to be aware that he may stir up a rival Liverpool and Manchester line, through the disappointed feelings of the Manchester people urged on by Stephenson'. Loch denied all this firmly.[27]

In Loch's view, the railway companies had brought most of the trouble on their own heads. They boasted too much of their probable profits and 'even our president and sound-head friend Rathbone boasted forth his prospects of visionary gains and cheap carriage'. Instead of boasting they should, he asserted, improve their facilities, especially in Manchester where local feeling was running high. In all the controversies—which related to a confusion of different issues—there was a hard element of personal animus. As one spokesman put it, there was an unholy league of the Croppers, Rathbone, Earle, Hodgson and the Quakers against Stephenson, in particular, which was based on the most selfish and vindictive feelings.[28]

'We are bothered out of our lives with Railways', moaned Loch in March 1837; it was 'a controversy and a plague'. Ever the conciliator, he used his influence towards compromise and by mid-1837 many of the disputes had quietened. 'All the irritation', he wrote, 'that has and does exist ... appears to prevail in exact proportion as they missed the opportunity of making a satisfactory arrangement.'[29]

[26] SC, Earle to Currie, 11–10–1836; Booth to Loch, 17–10–1836, 5–11–1836; Loch to Currie, 23–7–1836, 28–7–1836, 10–2–1837, 7–2–1837; Loch to Rathbone, 7–2–1836, 23–2–1837; Loch to Sunderland, 24–2–1837.

[27] SC, Rathbone to Loch, 20–2–1837; Loch to Currie, 17–2–1836.

[28] SC, Loch to Currie, 7–2–1837; Sandars to Loch, 10–3–1837; Currie to Loch, 9–2–1837. See also Holt, op. cit., 14–15.

[29] SC, Loch to Booth, 13–3–1837, 29–4–1837; Loch to Ridgeway, 23–3–1837; Loch to Sandars, 18–3–1837; Loch to Currie, 1–3–1837; Fenton to Loch, 21–4–1837; Rathbone to Loch, 3–4–1837, 21–4–1837.

In the middle of the railway negotiations of early 1837 came a turn in the affairs of the Bridgewater Canal. Three years earlier Lord Francis had been compelled, against his will, to accept James Sothern as canal superintendent. Sothern had continued to defy his wishes. Co-operation between the canal and the railways had repeatedly foundered on Sothern's intransigence. In January 1836 Lord Francis told his brother that he was determined to oust Sothern, 'who is I believe mad and has exhausted my means of forbearance'. In July Loch had fervently hoped for some means of bringing the canal and railway interests 'to concur in some plan embracing all'. But, to accomplish anything of this order, Sothern had to be removed. It seems that Lord Francis took the case to the Court of Chancery in August 1836 on the grounds of Sothern's mismanagement of the Bridgewater Trust affairs. Although not fully successful, the case appears to have given Lord Francis more direct control over Sothern, who was then pressed into thinking of resignation.[30]

Negotiations with Sothern proceeded during January 1837, by which time Sothern had agreed in principle to resign, but the arrangement was not formalized until March when, apparently, it was accepted that Sothern should receive £45,000 as a kind of golden handshake. Loch, who had undertaken the campaign for Lord Francis, reported that 'In order to prevent the same thing taking place again, I am named superintendent.' A deputy, Richard Smith, was appointed to manage the canal at a salary of £1,200 a year. It was a vital (if very costly) take-over, since it prepared the ground for a greater element of co-operation in the tri-partite co-existence between the canal, the railway and the Old Quay Company.[31] Once more James Loch found himself as the effective liaison between the parties—a further burden to add to his administrative responsibilities. He immediately set about the renovation of the canal management. Within a year trade had certainly improved, and Loch claimed it was partly the result of 'a more active management, our Agents being trusted like Gentlemen'. Similarly, relations between

[30] SC, Loch to Moss, 27–7–1836; D593/P/20, Loch to Countess of Sutherland, 21–5–1836, 1–8–1836, 5–8–1836, 8–8–1836, 12–8–1836; D593/P/22/1/5, Lord Francis to Sutherland, 23–1–1836.

[31] SC, Loch to Lewis, 7–3–1837; D593/P/221/5, Lord Francis to Sutherland, 2–1–1837, 9–2–1837; EBC X3695, Loch to Smith, 30–1–1837; Loch to Lord Francis, 30–1–1837; Brownlow to Lord Francis, 11–2–1837. Mather, op. cit., 142. H. Reeve (ed.), *The Greville Memoirs*, II, 303–4. Spring, op. cit., 93.

the Bridgewater Canal and the Liverpool and Birmingham Junction Canal, which had been decidedly strained under the Sothern regime, were slowly healed. 'We are still in the same boat', Loch told Lord Clive in 1838, 'and there is nothing now likely to induce us any more to be in half-confidence with each other, a painful condition to be in.' The age of Bradshaw and Sothern was over.[32]

The rules of the game of collusion played between the transport interests were frequently flouted by one party or another in the 1830s—and so the rules were re-written several times. There is every indication that, of the three companies concerned, the Old Quay was the most desperate and demanded that it should charge the lowest rates of the three as the only chance of keeping its share of the trade. Shares in the Old Quay Company fell from £1,250 in 1826 to £570 in 1836. In March 1837 Loch made a survey of the competitive position of canals in general. Between Liverpool and Manchester the railway had doubled its traffic from 1832 to 1836, while the Bridgewater Canal's had increased by about 60 per cent—the lowering of freight rates in 1832 'had increased the amount of goods carried by the Trustees, without checking the increase by the railway'. The canal continued to carry very much more than the railway. The situation was reasonably satisfactory save for the fact that the Old Quay Company had successfully demanded that it should carry at rates 20 per cent less than the railway and about 10 per cent less than the Bridgewater Canal. One consequence was that the Old Quay had thereby eaten into the Irish trade of the Bridgewater Canal. Loch felt the situation to be unfair and attempted to find a new equilibrium—the time was ripe for an increase of rates on the waterways, though it would not be necessary for the railway to increase. Unfortunately there was an atmosphere of mutual suspicion and the Old Quay, even after a new agreement in 1838 had been negotiated, continued to carry freight at rates lower than the Bridgewater. It was a very precarious equilibrium; the Old Quay Company was increasingly unco-operative and the Railway Board was becoming more and more uneasy about Loch's close alliance with the Bridgewater Canal.[33]

Within the Railway Board the squabbling continued unabated. This derived largely from the fact that a considerable number of

[32] Spring, op. cit., 92–3. SC, Loch to Clive, 25–1–1838, 25–4–1838.

[33] SC, Loch to Currie, 29–2–1836; EBC X3695, Loch to Lord Francis, 10–3–1837, 2–4–1837, 13–5–1837, 19–11–1838; Smith to Loch, 8–5–1837; Loch to Smith, 11–5–1837. Donaghy, op. cit., 99–100. Wheeler, op. cit., 282.

the directors were also involved in the Grand Junction Railway (which opened in July 1837). Another group, perhaps feeding on personal jealousies, were bitterly opposed to the Grand Junction which, they sneered, was 'only a branch' of the London and Birmingham. In September 1837 a crisis occurred and half the Board resigned, led by John Moss who commented that a magnificent concern was being torn to pieces by dissension. James Loch condemned the whole affair as childish and hasty, and when the breach was joined he reported, somewhat didactically, that 'the late gale has blown over . . . we shall again proceed as before. I think that it will be of use, it will make them more circumspect . . . before they again attract public notice by following the same conduct—it was very unlike that of prudent considerate men of a certain time of life.' [34]

The real solution, Loch knew, was a permanent amalgamation of the Liverpool and Manchester with the Grand Junction, and he threw his efforts into achieving this end. He analysed the advantages of one 'grand union'. It would give a firm and united management; it would end the mutual distrust and insinuations, and create a complete identity of interest; it would give peace and repose to the public; there would be economies of scale, especially on the use of locomotives; it would provide uniformity of rates; most important of all it would give security against the attacks of rival lines. In 1837 an amalgamation of this nature was little more than a pious hope and, when Loch's efforts were frustrated, Moss bitterly condemned all railway directors as petty tyrants who would make the railway concerns the object of public abuse. Nevertheless, despite the irremovable problems of personality, a lesser arrangement was achieved in late 1839—'a system of mutual reciprocity'—which was an important step towards a fuller union. [35]

Loch's experience of the opening decades of the railway age had led him to various inescapable conclusions. He had come to realize that no individual could significantly influence the course of the railway as a business entity. Alluding to the arrangement made with the Grand Junction, he said that 'No event in the history of railways

[34] SC, Sandars to Loch, 9–9–1837; Loch to Sandars, 9–9–1837; Currie to Loch, 4–12–1837, 6–12–1837; Moss to Currie, 1–12–1837; G. Loch to Loch, 1–12–1837; Loch to Currie, 6–12–1837, 9–12–1837, 15–12–1837, 5–12–1837.
[35] SC, Loch to Moss, 2–1–1838, 17–2–1838; Booth to Loch, 6–4–1838; Loch to Cropper, 23–1–1838, 17–6–1838; Loch to Currie, 23–1–1838, 17–3–1838; Moss to Loch, 13–2–1838, 19–2–1838, 23–4–1838; Currie to Loch, 18–11–1839; Loch to Fenton, 16–11–1839.

so completely proved the vast nature of the practical monopoly of the present system and the unpracticability of even a large body of wealthy individuals to contend with an established and prosperous Company.' Monopoly was the inevitable and real groundwork of the railway system—and it was, therefore, perfectly rational to make the management as large and as extensive as possible but, he insisted, there must be a proportionate increase in 'the stringency of some superintending power'. Monopoly was inherent and necessary in railway operations and, to Loch, this fact of life made government intervention unavoidable. [36]

During his lengthy deliberations on the problems of railway management, Loch toyed with a plan to combine the administration of the many railways involved in the trade of Lancashire. This would create a more efficient system and the public interest would be enhanced so long as it was subject to a superintending power. His son, George Loch, saw the advantages of the idea but thought it unworkable; all their experience had proved 'how utterly impracticable it would be to reconcile the conflicting pretensions of so many lines'. The individual railway boards would never voluntarily relinquish their separate autonomies. As an alternative, he suggested 'a sort of Congress or Diet of the several "confederated" railways', possessing limited powers of general regulation, to which each railway would send a delegate. One thing was clear to father and son. If the railways were to operate as a system for public and private benefit some kind of comprehensive guidance was imperative. [37]

James Loch pursued the logic of his argument into parliament. With Lord Seymour, he introduced the Railway Regulation Bill in 1840. This was not only a landmark in the growth of the modern state, but also the end of the years of governmental indecision towards the railways. [38] Loch's conclusions sprang from his experience of the coming of the railways: by their sheer size the railway enterprises appeared to have outgrown the existing conventions and restraints on business organization. In 1825 it had been perfectly reasonable to believe that a wealthy aristocrat could guide a major railway along acceptable lines; in 1840 such an idea was almost unimaginable. The railways had added an entirely new dimension to the problems of control of industrial organization.

[36] SC, Loch to Fenton, 16–11–1839; Loch to Garett, 11–3–1840.
[37] SC, Loch to G. Loch, 24–1–1840; G. Loch to Loch, 26–1–1840.
[38] See Parris, op. cit., chapters 1, 2.

XI

Into and Out of the Vortex

Collusion between the transport interests on the Liverpool and Manchester route had been a feature of the events of the 1830s. Despite all manner of difficulties, open war had largely been avoided. James Loch had been instrumental in perpetuating a surprising degree of compromise and, even in the face of ill-will in the policing of the regulations, the Carriers' Agreements had generally prevailed. Loch fought every inch to preserve co-operation and to prevent unilateral rate-cutting. His first premise was that 'to run against each other is advantageous to neither.' Since he represented both canal and railway interests Loch had every reason to adhere to such a notion. However, in the generally depressed conditions of industry between 1839 and 1842, falling prices and reduced profits added a new severity to the contest for survival. The uneasily co-existing rivals broke apart under economic strain.[1]

The rift began in July 1840. Trade on the railway was declining despite the fact that the total cotton traffic was increasing. It was clear that the cause was the successful competition of the waterways, and since the profits of the Old Quay had 'decidedly diminished', it was inferred that the Bridgewater Canal 'got the difference'. George Loch suggested that the reason was the superior management of the canal, which took great pains to attract business. He said it was absurd for the railway board to 'complain of them for managing their affairs so well as to deprive us of business' when the railway 'took so little pains'. He insisted, in effect, that the canal was pursuing a perfectly legitimate policy, competing not in price but in service. But Henry Booth believed that some of the private carriers

[1] SC, Loch to Cropper, 17–6–1839. See also Mather, op. cit., 143–4.

on the waterways had not acted in good faith and 'that they either charged lower than the rates fixed on, or make some abatements afterwards', though he absolved the Trustees themselves from the imputation. The suspicion was there, and it grew. John Moss declared that the railway should make preparations for a freight-war and that a fund for this purpose should be set aside.[2] Moss was a man to reconcile. It was at this time that Loch wrote him an invitation to accompany him to Sutherland to view 'the finest European scenery to be seen ... I undertake neither the Railway or Canal shall be pronounced in your hearing the whole time.'[3]

Loch was unwilling to allow the agreement to lapse simply to appease the more truculent members of the railway board. 'I consider it a very serious misfortune', he said, 'that the Carriers' Agreement which I took, in conjunction with the aid of others to effect, should be put an end to—and every influence I possess shall be exerted to give it continuance and support'. The question, he contended, had not been fully investigated—there were a thousand things to consider—for example, the general decline of trade, and the distinct possibility that the current Manchester trade did not 'require the speed of railways'—a point which had been overlooked. Loch's son pointed out that changes in the marketing of cotton had favoured the canals, which were able to supply direct to the warehouses, while the insurance companies had been attempting to spread their risks more widely between the carriers. He also admitted that some of the allegations of price cutting were not entirely without foundation. But the elder Loch insisted that the management of the Bridgewater had 'acted up to ... the spirit and letter of the arrangement'.[4]

It was all in vain. The Old Quay Company had already opted out of the agreement. Evidence was produced to substantiate the allegations against individual carriers; it was taken for granted that the agreement was moribund, and Moss looked 'for fighting ... with complacency'. Trade was generally declining, yet the canals were carrying more cotton than before—*ipso facto* they were cheating. The agreement was dissolved and the railway lowered its rates. The

[2] SC, G. Loch to Loch, 27-7-1840; Loch to G. Loch, 27-8-1840; Gatty to Loch, 15-8-1840.
[3] SC, Loch to Moss, 1-9-1840.
[4] SC, Loch to G. Loch, 28-7-1840; G. Loch to Loch, 30-7-1840, 10-8-1840, 19-8-1840, 3-8-1840, 1-9-1840, 12-9-1840; Loch to Booth, 21-8-1840, 22-8-1840, 24-8-1840. See also Clapp, op. cit., 155-6.

battle was on. Loch predicted that 'the more goods that are carried the greater will be the loss', and resignedly noted, 'I have done my best to keep all quiet.' The revocation of the Carriers' Agreement, he said, was based upon 'vague surmises'; it was illogical, it was a means of penalizing the Bridgewater Canal for its new efficiency.[5] It was still more a negation of the policy that Loch had steadfastly pursued for fifteen years.

Other aspects of the dispute caused Loch further alarm. He saw the railways using high passenger fares to make up losses on their goods traffic—which appeared to confirm his belief that 'they could not carry heavy goods at a profit.' It was grossly unfair trading and he told the House of Commons that the Liverpool and Manchester Railway 'was obliged to charge a premium on the conveyance of passengers, to make up for loss in the carriage of goods'. Loch also warned Labouchere, at the Board of Trade, of the dangers implicit in the struggle. It would end, he said, in a combination against the public interest. Loch thought the government should act, but he realized that 'with your present powers, your Board can do little direct good'. Nevertheless, he believed that Inspectors should be appointed to investigate the practices of the carriers. Other canals feared 'being drawn into the vortex', yet a failure to resist would be 'absolutely suicidal'. Loch declared that 'our relations stand in nearly as perilous a condition as those of England and France.' It was essential to put an end to the contest that had unhinged the whole carrying trade of the country. Henry Booth, the railway-master, believed that a few months of rate cutting would cure the waterways of their disorderly conduct.[6]

After some months a compromise was arranged between the transport interests. But it was an uneasy time. Even when the railway was maintaining its share of the traffic it was difficult to persuade certain 'jealous people' of the incontestable facts. By the terms of the new agreement the railway carried various goods (including cotton) at a rate 10 per cent higher than the waterways. Very soon the railway board became dissatisfied and demanded an equalization of all rates, and threatened unilateral action. The Old Quay Company was again subverting the agreement by 'making many indirect

[5] SC, G. Loch to Loch, 31–8–1840; Loch to G. Loch, 10–8–1840; Loch to Moss, 1–9–1840.

[6] SC, Loch to G. Loch, 12–9–1840, 15–9–1840; Loch to Powis, 19–9–1840, 26–10–1840; Loch to Labouchere, 19–9–1840; Powis to Loch, 21–10–1840; Booth to Loch, 22–10–1840. Hansard, July 1840, 924–5.

allowances or affording indirect advantages, such as letting the
carriers carry greater weights for less money ... and ... by every
inducement and allowance that they can, short of open and direct
reduction of tonnage'. Loch again used all his conciliatory influence.
Out of the resulting compromise, yet another agreement was improvised in April 1841 which specifically forbade the use of dis-
counts.[7]

Had the general economic environment become less intensely
competitive in the following months, the fragile rate agreement
might have held. But it was not to be. New lines of railway were
coming into operation—and competition between the railways
inevitably began to affect the canal trade. Freight traffic was being
syphoned away from the Bridgewater Canal in this way. In another
area, the Trent and Mersey Canal was losing money heavily and
demanded a reduction of rates.

Loch analysed the pressures which placed the agreement in
jeopardy. The reasons were: first, that new and unexpected channels of
communication had opened; second, the low freights were aggravated
by railway competition; and third, the 'restricted conditions of trade
in the country' depressed all transport enterprises. The position of
the canals was particularly serious since if trade 'once escapes us, the
competition is so great, that I am convinced we should never be able
to get it back—at least without an immense sacrifice.'[8]

In December 1841 the Carriers' Agreement once more collapsed.
Feeling ran high. The railway directors openly denounced the
waterways. Railway rates were reduced by 15 per cent and a Traffic
Committee was established to direct the attack. They believed that
the private water carriers had culpably infringed the terms of the
agreement: 'they must now learn the consequences of their bad
faith', said one; 'the reductions we have determined on will make the
lesson a severe one.' James Loch deplored the contest. Moss admitted
that it was costing the railway company 'some thousands a week'.
Loch regarded it as a futile exercise provoked by impetuosity, and he
warned that if it continued for long 'the public will interfere and
prevent any return to higher tonnage.' The canals were not broken

[7] SC, G. Loch to Loch, 2–11–1840, 18–12–1840, 8–12–1840, 1–3–1840, 5–4–
1841; Loch to Booth, 12–3–1841, 7–4–1841; Booth to Loch, 4–4–1841; Loch to
Lawrence, 6–4–1841; Loch to G. Loch, 6–4–1841, 27–4–1841. EBC X3695, Loch
to Lord Francis, 9–12–1841.
[8] SC, G. Loch to Loch, 26–7–1841, 2–8–1841. Twenlow Papers, September
1841. SC, Loch to Powis, 29–10–1841; Moss to Loch, 10–2–1841.

by the struggle and in April 1842 yet another agreement was signed. The price of the railway shares had fallen, the dividend was reduced below the normal 10 per cent and, reported Loch, 'this is entirely owing to the foolish contest with the canals, we thereby lost £10,000.'[9]

Loch did not conceal his opposition to the warfare between the canals and railway. He told Henry Booth that his duty was to protect the property and interest of the Duke of Sutherland. His Grace required a steady, secure income from his large investment. He could not sanction any 'experiment or contest with other concerns', for his income was thrown into jeopardy by such action. As the rate-war intensified Loch stated candidly that the Duke of Sutherland would be forced to reconsider his investment in the railway company.[10]

Increasingly Loch found himself opposed to the policies of the Railway Board—not only on rate policy but also on relations with the new railways. He considered that the management lacked a 'singleness of view'. He deplored the manner in which the Board was being swayed by petty influences. On the other hand, many of his fellow directors believed Loch was attempting to protect the canal interests, and he became the butt of their abuse. Loch was accused of deliberately selling Sutherland's surplus shares to canal interests without regard for the best interest of the railway. In 1841 a 'Manchester Citizen' declared that the national interest was being 'sacrificed to pander to the cupidity of an already infinitely over-paid member of the aristocracy'—on the grounds that the Sutherland directors had opposed certain connections with new railways. On several issues Loch's wishes were contravened and the Board voted heavily against him. It signified a perceptible diminution of the influence of Loch and Sutherland in railway matters.[11]

Very serious consideration was given to the idea of reducing Sutherland's shareholding in the railway, even to the extent of selling out altogether. Indeed, the threat of a sale was thought to be a useful weapon to wield against the 'very injudicious proceedings for the

[9] SC, G. Loch to Loch, 16–2–1842, 2–3–1842, 21–4–1842, 5–7–1842; Moss to Loch, 26–2–1842; Loch to Lawrence, 25–3–1842. EBC X3695, Loch to Lord Francis, 6–5–1842. Donaghy, op. cit., 100–3.

[10] SC, Loch to G. Loch, 5–4–1841; Loch to Lawrence, 6–4–1841, 25–3–1842; Loch to Booth, 9–11–1840.

[11] SC, G. Loch to Loch, 26–3–1842, 8–4–1842, 14–4–1842. Loch and Laws, op. cit., *passim*. Holt, op. cit., 15–17.

permanent interests of the railway'. Arguments about 'having too many eggs in one basket' were repeated. Moreover, there were other threats to the future security of the railway interest. In 1841 Loch warned Booth that 'The Manchester Ship Canal is very seriously entertained by a large body of wealthy and respectable men and it obtains daily converts.'

There were two major reasons for a sale of shares by Sutherland. First, the interest had been alienated by the almost ceaseless acrimony of railway affairs; and, second, the House of Sutherland faced a number of financial problems which necessitated a sale. In the upshot it was decided to sell only the new half and quarter shares, and this was effected in 1843 and 1844.[12]

In April 1844 Booth proposed another share-issue to convert the existing debt of £454,000 into share-capital. He explained to Loch that the market was ripe for a new issue and the share-price would not be affected seriously; the new shares, he said, would be 'so much clear gain' to the proprietors. The company was currently paying its legal maximum dividend of 10 per cent. The express object of Booth's share-issue was to provide an 'enlarged surface over which it [the profits] has to be spread'. The share-issue went forward and it was decided to sell some of Sutherland's allocation—the shares were at 'an absurdly high price' on the market. George Loch was jubilant: the transaction had realized £59,800 and he had 'little doubt that the 10 per cent dividend will continue, and the original shares remain at the same value they bore previous' to the new issue. It was exactly as Booth had planned.[13] The 10 per cent clause was never regarded as 'a minor matter' by the railway proprietors. H. Pollins has written that 'since the Company did not pay a dividend higher than ten per cent, the original clause was never operative'—but this was the precise intention and consequence of the policy sanctioned by the railway board.[14]

The Liverpool and Manchester Railway Board found that there were two major sources of trouble in its operations. First, its relations with the Grand Junction had never been fully satisfactory, and,

[12] SC, Loch to G. Loch, 15–4–1842, 16–5–1842, 26–7–1842, 27–7–1843; G. Loch to Loch, 21–4–1842, 16–5–1842, 26–7–1843, 24–9–1843, 25–12–1843; Booth to Loch, 3–4–1843, 12–4–1841; Loch to Booth, 7–4–1841; Drummonds to Loch, 16–1–1844, 23–1–1844, 24–1–1844.
[13] SC, Booth to Loch, 27–4–1844; G. Loch to Loch, 13–8–1844, 14–9–1844.
[14] Pollins, op. cit., 94, 95–6.

Elizabeth Gordon, 1765-1839; Countess of Sutherland in her own right, Duchess/Countess of Sutherland from 1833. Also known as Lady Stafford between 1803 and 1833.

George Granville Leveson-Gower, 1758-1833; Marquis of Stafford in 1803, 1st Duke of Sutherland in 1833.

Harriet Elizabeth Georgiana Leveson-Gower, 1806-68; Duchess of Sutherland from 1833.

second, its attempts to stabilize freight rates had been persistently frustrated by lack of co-operation, especially from the Old Quay Company. The solution to neither problem appeared to be in sight in 1842.

The rate agreement which had been negotiated in April 1842 did not hold for more than a few months. In September the Railway Board once more accused the private carriers on the canals of infringement of the agreement. The railway share of the cotton trade had fallen to 12 per cent when once it had been 30 per cent. The Old Quay carried less than either the railway or the Bridgewater. George Loch believed the reason was as much in 'superior dealing as in unfair dealing'. Negotiations were reopened between the three parties. There were large difficulties. Loch believed that the railway was putting 'everything in jeopardy for cotton alone'. Loch himself concocted a plan to divide the trade with penalties on over-carrying. But this raised the question of how 'to decide what was and was not the proportion of the whole trade to which each of the three bodies were entitled'. The division of the trade between the oligopolists was entirely an arbitrary matter, for there was no general criterion. The previous contest had cost the railway £10,000, the Bridgewater, £4,900, and the Old Quay probably as much.

In May 1843, after a good deal of ill-tempered haggling, another agreement was made. This proved as temporary as its predecessors. The contest reached a final climax in the last few months of 1843. The Old Quay broke away in August and reduced rates by 50 per cent, to which extreme provocation the railway reacted in kind—the railway board, despite Loch's efforts, believed that the railway could fight a final contest with little cost. Booth seems to have welcomed the possibility of a severe struggle. Loch again said that the rate-contests lost money, and gave no credit to any party, but 'an infinite evil ... to all'. A ruinous round of reductions followed and Loch reflected on the fact 'that the present excellent state of the trade should afford no remuneration to those concerned in it.' He also stated that such mutually-damaging contests were 'inevitable as long as there are three independent concerns between Liverpool and Manchester'.[15]

[15] SC, G. Loch to Loch, 21–9–1842, 7–3–1843, 14–3–1843, 20–3–1843, 20–4–1843, 22–4–1843, 25–4–1843; Loch to Lawrence, 21–8–1843. EBC X3695, Loch to Lord Francis, 16–3–1843, 18–3–1843, 3–4–1843, 11–4–1843, 19–4–1843, 22–4–1843, 5–5–1843, 27–6–1843, 8–8–1843, 22–8–1843, 28–8–1843, 3–9–1843, 18–9–1843, 22–9–1843, 26–9–1843; F. Smith to Loch, 8–11–1843; Loch to F. Smith, 14–11–1843.

The extreme action of the Old Quay Company was a symptom of its competitive weakness. George Loch had said, in March 1843, that the Old Quay did not really want an agreement; the only purpose of its tactics was to compel the Bridgewater Canal 'to take their line off their hands, for they can make nothing of it themselves and . . . never will'. They had already flirted with the Leeds and Manchester Railway in hope of a take-over. In April Loch had suggested to Lord Francis that it might be worth his while to buy into the Old Quay himself—'it would be better to lose £2,000 a year by making a bad bargain with the Old Quay for a lease than £4,900 a year in a contest.' The Manager of the Old Quay, Linguard, knew that the concern was bankrupt and, said Loch, 'wishes to show its value as an instrument of annoyance. This he does not conceal.'

In December 1843 agreement was reached. Loch had undertaken 'a nervous though a necessary negotiation' with the concurrence of the railway board. On behalf of Lord Francis he had purchased the Old Quay Navigation Company. 'I have dreamt for 3 nights successively and 3 times every night', he confided to Lord Francis, 'that I have got into the barge on the Canal and have been forcibly taken and put on board a passage boat on the Old Quay. I think that this is a puzzler for the readers of dreams.' Lord Francis is said to have paid £550,800 for the Old Quay, which had once been offered to the Duke of Bridgewater for £10,000. The dissident party in the rate agreement was thereby effectively removed. Loch was congratulated on his coup—particularly in the face of 'Mr. Linguard's conduct'. 'Buying Mr. L. off at 6 years purchase, as it were, is certainly cheap, and at the same time getting rid of a very awkward person to deal with', Loch was told. 'I trust that all your anticipation of the great benefits to be gained by the acquisition of the Old Quay will be amply realized . . . it will be a step worthy of a life of toil.'[16]

Within days of the purchase Loch set about the rationalization of the management of the Old Quay and the Bridgewater Canal. Linguard was dismissed with compensation. It was discovered that the 'great loss' previously experienced on the Old Quay was largely the result of maladministration of tonnage registration. In a few months Loch was well satisfied with the acquisition: 'I was not aware that we had so formidable a rival—it should have taken the lead',

[16] SC, Loch to Mackenzie, 6–12–1843; Loch to Sutherland, 10–12–1843; Loch to Duchess of Sutherland, 9–1–1844; Hothern to Loch, 6–1–1844. Malet, op. cit., 174. EBC X3695, Loch to Lord Francis, 1–1–1844, 3–1–1844, 8–1–1844.

he commented in May 1844. In fact, in 1844 the Old Quay carried more freight than it had ever done before and its success promised to help 'to keep off any desire to have direct additional lines of communication' between Liverpool and Manchester. Most important of all, the unification of the two waterways cleared the air for a much more peaceful co-existence with the rival railway company.[17]

'I am the last canal or nearly so which can be said to exist in England', wrote Lord Francis Egerton in 1845, 'and I do not suppose anybody in Manchester would give me three years purchase for the article'. The purchase of the Old Quay had involved him in 'vast debt'. A year earlier he had written in the *Quarterly Review* on the relative prospects of rail and water carriage, stating that 'some dozen years of experience enable us to say that there is an inherent force of vitality in the latter, which will at least secure it an honourable death and respect from its conquerors . . . such an euthanasia, is, we trust, for the present postponed.' George Loch did not accept this pessimistic view for the Bridgewater concern—'its position, the nature of its trade, and its shortness must always command a great traffic', he said; 'it is very differently circumstanced from those other canals which are seeking to convert themselves into railways.' It was a peculiar case since the 'time required for the transit is little more than that occupied by the Railway'; it required no repairs on its river sections and the handling-costs onto sea-boats were less than those of the railway.[18] F. C. Mather has recently demonstrated the essential resilience and vitality of the Bridgewater concern—even in the 1840s, when its profits were falling, it continued to carry two-thirds of the traffic between Liverpool and Manchester. Indeed, it was too successful in that it wrested traffic from the railway and thereby jeopardized the freight agreement. In 1845 the trade had been divided between the railway and the canal, with a penalty of 2*s*. 6*d*. per ton for any excess tonnage carried. The canal 'generally exceeded' its allotted portion, and in the five years 1845–9 it paid £13,000 per annum in excess penalties to the railway. The reason was that the individual carriers on the canal undercharged their customers. The system worked well until the railway found itself in competition

[17] EBC X3695, Loch to Lord Francis, 3–1–1844, 6–1–1844, 11–1–1844, 5–4–1844, 9–4–1844, 10–6–1844, 24–8–1844, 7–11–1844, 19–10–1845; G. Loch to Lord Francis, 16–10–1845. Donaghy, op. cit., 104.

[18] Earl of Ellesmere, op. cit., 244. EBC X3695, Loch to Lord Francis, 10–4–1844, 19–10–1845; G. Loch to Loch, 14–6–1845, 23–10–1845; Lord Francis to Barry, 20–10–1845.

with new railways and a new contest began in 1849. Once again, Loch remarked, the railways had to learn the strength of the canals —and 'that they could not annihilate the Canals'. Eventually, 'the foundation of a lasting agreement with the railway' was established. In forty years of technological change in the provision of transport services between Liverpool and Manchester, the element of oligopolistic collusion remained as the predominant *modus vivendi*.[19]

In the early 1840s the Liverpool and Manchester had lost its supremacy in railway affairs. No longer could it dictate terms to infant companies or growing rivals. The railway board lacked leadership and its future was overshadowed by its more powerful neighbours. Loch believed that it was 'destined to be swallowed up either by the Leeds or the Grand Junction and unless they [the Board] put themselves in a state of actual exertion they will be appropriated by the one or other without them being hardly aware of it.' Although relations with the Grand Junction had been kept 'at an irritable and unsatisfactory state', Loch favoured an amalgamation with this 'natural and old connection ... it would secure peace for many years.' Most importantly it would help remove the renewed threats of north and south lines to Manchester. But it was a very delicate business, requiring subtle diplomacy; 'we have most slippery and unscrupulous people to deal with on both sides', remarked Loch.[20]

It was a time of amalgamation and extravagant projects. There were too many 'ill-conceived projects now afloat', wrote Loch in April 1844, 'which will be alike injurious to the public interest, to the enjoyment of public property and the safety of that vast capital that has been already invested'. The speculation, thought Loch, would lead to the 'moral injury of a vast body of the educated classes of the Community'. It was therefore essential that the existing railways reach some general understanding to check the public evil. Amalgamation would help since it would bring safety and security to railway property. The negotiation, despite the 'usual shilly-shally conduct' and the perennial difficulties of personality, proceeded, and in

[19] Mather, 'The Duke of Bridgewater's trustees', 150. SC, Loch to Sutherland, 8–12–1849. Spring, op. cit., 94. Jackman, op. cit., 740–1.
[20] SC, Loch to G. Loch, 7–1–1844, 23–1–1844, 22–10–1844; G. Loch to Loch, 21–1–1844, 7–3–1843; Loch to Lawrence, 27–2–1844, 30–8–1844; Loch to Duchess of Sutherland, 10–1–1844. EBC X3695, Loch to Lord Francis, 24–8–1844, 5–11–1844, 7–12–1844, 18–11–1844, 29–11–1844, 12–2–1845, 4–3–1845, 16–10–1845.

October 1845 the Liverpool and Manchester and the Grand Junction were amalgamated. In the following year the concern became a component part of the London and North Western Railway. The Duke of Sutherland, it was said, gained £70,000 on the transaction, 'and ... no fear of his old dividend'. Twenty years later, in 1865, with perfect irony, a group of Liverpool bankers and merchants were heard to cry loudly against the excessive rates charged by 'that leviathan monopolist', the London and North Western.[21]

As the structure of railway investment became more monolithic by the process of amalgamation, so the influence of individual shareholdings diminished. After 1845 the Duke of Sutherland was little more than a recipient of dividends. In 1846 he possessed £205,000 of railway stock (at par) which, at the prevailing market price, was worth £526,593. The panic of 1848 caused Loch some consternation, but he consoled Sutherland with the thought that 'Your Grace stands better off than most, I could say almost any other Railway Proprietor, for you got all your shares at *par*'—and could get back his original outlay at any time. More important than the reduced capital value was the loss of annual dividends. The dividend had fallen to 7 per cent—which, although a better return than practically any other investment, was an embarrassment to the Sutherland finances. The Duke wanted a stable income and the unpredictable fluctuations made him 'much against any extension' of his commitment to railways. There were, of course, other strongly competing demands on the 2nd Duke's capital—notably in the Scottish Highlands and in the maintenance of his prestige in aristocratic society.[22] By way of contrast, his brother, Lord Francis Egerton, did buy his way into new railway promotion—not as a straightforward investment of capital, but as a means of minimizing future competition for his Bridgewater Canal.[23]

In the late 1840s railway dividends represented about 12 per cent of Sutherland's total annual income—in 1848 the dividend income

[21] SC, Moss to Loch, 15–4–1844; Loch to Moss, 19–4–1844, 20–4–1844, 27–4–1844; Loch to Sutherland, 9–6–1844, 4–11–1844, 23–7–1845; Sutherland to Loch, 3–8–1845; G. Loch to Loch, 5–9–1845, 27–10–1845; Loch to G. Loch, 22–10–1845; Langton to Loch, 12–10–1845: Loch to Rotheram, 12–6–1845; Loch to Lawrence, 12–9–1844, D593E/7/21. Jackman, op. cit., 738. EBC, Loch to Lord Francis, 14–6–1845.

[22] See below, chapter XVIII.

[23] SC, Drummonds to Loch, 18–2–1846; Loch to Langton, 15–9–1846; Creed to Loch, 21–2–1848; Loch to Sutherland, 19–10–1848, 1–11–1848; Sutherland to Loch, 3–11–1848. Mullineux, op. cit., 30.

was £16,809, while total gross income was £135,763. Falling railway income helped to force important retrenchments on the Sutherland estates in 1850. The financial position was epitomized by the 2nd Duke in a comment to Charles Kirkpatrick Sharpe in October 1849 when he said that 'destitution on our West Coast has required outlay, and I spend £92,000 in one year in Sutherland—more than three times the income; and in England railway shares have fallen, and I have been obliged repeatedly to sell out of the Stocks, and am now *in forma pauperis*'.[24]

Between 1825 and 1845 the House of Sutherland had clearly exerted a formative influence on the coming of the Railway Age. The Sutherlands are the most obvious exception to the generalization that the aristocracy, while reaping lucrative capital gains from land sales, gave little support to railway investment. Moreover, the family did much to create the context within which the new technology of railways was accommodated. Throughout the first two decades of the Railway Age James Loch was able to temper the expected onslaught on canal property by a consistent policy of compromise. Extraordinary opportunities were created for the canals to buy a very large role in the extension of the system in the early 1830s but, for the most part, entrepreneurial inertia, the immobility of canal capital, and the force of traditional allegiances prevented the realization of Loch's anxious expectations. As with any situation convulsed by technological innovation, uncertainties of the future made decision-making exceptionally hazardous. Lacking the support of other canal proprietors, the Sutherland family did not partake in the enormous expansion of railway capital after 1833. Instead, the family continued to divert its capital to the northern Highlands of Scotland, where there was an infinitely greater degree of control, but a rather more dubious return on capital.

In the transport world Loch's efforts were devoted to maintaining equilibrium in the trade between Liverpool and Manchester. The policy was generally successful and the Bridgewater Canal remained viable even during the sporadic periods of severe competition with the railways. However, it would be unwise to generalize from the Bridgewater case to statements concerning the survival capacity of

[24] SC, Memo, 25–1–1849; Loch to Duchess of Sutherland, 26–12–1849; Loch to Sutherland, 21–1–1850, 28–1–1850, 14–3–1851, 13–10–1851, 16–12–1851. Allardyce, op. cit., II, 598.

all canals or the aggregate net benefits of the railways to the British economy. The Bridgewater Canal was essentially atypical, and, in any case, it bought its successful survival at a high price.[25]

Without the income of first, the Bridgewater Canal, and second, the railway, it is difficult to see how the House of Sutherland could have even contemplated its 'improving policies' on its territorial empire in Scotland and England. In 1848 Loch gave a brief history of the family involvement in the railways. He recounted that the 1st Duke (Lord Stafford) had invested £100,000 in the Liverpool and Manchester Railway in 1825, which Loch described as 'the greatest and the most successful mercantile transaction that has perhaps ever taken place'. From the original investment, the 1st and 2nd Dukes had 'received above nine per cent including those years wherein none was paid when constructing'. In addition, the capital value of the shares had greatly appreciated, and the new shares had cost nothing 'because sales of shares had paid for the new issues retained'. Furthermore, the periodic sales of shares had enabled the Duke 'to build Dunrobin', and to relieve the acute distress in Sutherlandshire.[26]

Thus the profits of the Lancastrian transport sector helped finance the great Sutherland expenditures in the nineteenth century. Moreover, there may have been a deliberate effort to emulate the profitability of the Bridgewater Canal in the development plans undertaken in the northern Highlands. It is not unlikely that strong family reasons—the prestige of the Countess, and the future income of the heir, Lord Gower—may have dictated the deployment of the great Sutherland fortune in the north. This notion was pursued by a very

[25] It may be noted that these conclusions are in opposition to some of the important and detailed work of F. C. Mather in his new book, *After the Canal Duke*. He believes that the practical result of Lord Stafford's purchase in the Liverpool and Manchester Railway was detrimental to the interests of the Bridgewater Canal. He contends that this investment created inner conflicts in the Bridgewater interest and 'paralysed so many exertions for self-defence' (82). Mr Mather is especially critical of Loch, whose management, he suggests, minimized the competitive efficiency of the canal. As seen in the chapters above, Loch's achievement was very considerable and—given the natural oligopoly circumstances of the route—was basically successful in dividing the trade to the mutual advantage of the two brothers. It is unfortunate that Mr Mather has not specified a 'hypothetical alternative' set of tactics against which to judge the policy that Loch actually pursued.

[26] SC, Loch to Sutherland, 6-11-1848. Loch assured the Duke 'that this investment is one of the most advantageous arrangements of capital . . . that can be quoted . . . as the holder of these shares you have been a great gainer.'

hostile critic of the family's northern activities—a correspondent of the *Military Register*—in October 1815. He may not have been far from the mark when he claimed that the policies followed in Sutherland were:

to be understood to be bottomed in a consideration of the relative prospective fortunes of the two sons of the present Marquis of Stafford . . . The present Earl Gower . . . will come to the Marquisate with but the Stafford and Sutherland estates which will indeed be considerably less than the inheritance to which his younger brother will succeed, and therefore the noble parents are understood to be desirous that during the incumbency of the present Marquis, the fortunes of the two sons should be brought as nearly on an ultimate par as may be.

Although the main drama in the struggle between the canals and the railways came in the 1820s, the profits of the Bridgewater Canal had been flowing to Lord Stafford since 1803. The writer in the *Military Register* asserted that William Young (Loch's immediate predecessor in Sutherlandshire) had 'sworn that he would make the Sutherland Estate, in a given time, to equal the *Lancashire canals*'.[27] As the next section shows, James Loch took over and consolidated the long-term plans for the development of a regional economy in the Highlands. Thus the railways and canals competed with the Sutherland involvement not only for Lord Stafford's capital, but also for Loch's own time and energy.

[27] 'Highlander' in the *Military Register*, 31 October 1815.

Part Three

The Sutherland Clearances

Eschew that damnable wyce of awarice, which bringeth ewer with it heatred, extortion and oppression. . . . Beware thou spend not abowe 3 of the 4 parts of thy revenue . . . otherways yow shall leive lyke a riche begger in continuall wants . . . Let no man tyrranise ower your tennents, yea, not your owne brother . . . Do few bussines with your countreymen by the intercession of others . . . for they will suck the margh and substance of your tennants, and your reputation shall be thereby diminished . . . Yse your diligence to take away the reliques of the Irishe barbaritie which as yet remains in your countrey, to wit, the Irishe language and the habit . . . Setle also a summer market in Broray, that so yow may bring money into your countrey . . . for your marts, wooll and other commodities. (Letter of Advice by Sir Robert Gordon to his nephew, John, Earl of Sutherland, c. 1620, in W. Fraser, *The Sutherland Book*, II, 340, 345, 354, 359, 362.)

I wish to possess authentic information relative to the CLEARING affair for, though it took place twenty years ago, it may be just as necessary to inquire into *the means that were used to effect* the CLEARING; and if anyone will have the goodness to point out to me the authentic sources of information on the subject, I shall be extremely obliged to him. (William Cobbett, 1832, *Rural Rides* (1930 ed.), III, 877.)

the literary record is characterised by the purging of guilt, the urge to justify or accuse, and the overemphatic protestations which paralyse any attempt to tell the story plainly and in a way that would be more eloquent of the true suffering involved. (M. Gray, 'Settlement in the Highlands 1750–1950', *Scottish Studies*, VI (1962), 149.)

there is no economic case for the development of the Highland area . . . the economic solution to the 'Highland Problem' is to induce the movement of labour out of, and not the movement of capital into, the area. (D. J. Mackay and N. K. Buxton, 'The north of Scotland—a case for redevelopment', *SJPE*, February 1965, 23.)

'To give a proper account of the Sutherland Clearances would take a bulky volume.' (A. Mackenzie, 1883, *History of the Highland Clearances* (1914 ed.), 19.)

XII

‧‧‧

Sutherland and the Highland Problem

‧‧‧

The environment of the Liverpool and Manchester Railway was a world removed from that of the Highland clearances. A greater contrast in the Victorian economy would be hard to find. The economic experience of the Highlands was set squarely in a pre-industrial context—yet the clearances were as much an expression of the 'Age of Improvement' as the promotion of railway capital in Lancashire. Both were responses to the burgeoning demands of the growing national economy; both were essentially experimental, speculative and capital-intensive. But there the similarity ends. The railway experiment carried all before it; the Highland experiment yielded little evidence of positive achievement, and many people regard the clearances as an unmitigated disaster. Pre-industrial economic history is littered with unfulfilled projects for development—one of which was the policy of clearance in Sutherland. Speaking of Sutherland in 1815, James Loch declared that 'in no country in Europe, at any period in its history, did there ever exist more formidable obstacles to the improvement of a people arising from the feelings and prejudices of the people themselves.'[1] Its problems were those of Highland economic development.

During the age of the Industrial Revolution most regions of Britain achieved a socially desirable integration into the mainstream of the national economy. The Highlands, however, were confirmed in their economic isolation. Many substantial efforts to promote economic advance failed, and the far north became 'the sore little finger'[2] of

[1] Loch, *Account* (1815), 4.
[2] F. F. Darling (ed.), *West Highland Survey* (1955), viii. See also A. Collier, *The Crofting Problem* (1953), chapter I, and p. 24.

151

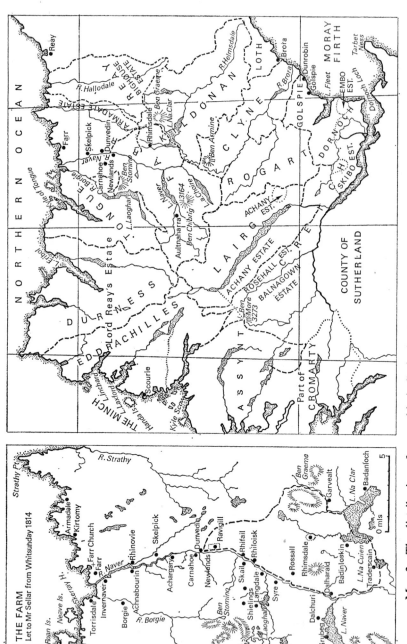

Map 3   The distribution of ownership in Sutherland in 1810 and the new sheep farm of Patrick Sellar in Strathnaver in 1814

the British environment. But the Highland problem is not merely economic; it is a tangle of social, political, even racial[3] issues. As M. Gray has written, the Highlands in the early nineteenth century experienced 'the total impact of the powerful individualism and rationalism of industrial civilisation on the weaker semi-communalism of the recalcitrant fringe'.[4] Nowhere was the impact greater than in Sutherland at the time of the clearances.

Life in the Highlands before the clearances was characterized by scattered cultivation, low *per capita* incomes, high birth and death rates, poor communications, little capital per head, a high dependence on agriculture, major inequalities in the distribution of income, and a strong attachment to 'traditional' attitudes. Sparsity of resources and geographical isolation, coupled with an ancient social system and a primitive technology, enforced an equilibrium of low-level subsistence.

Land-ownership was concentrated in the hands of a few large proprietors who dominated a patriarchal society which was based on the vestiges of a kinship system. In the words of Samuel Johnson, the form of tenure still subsisted, but without its 'primitive stability'.[5] The unequal distribution of income made possible the accumulation of capital in the hands of the landlord class. But, more often than not, the Highland landlords squandered the internally accumulated capital on personal consumption in Edinburgh and London— especially in the late eighteenth century when rising rents inflated their social pretensions.

Agriculture was generally based on the communal runrig system. Oats and barley provided most of the tenants' subsistence requirements. Cattle, the only major export of the Highlands in the mid-eighteenth century, produced income for rent and a small cash surplus. In some parishes personal service persisted until the end of the century.[6] The high ratio of population to arable land and the repeated subdivision of the land were fundamental obstacles to radical changes in productivity. Initiative and capital were also deficient.[7]

[3] See the genocide thesis stated by I. Grimble, 'Gael and Saxon in Scotland', *Yale Review*, LII, 118–22; Cf. J. S. Blackie, *The Scottish Highlands and the Land Laws* (1885), *passim*. SC, Loch to Trevelyan, 16–1–1848.

[4] M. Gray, *The Highland Economy, 1750–1850* (1957), 246. Collier, op. cit., 4.

[5] *Journey to the Western Islands of Scotland in 1773* (1930 ed.), 78.

[6] In Loth, Sutherland, in 1791 it was reported that the commutation of 'bodily service' into money rents was difficult because the means of payment did not exist. *OSA*, VI, 315–17.

[7] See H. Hamilton, *The Industrial Revolution in Scotland* (1932), 55. T. C.

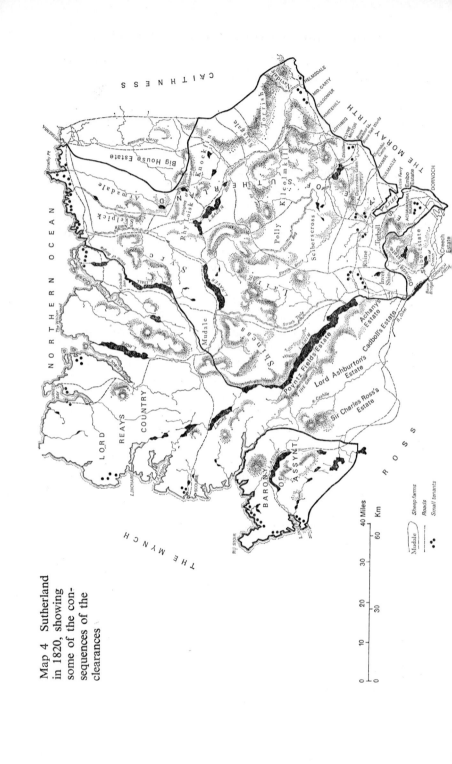

Map 4 Sutherland in 1820, showing some of the consequences of the clearances

Thomas Pennant in the 1770s pointed out that major areas of the Highlands were able to subsist only by large imports of meal. Despite the widespread adoption of the potato, the strategic reliance on meal imports increased as population grew. The margin beyond subsistence was dangerously small, and in poor years (of crop failure, or low cattle prices) the community was thrown into a parlous position.[8]

P. Gaskell has recently suggested that the eighteenth-century Highlander lived 'not in picturesque rural felicity, but in conditions of penury and squalor that can only fairly be compared with those of a famine area in contemporary India, and that were tolerable only because they were traditional and familiar.' But opinion is divided. I. Grimble writes of the 'joy and richness' of the 'elegant untroubled poetic world' of a Highland society in the same century. Many reminiscences of the early nineteenth century contain nostalgic yearnings for a lost 'golden age'. It is possible that the latter refers to a particular quality of life rather than to the security of subsistence.[9]

In the late eighteenth century growing population pressed heavily against the region's resources. There were many signs of overpopulation[10] and yet, prior to 1815, most landlords continued to believe that a larger population was essential for economic progress. While the ancient way of life crumbled the new economic order failed to provide sufficient employment opportunities. And thus the population dilemma reached very much larger dimensions at the end of the eighteenth century.

The humiliations following the 1745 rebellion helped to weaken the integrity and resistance of the old order. This favoured the spread northwards of rational, capitalistic farming on the impetus of rising prices and the promise of increased rentals. The communal runrig system was assaulted by a new, universal fashion—by which each tenant was allotted a separate, independent piece of land.

Smout and A. Fenton, 'Scottish agriculture before the improvers', *Agricultural History Review*, XIII, 86, et seq. Gray, op. cit., 12–18, 29.

[8] Gray, op. cit., 25, 35, 42–4. See also 'Mr. Kemp's tour to the Highlands', *Scots Magazine*, February 1792.

[9] P. Gaskell, *Morvern Transformed* (1968), 9. I. Grimble, 'Emigration in the time of Rob Dunn, 1714–1778', *Scottish Studies*, VII, 150–1. Cf. M. I. Adam, 'The eighteenth-century Highland landlords and the poverty problem', *SHR*, 1922. Article VII in *Edinburgh Review*, October 1857.

[10] See Gray, op. cit., 35, 53, 60–2. John Walker, *An Economical History of the Hebrides and Highlands of Scotland* (1808), I, 84.

Tenants were uprooted; some were resettled, others were evicted without compunction; rents were raised; some holdings were expanded; the middlemen (tacksmen) were banished. The entire agrarian structure was revolutionized. The initiative came almost entirely from the landowners who were, to begin with, perplexed to find that their 'improvements' were attended by widespread internal and external migration.[11] This process was substantially reinforced by three other tendencies—the inexorable growth of population, the widespread introduction of sheep, and the rise of meal prices[12] in the later eighteenth century.

Demographic pressure rendered even more vulnerable an economy already precariously balanced near famine conditions. Acute land shortage was perhaps temporarily mitigated by the introduction of the potato into the peasant diet. The rise of the linen, kelp and fishing industries also gave a transient, illusory hope of a solution—especially where it was thought that it would help to detach a portion of the population from the land, 'leaving a thinner but stronger rural population'. But, while population continued to increase,[13] the industries tragically failed after 1815. The population became more vulnerable than ever.

A new era of capitalistic sheep farming began in Scotland about 1750. In 1762 the introduction of sheep farms in Perthshire and Dunbartonshire had caused depopulation. The greatest stimulus came from the doubling of wool prices in the decade 1785–95. In 1795 Sir John Sinclair asserted that 'under sheep, the Highlands would be six, if not ten times more valuable than under cattle'.[14] The resettlement of tenants gained in urgency, but the benefits of sheep-farming to the peasantry were minimal: 'The tragedy . . . was not that sheep came but that the great increase in production was achieved by inhibiting rather than releasing the energy of the peasants.'[15] The Highland economy moved from one extreme (small-scale, labour-intensive communalism) to the other (large-scale, land-intensive individualism). Sheep-farming entrepreneurs brought high

[11] Gray, op. cit., 63, 68, 75. See also 'A Highlander', *The Present Conduct of the Chieftains in the Highlands of Scotland* (1773), *passim*.

[12] See R. Mitchison, 'The movement of Scottish corn prices in the seventeenth and eighteenth centuries', *EcHR*, 1965.

[13] Gray, op. cit., 58–66; R. Mitchison, *Agricultural Sir John* (1962), esp. 86–7. Darling, op. cit., chapter 3. Gaskell, op. cit., 6–7.

[14] Sir John Sinclair, *General View of the Agriculture of the Northern Counties* (1795), appendix VII, 41.

[15] Gray, op. cit., 86.

rents and capital imports. The small tenant's holding was required for wintering. His land was forfeited; he was evicted or 'cleared' from the interior straths and (in some cases) was given a 'lot' on the coast. It was, in one view, a 'violation of the fundamental Highland belief that land is the property of the community'.[16]

A great deal of opinion holds that the clearances were catastrophic since they robbed the common people of their land, deprived them of the means of life and exposed them to the fate of starvation. In 1852, for instance, Donald Ross stated that there was no redundance of population in the Highlands: 'It is overflowing without being full— an excess of numbers before the country has been nearly peopled to the full extent of its resources.' Its resources had been engrossed by the landlords who were responsible for the current destitution.[17]

The economic consequences of the clearances are not easily disentangled from those of other, concomitant, changes in the Highlands. The clearances reduced the cattle population of many areas. Even where provision was made for the resettled people, the critical ratio of arable land to population probably deteriorated. Where provision was made the reception areas were frequently extremely congested and lacked sufficient employment opportunities. Large-scale emigration, which had a long pre-clearance history, was given an added cause.[18] But the clearances cannot bear the entire responsibility for the ensuing destitution. After 1815 many of the props of the Highland economy collapsed—kelp declined calamitously, domestic linen production died away, cattle prices fell, whisky distilling probably diminished, fishing fell short of earlier expectations, road construction decreased, even wool production became less profitable and, finally, the potato succumbed to its fatal disease. There is a case for saying that the evictions were subsidiary in their repercussions when compared with the larger forces of price change and population growth. R. H. Campbell has remarked that by compelling the tenant to move, the landlord 'was frequently only forcing a tenant to act as he would have to do eventually'.[19]

[16] F. Gillanders, 'The West Highland economy', *TGSI*, XLIII, 252–5.

[17] D. Ross, *The Scottish Highlanders; their Present Sufferings and Future Prospects* (1852), 16. See also Angus McLaine, *Population of the Highlands of Scotland, their deterioration and its cause* (1857).

[18] See the excellent contemporary analysis of Highland emigration in *Writings of Francis Horner* (ed. F. W. Fetter, 1957), 115–32.

[19] R. H. Campbell, *Scotland Since 1707* (1965), 8. See also, Gaskell, op. cit., 117. W. Singer, 'On the introduction of sheep farming into the Highlands', *Transactions of the Highland Society of Scotland*, III (1807), 537 ff.

Even during the period of rapidly rising rents, landlord indebtedness did not diminish; consumption aspirations outstripped the growth of estate incomes. After 1815 falling prices decisively undermined the finances of many estates. The population dilemma was accentuated and reduced income narrowed the range of action of many proprietors. It was quickly reflected in the final abdication of many landlords—property changed hands on an unprecedented scale.[20] The general circumstances of the economy had deteriorated and emigration was regarded increasingly as the only real solution. And thus began the absolute decline of population in the Highlands in the second half of the nineteenth century.

The case of Sutherland is part of the general experience of the Highland economy before 1850; the broad determinants and tendencies were at work but the strains and tensions were heightened by the calculating deliberation and coercive execution of landlord policy which sought to accelerate the transformation of the local economy. All Highland history of this period is controversial, but the Sutherland episode is the most heatedly disputed. The literature on the subject is notable for its persistent tone of emotive and strident polemicism. There are many problems—the presently available statistics are meagre, and much of the literary evidence is of an equivocal nature. There prevails, also, a vitiating confusion of criteria, a jumble of economic, social, political and moral judgments. The controversy relates to the clearance policies sanctioned by the Sutherland family both before and during the agency of James Loch, whose administration began after 1812.

In the history of the Highland clearances the events which took place in Sutherland usually form the centrepiece. Historical discussion has concentrated on two main issues: first, an explicit or implicit comparison of the material and cultural conditions of life before and after the clearances; and second, a description of the methods actually employed in implementing the clearance schemes. Since the Sutherland clearances occurred mainly between 1806 and 1820 the clarification of these two issues hinges, in large part, on the availability of evidence for the period before the 1820s. It is unfortunate that the published material for the pre-clearance period is almost entirely reminiscent in character rather than con-

---

[20] J. Barron, *The Northern Highlands in the Nineteenth Century* (3 vols, 1903–1913), II, appendix E.

temporary. Memories revived after the lapse of two or more decades form very sandy foundations for any historian. Indeed, some of the most important sources for the history of the Sutherland clearances fall into this category. Much of Donald Sage's widely read volume *Memorabilia Domestica* was the product of an extremely erratic memory recalling events that had occurred several decades earlier. Donald Macleod's *Gloomy Memories* were at least thirty years old when he committed them to paper; Hugh Miller's recollections were those of a very early childhood in Sutherland, and those of Joseph Mitchell were not much fresher; the vivid accounts presented to the Napier Commission on Crofters in 1884 were often memories of a time seventy-five years earlier. Such evidence may be extremely valuable but, by its nature, it requires the most careful cross-checking.

Even more difficult is the problem of bias in so much of the literary evidence. When in 1820 James Loch issued his *Account of the Improvements on the Estates of the Marquess of Stafford*, it was transparently an apologia from the landlord's camp—on its own it is clearly a dangerous source. Similarly, many of the ostensibly documentary accounts of the clearances published in the nineteenth century went far beyond the plain reporting of events. More often than not the object was to stir men's consciences and to promote political action. Doctrinaire issues also cast their shadow across the evidence. A good example was that of Dr John MacCulloch who, in 1824, castigated what he termed 'the cant of the poets and romancers' in their sentimentalization of the way of life before the clearances. He wrote:[21]

Idle tourists, ignorant of the country, ignorant of political economy, and copying in succession from each other, have continued to propagate their false and foolish views ... Had Adam Smith, by good fortune, and with the added advantage of being 'a Scotchman' given but one brief chapter to the Highlands, a world of ink and ill-humour would have been saved. Instead of this, the philosophy has been sought in the economics of Oliver Goldsmith.

Similarly, the survival of contemporary evidence has been arbitrary—tending inevitably to favour the rich and the literate. The common people of the Highlands have probably suffered as much as any from what E. P. Thompson has termed 'the enormous condescension of history'. Those of Sutherland have left few literary

[21] John MacCulloch, *The Highlands and Western Isles of Scotland* (1824), IV, 125.

records—except perhaps through the mouthpiece of a London newspaper, the *Military Register*, which published a series of letters from Sutherland at the time of the clearances. Where it can be checked it tended to be relatively accurate in reporting events—despite its highly polemical tone. The most recent development in the search for evidence has been the employment of archaeological techniques. In this case tangible evidence of destruction by fire in the cleared townships has been sought. So far no evidence of conflagration has been discovered, and the results[22] have been negative. This alone, however, does not disprove the use of fire by the men who implemented the Sutherland clearances.[23]

Viewed as an episode in economic and social history—as the adjustment of the Sutherland economy to the impact of the Industrial Revolution—there are further difficulties in the special dearth of statistical evidence. As in all the other aspects, the evidence that survives has to be very critically evaluated. Fortunately, some of the surviving pieces of the jigsaw puzzle are especially suggestive of the overall pattern.

The existing literature contains two predominant attitudes. The Sutherland policies are seen as *either* the draconian, class-oriented actions of an alien aristocrat who sacrificed a dependent peasantry in the ruthless pursuit of capitalistic profits *or* the misinterpreted benevolence of an ideal landlord who was willing to forfeit his short-term ends in order to undertake his paternalistic duty of ameliorating the plight of his famine-doomed tenantry. Such a summary is not a caricature—though there is a further variation which sees the Sutherland clearances as a policy which was necessary, but executed in a cruel, inhumanitarian fashion. Certainly, the questions of motivation and method have held positions as important as that of the net effect of the clearances.

The condition of Sutherland prior to the clearances, which largely occurred after 1800, is not entirely clear. There are various accounts written by curious and rather incredulous southern visitors—for instance, in 1658 Franck, a Cromwellian trooper, spoke of Strathnaver 'where a rude sort of inhabitants dwell (almost as barbarous

[22] See Horace Fairhurst, 'Rosal, Strathnaver, Sutherland', *University of Glasgow Gazette*, no. 4, March 1963, 9; and the anonymous review of J. Prebble's *Highland Clearances*, in *The Times Literary Supplement*, 7 November 1963, 904.

[23] Compare with the literary evidence in chapter XIII below.

as cannibals) who, when they kill a beast, boil him in his hide, make a caldron of his skin, brawis of his bowels, drink of his blood, and bread and meat of his carcase.' More than a hundred years later the writer John Knox observed that Sutherland was 'the most remote and the least improvable' country he had witnessed; 'the poverty of the soil utterly precludes improvements in agriculture of any consequence, and nine parts out of ten in this great county must unavoidably remain an inhospitable, sterile desert to the end of time.'[24]

The county of Sutherland contains a little more than $1\frac{1}{3}$m. acres of which the infant Countess of Sutherland inherited about $\frac{3}{4}$ m. acres in 1766. During her minority the estates were administered by a body of Tutors or guardians. The Countess apparently did not visit her Highland inheritance until she was seventeen. In 1771 surveyors were appointed to make a thorough investigation of the estate.[25]

Significant emigration from Sutherland had occurred several decades before sheep or clearances had affected the structure of the local economy. In 1763 and particularly in the harsh winter of 1771–1772 there was large-scale emigration—especially from Strathnaver to the American colonies. It was described as 'a sort of madness among the Common People', provoked by the 'want of Victuals' and 'the oppression they meet with from their Masters the Tacksmen'.[26] Pennant described crowds of poor people 'dispirited, and driven to despair by bad management . . . emaciated with hunger' who trekked to the east coast in search of a reported meal ship. 'Numbers of the miserable of this country', he wrote, 'were now migrating: they wandered in a state of desperation; too poor to pay, they mostly sell themselves for their passage, preferring a temporary bondage in a strange land, to starving for life on their native soil'.[27] Yet in 1773 the *Edinburgh Evening Courant* claimed that the 1,500 Sutherlanders who had departed for America in the previous two years 'had taken with them an amount larger than a year's rent for the entire country'.[28]

[24] SC, D593/V/10/119.
[25] Sinclair, op. cit., 136–7. Grimble, *Trial*, 137. R. J. Adam, op. cit., xix.
[26] R. J. Adam, op. cit., xix, xxiv, xxvi.
[27] Ibid., quoted xxvi. Cf. Fraser, op. cit., I, 446–7.
[28] D. Meyer, *The Highland Scots of North Carolina, 1732–1776* (1957), 55. D. M. Sinclair, 'Highland emigration to Nova Scotia', *Dalhousie Review*, July 1963, 2, 9. Further conflicting evidence is given in *The Scots Magazine*, XXXIV (1772), 395, which ascribed Sutherland poverty to 'opulent graziers engrossing the farms, and turning them into pasture'. See also J. P. Maclean, *An Historical Account of the Settlements of Scotch Highlanders in America Prior to the Peace*

The estate management made a concentrated effort to stem the outflow: tree planting and trenching were undertaken to provide employment, and grain supplies were imported from neighbouring counties. At this time, more than one-third of the total rental of £3,000 per annum was paid in kind, and arrears increased. But migration continued and the estate ran into acute financial difficulties. R. J. Adam is certain that pressure from the landlord was not part of the cause of emigration—there was a great reluctance to lose tenants.[29] The management was optimistic of the long-term viability of the estate—a belief supported by the possibility of improved agricultural efficiency and the rise of the native fishing and kelping industries. Tacksmen were regarded as the major cause of oppression and migration—and as early as 1768 their powers of sub-letting were reduced. The estate raised rents (in Assynt, from £550 in 1759, to £657 in 1775) —though the sub-tenants paid no more than they had previously paid to the tacksmen. The policy did not prevent further emigration though the American War of Independence checked the exodus for many years. Population continued to grow—probably the most reliable vital statistics are those for Assynt which contained 1,718 people in 1774 and 2,479 in 1811. Like most of Sutherland, Assynt was almost exclusively agricultural: 'Beyond black cattle, herring and salmon, Assynt had little of its own to offer the outside world.'[30]

The rate of population growth was undoubtedly considerable despite emigration, and a comparison of the estimates of Webster in the mid-1750s (20,774) and the *Old Statistical Account* in the early 1790s (22,961) probably understates the real increase. Most of the contributors in the latter source refer to substantial population growth, but there were variations between the fourteen Sutherland parishes; in four cases a decline of total population was claimed. The

---

of 1783 (1900). The best available evidence is the 'Reports of the Examination of Emigrants from the Counties of Caithness and Sutherland', at Lerwick, 1774–5, PRO (T47/12). These give a vivid impression of life in Sutherland, and of the motives of the emigrants. They are conveniently accessible in typescript as 'Emigrants from Scotland to America, 1774–1775', compiled and indexed by Viola Root Cameron, 1930 (microfilm of the Scottish Central Library, Lawnmarket, Edinburgh).

[29] R. J. Adam, op. cit., xxiv-xxx. Fraser, op. cit., I, 483. Cf. Grimble, 'Emigration'; I. C. C. Graham, *Colonists from Scotland* (1956), *passim*.

[30] R. J. Adam, op. cit., xxiv–xxx—this is the best documented study of any part of Sutherland in the eighteenth century, based on records at Dunrobin Castle.

reasons offered for growth are equally obscure. In Durness the introduction of smallpox inoculation (in the 1760s, and generally by 1780)
was said to have reduced the infantile death-rate; in Tongue 'a
gentlewoman' in the late 1780s 'had inoculated 99 with her own hand,
and paid them such attention, during the progress of the malady,
that, except one, they all recovered.' Yet in Assynt, where population
had grown rapidly, smallpox inoculation was 'not yet universally
introduced, on account of vulgar prejudice', and similarly in Criech.
Other reasons ascribed were the fecundity of the women, improved
medical treatment, youthful marriage, the 'advancing culture of
small crofts', and perhaps most importantly—the subdivision of
farms 'which, by affording employment and provision for a greater
number of people, encourages industry and early marriage' (Tongue).
But, on the rather dubious demographic evidence of the *Old Statistical Account*, the birth-rate was not much more than 30 per 1,000 in
the early 1790s. However, the meagre evidence for family-size
(Farr 6–7, Criech 7–8, Golspie 9—presumably all including parents)
may suggest a crucial decline in infant mortality, especially when set
against Adam Smith's well-known remarks of 1776 about half-
starved Highland women commonly bearing twenty children 'not to
have two alive'. The demographic determinants remain very little
understood. [31]

The reporters to the *Statistical Account* made no explicit connection between the widespread introduction of the potato and the rise
of population in Sutherland, though they did relate potatoes to the
subdivision of arable land. Dependence on this relatively recent
addition to the diet had become pronounced in many parishes:
in Tongue and Durness it was the principal food of the people.
Sales of cattle from the people in the wide straths continued to provide a major part of rent payment, but service and victual payments
were also exacted. A recurring complaint in the reports was the
widespread lack of employment opportunities and the deficiency of
arable land. Apart from some flax spinning, in some parts kelp
burning, and whisky distilling, there was a widely deplored dearth of
non-agricultural industries. In good years most parishes appear to
have been self-sufficient, but the general poverty (which one reporter
said 'need hardly be mentioned') and the fear of poor harvests

---

[31] *OSA*, III, 538–43, 565, 581–2, 409; IV, 281–3; VII, 574; VIII, 7–8, 367–9;
IX, 28; X, 298–300; XI, 571; XVI, 315–17. A. Smith, *The Wealth of Nations*, I,
70. Cf. 'Mr. Kemp's Tour', 57.

created an all-pervading anxiety. Some fishing was undertaken, but, on the whole, the people 'are for a military, but not a seafaring life'—in Loth the fishing was primarily undertaken by alien boats.[32] Many of the accounts refer to migration to America and increasingly to the cotton mills of central Scotland, but equal emphasis was given to seasonal migration—a clear indication of a growing incapacity of the local economy to provide sufficient employment. The lack of employment opportunities may also explain, in part, the apparently high preference for leisure. The minister of Rogart wrote that the 'people seem to be much more inclined to idleness than to industry. They are extremely frugal of the little they have; but as to earning anything more, it is a melancholy fact, that a poor tenant, who rents land only to the value of 20s. or 30s. and whose labour could well be spared from his little farm many days in the year, will rather saunter, or sit idle at home, than work for 6d. a day, which would be a considerable addition to his own and his family's scanty meal'.[33]

Sheep farming had affected Sutherland but little before the 1790s, yet there were already signs that large-scale grazing was introducing a new pressure on the availability of land for small tenants. In the 1780s rising cattle prices had given occasion in Edderachyllis on the Reay estate 'to some gentlemen, not residing in the parish, to take leases of extensive grazings . . . which they manage with few servants'. The old possessors had been removed, and many had migrated south to the cotton mills. In Criech sheep farmers had begun to take the place of the small tenants with their cattle and horses. However, in Farr, a parish largely untouched by engrossing graziers, migration had also been great, seasonal migration common, the level of pauperism high, and the 'general want of employment' was a grave source of anxiety.[34] Pressure from the landlords seems to have exacerbated the problem since real rents in the county apparently rose from £9,754 in 1798 to £16,216 in 1808,[35] but this may be partly accounted for by new rents from sheep farming, the conversion of service and victual rents into money rents, and the extinction of wadsets.[36]

Almost all the evidence seems to confirm the idea of the persisting

[32] *OSA*, VI, 317. Cf. *The Tour of Dr. Richard Pococke . . . Through Sutherland and Caithness in 1760*, ed. D. W. Kemp (1888), 18–19.

[33] *OSA*, III, 566.

[34] Ibid., IV, 281; VIII, 368; III, 540–3.

[35] John Henderson, *General View of the Agriculture of the County of Sutherland* (1812), 178–81.

[36] SC, D593K/1/8/20, R. M. Brereton to G. Malcolm, 23–3–1888.

economic backwardness of Sutherland, and to contradict the retrospective view of Hugh Miller that the people were 'in very comfortable
circumstances' before the clearances.[37] Recurrent famine must be
regarded as an established characteristic of the economy. In 1782–3,
for instance, frost and mildew created a severe crisis, and many
people survived on cockles and mussels, while others bought imported foreign victuals from the estate Tutors at inflated prices, and
5,849 people were relieved by charity.[38] Lesser crises occurred between 1783 and 1807. In the latter year a particularly harsh winter
decimated the black-cattle population of the interior straths. In the
following year Lady Williams Wynn wrote:[39]

At present nothing can exceed their poverty and misery, and yet, there is
hardly a day Labourer in the County of Sutherland. Every family has a
small farm which they are too poor to stock with sheep or cattle, and in a
bad year, as the last, when all their Oats were spoilt with the rain, they are
reduced to absolute Starvation. I have seen misery in Wales, but till I
came into this Country, I had no idea of human or indeed any other
Creature existing in such habitations as I have seen, and their food is, if
possible, still worse.

At much the same time John Henderson, the agricultural reporter,
said that even in the best seasons 'the produce of grain in this county
does not subsist the inhabitants' and imports from the south and
from Caithness were always required. He stated that the people of the
interior straths were unable to produce more than one half of their
yearly grain requirements and were dependent on supplies from the
coast-side farmers—but their livestock holdings were often considerable, as, for instance, in Strathnaver where each family possessed
an average of 12 cattle, 6 small horses and 15–20 sheep—valued at
about £75 in 1811.[40] In 1786 Knox could find no roads in the county
—'through a considerable part of the year the inhabitants of each
respective glen or valley may be considered as prisoners strongly
guarded by impassable mountains on one side, by swamps and furious

[37] H. Miller, *Sutherland as it was and is, or, How a Country may be ruined* (1843),
1–16. Miller was born in 1802. See comments of Margaret M. McArthur, 'The
Sutherland Clearances' (Ph.D. thesis, University of London, 1940), 156–237, 302.
[38] *OSA*, III, 522, 412; VIII, 14, 37–2. F. T. Smith, *The Land of Britain*, part 3
Sutherland (1939), 172. D. F. MacDonald, *Scotland's Shifting Population,
1770–1850* (1937), 6.
[39] R. Leighton (ed.), *Correspondence of Charlotte Grenville, Lady Williams
Wynn* (1920), 127. SC, Grant to Loch, 11–6–1845.
[40] Henderson, op. cit., 26, 68–71, 104–5, 205. Sinclair, op. cit., 138, 151.

torrents on the other.'[41] Joseph Mitchell, in a rather coloured account, recalled that in 1809:[42]

the whole of Sutherland and Caithness were nearly destitute of Roads. The country imported corn and meal in return for a small value of Highland Kyloes, which formed its almost sole export. The people lay scattered in inaccessible straths and spots among the mountains, where they lived in family with their pigs and kyloes, in turf cabins of the most miserable description, spoke only Gaelic, and spent their whole time in indolence and sloth.

A contemporary account claimed that famine conditions occurred 'every three years'.[43] The termination of periodic famine was to be regarded as the most fundamental justification of the Sutherland clearances.

Elizabeth, Countess of Sutherland, married Earl Gower in 1785. In 1787 Gower was introduced to local landowners at Dunrobin Castle. One of the proprietors, George Dempster, reported that the Englishman was 'a man of taste, virtu, reserved and very well bred', but 'he does not like the bagpipe and says so and shews it indeed, for he has converted the piper into a porter. We may give the more credit to another declaration of his, that he likes Dunrobin and Sutherland as well as Staffordshire.' Dempster had spoken of setting the country on its legs, but remarked that 'the noble personages cannot enter into the spirit of improvement or see its importance, unless it were by inspiration. The disposition of both however seem good.'[44] The deficiency of inspiration was, however, less important than the deficiency of capital—for Gower did not inherit the Bridgewater and Leveson-Gower fortunes until 1803. The Sutherland estate itself was far from lucrative. Very little alteration or improvement occurred on the Sutherland estate before the turn of the century.[45]

George Dempster was a leading spirit in the improvement movement in the area. He encouraged Sir John Sinclair in his efforts to 'kentify' Caithness, and he possessed a prodigious optimism for the

[41] A. R. B. Haldane, *New Ways Through the Glens* (1962), 12.

[42] Ibid., 138–9. See also Anon. [James Loch], *Facts as to the Past and Present State of the Estate of Sutherland* (1845).

[43] H. Fairhurst, 'The surveys for the Sutherland clearances, 1813–1820', *Scottish Studies*, VIII, 11–12. Barron, op. cit., I, 168. See also T. Sellar, *The Sutherland Evictions of 1814* (1883), 2 ff.

[44] J. Fergusson (ed.), *Letters of George Dempster to Sir Adam Fergusson, 1756–1813* (1934), 166.

[45] Sinclair, op. cit., 129.

future of the far north.[46] He recognized two basic facts of life: first, the poverty and the increasing under-employment of the population, and, second, the practical inevitability of large-scale sheep farming. He believed that the introduction of sheep farming must be simultaneously accompanied by the promotion of manufactures in the county—taking advantage of the labour availability and thereby ameliorating the deteriorating position of the people.[47] Roads were imperative for the success of the cattle and sheep trade, he told a Sutherland estate factor in 1794, but he said, 'it is from the introduction of manufactures into the County that I have always looked for its improvement and the solid increase of rents.' He considered the introduction of linen manufacture particularly promising in view of the wartime stoppage of cotton imports.[48] He spoke of converting 'Sutherlandshire into a Lancashire', and in 1809 of founding 'cities to rival Rome in its splendour'.[49] At the heart of his thinking was the theme that 'the people need not be driven out of the country because the sheep are introduced into it. Villages may be built for them, where they might be employed in manufactures.' It was a plan to diversify the economy by promoting manufacturing villages along the coasts. One such village was promoted at Spinningdale on the Kyle of Dornoch in the early 1790s by the efforts of David Dale with the assistance of Dempster and, in a lesser way, Lord Gower. It employed one hundred hands in cotton spinning, but it was uneconomic and in 1806 the mill burnt down and the project never recovered, apparently due to the competition of English industry.[50]

Despite the failure of Spinningdale and despite the gloomy predictions of the Earl of Selkirk, optimistic plans for the development of Sutherland resources continued to be promoted. It seemed that a judicious combination of sheep farming and manufactures would solve the growing economic dilemma of the county. The high prices of wartime inflated all prospects of success and this was the essential background to the schemes. Two things only seemed to be lacking—capital and initiative: when the husband of the Countess of Sutherland inherited his fortune in 1803 the first deficiency was

[46] Mitchison, *Agricultural Sir John*, 27.
[47] Henderson, op. cit., 227 ff. *OSA*, VIII, 374–83.
[48] SC, D593/2/1–3.
[49] Fergusson, op. cit., 252, 316.
[50] *OSA*, VIII, 381–3. C. H. Herford, op. cit., 132. Henderson, op. cit., 13, 117. Earl of Selkirk, *On Emigration and the State of the Highlands* (2nd ed. 1806), appendix K.

removed, and initiative was easily imported. Large plans were hatched and the idea of villages was given high priority. A vital element which Dempster had emphasized in 1795 was given little notice. He had warned that 'it is one thing to build a village, to which people may resort if they choose it, and another to drive them from the country into villages where they must starve, unless they change at once their manners, their habits and their occupations.'[51]

[51] *OSA*, VIII, 380–1; see also Sir George Mackenzie of Coul, *Letter to the Proprietors of Land in Ross-shire* (1803), esp. 17.

XIII

+++

William Young and Patrick Sellar

+++

The cheviot sheep had been first introduced into Sutherland in 1794 by a company of southern sheep farmers on the estate of Lord Armadale. The experiment was successful and it was commended because the population of the estate had actually increased and because the people were 'encouraged . . . to improve and be industrious seamen'. Other removals were also engineered by neighbouring landowners. Lord Reay marked out forty acres near Sandgoe on the north coast to accommodate twenty families, while on the Strathy estate eighteen families who had paid £185 rent in the high strath were replaced by a sheep farmer paying £400. The sheep population of the county grew rapidly to an estimated 94,750 in 1808 and large numbers of families were pressed out towards the coasts—at Portskerra there were twenty-nine families living off twenty-three acres of arable land and the fish they could catch, to which was added a further eleven families of new settlers. In Edderachyllis, fifty families were removed 'and their places occupied by sheep'; those thus removed seem to have been left to their own devices which meant that the coastal areas were increasingly congested with families living on less than two acres each.[1]

The estate of the Countess of Sutherland did not follow the general trend until about 1806. There were two reasons for the delay—the husband of the Countess did not inherit his fortune as Lord Stafford until 1803, and most of the estate was tied up by leases which were not expected to run out until 1807. Plans, however, were considered in the 1790s. In 1799 furtive communications were passed between

[1] Henderson, op. cit., 17–18, 189.

169

agents and the Countess outlining a policy of removals on the expiration of the leases, subject to the assent of her husband—with the hope that 'when a considerable thinning comes to take place, may not many of the people be preserved, and with advantage, by making a village on the coast of Assynt?' Earlier in 1791 the efforts of George Dempster to introduce cotton manufacture into the country were viewed with keen interest—and the estate factor speculated that 'if it succeeds Lord Gower can enlarge the plan on going into the county.'[2]

The first clearance of the Sutherland estate seems to have occurred in 1806 when the Northumbrian sheepfarmers, Atkinson and Marshall, took over a large tract of land in Lairg and Strathnaver. It is likely that many of the men of these districts were absent, fighting in the Countess's own regiment against France; it is equally probable that they believed that their tenancies were secure by hereditary customary succession.[3] About seventy-seven families were evicted from the upper parts of the strath; no land appears to have been reserved for them and they congregated on the northern coastside which was already at least partly occupied. No village had been created for their future subsistence; in fact, many decided to emigrate to America; the ship carrying them and its 140 passengers were lost in a storm off Newfoundland.

In the same year the Countess (now also known as Lady Stafford) reported that her husband, Lord Stafford, was 'seized as much as I am with the rage for improvements, and we both turn our attention with the greatest energy to turnips.' Plans for the accommodation of the removees were in the making but, before 1809, they lacked real direction, and meanwhile more southern entrepreneurs were being introduced to exploit rising sheep and wool prices. The Countess in 1808 declared that she was much occupied in plans for improvement; she described her estate as 'a wild corner, inhabited by an infinite multitude roaming at large in the old way, despising all barriers and all regulations, and firmly believing in witchcraft'. Two months earlier her guest, Lady Williams Wynn, observed that the Countess had 'been very much abused for turning off last year a great number of

---

[2] Fraser, op. cit., I, 483–4. SC, D593/N/4/1/3, letter from Gilchrist, December 1791.

[3] Henderson, op. cit., 4, 23–6, 104–6, 175. No analysis of the Sutherland economy of these years should ignore the large number of men involved in the armed forces. It would be difficult to over-estimate the importance of the employment and income that this actually provided until about 1815. See the early chapters of A. E. J. Cavendish, *An Reisineid Chataich* (1928).

small tenants who had held land under the family for upwards of two hundred years, and making sheep farms but I doubt whether in a few years, they will not feel the advantage of this new plan.' The guest also recorded that the Countess was doing all she could to make the people 'more comfortable by building better cottages and encouraging them to fish on the coast, but they are too much addicted to filth to enjoy the former, and too idle to attempt the latter.'[4]

In 1809 a close liaison developed between the Countess and two Morayshire capitalists who were projectors in a scheme to run a packet vessel across the Moray Firth designed to open up the trade of the northern Highlands. The two men, William Young and Patrick Sellar, brought with them an assortment of panaceas for the economic problems of the Sutherland estate and soon began to exert a major influence on the Countess.

During the previous decade Young had obtained very cheaply the occupancy of considerable tracts of desolate coastal land in Moray. Applying novel methods of drainage and ploughing, he reaped quick returns in the production of grain. He built canals and roads; he accidentally discovered limestone; and, eventually, he built a new fishing village at Hopeman. Here he constructed a harbour in order to export the product of his corn-mill and calcinated limestone and also to import coal. Within four years Hopeman accommodated 200 people 'in neat buildings on a regular plan, with a suitable garden appertaining to each dwelling'. Fishing crews were established and the corn crops were large. Young quickly gained a formidable reputation as a scientific improver; his fame reached the notice of the Stafford family who were soon persuaded that his methods could be applied with equal success to the coasts of Sutherland.[5]

Young and Sellar visited Sutherland in May 1809 and were impressed by an almost boundless prospect for coastal improvement consequent upon the conjunction of new roads and the new packet service. In July they made a joint offer to the Countess for a 300-acre farm at Culmailly (south of Golspie) at a rent 25 per cent higher than that of a neighbouring leaseholder, Robert Mackid, the Sheriff-Substitute of Sutherland. Their proposal was 'to settle as many of

[4] Allardyce, op. cit., I, 281, 345–6. Leighton, op. cit., 127.
[5] W. Leslie, *General View of the Agriculture of the Counties of Nairn and Moray* (1813), 262–3, 275–6, 406, 410. R. Young, *Annals of the Parish and Burgh of Elgin* (1879), 305. *NSA*, XIII, 43, 96, 155.

the present tenants as might choose to make themselves useful, in neat cottages at the bottom of the farm near the road, and to enclose the rest of the farm and put it into an improved mode of culture'. They would, they declared, set an example to the rest of the county. Shortly afterwards a 21-year lease was signed. Young and Sellar, at this stage, were exclusively concerned with the development of the coastal economy and they gave the Stafford family a flood of optimistic advice on this subject—they were not involved in the sheep farms which were being let in 1809. Their plans hinged upon the introduction of extensive land drainage and the construction of threshing, flax and wool mills. Flax cultivation was especially vital. 'It surprises us', they wrote, 'that in a country apparently so well adapted for the growth of flax as the great part of the shade of land along the coast of Sutherland is, no attempt has been hitherto made to raise flax. We shall certainly make the experiment ourselves.' Flax would provide a paying crop for the coastal farmers and a great source of employment to ameliorate the common people. Young told Lord Gower, who was taking an important personal role in the planning of the estate, that the people removed from the interior by sheep farmers could be accommodated in coastal settlements if sufficient enterprise was imported—particularly manufacturing enterprise. 'Your Lordship will perceive that I am advocate for a Village system and Sutherland seems favourable for it'—but he warned against overcrowding. He and Sellar were 'pleased beyond measure with the beauty of the country, its susceptibility of improvement and the disposition of the common people to get forward'. They were impressed with the specific desire of the Sutherland family to alleviate the sufferings of the people which, they opined, could be combined with the pursuit of pecuniary gain.[6]

Patrick Sellar was particularly excited by the prospect; expedient plans could produce rapid results—Young had proved it in Moray where, in four years, he had 'settled nearly 300 souls on the spot at Inverugie, which, when he began, was perfectly barren, and a considerable tract of ground near the village is, in consequence of their industry (in a great measure) risen in rent from something like 2/6 to nearly £3 per acre.' In Sutherland, they claimed, the people were

[6] SC, D593/P/22/1/21, Minute of Lease between the Marquis and Marchioness of Stafford and William Young and Patrick Sellar, 1809; Young and Sellar to Lady Stafford, 5–7–1809, 3–8–1809, 19–8–1809; Young to Gower, 19–8–1809; Sellar to Lady Stafford, 31–8–1809.

James Loch, 1780-1855.

Patrick Sellar, 1780-1851.

incapable of producing their own subsistence, and 'they must have perished but for your Ladyship's bounty. Their unavailing efforts to perform that for which *they are not fitted* has damped and depressed their industry. Your Ladyship has lulled asleep their care ... they have sunk into despondent security.' Sellar and Young were inspired by a vision of the future.[7]

The Country in its time may not produce gold or silver or wine or oil, but [they assured the Countess] if it produce industry all these things will be added unto it. If your Ladyship can lead the people from destroying the Soil, and from starving every creature on it, to settle in villages; if you can introduce a few Mechanics and manufacturers among them; induce the farmers to the cultivation of flax; set a woollen manufacture such as we have at Elgin, agoing; and get the sons and daughters of the present generation into the employment of those who can teach them industry and which considering the pliability, and the acuteness too, of the people, seems no very Herculean undertaking, the present enchantment which keeps them down will be broken, and Sutherland may enjoy as many comforts and pay as fair rent as any of her neighbours.

The vital assumption concerning the pliability of the removees was not borne out by the experience of the main Sutherland factor, Cosmo Falconer. He had attempted, without success, to persuade people removed from the interior to take crofts reserved for them at Achavandra on the moors near Dornoch. Falconer, who had doubts about the experiment, spoke of the people's tendency to 'obstinately resist any endeavours to connect them with work'—'only a determined plan which will drive them to a change' would be effective, he said. The people had been subject to 'a stirring up by some disaffected people' which had prompted some of them to leave the estate. The Stafford family apparently decided to postpone further removals for six months. Meanwhile lengthy discussions continued on the subject of the location of new villages on the east coast— sites at Culgower, Helmsdale, Golspie, Brora, Kintradwell, Wester Garty, Skelbo and Knockglass were considered. William Young favoured Helmsdale as a perfect natural harbour for a fishing station, and Achavandra where 'Fishing, manufacturing and agricultural pursuits might all combine, while the *improvable* moors behind hold forth a lasting fund for employment to the people and of emolument to the Estate.' The untouched moors of the south-east, he said, could

[7] Ibid., Young to Gower, 21–10–1809; Young and Sellar to Lady Stafford, 20–9–1809, 2–11–1809, 23–11–1809; Young and Sellar to Gower, 9–12–1809, 13–1–1810.

easily produce large harvests of grain. He had already printed a hundred copies of Benjamin Franklin's *Way to Wealth* in order to spur the people to industry. Young's enthusiastic predictions flowed into Dunrobin Castle in the later months of 1809—he spoke of harbours, canals, carding and flax mills, woollen manufacturing, fishing colonies, 'a bustling seaport' and the export of grain and light manufactured goods, coal and salt, timber and lime. Lord Gower's one great motive, the comfort of the people, he said, would be fulfilled; the people would be happier on the coast; and, moreover, there would follow an increase of 'rents and prosperity ... beyond our most sanguine expectations'.[8]

Though their enthusiasm ran on unabated, Young and Sellar slowly came to realize the practical problems of their ventures. In November 1809 Young remarked that it would be necessary 'to stigmatize the slovenly', and that he foresaw 'a world of outlay before any pecuniary returns can be got'. He recommended that Gower should spend £1,000 on trenching operations at Achavandra 'which would afford employment to settlers who in this way would in return be able to pay a corresponding rent'. Falconer, the factor, commented rather biliously that 'at least it would shut their mouths against clamours and prevent a plea of hardship'. Increasingly, Sellar and Young spoke of the indolence and inefficiency of the common people: they described the seasonal migrant who went south in summer and returned home in October with perhaps £10 in his pocket, merely to dig his potatoes, repair his cottage, buy a pig and 'make himself snug for the winter'. Many lived idly on remittances from sons who had migrated to America: they knew '20 families in this neighbourhood enriched by emigrations from their father's or their uncle's house'. There was too much 'erroneous application of labour', they insisted, especially in seasonal migration and peat cutting—Sutherland farmers spent the three best months digging peat, using perhaps fifteen horses which ate all the food 'and die in winter'. Consequently, they reasoned, the farmers got into debt and paid only a quarter of the real rental value of their land. If instead the farmers cultivated turnips, forgot their 'ruinous system' and broke with 'immemorial custom' and imported coal— landlord and tenant would be infinitely more secure. For themselves, Young and Sellar announced that they could demonstrate the

[8] Ibid., Falconer to Gower, 29–8–1809, 4–9–1809, 12–9–1809, 11–10–1809, 8–11–1809; Young to Gower, 21–9–1809, 2–11–1809.

efficacy of their methods, and (within ten years) they would pay quadruple the rent of any coastal land they took for themselves—and provide employment for the displaced population.[9]

The unrestricted optimism of Sellar and Young was thus matched by their denunciation of the existing situation. They were notably critical of previous clearances in the county—when the people from the sheep walks had been 'crammed ... into hamlets ... without *any new tract being pointed out for their industry*, and wanting, we fear, the full supply they formerly enjoyed on their boundless pastures—depression, debility, sloth, filth, are the consequences—disease follows; contagion spreads; and where all are predestinarieans careless of precaution, and little aid is to be procured, it is not wonderful that much mischief is done'. It was utterly essential, they said, to chalk out new holdings for the poor people dispossessed by sheep farming.[10]

It is clear that during 1809 and 1810 the Stafford family had encouraged Young and Sellar to investigate their property; they listened receptively to their plans. The obvious consequence was that the authority of their factor, Cosmo Falconer, was undermined. In February 1810 Sellar observed to Lord Gower that Falconer had 'not properly courted the people'. In the previous November Young and Sellar, referring to their improvement proposals, candidly assured the Countess that they could 'no more see how these things are to be carried through, under the present management, than how a camel is to go through the eye of a needle'. In August 1810 Sellar alleged that Falconer had misused his powers by selling meal for his own personal profit against the interest of the Sutherland family. Another family associate condemned Falconer's 'want of an active and well directed mind'. Some time after this Falconer was replaced by William Young, who became factor of the Sutherland estates, and was thus given full rein in his plans for comprehensive improvement. Patrick Sellar was also involved apparently as legal agent and accountant—he collected rents and followed the instructions of Young.[11]

Concurrently, more sheep farms were advertised and the improve-

---

[9] Ibid., Young to Gower, 23-11-1809, 25-1-1810, 11-2-1810, 21-2-1810; Sellar and Young to Gower, 4-11-1809; Sellar to Gower, 18-11-1809.

[10] Ibid., Sellar and Young to Gower, 16-5-1810.

[11] Ibid., Young and Sellar to Lady Stafford, 2-11-1810; Sellar to Gower, 21-2-1810, 13-8-1810; Mackenzie to Loch, 10-8-1820. P. Sellar, *Statement by Patrick Sellar* (1826), 2.

ments at Culmailly and Achavandra progressed—slowly, since the construction of cottages was delayed by a lack of skilled labour in the county. Advertisements were printed which invited small tenants from the interior to settle in the cottages at Achavandra on improveable crofts of three acres. They were expected to trench the land, for which they would receive a gratuity of £10 per acre and a 10-year lease. The tenant would pay £2 10s. 0d. rent and would follow a strict rotation. This was to be the pilot-scheme for other reception areas along the coasts of Sutherland.[12] There were formidable costs involved for, as Sellar told Gower in 1810, 'by your Lordship's plan, at Achavandra, each cottage and lott will cost £50 and to provide for one thousand families in this way would require £50,000; but there are many thousand families to provide for in Sutherland.' Moreover, the infra-structure of the new economy had to be created. In August 1811 the agricultural reporter Henderson was able to report admiringly on the co-ordinated plans of the Sutherland estate on which sheep farming was being introduced 'without decreasing the population'. At that time both coastal and interior villages were being planned: 'fishing stations, in which mechanics will be settled, inland villages with carding mills'. Scientific rotations and new breeds of horses and cows had been introduced; salt was to be made at Brora where an eminent Welsh engineer was superintending a renewed search for coal; willow plantations were planned for the manufacture of baskets; fairs were being established to facilitate trade; houses were to be provided to attract experienced fishermen from the south of Scotland.[13]

In 1811, then, the scene was set for the forthcoming transformation of the Sutherland economy. The capital of Lord Stafford was beginning to flow into the improvement of the coastal villages and the development of transport connections. Urged on by the persuasion of Sellar and Young, the family believed that the animal and human populations of their estate were not only compatible but mutually supporting. The broad outline of the plan was established, the details would follow. Lord Gower was closely involved in the plan (he had taken the lease of a farm himself) and in October 1811 he accompanied Young on a tour of North Wales (to view a sea embankment at Tremadoc) and the Lancashire collieries. His mother, the Coun-

[12] SC, D593/P/22/1/21, Young to Gower, 14–3–1810, 30–4–1810, October 1810; Sellar to Gower, 13–8–1810; advertisement of Sutherland Farms, July 1809.
[13] Henderson, op. cit., 131–58.

tess, wrote to Sir Walter Scott: 'I have great hopes at present', she told him, 'from the abilities of this Mr. Young, of considerable improvements being effected in Sutherland and without routing and destroying the old inhabitants, which contrary to the Theories respecting these matters, I am convinced is very possible.'[14]

For the years 1811 and 1812 the documents of the Sutherland estate are not presently available for inspection, but it is clear that the clearance schemes hastened. As Mackenzie put it, 'a new era of depopulation commenced, summonses of removal were served on large portions of the inhabitants. The lands were divided into extensive lots and advertised to be let for sheep farms.'[15] More sheep farmers came to the county[16]—men who were considerable capitalists able to invest in large scale pastoral operations. The year 1812 produced another subsistence crisis in the northern Highlands when appalling weather conditions destroyed crops in the interior straths. Sellar later remarked that 'it was the mildew 1812 that convinced us of the impolicy of keeping a highland population on land fit only for grass.' William Young supervised clearances from the parishes of Dornoch, Rogart, Loth, Clyne, Golspie and Assynt before the end of 1812, apparently without resistance. Much less is known of the conditions in the reception areas along the coasts—thirty years later Donald Macleod referred to the provision 'of miserable allotments', and although landlord money was being spent on the development of the village system, it is unlikely that elaborate preparations had been arranged by 1812. Construction at Brora had started but there was no fishing at Helmsdale until 1814. At much the same time the Stafford family continued its policy of buying out neighbouring landlords—in 1812–13 it spent at least £27,000 in this manner, largely to obtain coastal land for resettled population.[17]

Another significant development before 1813 was the emergence of Patrick Sellar in the role of sheep farmer—the role in which he achieved an almost unparalleled notoriety in Highland history.

[14] NLS, Letters to Sir Walter Scott, MS 3881, f. 89 (22–10–1811).
[15] Mackenzie, op. cit., 10.
[16] For the period as a whole the majority of the new sheep farmers were actually local men from Sutherland and adjacent counties.
[17] J. Loch, 'Dates and Documents'. SC, D593/N/4/1/1d, Young to Loch, 7-2-1813. SC, Sellar to Loch, 11-12-1816. Sellar, *Statement*, 3. *Inverness Journal*, 29-11-1811, 10-4-1812.

Sellar's father had been a law agent in Elgin for various landed proprietors including Russell of Westfield whose estate he bought in 1808 for £19,500. He had also invested in the Burghead harbour and road construction, and had pursued an improvement policy similar to that of William Young. His only son, Patrick, educated at Edinburgh University for the legal profession, joined his father's business in 1803 and was Procurator-Fiscal from 1806 to 1810, when he concentrated his activities in Sutherland. Sellar claimed that before he visited Sutherland he had regarded Highland sheep farming as 'one of the most abominable and detestable things possible to be imagined', and that 'the inroads then making on the ancient habits and manners of the children of the Gael were cruel and impolitic in the extreme.' It seems that, in August 1810, on a journey to Strathnaver with Young and Telford, his attitude was transformed. He obtained a loan of capital from Lord Stafford and, before long, he had negotiated a lease for sheep-walks including some uncleared parts of Strathnaver which were marked down for clearance in the years 1812–14. Meantime, he continued as William Young's right-hand man, assisting in eviction and collecting rents. Sellar was not an attractive man—his daughter-in-law remembered him as 'a man of iron will' —his expressions and his actions were arrogant and insensitive.[18]

Another change concerned James Loch, who became central commissioner of the affairs of Lord Stafford in late 1812. His duties were concerned with the co-ordination of the dispersed administration of Stafford's property. He did not visit Sutherland until 1813 and William Young retained direct control over the policies which he had initiated. During the course of the previous two years, Young had also been asked to recommend improvements on the English estates of Lord Stafford. In November 1812 Loch described Young as 'a very first rate Highland improver, a strong-headed intelligent Scotchman'. The substance of Young's report on the English estates, Loch reported, was 'that everything that differed from Moray was wrong and everything was to be improved by the total eradication of the present tenants and the introduction of Scotch farmers ... a vast and immediate rise of rent is expected.' Rather taken aback, Loch commented, 'A tenantry of 200 years standing Mr. Young did not consider as deserving of attention.'[19]

[18] SC, D593/P/22/1/21, Young to Gower, 12–8–1810; Sellar to Gower, 13–8–1810. T. Sellar, *The Sutherland Evictions of 1814* (1883), 24; R. Young, op. cit., 581. E. M. Sellar, *Recollections and Impressions* (1907), 38.
[19] SC, Loch to Adam, 7–11–1812.

Loch had hardly settled the terms of his commission when, in February 1813, he received confusing news from Young that the people of Kildonan had violently resisted his authority. This was virtually Loch's first contact with the affairs of the Sutherland estate. It was not, however, the first instance of popular resistance to clearances: in 1792 there had been anti-clearance riots in Ross-shire.[20]

The disturbance concerned Young's preparations for a forth-coming clearance of about seventy families from an interior area of Kildonan. He planned to resettle them on the recently acquired Armadale and Strathy estates on the north coast 'where crops are sure to ripen' and where 'the sea would have afforded constant supplies of fish both for the people and for export'. The Kildonan people who, he said, subsisted only by the profits of smuggling, 'rose in a body and chased the valuers off the ground and now threaten the lives of every man who dares to dispossess them.' The incident had developed into a confrontation between the estate administration and the inhabitants threatened with clearance. The situation was grave, Young warned Loch; he complained that virtually all the inhabitants were hostile to any plan for improvement and that he was compelled to do everything 'at the point of the sword'; they were absolutely a century behind and lacked common honesty but, he said, 'I had brought them wonderfully forward and had calculated that in two years I should have all the estate arranged.' 'In short', he continued, 'such a set of savages is not to be found in the wilds of America ... if Lord and Lady Stafford do not put it in my power to quell this banditti we may bid adieu to all improvement.'[21]

Loch, who was several hundred miles away in England, was seriously perturbed and promptly contacted Lord Sidmouth at the Home Office. He wrote also to the Sheriff of Sutherland, Thomas Cranstoun, to warn him of the danger that the spirit of insubordination could easily spread across the entire county: 'the whole people are anxiously watching the issue of this contest, for so it must now be called, some to resume farms they have formerly possessed, others to follow the same plan of resistance in other projected arrangements.' Cranstoun, however, was absent from Sutherland and his duties were being undertaken by his deputy, Mackid. Mackid had failed to obtain obedience from the people and, though he took a precognition, its contents were only tardily communicated to his superior.

[20] See Stewart, op. cit., I, 416.
[21] SC, Young to Loch, 7–2–1813.

179

Cranstoun resolved to travel north to investigate the crisis, and he obtained authority to call on troops from Fort George. Loch, though he had not been to Sutherland himself, assured Cranstoun that the people to be removed would be provided with new houses on 'small but comfortable arable farms on the lea coast of Armadale'; moreover, Lord and Lady Stafford were prepared to delay the removal until the people could sell their cattle at the best prices. Loch also reassured Young that the Staffords 'give their authority and approbation to every measure you may hereafter find it necessary to adopt to carry your proposed arrangements into full and complete effect'.[22]

On 20 February 1813, when the news of possible military intervention was known, Young met the ringleaders of the riot and extracted from them 'partly from fear . . . a petition to Lord and Lady Stafford begging forgiveness'. It seems likely that a further disturbance occurred but, when the troops arrived in the middle of March, the Kildonan people 'became perfectly submissive'. The ringleaders were rounded up but later released. Young and Gower met representatives of the people, explained their intentions and tried to conciliate their feeling and remove their fears. Patrick Sellar believed that the management had, in effect, capitulated to the riotous conspirators, who got off scot free: 'I saw six of the ringleaders feasted in Rhives parlour, Mr. Young drawing ale for them,' he recalled later. The Kildonan people also sent a deputy, MacDonald, to London to deliver a petition to the Regent and to remonstrate with Lord Stafford with the object of either preventing the clearance or obtaining assistance for migration to Canada. MacDonald was received with condescending civility at Cleveland House; Loch made it clear to Young that they could not afford to alienate public opinion especially in London; 'wicked libels' had already appeared in the *Star*.[23] Lord Stafford, however, refused to accept the petition because 'all the signatures were in one handwriting'. MacDonald had spoken well of Young and said that the Kildonan complaint 'was against Sellar and Dornoch law'. Loch also contacted the Home Office to deny the various allegations of cruelty complained of in the petition.

---

[22] SC, Loch to Cranstoun, 15–2–1813, 18–2–1813; Cranstoun to Loch, 10–2–1813; Loch to Young, 15–2–1813; Mackenzie to Loch, 21–2–1813; Mackenzie to Lady Stafford, 15–2–1813; Young to Mackenzie, 16–2–1813; Loch to Mackenzie, 18–2–1813. Home Office (Scotland) correspondence, RH 2/4100, f. 82, 93, 105.

[23] The *Morning Star* carried a number of items on Sutherland—see 16–3–1813, 22–3–1813, 24–3–1813, 4–5–1813.

All that was asked of the people, he wrote, 'is that they should live in new houses in place of old, that they should occupy farms which will produce corn in place of farms fit only for sheep, and that they will become industrious subjects in place of continuing vagabonds and breakers of the law.' He claimed that, while the Stafford family were spending enormous sums on the relief of the poor, 'these fellows are buying up all the barley in the country for the purpose of illicit distillation'—Loch claimed that MacDonald had told him that there were 300 illegal stills in the vicinity and that so much whisky was produced that it had to be 'shipped by sea'. Lord Sidmouth found the explanations perfectly satisfactory. But although the estate administration gave various concessions to the people a large number decided that resettlement in Lord Selkirk's scheme in Canada was preferable to the lots on the north coast of Sutherland. Selkirk received applications from 700 souls and by July 1813 more than 100 had left the estate.[24]

Writing from Sutherland in June 1813, Selkirk noted that the introduction of sheep had been 'pushed on with considerable harshness and has excited very general discontent'. The Kildonan people possessed 'so much of the Old Highland Spirit as to think their land their own'. They had been delighted with Selkirk's tempting proposals for emigration, and he observed that 'The Sutherland men seem to be both in person and in moral character a fine race of men: there are great numbers among them who have property enough to pay their passage, and settle themselves with little or no assistance and many capable of paying in cash for their lands.' Selkirk thought their riotous behaviour excusable: 'According to the ideas handed down to them from their ancestors, and long prevalent among high and low throughout the Highlands, they were only defending their rights and resisting a ruinous, unjust and tyranical encroachment on their property.'[25]

During the course of the Kildonan incidents the Sheriff-Substitute, Mackid, had clashed with Sellar and had insinuated various allegations against him, apparently concerned with the methods Sellar

[24] SC, Young to Loch, 21–2–1813, 20–3–1813, 27–3–1813; Loch to Young, 3–4–1813, 12–3–1813, 16–3–1813; Inglis to Loch, 11–3–1813; Loch to Cranstoun, 6–3–1813; Sellar to Loch, 7–5–1813; Loch to Inglis, 6–3–1813, 9–3–1813. Allardyce, op. cit., I, 76–7. Chester Morton, *Lord Selkirk's Work in Canada* (1916), 57.
[25] Selkirk Papers, Public Archives of Canada, Ottawa, M.G. 19, E1, 1, 650–61, Selkirk to MacDonell, 12–6–1813.

had used to collect rent. Sellar remarked that 'Mr. Mackid . . . would very gladly fish out anything improper in my conduct.' Young defended Sellar saying that he knew him too well to allow himself 'to think for a moment that he could be capable to extract a single shilling improperly from the people, far less to put it in his own pocket. I have formerly had occasion to ask him about similar charges and always got a satisfactory reply.' Mackid and Sellar were enemies—Sellar had caught Mackid poaching on at least one occasion, and Mackid believed that Sellar was ambitious to take over his position as Sheriff-Substitute. Two years later Mackid made much more serious charges against Sellar.[26]

It was not surprising, in view of the civil disorder, that William Young attempted to justify the Kildonan clearances to Sheriff Cranstoun. No one, he claimed, could say that oppressive measures were pursued. The people had been repeatedly told of the plans and of the provision for their resettlement. Kildonan was utterly unsuited for crofting: 'the situation is black and cold, and grain and potato crops are attacked either by early frosts or land floods almost every third year . . . the people are reduced to the utmost distress both for provision for themselves and their cattle.' Only sheep could thrive there, and sheep provided raw material for national manufactures, and an additional supply of food. Young stated categorically that 'it was never Lord Stafford's intention to send a single individual out of the Sutherland Estates, fortunately it admits of giving the whole (numerous as the population is) situations where in by industry and labour they can earn decent subsistence and in all the arrangements hitherto made it is not believed that 40 families have left the Country.' Assynt had been 'almost entirely remodelled and put under sheep stock', yet no one had migrated. The inhabitants had become fishers, kelp makers, and labourers, with 'ample remuneration for their services, and live in comfort with about two acres of arable land and a sufficiency of pasture for two cows and the same number of young cattle, for which they pay moderate rents'. The Kildonan plan had been similar—each settler would receive three acres of good arable and some pasture land on the coast, with nineteen-year leases, and loans for the building of dry-stone houses. Special provision was to be made for the old and infirm; employment on road making and ditching was available for those without other employment. Young

[26] SC, Sellar to Young, 25–3–1813; Young to Loch, 27–3–1813. See Prebble, op. cit., 94–5.

concluded that 'besides the money annually contributed by Government for roads . . . Lord Stafford is laying out the whole rents of the Estate . . . about £15,000 annually, in improvements and which is almost solely paid out for labour, and I have besides got several thousand pounds of his Lordship's money for similar purposes.' Such was the justification of 1813.[27]

William Young described the Assynt people as sober, industrious and uncorrupted by illicit whisky. In July 1813 Young accompanied a newly appointed minister to his parish of Assynt. Young reported that they had been set upon by more than a hundred 'mountain savages . . . and it was ten to one that lives were not lost'. The rioters had narrowly failed in their intention of handcuffing Young 'to be sent in that state to sea in an open boat.' Once more Cranstoun, Mackid and the militia were mobilized—a King's Cutter with 150 men of the Norfolk militia was despatched from Leith Roads to Lochinver—but when it arrived the commotion had subsided and five ringleaders had been incarcerated by Mackid.[28] Three parishioners were subsequently tried by an Inverness court and imprisoned for nine months.

Undeterred by the unpleasant and inconvenient commotion of 1813, the Sutherland management pressed on in its resolution to clear large areas of the estate at Whitsun 1814. It was primarily concerned with the remaining uncleared parts of Strathnaver which would become a sheep walk for Patrick Sellar. Strathnaver became a 'man-made wilderness', and the evictions were, writes F. F. Darling, 'of the order of brutality expected of a Norse raid a thousand years earlier'— the name Strathnaver 'became a symbol, and some of the hidden bitterness which may so easily flare up in Highland affairs today is referable to that time'.[29] There was a long sequence of events— Sellar cleared Strathnaver in May and June 1814; a year later, after a series of petitions and a precognition, Sellar was arrested and imprisoned by Mackid and charged with a long list of atrocities

[27] SC, Young to Cranstoun, 28-2-1813. See also *Edinburgh Advertiser*, 7-5-1813.
[28] SC, Young to Loch, 11-7-1813; Cranstoun to Loch, 8-8-1813; Loch to Cranstoun, 7-8-1813; Young to Mackid, 7-8-1813; Allardyce, op. cit., 84-5. Home Office (Scotland) Correspondence, RH 2/4 102, f. 381, 383, 385, 389, 399. See also W. Daniell, *A Voyage Round Great Britain* (4 vols, 1814-20), IV, 75-6.
[29] Darling, op. cit., 6. H. Fairhurst and G. Petrie, 'Scottish Clachans II', *Scottish Geographical Magazine*, LXXX (1964).

including 'culpable homicide, oppression and real injury'. Sellar was bailed out (after a delay) and there followed a second precognition. In April 1816 Sellar was tried by jury at Inverness.

Between November 1813 and April 1814 Sellar had perambulated the Sutherland estate collecting rents and serving removal notices on the people. He spoke no Gaelic and was assisted by guides. The weather was appalling and one of the guides lost several toes by frostbite—the new merino sheep, noted Sellar, had fared very much better. Young looked forward to the forthcoming changes—'we shall have a glorious summer of it and full work from sun to sun'— on the coal, brick, tile, salt and lime works, on drainage and the creation of coastside farms, and on the removals from Strathnaver and Strathbrora. Previous quarrels, he said, were due to the idle and grovelling character of the people, but 'now they begin to see I am right and that even Lord Selkirk and his Red River are wrong, and we shall have 120 men at sea from Port Gower alone in the ensuing season in search of the friends of the people (Herring).' The year 1814 was to be the great leap forward for the Sutherland economy. [30]

In May 1814 William Young described the actual process of removal. There had been great activity: 'I shall for the next 14 days be altogether in Strathnaver and Brora where we have at least 430 families to arrange in different allotments, to double their present rents and put them in a more industrious way of life.' He warned against hopes of instant success:

One would not quarrel with a child because it could not read the first time a book is put into its hand; give them a thorough knowledge of right and wrong, show them that they must earn their bread by the sweat of their brow, hunt down all vagabonds and the thing will come round—the changes already brought about are wonderful, and the Kildonan men *of last year* are now industrious herring fishers.

Neither Sellar nor Young made any mention of disturbances during the current clearances. Young was more worried about low cattle and sheep prices, and Sellar continued to muse on the cunning and lazy traits of the native Sutherlanders. 'They require', said Sellar, 'to be thoroughly brought to the coast where industry will pay, and to be *convinced* that they *must* worship industry or starve.' [31]

[30] SC, Sellar to Loch, 3–3–1814; Young to Loch, 3–3–1814; Loch to Gower, 15–5–1814; D593P/22/1/28(1), Young to Gower, 6–10–1815.
[31] SC, Young to Loch, 24–5–1814, 10–6–1814; Sellar to Loch, 1–8–1814.

184

However, soon after the clearance, in July 1814, some of the tenants of Strathnaver had raised a petition complaining that Sellar had illegally pulled down their houses and set fire to their heaths—apparently no mention was made of murder. The petition was transmitted to Lord Gower by Mackid. The Stafford family had replied that 'it is always their wish that justice should be impartially administered' and advised that the case should be brought to the notice of Cranstoun, the sheriff deputy, to 'let him award what pecuniary damages he might see due, after a full investigation'. Sellar had agreed to this course of action. Cranstoun, absent in Edinburgh, directed his substitute, Mackid, to undertake a precognition. Meanwhile the Strathnaver people, urged on by a popular anti-eviction newspaper, the *Military Register*, had raised a subscription for the purpose of prosecuting Sellar. Having taken the precognition, Mackid then arrested and jailed Sellar at the end of May 1815. Mackid wrote to Lord Stafford that 'a more numerous catalogue of crimes, perpetrated by an individual, has seldom disgraced any country, or sullied the pages of a precognition in Scotland! ! !' Sellar was alleged to have set fire to the houses, property and food of the people and to have caused the death of three of the inhabitants. [32] In 1841 Donald Macleod of Rossal recounted the worst of the alleged atrocities. Sellar and his removal party came to the house of an old woman. Macleod recalled that 'on his arrival I told him of the poor old woman being in a condition unfit for removal'—the woman was a hundred years old. Sellar replied, 'Damn her, the old witch, she has lived too long, let her burn'. Fire was immediately set to the house, and the blankets in which she was carried were in flames before she could be got out . . . she died within five days. [33]

When the charges against Sellar were made public, Loch demanded to know the worst from Young of what he called the 'hurried and improvident ejection of the people'. Loch acknowledged the possibility that Sellar had acted too hastily; there had been many complaints against him; Sellar was extremely unpopular—'he has', said Loch, 'a quick sneering biting way of saying good things in the execution of his duty which I do not think has made him popular

[32] The *Military Register* (21-6-1815) reported that 'the Sheriff was so affected by the detail that he fainted in court, overpowered by his feelings.'

[33] *The Trial of Patrick Sellar,* ed. A. Mackenzie (1883); Mackenzie, *Clearances* 10. The *Military Register*, 14-6-1815.

with anybody'. Loch indeed advised Sellar to 'avoid a certain ironical mode of expression, which does you more mischief than you are aware of'. Loch contacted his uncle, Lord Chief Commissioner Adam, to make it clear that Lady Stafford had no wish 'to screen Mr. Sellar in doing any illegal act'. Nevertheless, he considered Mackid an extremely 'unfit man' for the precognition. Mackid had refused bail on a bailable offence, he had also written an improper letter to Lord Stafford. Moreover, Mackid hated Sellar, and he possessed the 'local prejudices in favour of the people and against the system of improvement'. Loch told his uncle that 'I am far from thinking that Sellar has not acted hastily or inadvisedly but that he has been guilty of crimes (even that of murder) which are insinuated rather than alleged by Mackid against him, I totally disbelieve, and I look upon them as the pure offspring of jealousy and ill nature.'[34]

Young agreed. Sellar had many enemies and he should have 'steered a middle course' in the removals in Strathnaver. Mackid had told him that the people 'wished to see Sellar hanged or sent to Botany Bay'—and if they succeeded, said Young, it would be the 'death-blow to the improvement of this princely property, for the *good old system* of sloth and indolence cannot do although they believe it is now on the eve of returning ... the people suppose they got a complete victory.' Young also reiterated that the re-movees were perfectly comfortable in their new coastal crofts; at Skelbo 'after three years trial they feel their situation so comfortable that if their old places were offered they would not exchange.'

Sellar himself described Mackid's action as diabolical and illegal, and demanded an investigation by an impartial judge. He claimed that none of the witnesses at the precognition had been willing to swear to the statements that Mackid had extracted from them—Sellar was willing 'to give them battle'. Sellar also claimed that he had evidence that Mackid had not only dictated the original petition himself, but that he had intimidated witnesses and had told numerous people 'that I should certainly be hanged'. He spoke of 'these barbarous hordes', and described his precognition as 'a base machination of bad men, and without the slightest ground or foundation'.

Sellar gave his own account of the 1814 clearance. The people had been given full warning of the eviction in the latter months of 1813. He had sent legal warning in March 1814. In May the people told

[34] SC, Loch to Young, 9–6–1815; Loch to Adam, 10–6–1815; Loch to Lady Stafford, 9–6–1815; Adam to Loch, 21–6–1815.

Sellar's shepherd that he would never gain possession of their land. Sellar therefore took out a warrant for their ejectment which he did not enforce until 16 June. Several hundred cattle remained in the Strath 'while my ewes were dying in Culmailly . . . which forced me to send a great proportion of these to the knife at one third of their value.' He referred to the fact that the coastal settlements for the people (Young's responsibility) had not been ready until May 1814—due to the incompetence or illness of the surveyor Roy—and the people had no opportunity to plant their new crofts. 'But when Mr. Young at length did lay off the allotments . . . the people had nothing to do but to carry their trash there'. Instead they continued in 'violent possession of my ground', and harassed his agents. Sellar described the subsequent forceable removal of the people and he readily admitted that fire was used to destroy the dwelling of William Chisholm. Chisholm, said Sellar, was a bigamist, a squatter and a sheep thief, widely disliked by the local population. Sellar vehemently denied that any other 'hut or one stick . . . *was burned by any person in my employ*'. He had given strict orders that sick people should be left undisturbed in their houses. He remarked that he had once been 'a passionate declaimer' against the clearance system, but he was now more convinced than ever of its supreme utility. He concluded his account with a characteristic swipe at the Highland peasant who, he said, followed his ponies, 'cocked bonnet on his head and a red top to it, and a ragged philibeg reaching halfway down his leg, afflicted I doubt not by a hereditary itch which all the brimstone in Scotland would be tardy to cure'.[35]

Patrick Sellar was certainly aware of his own unpopularity. Before his arrival, the estate, he said, was 'in the possession of middlemen, sub-tenants, turfcutters and whisky smugglers, who poach the game, destroy the woods, destroy the surface of the ground, and pay their rents . . . as they please, while the factor gets fat and full'. Sellar pictured himself as the

keen thin man who trounces the poachers high and low from the Sheriff [Mackid] on his seat of justice who kills five partridges . . . to John Gunn of Knockfin selling game on the streets of Thurso. He places officers and spies in every parish, scours the country himself, checks the woodstealing, makes every man pay interest and is the immediate instrument in turning out the people of every parish from the rent free possessions to fishing

[35] SC, Young to Loch, 15–6–1815 (2); Young to Lady Stafford, 18–6–1815; Sellar to Loch, 15–6–1815, 28–6–1815, 15–8–1816; Sellar to Lady Stafford, 17–7–1815; Sellar to Adam, 24–5–1815.

allotments, the then object of their detestation. Can such a man [he asked], fail to have conspiracies against him?

Referring directly to the accusation of murder, Sellar asked Loch:

Can you believe, my good sir, that I, a person not yet cognosced or escaped from a mad house, should deliberately, in open day, by means of an officer who has a wife and family, with three witnesses *called to attest the process*, burn a house with a woman in it! or that the officer should do so, instead of ejecting the tenant—the said tenant and woman being persons of whom we know nothing, and against whom we could have no felonious intent, no malice or ill will?

Sellar received some support from Robert Gordon, the tacksman of Langdale. Writing to William Munro of the Highland Society, Gordon said:

It was told us that in consequence of Mr Sellar's cruelties 3 people lost their lives, now let me tell you that one of those 3 are still living, the other was never born (an abortion) but the 3rd who was an old woman died about four days after being removed out of the place she dwelled in, without receiving any known injury ... this business would never have made such a noise were it not for an old game grudge between the Sheriff-Substitute and Mr Sellar.

Gordon insisted that there was a conspiracy against Sellar and he denied the current belief that there had been mass emigration from the parish. [36]

Lady Stafford believed that the clearances should continue regardless of the Sellar affair. She asked Loch 'to encourage Sellar in trouncing these people who wish to destroy our system . . . I do hope the aggressors will be scourged.' It was essential that Sellar should exculpate himself, preferably without a full-scale trial. Lady Stafford described Mackid as 'a man of acknowledged bad character, and a passionate enemy of Sellar'. Loch had the difficult task of convincing the world that the House of Sutherland was not attempting to influence the course of justice, that 'they do not wish to protect Sellar if he has done what was wrong.' He repeatedly pointed out that Sellar had undertaken the Strathnaver evictions in his capacity as tenant, not as estate factor. Loch also insisted that the motives of the general improvement policy were beyond reproach even though 'a hasty or inaccurate execution of these orders have been given the appearance of harshness when every attention and tenderness was

[36] SC, Sellar to Loch, 13–10–1815, 16–10–1815; Gordon to Sellar, 12–2–1816; Gordon to Munro, 12–2–1816. Cf. Donald Macleod, *History of the Destitution in Sutherlandshire* (1841).

... intended and shown.' The Stafford family were particularly worried by the effect of current reports on public opinion—the *Military Register* was more vocal than ever, the *Annual Register* reported Sellar's case as though his guilt had already been proven, and even the government-authorized *Public Gazette* had stated that Sellar was guilty of murder. Lady Stafford was prepared to believe Sellar's assertion that there was a conspiracy abroad to injure him— led by Mackid and Alexander Sutherland, the supposed author of the articles in the *Military Register*. In July 1815 the Stafford family authorized Loch to prepare an *Account of the Improvements* to defend their policies against the current libels. The family also promoted Sellar's demand for a new precognition which would exculpate Sellar and destroy the career of Mackid. A precognition would reveal their policy in its true colours—but only if undertaken by 'a man of such rank and character not connected with the Highlands'. Mackid was not such a man. [37]

Cranstoun apparently agreed. He wrote to Loch in August 1815. Cranstoun said that he was displeased with Mackid for writing to Lord Stafford and disclosing the substance of the precognition and stating that Sellar was guilty of various crimes. The letter was improper and its style was 'mean and disgusting'. Mackid must have known, he said, that a precognition was to enquire into grounds for trial, not to convict. Cranstoun said that the precognition had been rendered indispensable because Lord Gower had officially laid before him the Strathnaver petition. Mackid had erred and Cranstoun decided that he would personally conduct a new precognition—which pleased Loch who believed that it would enable Sellar to 'exculpate himself from all blame'. Sellar was indignantly confident, remarking 'I don't fear the investigation of the holy Inquisition, although I confess I have felt something not very different from the procedure of that venerable court.' However, a few days before the new precognition, the Rev. David Mackenzie (who is sometimes regarded as a 'quisling' minister at the beck and call of the Stafford family) pointedly refused to deny 'the circumstances regarding Mr. Sellar since they have a foundation, however highly exaggerated'. [38]

[37] SC, Lady Stafford to Loch, 24–7–1815, 15–7–1815; Lady Stafford to Sidmouth, 14–8–1815; Sellar to Lady Stafford, 17–7–1815; Lady Stafford to Adam, 25–7–1815; Young to Lady Stafford, 17–7–1815; Loch to Adam, 6–7–1815, 7–7–1815.

[38] SC, Cranstoun to Loch, 7–8–1815; Gower to Loch, 29–9–1815; Mackenzie to Loch, 25–8–1815; Sellar to Loch, 11–9–1815, 13–9–1815.

Cranstoun began his precognition on 13 September 1815. To Sellar's mounting horror Cranstoun refused to examine witnesses for his defence. Sellar had named six witnesses: 'the Sheriff Officer, three instrumentary witnesses to the ejection, and two indifferent spectators, John Burn, a farmer in Caithness, and Donald McLeod, mason in Rossal'. The last name is astonishing—Macleod is presumably the same man who published a vehement denunciation of Sellar in 1841—a graphic eye-witness account of the alleged atrocities. Sellar described Macleod as an accidental witness 'who happened to be present'. Cranstoun confined himself to an interrogation of Mackid's earlier witnesses. Sellar believed that Cranstoun was 'screening Mackid by verifying the Precognition'. Sellar alleged that Mackid had again intimidated the witnesses. The outcome of Cranstoun's investigation is not clear but Sellar was roused to a new peak of indignation. Loch tried to quieten him and defend Cranstoun as being 'incapable of doing anything but strict justice between the parties'. Sellar felt differently and remarked, 'As Mr. Cranstoun refused to cite my witnesses and to hear them, I see no course left but to force on my Trial.' This he did—it was the action of a man supremely confident of his own innocence, or else equally confident of his ability to manipulate the course of justice. In the latter case, he could expect little aid from the Stafford family—for more than twelve months they refused to allow Sellar a copy of Mackid's self-incriminating letter of May 1815. Nor was the verdict of the trial a foregone conclusion. In March 1816, Lady Stafford wrote of Sellar that 'we have only to hope he will come out clear.' But, while Sellar was eager for a trial, the people of Strathnaver were also adamant. Lady Stafford reported that 'the Lord Advocate tried to make the People enter into a compromise or submission with Sellar . . . they refused . . . and therefore he was obliged to order a trial.' The trial was set for April 1816. [39]

Although Loch attempted to divorce the Sellar case from the general Sutherland policy, it was clear that not only was Sellar on trial—the policy itself was no less so. In early 1816 Loch's anonymous *Account* defending the policy was distributed. He also wrote numerous

[39] SC, Gower to Loch, 29-9-1815; Loch to Sellar, 3-10-1815, 10-10-1815, 26-10-1815, 30-10-1815; Sellar to Loch, 11-9-1815, 13-9-1815, 14-9-1815, 24-9-1815, 13-10-1815, 5-11-1815; Sellar to Lady Stafford, 28-9-1815; Young to Loch, 17-9-1815; Loch to Lady Stafford, 8-10-1815; Lady Stafford to Loch, March 1816. The *Military Register*, 4-10-1815.

letters demonstrating how the population had increased 'while the people have by being moved to the Sea coast become more industrious'. The land they vacated would supply large amounts of wool to English industry. He reiterated the philosophy of improvement to William Young—that the 'pleasure and delight attending his Lordship's improvements in Scotland was that they were calculated to improve and increase the comforts and happiness of the lower orders while they added to his Lordship's wealth and dignity ... what in fact is the object of all improvement and industry but the increase of the comforts of life to the lower ranks and the elegances of life to the higher.'[40]

But great caution was needed. The Sellar affair had already delayed by several years a new round of clearances. For the future, Loch instructed Young to move people to the new village of Helmsdale in a way that would not 'create any real or alleged hardship'. Loch had heard rumours in Edinburgh that in earlier removals the people had not been given sufficient notice. Another set of complaints could not be tolerated—'if another disturbance takes place at Helmsdale you may depend upon it becoming a subject of Parliamentary enquiry.' William Young, affronted by the implied criticism of his factorship, threatened to resign. He replied hotly, 'take my situation all in all, consider what I have had to encounter in every arrangement great and small among 15,000 people, most of them hostile to change, to industry and the advance of rent, see what has been effected in a short space of four years and tell me if the like was ever done in Britain.' Young went on to say that 'the Strathnaver people certainly got too short notice and should have had longer time to move off, I admit it but the fault was none of mine.' The fault belonged to the sheep farmers (especially Sellar) who had taken over their farms without conceding that they could expect little benefit during the first summer of the lease. 'Sellar ought to have known this', added Young, 'but dearly has he paid for his rashness ... no poor Highlander ever charged me with cruelty or hardship.' Taking the accounts of Sellar and Young together it is evident that there had been a failure of communication between the two men at the time of the Strathnaver clearance. Sellar had proceeded with the eviction on the understanding that Young would have the coastal lots ready for the evictees. Young claimed that Roy, the surveyor, had told

[40] SC, Loch to Stafford, 24–8–1815; Loch to Young, 14–2–1815, 15–2–1815, 12–1–1816; Young to Lady Stafford, 5–1–1816; Loch to Sellar, 9–2–1816.

Sellar that a delay was advisable, but Sellar had left the responsibility in Young's hands. In the event, the lots were not ready until about three days before the ejectments. Loch advised Lord Stafford to delay the next removal for twelve months and to allow the removees eighteen months rent-free occupation before they settled in Helmsdale. The Sellar affair, via its effect on public opinion, certainly induced more stringent preparation for future removals.[41]

Loch was noticeably cool towards Sellar during the period immediately before the trial. The position of the Staffords was one of delicacy: if Sellar was guilty they did not wish to be implicated; if he was innocent they must keep clear of the legal proceedings to avoid any taint of using undue influence on his behalf. Sellar received little aid, if any; Loch was generally unco-operative and not especially encouraging—he took great pains to make it clear that Sellar had acted in his capacity as tenant, not as under-agent, during his evictions from Strathnaver. Sellar appears to have been left to his own devices. There was a deliberate and conspicuous absence of representatives of the Stafford family at the trial, and Loch's closest informant in Inverness remarked: 'I look with great anxiety to the issue of the trial', for, though he thought that the charge was exaggerated, he feared that Sellar's conduct 'may have been culpably harsh'.[42]

In the outcome, the jury of fifteen 'gentlemen' at the Inverness trial unanimously found Sellar not guilty and the legality of the removal process was upheld. The story of the trial has often been told and it remains very much a *cause célèbre*. At the time Loch and the Stafford family were jubilant. Loch wrote to Sellar that 'such a termination was equally essential for the future progress and prosperity of Sutherland as it was for your comfort and happiness ... I went to Cleveland House where I found everyone most happy.'[43]

Though Sellar was acquitted, many writers have questioned the impartiality of the judge and the jury—and Sellar continues to be found guilty by many historians. The controversy flared up many

[41] SC, Loch to Young, 29–11–1815, 10–12–1815; Loch to Stafford, 30–11–1815; Young to Loch, 8–12–1815.

[42] SC, Loch to Grant, 3–2–1816; Grant to Loch, 7–3–1816, 12–3–1816, 6–4–1816, 25–4–1816; Loch to Mackenzie, 1–4–1816; Mackenzie to Loch, 21–4–1816; Loch to Sellar, 8–4–1816. Cf. the letter of David Stewart of Garth, 9–6–1817, quoted in 'More about Sellar and the Sutherland clearances', *Celtic Magazine*, IX (1884), 489.

[43] SC, Loch to Sellar, 29–4–1816.

times in the years after the trial; Sellar was persecuted throughout his life, and for posterity he has become the archetypal villain of Highland history. Writers from Donald Macleod to Karl Marx, and from David Stewart to Hugh Miller, have waxed eloquent in their denunciation of the Sellar affair. Yet doubts remain. It is impossible to say whether Sellar or his adversaries lied. Sellar was certainly an objectionable and provocative man; he had intruded into the life of Strathnaver without delicacy or sympathy; the accommodation for the people he removed had not been ready until a matter of days before their forcible ejection; and Sellar had certainly set fire to one house in the Strath. Equally certain is the fact of Mackid's long-standing feud with Sellar; Mackid's legal proceedings against Sellar were highly irregular; the Strathnaver people had been incited to opposition by skilful propaganda; and there was a popular 'conspiracy' to teach Sellar a lesson.

The forced resettlement of 430 families was bound to create cases of appalling hardship. Moreover, Sellar's closest associates believed that he was capable of culpable hardship in the use of his authority. Yet, balancing the probabilities, it is difficult to imagine this pedantic, calculating man committing acts of pointless, sadistic cruelty against the Kildonan peasantry. For their part the people abominated the clearance system. They were on the edge of hysteria and violence. In the belief that they could stop the clearances it is possible that they were persuaded to inflate their complaints into charges of homicide against the hated Sellar. They had been provoked by Sellar's arrogance. But their action was also the consequence of an economic policy that entailed the instant transformation of an ancient way of life.

Immediately after the trial Sellar instituted a legal action against Robert Mackid. Already the *Military Register* had denounced the trial as a farce and Sellar was anxious to break, once and for all, the conspiracy which he believed had had a continuous existence since 1812. During the trial the throats of twenty of Sellar's sheep had been cut, together with that of 'Lady Stafford's Thibetan Goat'. Sellar made preparations to remove the remaining refractory people from Strathnaver, remarking 'I suppose military power may be necessary.' Sellar advised that the trouble-makers among the people should be rooted out; 'now is the happy hour to give them battle', he said. He also made a strong request to take over the farm

of Mackid, who decided to leave the country—a thought which horrified Loch, who told Lady Stafford that 'it shows much too greedy a
disposition upon Sellar's part . . . and might lead to such misrepre-
sentation as to be productive of very bad effects by keeping up this
unsettled irritation of these men's minds'. However, Loch believed
that 'the neck of resistance' had been broken and that the improvement of the county could go forward once more: meanwhile he
advised Sellar to avoid taunting the people. [44]

During 1816 and 1817 Sellar continued his pursuit of Mackid who
had relinquished his position as Sheriff-Substitute. 'I am very much
of Buonoparte's creed in one thing', declared Sellar, 'that a first
point is to make the enemy pay the *expenses of the war* . . . I think I
may count on £1500 or so. If the defendant don't become bankrupt
within 60 days of the arrestment I secure a preference on his funds.'
Mackid was certainly a broken man and, in September 1817, Sellar
finally settled with him: 'I found the miserable man involved in such
difficulties on all hands; and his family of I believe 9 or 10 young
children so certainly about to be beggars by my bringing him to
Trial that I am well pleased to wash my hands of them.' In the settlement Sellar was able to extract a confession from Mackid to the
effect that the precognition he had taken was full of falsehoods for
which he was 'thoroughly ashamed'. [45]

There was a second sequel to the Sellar trial. Within four months
Loch had expertly removed 'the disuniting and clashing authority'
of Young and Sellar from the administration of the Sutherland estate.
The two men resigned under pressure—they were both in disgrace. [46]
There had always been an element of mutual jealousy between
Young and Sellar, and Loch considered them both unfit for their
responsibilities. Moreover, Loch felt the whole policy needed to be
rethought from first principles—Loch was given more direct control
and Young was unwilling to submit to the consequent restrictions.

Young was criticized for his 'impatience of delay and an eternal
fidget to be moving'—and for a failure to attend to detail which had

[44] SC, Grant to Loch, 26–5–1816; Sellar to Loch, 7–5–1816, 25–5–1816,
27–5–1816, 31–5–1816; Loch to Sellar, 15–5–1816, 25–5–1816; Sellar to Lady
Stafford, 17–5–1816, 2–6–1816; Young to Loch, 11–5–1816, 15–5–1816; Loch to
Adam, 21–5–1816; Loch to Young, 7–5–1816, 30–5–1816; Loch to Grant,
31–5–1816; Loch to Lady Stafford, 15–5–1816. The *Military Register*, 5–6–1816.

[45] SC, Sellar to Loch, 2–6–1816, 24–9–1816; Lady Stafford to Loch, 9–10–1817;
Sellar to Grant, 23–9–1816. See also Prebble, op. cit., 102.

[46] See the triumphant and basically accurate report in the *Military Register*,
30–10–1816.

'not only hurried on many improvident arrangements before their time', but also produced many cases of hardship. Young was also a poor planner: he had, for instance, spent almost £40,000 of Lord Stafford's money at Brora 'without any steps having been taken to ascertain the extent of the field of coal'. Loch was appalled by Young's methods of auditing.

His criticisms of Sellar were even more outspoken. Loch told Lady Stafford ('on the most sufficient grounds') that Sellar possessed 'less discrimination than it is easy to believe, and was really guilty of many very oppressive and cruel acts'. Sellar possessed 'irremediable defects of . . . character'. In a rigid and formal way Sellar was efficient, but he was deficient beyond measure in 'taste, temper or feeling'—and Loch concluded that 'he is the most unfit and dangerous person from these defects to be entrusted with the management and therefore the character of any ancient and distinguished family.' To his uncle, Lord Advocate Adam, Loch wrote, 'You have no idea either of the inaccuracy and unsteadiness of execution, the total want of plan, the lavish expenditure, or the total disregard to the people's feelings which characterised the whole management.'

Young resigned in September 1816 and Sellar was grudgingly given temporary control until July 1817 when Francis Suther took over the management. Suther, an asthmatic lowland Scot, was a protégé of Loch and was previously agent for the English estates of Lord Stafford in the counties of Salop and Stafford. Under the factorship of Suther, Loch was able to undertake a reorganization of the northern affairs. After 1816 Loch was fully responsible for the Sutherland policies.[47]

[47] SC, Grant to Loch, 10–6–1816; Loch to Grant, 31–5–1816, 8–6–1816, 1–7–1816; Young to Mackenzie, 27–7–1816; Lady Stafford to Loch, 8–9–1816, 26–9–1816; Loch to R. H. Bradshaw, 1–9–1816; Mackenzie to Loch, 9–10–1816; Loch to Lady Stafford, 3–10–1816, 11–10–1816; Loch to Adam, 28–8–1816, 3–10–1816. Cf. T. Sellar, op. cit., 41.

XIV

The Reaffirmation of the Sutherland Policy

The programme for the Sutherland economy consisted of a sequence of clearances from the interior straths, and a simultaneous creation of vigorous coastal settlements which would generate a diversified range of employment opportunities for the majority of the population. It had been launched on the wave of improvement which, with the help of Dempster and Sinclair, reached Sutherland before the turn of the century—years of optimism and rising prices. The drive of Young and Sellar, and the deteriorating economic condition of the inland peasantry, gave added impetus and urgency. The implementation of the policy had met both passive and active resistance from the common people, and an increasingly hostile public opinion.

Having inherited this policy, James Loch publicly defended it. His *Account* was circulated to many influential people, one of whom was Sir David Dundas. Dundas told Loch that it was an example of the effect of a landlord making the most of a great domain for himself and the public weal, and commendable 'as the death-blow to the feudal system'.[1] The Sellar affair, while it provoked some heart-searching and some delay, failed to alter Loch's conviction that the removals were utterly imperative in every light.

It was in these years that Loch's energies became increasingly consumed by the problems of the Highland properties. But he was not able to disengage himself from other, competing, demands on his time—and on Lord Stafford's capital. In particular Loch was

[1] SC, Dundas to Loch, 17–1–1816.

concurrently involved in the conversion of the Lilleshall and Trent-ham estates into showpieces of aristocratic rural economy. He con-tinued to supervise, in extraordinary detail, all these agricultural improvements—from the design of ploughs to the wording of rota-tion clauses. He also found himself testing his nerve against striking Staffordshire colliers, in rallying local ironmasters and landowners in Salop to maintain employment in the hard times that followed the French Wars, and not least in facing the current of radicalism that seemed to threaten the industrial Midlands in these years. Such problems were small only in comparison with those emerging on the Sutherland estates of Lord and Lady Stafford.

The Sutherland plan depended entirely upon the prodigious financial assistance which Lord Stafford was able to give his wife's estate. Under Loch's aegis a more stringent control of finance was instituted. Thenceforward, Stafford's expenditure was to be confined to a great series of improvements which would 'add to the permanent interest and consequence of the family'. Loch defined the economic strategy with his usual clarity: 'Lord Stafford has such an income as no other proprietor will have, so long therefore as his Lordship is placed to expend part of his income there, it ought to be upon those things which a proprietor of lesser means could not do, leaving those things which any and every proprietor and many tenants could accomplish.' In effect, Lord Stafford was fulfilling the role (now-adays usually reserved for the State) of establishing the fundamental conditions for the future advance of the economy—providing the heavy capital investment items (such as roads, harbours, settlements) which were beyond the normal means of individual entrepreneurs, but which would, in the long run, reap returns to the whole re-gional economy—especially by way of external economies. Once the basic equipment of the economy had been established, it would function of its own accord; *laissez-faire* would become appropriate.

Thus it was that the clearances and the resettlement of the last months of Young and Sellar were followed by renewed plans under Loch and Suther. Discussion within the Sutherland management was confined to the questions of how quickly the clearances could be implemented. Loch's confidant, Grant, counselled a gradual approach: 'In this respect I differ a little from you', he told Loch in 1816, 'I confess that my nerves are hardly equal to the contemplation of removing 1,056 families at once, even supposing you could acquire the means of their accommodation.' These difficulties were implicit in the policy which Loch now reaffirmed as the answer to the economic and social problems of the estate.[2]

In 1815 Loch sanctioned further clearances from Kildonan to Helmsdale for the following year. The people, he said, would always be sheep stealers or whisky smugglers while left in the mountains; Young was instructed to 'prepare the people thoroughly beforehand'; they were to be shown their new coastal lots at least six months before their removal, and they were given eighteen months rent-free occupation—in order to put them 'in good humour' and to avoid 'a fracas'. By the end of May 1816 Young was able to report a successful resettlement. The Helmsdale lots were in great demand—so much so that Young was 'obliged to reduce some of the lots to *an acre for tradesmen*'. The new occupier of the cleared land, Major Clunes, was able to take possession 'at a rent which no other sheep farmer would give'. Young also indicated that 'all the coast side lands suitable for lotting out are now brimful' and that Loch would be unwise to think of more removals before 1818. Loch's urgent desire to press forward with the policy was frustrated by the fact that much of the coastal land was tied up with leases dating from the time of Cosmo Falconer. The Sutherland management accepted that clearances were unworkable without resettlement accommodation. But the availability of land was not the only factor to be considered. For, as Loch told Lady Stafford, 'I am afraid both from the temper of the people at large as well as the feeling of government we must get them out of the hills gradually though the other course would be most for their own happiness and comfort.' Loch was unable to escape the perennial paradox of the Sutherland policies—the need to compel people to do what was designed for 'their own happiness and comfort'.[3]

In 1816 Loch drew up long-term plans for the future remodelling of the estate. He acknowledged that Falconer's leases (many of which would not expire until 1830) prevented 'the people being moved at once to the seaside, and so long as the measure is incomplete and in progress, so long will the clamour and discontent prevail even if there are no external exciting causes.' The vast numbers involved prevented the idea of comprehensive clearance—

[2] SC, Loch to Gower, 17–6–1816; Loch to Lady Stafford, 18–6–1816; Loch to Grant, 1–7–1816, 12–7–1816; Grant to Loch, 5–7–1816.
[3] SC, Loch to Young, 26–10–1815; Loch to Lady Stafford, 27–11–1816; Loch to Lord Stafford, 30–11–1815; Young to Loch, 26–5–1816, 8–6–1816; Loch to Adam, 11–6–1816.

'some must never be moved at all', admitted Loch. Nevertheless, Loch was able to designate large areas as appropriate for clearance in the coming years, and he instructed his agents to tell the people of the proposed changes. Loch's resolution was given solid support by the sheep farmers who were already severely troubled by the post-war decline of sheep and wool prices. Atkinson and Marshall, in early 1817, for instance, complained bitterly of the conditions they faced in Sutherland—they had lost a fortune, they claimed. Having spent enormous sums establishing their concern, they had suffered 'ruinous losses of sheep' by the 'destructive ravages of dogs, foxes, eagles . . . and the enmity of the natives'—they had lost 7,500 sheep since 1811 in this way. If, at the beginning, they had contemplated spending 'one half of the reality, no earthly consideration would have induced us to embark on it', they lamented; 'it has produced up to the present moment only an accumulation of anxiety, vexation and disappointment.' They recalled the time when they had been graziers 'in the wildest and stormiest part of the Cheviot Mountains'. The sheep losses had been equally large—but the Cheviot shepherds had been accountable for the losses. In Sutherland, the law was not enforced and, moreover, the shepherds obtained 'the most enormous and extravagant wages ever received . . . by any shepherds in the Kingdom'. If sheep thefts were not prevented, and if rents were not abated, they warned, sheep-farming in Sutherland 'will not prove an object worthy of attention of people of capital and skill'.[4]

Patrick Sellar was of similar mind—he had also suffered losses of sheep and complained that returns to his Strathnaver farm were unsatisfactory. As a result of this, together with his deteriorating relations with Loch, he threatened to give up his farm in 1816. But Loch was adamant—it would be a bad precedent to allow a tenant to 'give up his farm the moment he tires of it, especially as it was his [Sellar's] taking his farm and his dispeopling it rather in too great a hurry which produced all the unpleasant discussion last year. It might lead to the conclusion that the measure in its principle was *unwise* and was to be abandoned.' Sellar remained. Loch assured him that the sheep stealing would end once the hills were completely cleared of people. Sellar declared that further 'Ejectment' was the only remedy for sheep stealing and that sheep farmers should be

---

[4] SC, Atkinson and Marshall to Loch, 30–1–1817, 16–2–1817; Loch to Grant, 8–6–1816; Matheson to Loch, 28–7–1817.

compelled to clear their land as a condition of their tenure. It would, he said, end the situation in which 'every fourth year, they [the interior inhabitants] are maintained by imported victuals.' Loch apparently agreed, and in July 1817 Lady Stafford concurred in the plan for a second round of clearances. A grave problem, she believed, was 'the quantity of people fixt on the estates as a sort of beggars in black huts without any holdings'. Such squatting was the result of the 'stupid and lax management' of William Young. However, during the discussion of the problem Loch had consulted a tacksman of the interior, Captain Mackay, who stated cogently that a removal to the north coast at the mouth of the Naver was quite impracticable since the lots were already full. He also suggested that Sellar's sheep had not been stolen by the people, but had been drowned, or injured in sheep-drains or taken by Sellar's own shepherds. Lady Stafford was at least half-convinced, saying that Sellar 'exaggerates in everything relating' to the people. The clearance was thus delayed until more adequate accommodation should be available. She also demanded that the most elaborate preparations should be made to effect the removal 'without cruelty to the inhabitants'. Although Sellar had to accept delay (until 1819) which would cost him £1,000, he was happy with the plans—'I thank God the thing is so near a termination.'[5]

The problems of clearance and resettlement were undoubtedly aggravated by the existence of large numbers of 'squatters' on the estate. Loch stated that there were '408 families comprising about 2,000 people who had squatted on the estate and paid no rent'. He claimed that they were victims of earlier clearances in Ross-shire where no provision for removees had been made.[6]

While Loch made plans for the new clearances, yet another subsistence crisis occurred. The grim winter of 1816–17 produced widespread destitution in the Highlands. Once again the supply of oatmeal failed. Relief was imperative—and the landlord was the only person able to provide it. In September 1816 a Highland proprietor told Loch that he had secured 'some meal for my people but I expect no rents to enable me to pay for it, and how Highland

[5] SC, Loch to Sellar, 15–5–1816, 2–4–1817, 8–10–1817, 3–12–1816; Loch to Young, 30–5–1816; Young to Loch, 31–5–1816; Loch to Lady Stafford, 15–5–1816, 18–12–1816; Loch to Suther, 18–10–1817, 13–12–1817; Loch to Mackay 27–9–1817; Loch to Gower, 27–10–1817; Sellar to Loch, 27–2–1817, 23–3–1817 4–7–1817, 24–8–1817, 6–9–1817, 16–10–1817; Lady Stafford to Loch, 5–7–1817 11–7–1817, 31–8–1817, 31–10–1817; Mackay to Loch, 16–10–1817.

[6] SC, Loch to MacNeil, 22–2–1851.

lairds are to live this year I am at a loss to conceive.' In the same month Sellar reported that 'the mildew has completely destroyed the potatoes in the interior; and the useless part of the population must, for the ensuing year, either be in great part fed by Lord and Lady Stafford, or starve, or leave the country.' Sellar spoke of the intentions of many Strathnaver tenants to emigrate to America, commenting that 'they are just in that state of society suited for a savage country.' In August Lord Stafford directed that, from the poorer tenants, 400 cattle be purchased, to be driven south to the English estates. Meal supplies were ordered but the crisis deepened and by November a full-scale relief operation had become imperative. Loch told Lady Stafford that 'the future state of this population becomes every day a more important and anxious subject'—he believed that assisted emigration would have to be considered. Sellar reported that the people were panic-stricken and that in return for meal the estate factors could take 'the *only* thing the people have to give—labour'. Sellar suggested a plan to employ 3,000 men on road construction to be paid by allowances of food—otherwise, he said, between 12,000 and 15,000 people would be 'destitute of three or four months food'. And, although Sellar's plan was not accepted, vast quantities of food were imported by the estate management, rent collections were postponed, and road construction proceeded. Loch was uneasy about the situation since he believed that 'if you give full work and wages to the people, they will lose all habits of economy and will not feel the inconvenience of their present situation among the hills ... Lord Stafford has no intention of doing more than merely supplying the most urgent wants of the country.' The problem was exacerbated by difficulties experienced in the new fishing industry at Helmsdale—though Sellar claimed that the coastside inhabitants were the only people unaffected by the destitution. Loch could not allow the fishing to lapse—'if such an unfortunate event were to happen', he wrote, 'the settlers on the coast would be reduced to the same or nearly the same helpless condition and become a similar burden upon the estate as the inhabitants of the mountainous districts.'[7]

Lord Stafford is said to have spent more than £10,000 on relief in

[7] SC, Young to Loch, 15–5–1816; Grant to Loch, 17–9–1816; Sellar to Loch, 30–9–1816, 16–10–1816, 20–10–1816, 27–10–1816, 29–12–1816; Lady Stafford to Loch, November 1816; Mackenzie to Loch, 14–11–1816, 16–11–1816; Sellar to Mackenzie, 16–11–1816; Loch to Lady Stafford, 28–11–1816, 6–12–1816, 8–12–1816; Loch to Sellar, 3–12–1816.

1817.[8] Its administration was very selective. None was gratuitous, all was to be paid for by labour. The coastal settlers were given first priority, followed by direct tenants in the interior. No relief was given to sub-tenants who, said Loch, were the responsibility of the tacksmen—'it is only common justice that those who are the occasion of such a population being created and multiplied, and who in better years derive all the advantage from their existence, should in the years of scarcity contribute to feed them and feel some of the disadvantages arising from too numerous a population.' It is also clear that anyone who had resisted the authority of the estate, especially sheep thieves and whisky smugglers, were refused relief and evicted for failure to pay rent. Famine put extraordinary power into the hands of the estate administrators.

In July 1817 Loch saw the effects of the dearth at first hand. He told Lord Stafford that 'during the last fortnight there has existed among some classes of the people the most extreme distress, many families having subsisted entirely on cockles, having already pawned all their blankets to the fishermen for fish. Such is the want of food that they came down in the evening, slept all night upon the shore to be ready for the arrival of the boats in the morning.' Cattle prices had fallen catastrophically and many of the animals had become too thin to sell. Loch was affected by the spectacle and ordered charitable allowances to the most distressed.[9]

Loch admitted that there was 'much dissatisfaction in the country because the quantity of meal has not been greater and that it has not been distributed with greater profuseness.' He rejected this criticism saying that the people had failed to sell their cattle when prices were high and they had refused to accept a more secure existence in the fishing villages. The basic problem, said Loch, was that the interior tenants 'had too liberal supplies in former years and the custom of importing meal for them annually, has tended to increase their numbers, their idleness and their attachment to their mountain spots'. For the future, Loch told the ministers of Sutherland, Lord Stafford would not supply the market—it would be left to private merchants—'the people . . . are never so well or so cheaply supplied as by fair and open competition between rival traders.'[10]

[8] Barron, op. cit., I, 168.
[9] SC, Loch to Mackay, 5–4–1817; Sellar to Loch, 22–3–1817; Loch to Lord Stafford, 22–7–1817; Loch to Sellar, 1–4–1817.
[10] SC, Sellar to Loch, November 1816; Sellar to Lady Stafford, 16–11–1816; Loch to Mackenzie, 5–11–1816, 25–11–1816; Mackenzie to Loch, 6–12–1816.

The destitutions of 1808, 1812 and 1817 gave the most fundamental justification for the clearance policies. Loch told Brougham that the people of the interior had been dying of starvation and that Lord Stafford had spent £13,000 on their relief. By contrast 'the people who have been lotted out upon the coast were ... in good plight and condition ... and paid their rents and added to the wealth of the community.' Similarly, the new factor, Suther, reported that the herring fishermen of Assynt paid their rents well, 'are in general well clothed and look healthy', while 'the people in the interior are quite the reverse and so poor that Mr. Gunn tells me he cannot get a farthing of money from them.' In Assynt, he said, the coastland was fertile, there was no mildew, and there were herrings 'at their door 8 months of the year, cod and ling at no great distance'—and in the interior 'they will starve and occupy land that a rent may be got for.' Lady Stafford was equally certain of the lesson of the latest famine: 'I should think the experience', she wrote, 'must do something with the people themselves in convincing them of the impossibility in the present state of the world of such a system of society continuing.' And so the plans for the great clearances of 1819–20 were pressed forward.[11]

The new clearances affected many parts of the Sutherland estate, but Strathnaver was again the most important case. From the upper Naver district (Grubmore and Syre) the people were to be moved to a proposed fishing community near the mouth of the river, and to lots extending along the northern extremity of the estate (from Farr Kirk to Bighouse). The inhabitants were given virtually two years notice; the lots were marked out well in advance; rent-free occupation was allowed for the period. The cleared land was to be added to Sellar's sheep farm and, to facilitate the resettlement, a new ground officer was sought—'a very active person who is not a native of the country, and who will be made to do his duty'. Other clearances were planned for the east and west coasts of Sutherland. Much of the northern coastal land was resurveyed—largely because in the earlier survey, by Roy, the rents had been 'calculated ... on the idea they were to be paid from the profits of smuggling'—in 1816 Sellar had claimed that more than 25 per cent of the total estate rent 'depended

[11] SC, Lady Stafford to Loch, November 1816; Loch to Lady Stafford, 21–6–1817; Loch to Sutherland Ministers, 29–9–1817; Suther to Loch, 28–10–1817; Loch to Brougham, 27–12–1819. Barron, op. cit., I, 29–7–1819.

on illicit distillation and the sale of black cattle'. Loch gave express instructions that rents of the coastal lots were to be made low enough to avoid dependence on whisky. The lots were also to be 'so small as to prevent their making any considerable part of their rent by selling a beast, their rent must not depend on that.' It was necessary, he said, to 'induce' the people to 'embark heartily' in fishing. At the same time, Loch wrote beseeching letters to Suther, to avoid haste, to take two years if necessary, to make the rents 'as moderate as your duty to the landlord and the real interest of the tenant will permit', and to give the people not even the slightest excuse for complaint. 'When you find any obstinacy in those who are to be moved and who owe money', Loch told Suther, 'you can manage by showing them that if they go quietly they may both get a cheaper lot and be excused their arrears ... I consider we must go on every year getting the interior free of the people ... the state of arrears they have got into gives us the right to do so.' Accumulated rent arrears on the estate had been £16,319 at the end of 1816 and they were rising rapidly.[12]

In March 1818 Loch received a letter from the Rev. David Mackenzie which questioned virtually all the premises of Loch's plan. It was true, he said, that the people of Strathnaver had suffered calamities during the famines which could well recur, and that they were grateful for Lord Stafford's generous relief. But, he insisted, the present coastside people had been equally afflicted by the dearth. Moreover, the coastal lands (excepting Strathy) were 'already thoroughly inhabited' as a consequence of Sellar's previous clearances—further removals would render the people 'more than ever indebted to the bounty of the landlord'. The coastal lands were extremely rugged, devoid of manure, and incapable of improvement for corn; the coastline (unlike the south-east) was rocky and dangerous and the people 'ignorant of seafarming their supplies from the Ocean'; they would have to build houses and boats and learn the art of fishing—and many of the people were simply too old. Mackenzie could not bring himself, in his pulpit, to tell the 220 families to be affected that the removal would 'be for their advantage'. Loch

[12] SC, Gordon to Sellar, 3–10–1817; Sellar to Loch, 3–10–1817; Lady Stafford to Loch, 11–8–1817; Mackay to Loch, 22–11–1817; Loch to Lady Stafford, 3–11–1817, 1–12–1817, 30–5–1818; Loch to Mackay, 8–11–1817; Loch to Morton, 1–5–1818; Loch to Suther, 3–11–1817, 9–12–1817, 16–12–1817, 25–12–1817, 7–2–1818, 8–2–1818; Suther to Loch, 6–12–1817, 22–2–1818; Loch to Marshall, 2–10–1817.

replied calmly that the proposed clearance was 'not undertaken in the mere wantonness of power'—it had been most thoroughly considered, with the benefit of the people foremost in the minds of the Stafford family. Even if he accepted Mackenzie's contention, Loch reasoned, it was a matter of indifference whether Lord Stafford supported the people on the coast or among the hills—and he would at least derive rent in the latter case, from sheep farmers in the hills. But, he said, the people on the coast would support themselves—not by corn, but by potatoes and fishing; he did not expect the old men to take to the sea, but he could think of no reason why the young should not do so. Loch asked Mackenzie to tell the people plainly that the plan would proceed and 'that they must make the best of the ensuing summer.'[13]

The summer of 1817 was a very favourable prelude to the clearances —cattle and sheep prices were relatively high and fishing on the north and east coasts produced record catches. In Strathnaver, however, the crops were again poor and when the people of Badinloch sent a petition concerning their poverty, Loch commented that it perfectly substantiated the case for their removal to the coast. In Langdale the tacksman Robert Gordon was compelled to relinquish his lease as a result of his accumulated arrears and he made preparation to emigrate with many of his people. Some of the interior tenants expressed a preference to leave the estate altogether rather than take their coastal lots, and they were told that their rent arrears would be ignored if they signed a voluntary declaration to relinquish all further claim on the estate. Loch estimated that 425 families would be removed on Whitsunday 1819 and 475 in 1820. In 1818 there was considerable reluctance to accept the resettlement— in Kildonan many of the people believed that Lady Stafford would reverse the policy before the ejection. There was an 'indescribable aversion' to the lots chalked out on the moors in the south-east at Dornoch and Evelix—which Loch admitted were in poor condition. The good arable land was reserved for the larger tenants. The lots at Helmsdale and Brora proved more attractive—largely because of the wider employment opportunities. It is also clear that previous lots at Helmsdale and on the north coast were being subdivided on Loch's instructions—in order to create more lots, and to compel the people to fish. 'Cultivation and fishing *cannot* be combined', asserted

[13] SC, Mackenzie to Loch, 17–2–1818, 19–3–1818; Loch to Mackenzie, 17–2–1818, 20–3–1818.

Loch. And although the people were showing few signs of moving to their new lots, Suther was able to report that he had experienced no resistance; the people were 'inoffensive and timidly pliant rather than otherwise' and 'the Ministers appear to look upon the changes quite coolly.'

Lady Stafford viewed the forthcoming evictions as the end of the phase of large-scale improvements. Expenditure had been too great, and she hoped that Loch would be 'able to close that Chapter in future'. She spoke of Lord Stafford's good-natured liberality in financing the projects, but she was perturbed that the financial returns were still inadequate to meet the current expenses of the estate. Loch, for his part, continued to reiterate the propriety of the policy, that the recurrence of destitution would be averted, and that the changes were dictated by the kindest feelings for the people. Loch told Sellar that steady progress in Sutherland would render 'the estate a very different thing to what it has been. I trust soon they will be the most distinguished tenantry in the north and the wealthiest.' He also told Sellar that 'you Highland gentlemen will make a fortune if these times continue', and that within two years most of the lotters would be safe on the shore. Sellar, who was rapidly expanding his sheep-farming operations into the estate of Lord Reay, was confident. He rejoiced in the fact that 'the common people are so effectively cowed that . . . I have . . . lost only one sheep by theft!' However, by the end of 1818 trouble was already brewing and Loch was again worried that the people were being kept in a state of irritation by agitators.[14]

In March 1819 Suther reported that most of the people of the interior were avidly taking up their coastal lots. All was well. But in April Loch (who was in London) heard the news that the constables attending the clearances had burnt down the houses of some of the recalcitrant tenants in the hills of Strathbrora. Loch was angered—it was a measure, he wrote, 'which I thought would never be acceded to, after the well-founded complaints which this conduct on the part of Mr. Sellar created [in 1814]. I can see no necessity for such a

[14] SC, Lady Stafford to Loch, 12–11–1817; Loch to Lady Stafford, 8–1–1819; Loch to Suther, 18–10–1817, 1–5–1818, 8–5–1818, 18–5–1818, 25–5–1818, 13–11–1818; Loch to Sellar, 4–11–1818, 1–5–1818; Loch to Wemmys, 3–12–1818; Mackay to Loch, 13–4–1818, 4–6–1818; Sellar to Loch, 13–4–1818, 19–6–1818; Suther to Loch, 23–4–1818, 24–4–1818, 17–5–1818, 26–5–1818, 26–11–1818; Gunn to Loch, 6–7–1818; Loch to Gilchrist, 8–6–1818.

measure having been resorted to; besides, I believe the custom of the country gives the people the property in roof timber.' The new burnings had provoked a well-founded 'animadversion' which Loch considered extremely unfortunate.[15]

Suther defended the action. He said that the removal had to be completed by 26 May so as to give the sheep farmers clear possession. Without the burnings, this condition could not have been fulfilled— it was 'a step rendered absolutely necessary by the apparent fixed determination of many not to move, and also to prevent them from erecting other huts ... which could not be otherwise prevented.' In Strathbrora 'a spirit of determined resistence was evident'; over forty persons had assembled to check the evictors, but Suther 'scolded and threatened them heartily' and they submitted. The following day their houses were destroyed—for, if the timbers had remained unconsumed by fire, the tenants would have continued to 'nestle in some part of the hills'. The people had been compensated for the loss of the timber, it having been valued by a 'sworn Appreciator'. Suther added that the reception lots at Helmsdale and Brora were six to twelve acres and the tenants were promised £5 per acre to improve them.[16] They were given inflated prices for their cattle, many had a whole year rent-free, and their arrears and meal debts had been written off. Fishing on the coast would be highly productive. Everything, said Suther, had been accomplished legally and with humanity.[17]

During the year of 1819, Suther and his under-agents achieved the removal of 704 families, 'nearly 4,000 souls, from eight parishes'. There had been no incidents of active resistance, but many families stayed in the hills until the last moment. A few returned to the hills and built huts with timber which had not been burnt in the fires. Captain Kenneth Mackay, who had assisted in the clearance, was gratified to report that 'my poor countrymen have acted in submission to the laws, and deference to the rights of their superiors. Many are going to America—as many to Caithness—and several to Glasgow.' Loch said that it was better for the people that they went to America, but since American emigration created a 'vulgar

[15] SC, Suther to Loch, 19–3–1819, 1–4–1819; Loch to Suther, 27–5–1819. The literary evidence leaves no doubt that fire was employed in these Sutherland clearances.
[16] On the operation of this system see the evidence of a satisfied removee, George Macleod in Poor Law Inquiry (Scotland) 1844, appendix, part II, 293.
[17] SC, Suther to Loch, 12–5–1819, 26–5–1819, 3–6–1819, 5–6–1819, 9–6–1819.

clamour' he was glad that more went to Caithness. Loch accepted Suther's explanation of the use of fire—that it could not 'be helped however much I could have wished it otherwise'. He assured Captain Mackay that he would never undervalue 'the pang that the people must have felt in leaving their homes', and he hoped that a greater proportion of the removees would settle on the coastal lots. Loch denied emphatically that he had given way to a 'rash and ill considered system, it is too serious a matter and the happiness of so many of my fellow creatures was not to be trifled with.' Referring to the current emigration, Loch told Suther it was 'a curious feature of the character and history of the Highlander—that he should when moved from his particular Glen prefer going to a worse or as bad a country at a distance and pay a higher rent, than remain on the shores of his own home.'[18]

What happened to the people removed from the mountainous interior at Whitsun 1819? Suther prepared the following analysis:

TABLE 1. *Sub-tenants and persons paying no rent removed at Whit-sunday 1819*

	Removals	Settled on estate	Settled on adjoining estates	Settled in the neighbouring counties	Emigrated	Uncertain where settled	Total left the estate
Tenants	2882	1974	195	604	61	48	908
Sub-tenants and persons paying no rent	449	330	31	57	22	9	119
Totals	3331	2304	226	661	83	57	1027

Suther explained that many who resettled in Caithness had become sub-tenants to a Dr Henderson who gave them five to twenty acres of arable land with stretches of hillgrazing for cattle—the latter being the crucial reason for their departure from the Sutherland estate. They received no lease and rents were high. Suther had 'lately found out that the people in the hills all consider themselves *farmers*

[18] SC, Loch to Suther, 3–6–1819, 3–4–1819, 8–5–1819, 18–5–1819, 8–6–1819; Loch to Mackay, 15–5–1819, 8–6–1819; Mackay to Loch, 20–5–1819; Suther to Loch, 29–5–1819, 5–6–1819; Gunn to Loch, 2–6–1819.

and took it as a degradation to be compared to Labourers or Fishermen'. Patrick Sellar, always ready with gratuitous advice, commented characteristically that 'Upon the whole Skibo and Caithness are two "receptacles" and they have unloaded you a great deal of trash, of which you are well rid.'[19]

Predictably enough, the new burning incidents in Sutherland elicited a public outcry which raged through 1819 and into 1820. Loch told Suther:

you have no idea the sensation the story of the burnings has made, one never to be obliterated and which no explanation can help . . . I wish to God you had only asked my opinion on the subject . . . the impression is as bad as in Sellar's time, and all the thought, arrangement and management which I have bestowed the last two years on this matter, and which I fondly hoped was to make my administration of the Sutherland affairs valued by the public has been cast away.

Suther had blundered.

The adverse publicity generated vigorous agitation within Sutherland and then extended its impact to opinion in Edinburgh and London. Virulent attacks on the Sutherland policy appeared in the *Scotsman* and the *Morning Chronicle*. Sir John Sinclair, who was generally favourable to the policy, believed that the clamour would inevitably be taken up in Parliament. Loch attempted to counter the ubiquitous 'misrepresentations' by writing many letters to influential people, and he began preparations for the publication of a second and much enlarged edition of his *Account*.

The main contention in Loch's somewhat despairing defence was that it was 'certainly rather hard that a nobleman who has not since 1811 touched any rents of an estate of £20,000 except to lay it out on the property itself for the amelioration of the country and its inhabitants . . . should be supposed capable of doing a harsh or cruel act to his tenantry'. Lord Stafford had spent 'many thousands' beyond the rent roll, and the vast majority of the removees were resettled on his estate; other landlords, like Lord Moray, evicted without compensation and without lots. At least Loch's old friend, Henry Brougham, was convinced of the case for the policy—he had never seen such a strong case, and, if necessary, he was prepared to vindicate Loch's measures in Parliament—'you know', he told Loch, 'I would not even for your sake, do any such thing if I had my

[19] SC, Suther to Loch, 3-2-1820, 23-6-1820; Sellar to Loch, 22-6-1819.

doubts—but I really think Lord and Lady Stafford *have* been ill-treated.' Loch also appears to have convinced (at least partially) both Wilberforce and McCulloch of the expediency of the policy.[20]

Loch believed that the clamour was the unhappy result of a blunder which had been inflated into an atrocity by Highland demagogy. Soon after Suther's 1819 evictions a very ominous situation developed in Sutherland which had many of the signs of an incipient popular revolt against the established order. It had been led by Thomas Dudgeon of Fearn in Ross. Dudgeon was the self-styled Secretary of a body called the Sutherland Transatlantic Friendly Society which existed ostensibly to examine the conditions of the common people and to raise money to promote emigration, apparently to Florida. In June and July 1819 Dudgeon (aided by a teacher and a publican) held meetings attended by more than 1,000 people at Meikle Ferry. It seems that extravagant promises were made to the people who were asked to subscribe 6d. and 1s. to promote the Association. Before long Dudgeon had prepared a petition to the Regent and to Parliament which asked for either 'a piece of muir to settle on' or aid for emigration. It complained of the inhumanity of the Sutherland policies. Loch alleged that nine out of ten of the people who signed the petition could not read English and did not know what they were signing. Dudgeon, he believed, was a swindler who was actuated 'by spleen and disappointment at not being appointed factor on the Sutherland estate'.

Whatever were Dudgeon's motives, he was able to rouse popular expectation in Sutherland. In August 1819 he published attacks on Suther claiming that hundreds of houses had been burned in the evictions, that the church had been debarred from giving the people shelter, that the lots provided were totally inadequate, and that atrocities had been committed. He claimed explicitly that Suther, by setting fire to houses in the hills, 'was to all human conception the direct and immediate cause of the delirium and death of Matheson's wife who is known to have been in a state of pregnancy at the time'. This last allegation was too vaguely worded to be actionable; it had not been supported by the precognition, and Loch believed it completely false—Matheson's house was still standing; it had not

[20] SC, Loch to Suther, 18–7–1819; Loch to Grosvenor, 19–7–1819; Loch to Brougham, 16–7–1819; Sinclair to Loch, 17–8–1819; Brougham to Loch, 30–12–1819; MacCulloch to Loch, 25–3–1820, 27–3–1820; Sinclair to Dudgeon, 29–7–1819; Loch to Mackenzie, 31–12–1819.

been burned, 'the woman was not in labour being too old for children', and she had died of an old complaint.[21]

While the allegations of cruelty were reiterated, Dudgeon's organization grew in confidence and he despatched representatives to remote parts of the county. Captain K. Mackay, who was to take some of the land cleared at Whitsun 1820, was gravely concerned. The people were about to combine to resist all law and order, he said, and were 'determined to have blood for blood in the struggle of keeping possession ... If I would not be considered by Mr. Loch as inconsistent and perhaps acting a dubious part—I would readily relinquish all prospect of getting these lands.' Loch, although he advised Mackay not to be intimidated, was prepared to believe that a sinister conspiracy was in the making, and that Dudgeon was 'connected with the numerous Radicals in the south'. Loch instructed Suther to send men to 'check' on the proceedings of Dudgeon's Association—he was perturbed by 'the present temper of the people's minds' and realized that intervention was rapidly becoming inevitable.

Dudgeon advertised a meeting 'to raise a loyal force for the government ... in a military capacity'—ostensibly to repudiate the 'wicked aspersions' that they were 'thieves and rebels'. The Magistrates of Sutherland (mainly landlords, sheep farmers and factors) immediately warned the people that the meeting was illegal. Apparently only about a hundred people assembled on the day appointed—4 January 1820—and Dudgeon himself failed to attend. The Seditious Meetings Bill was proclaimed, and the 'clause intimating the punishment in the case of their disobedience (7 years transportation) being read the people set off ... as fast as they could. Many of them cursing Dudgeon for not coming forward.'[22]

Dudgeon had been thwarted, at least temporarily. Shortly after-

[21] SC, Mackenzie to Loch, 20–6–1819; Sellar to Loch, 22–6–1819, 19–11–1819; Loch to Suther, 18–7–1819, 9–8–1819; Suther to Loch, 11–6–1819, 21–6–1819, 24–7–1819, 2–10–1819; Grant to Loch, 22–8–1819; Macleod to Loch, 14–8–1819; Dudgeon to Suther, 30–8–1819; Mackenzie to Loch, 30–9–1819; Loch to Lady Stafford, 6–8–1819, 23–9–1819; Loch to Mackenzie, 23–9–1819. Home Office (Scotland) Correspondence, RH 2/4, 127, f. 22.

[22] SC, Gunn to Loch, 27–9–1819, 26–11–1819, 18–12–1819, 25–1–1820; K. Mackay to Suther, 28–10–1819; Mackenzie to Loch, 10–11–1819, 27–12–1819; Loch to Gunn, 17–11–1819; Loch to Lady Stafford, 9–11–1819; Loch to Suther, 30–11–1819; Loch to Mackenzie, 31–12–1819; Suther to Loch, 2–1–1820, 4–1–1820. The *Scotsman*, 8–1–1820. On the connection with Radicals in central Scotland see Home Office (Scotland) Correspondence, RH 2/4, f. 255–6, 284. I am grateful to Mr Peter Holt for this reference. The *Military Register*, 4–8–1819, 24–11–1819, 29–12–1819, 5–1–1820, 19–1–1820.

wards the Association was disbanded and the subscribers lost their money. Loch was able to tell Brougham that fears of a Sutherland '*Rebellion*' were groundless. The people of Assynt, initially great supporters of Dudgeon, had sent a deputation to 'say that they were sorry for the part they had acted, but that they were ignorant and had been deluded by those whom they thought were respectable persons'. Even the Minister Sage (father of Donald Sage of Resolis), an important hostile critic of the estate policies, regarded Dudgeon as an impostor and had asked Suther to 'use your best measures to disappoint this Radical Demagogue'. Any known 'Dudgeonites' were summarily evicted from the estate. Twenty years later Dudgeon threatened to publish allegedly incriminating evidence against the Sutherland family. He demanded £30,000 from the family, to be distributed publicly, at his pleasure, among the sufferers of the removal policy—he would regard this as a mark of repentance and would desist from publication. Loch regarded the demand as conclusive evidence of Dudgeon's insanity.[23]

In August 1819 Loch had travelled north to Sutherland with Lord Gower and discovered that there had been 'only nine ejectments, and the people, except those that would rather they had not been turned out, are well pleased with what has been done for them.' He was delighted with the coastal villages—at Helmsdale he saw 'about 2,000 people most actively and usefully employed and very happy—those persons engaged in the Herring fishing there will make a very handsome profit and circulate a great deal of money through the country.' He wrote with irony that he had been in the county 'some days as had Lord Gower and we are neither burnt nor hanged'. In December 1819 it seems a number of evictees who had fled into Ross asked permission to return to Sutherland. This was interpreted as a triumphant answer to the current clamour, and unquestionable proof that the conditions in Sutherland were better than in other counties. In the same month the marriage of a daughter of the Stafford family gave the opportunity of providing the new settlers 'some whisky to drink her health' which, said Loch, 'will obliterate all those little heart burnings which the removals must, and naturally so, occasion'.[24]

[23] SC, Loch to Brougham, 27–12–1819; Suther to Loch, 15–1–1820; Loch to Suther, 22–1–1820, 27–1–1820; Mackenzie to Loch, 13–2–1841; Loch to Mackenzie, 15–2–1841.

[24] SC, Gunn to Loch, 31–12–1819, 11–3–1820; Loch to Lady Stafford, 15–8–1819, 10–12–1819; Loch to Grant, 17–8–1819; Loch to Gunn, 17–1–1820.

Yet there could be no erasing the impression of harshness that the word 'burnings' engendered. The issue even affected the county election contest for Staffordshire in March 1820, when Gower's opponents circulated the story that his father had burned the fishermen's huts (sic) in Scotland, and wherever Gower appeared the people cried 'Fire'. Loch commented ruefully that he did not think 'there is a single individual not connected with us, and not all of them, but what believe thoroughly in the people having been burned out of their houses.' Loch, though his conviction was unimpaired, was oppressed by the weight of public opinion. He looked anxiously to the conclusion of the removals of Whitsun 1820 when 401 families were to be removed, and it was decided to delay thereafter all further clearance plans for eight years—during which time 'the sheep farmers will continue discontented, and the straths full of sloth and smuggling'. Loch's frustration was profound; 'the people', he said, 'labour under great disadvantage—they are ignorant of our language, by nature and education suspicious, we cannot mend them accordingly.' The estate management was instructed to make every effort to renew the ancient feeling between landlord and tenant. 'I never supposed the removals could be liked by the people', wrote Loch, 'their necessity alone made it . . . imperative.' Loch explicitly prohibited the use of fire in all future Sutherland removals 'in any way whatever or at any time'.[25]

Two months before Suther's 1820 removals there had been an outburst of violent popular opposition to clearances which threatened to become a general rebellion against landlord policy. It occurred on the very border of the Sutherland estate—at Culrain in Ross on the properties of Munro of Novar. In February 1820 officers attempting to serve a notice of removal had been set upon by 'men in women's clothes . . . and threatened with the severest corporal punishment if they ever returned'. Three weeks later a posse of armed constables and militia had tried to enforce the law—but were confronted by a crowd of 500 people, summoned by 'the blowing of horns', and were pelted with stones. The posse was put to flight, especially by the women—'these women paid no regard to the fire arms, but rushed through knocking about them—one woman was shot and it is supposed mortally, another was badly wounded in the mouth and

---

[25] SC, Loch to Suther, 25–11–1819, 26–3–1820. For a description of a cleared village by a writer in sympathy with the Sutherland regime, see J. MacCulloch, *The Highlands and Western Isles of Scotland* (1824), II, 455.

eye by a bayonet, and a young lad was shot in the legs which immediately took him down . . . they did not regard the soldiers, daring
them to shoot as they would sooner suffer in that manner than
remove.' The rebellion was generally imputed to the influence of
Dudgeon. There were fears that a general rising, especially in
Sutherland, was imminent. At Unapool, in Assynt, a Sheriff's party
had attempted to evict a Dudgeonite and was 'beset by a party of
women who rushed on us like furies'—but the eviction was eventually
accomplished. The Culrain incident subsided within a few weeks.
The Sutherland estate factors were privately critical of the Culrain
removals, believing that the people had a case; the landlord was in
fact forced to a minor compromise. But the Sutherland factors
insisted that the disturbances were totally unconnected with circumstances in Sutherland. However, in June a further riot occurred
—even closer to the Sutherland estate—at The Gruids. There the
landlord had attempted to turn the people out 'without any place to
go'. The officer serving the summons was attacked—again by
women, 'for the men kept aloof . . . the women stripped him naked,
bound and began actually to burn him and would have ultimately
drowned him in the Shin had he not been rescued by a female more
humane than the others, his back is much burned in two parts and
much pinched all over the body.' It was, apparently, widely held that
'a woman can do anything with impunity.' As for the officer, it was
reported that he became a cripple.[26]

The haunting fear of 'blood for blood' had almost become a
reality when Suther began his second series of removals in May 1820.
Yet, somehow, the crisis passed. For the moment the violence did
not spread into the Sutherland estate. Suther appears to have accomplished his major removals without police assistance, and he was able
to tell Lady Stafford that 'the removals . . . have all been effected in
the most peaceable and easy manner. The people have behaved most
excellently.' A relatively minor removal remained for the following
year.

This, however, brought violence directly into the Sutherland
estate. In March 1821 the sub-tenants of Achness in Clyne rioted

[26] SC, Gunn to Loch, 18–3–1820, 4–4–1820; K. Mackay to Loch, 4–3–1820;
Suther to Loch, 3–3–1820, 5–3–1820, 15–3–1820, 19–3–1820, 26–3–1820, 27–3–
1820; J. Mackay to Loch, 11–3–1820; Mackenzie to Loch, 30–3–1820; Loch to
Suther, 9–10–1819, 23–3–1820; Kennedy to Loch, 15–4–1820. See also Loch's
Account (1820), xix-xx.

against an attempt to serve notice of removal upon them. Suther branded them as 'a turbulent set, complete Dudgeonites', and a vital link in a chain of smuggling areas. They followed the current example of resistance in Caithness and the Gruids where a sheriff's officer had again been 'stripped . . . to the skin'. Loch believed that there was 'a regular, organised system of resistance to civil power' in the northern Highlands, and he fully supported the introduction of fusiliers from Fort George who eventually restored law and order, 'like magic'. Several of the rioters were imprisoned, and the people were reported as much 'crestfallen'. The removals continued. The troops were retained for several weeks. Many of the Achness people, who had claimed that they had nowhere to go, refused their allocated lots and made preparation to migrate. Loch, who blamed the outbreak on the previously unchecked resistance, instructed Suther 'to be firm; and not vindictive' towards the rioters, and the succeeding removal was carried through in relative calm. In June 1821, Suther, with a sigh of relief, wrote that Strathbrora was 'effectively cleared of all its turbulent people. The removings were completed . . . and the houses demolished without a single word, indeed no business of this description had yet been done so quietly . . . Some are off for Caithness, but the bulk of them seem to have a wish to go to America . . . We are now, I think, settled for a few years.' As a sequel, there were allegations of cruelty—for example, Gordon Ross, a teacher, claimed that a drunken factor had turned out his children, suffering from whooping cough, into the north-east wind, with the result that one child had died. Ross later made 'the most ample recantation of his charge'. Even so Lord Stafford thought 'that Suther is not free from blame in this business'.[27]

In June 1821 Loch was able to say that the current round of removals had been completed. Looking back, he recorded that such an extensive arrangement had never previously been effected 'with so little individual misery'. The operation had been expensive and

[27] SC, Suther to Loch, 14–2–1820, 3–4–1820, 29–4–1820, 15–6–1820, 30–6–1820, 27–3–1821, April 1821, 27–5–1821, 4–6–1821; Gunn to Loch, 8–6–1820, 26–3–1821; Suther to Lady Stafford, 2–8–1820, 27–5–1820; Loch to Lady Stafford, 22–6–1820, 17–4–1821; Loch to Suther, 22–6–1820, 30–3–1821, 31–7–1821; Mackenzie to Loch, 14–8–1820, 20–3–1821, 30–3–1821, 31–3–1821, 14–4–1821; Grant to Loch, 17–4–1821; Loch to Grant, 5–4–1821; Loch to Mackenzie, 21–3–1821, 23–3–1821; Ross to Loch, 13–8–1821, 22–8–1821, 24–8–1821; Loch to Lord Stafford, 30–3–1821; Ross to Solicitor General, 15–4–1821; Gower to Loch, 20–7–1821; Lady Stafford to Loch, 23–7–1821; Loch to Lord Stafford, 28–7–1821, 19–8–1821.

the estate failed to yield any net income between 1811 and 1820. The most insistent demand after 1820 was to compel 'expenditure to fall considerably within the income of the Sutherland estate'.[28] The clearances had ended in the Achness Riots but, for the most part, resistance was passive. The Sutherland policy depended on threatened and actual compulsion; at various times between 1819 and 1821 the ordinary processes of civil power had proved inadequate to safeguard the implementation of landlord policy. However, the resistance was sporadic, unco-ordinated and virtually unarmed—the likelihood of a Highland rebellion was small in this dispersed and rural setting. An atmosphere of suspicion and hostility, and lack of co-operation, characterized the environment in which Loch attempted to promote the plan of economic development.

The Sutherland clearances almost certainly accelerated the movement for widespread emigration. Nevertheless, the population of the county continued to grow until 1831—although the increase was extremely small when compared with neighbouring Caithness. Emigration reduced the natural population increase.[29]

The clearance policy was designed to resettle population within the estate. It was not intended to compel emigration. However, during the acute distress of 1816–17, emigration appeared to offer one answer to the immediate problem. Sellar, in particular, believed that subsidizing emigration would be cheaper than resettling the people on the coasts. 'Would not Lord Stafford throw out some bait', he asked, 'to induce them to emigrate to America and carry a swarm of their dependants with them?' He recommended that Stafford purchase land in Nova Scotia (to be called New Sutherland) in order to induce people to emigrate from the interior. Loch believed that the magnitude of the distress required serious consideration 'of affording some of the mountaineers a comfortable settlement at the Cape or New South Wales or in Van Diemen's Land'. He wrote, 'I almost hope this summer may incline some people to emigrate.'

His attitude was significantly ambivalent. The open encouragement of emigration would imply a partial confession that the resettlement schemes were inadequate. Moreover, the Stafford family

---

[28] SC, Loch to Gower, 3–10–1820.
[29] H. Hamilton declares that 'From Sutherland alone 15,000 left between 1811 and 1820', but this figure is incredible since the total population in 1811 was only 23,629: *Industrial Revolution*, 72.

shared the general landlord aversion to the notion of losing population. Lady Stafford tentatively agreed that it would be desirable to assist young people who did not 'come under the list of useful inhabitants . . . to go off altogether rather than offer them lots'. Loch told Lord Bathurst of the population problem in the straths—emigration was difficult because of the inaccessibility of the area, while the population delayed the introduction of sheep farming. In wartime the Highland soldiers had been able to assist their families to exist in the hills; in peacetime it was increasingly difficult. Loch admitted that many would prefer to emigrate rather than exist on the coastal lots. [30]

But Loch did not regard emigration as a major solution—it was too expensive, for there were simply too many people. The real solution was to enable the people to support themselves on their coastal lots—in part by encouraging the cultivation of potatoes. In 1818 Loch told an itinerant migration agent that Stafford 'by no means wishes them to go, but rather they would take up their lots'. During the 1819 clearances, he warned Suther—'I regret . . . to find . . . that there is a very great migration from the estate to America and Caithness—*provided* this has arisen from any want of lots, or pains to have them settled upon them . . . I think at times you care less for getting them to remain than I could wish.' [31]

There were formidable problems facing people wishing to emigrate. The sea-passage to America was between £7 and £8. To receive Treasury or private assistance the people often had to demonstrate that they possessed a sum of at least £20. Yet the people most desirous of emigrating were those closest to destitution, possessing no assets and burdened with arrears of rent. Those with wage employment as agricultural labourers could rarely earn more than 2s. per day. Any offers of emigration assistance inevitably brought an eager response—as demonstrated by Dudgeon's schemes. Ship's captains and emigration agents scouted the county for potential migrants—frequently, the people pledged themselves to go and later changed their minds or found they could not raise the money. The Sutherland estate gave indirect assistance by waiving rent-arrears and giving good prices for migrants' timber and cattle—on the

[30] SC, Sellar to Loch, 27–10–1816; Loch to Lady Stafford, 28–11–1816, 27–12–1816; Loch to Lord Stafford, 20–10–1817; Loch to Sellar, 2–4–1817; Loch to Bathurst, 3–12–1817.
[31] SC, Loch to Suther, 7–12–1819; Loch to Gordon, 22–11–1818.

condition that the people relinquished all future claim on the estate. But the initiative came from the people themselves or from agents unconnected with the estate. The attitude of the estate was typified by the agent who wrote, 'I do not interfere in encouraging or preventing them.' In 1821, for instance, Loch was prepared to admit that emigration was a natural outlet for an increasingly super-abundant population—and 'the happiest thing for themselves and for the country'—but the organization of emigration was left in the hands of private individuals for, as Loch said, 'if it was known that we thought it better for them to go they would never move.'

Widespread accounts of the destitution and atrocities associated with the clearances brought offers of migration assistance from outside the county—in 1822 'The Expatriated Highlanders of Sutherland' in India offered aid to Joseph Gordon in organizing emigration. Any Sutherlander who could raise one third of his passage and who would solemnly swear that he was destitute and had been removed in the cause of sheep farming, was to be given assistance to Pictou. Gordon reported that the response had been too great—particularly from those 'who cannot contribute even the small portion I have required'. In fact, Lord Stafford gave £500 to assist the scheme—rather hesitantly since it was believed that Gordon had exaggerated the poor condition of the people on the coasts, and Loch was unhappy to lose any of the industrious lotters. It is clear, however, that settlers on the coast migrated as well as the interior tenants. Many of them did not participate in the fishing enterprises and were 'very miserable and would willingly embrace an opportunity of emigrating if they had the means'. Successful fishing families in Assynt migrated to America in 1820 because repeated phases of clearances had congested their settlements. Yet, as late as 1829, Loch continued to emphasize that the Stafford family did not wish to facilitate emigration.[32]

Generally, the Stafford family remained aloof. They took no part except to grant rent remissions. There was no compulsion. A fundamental tenet of Loch's thinking was that sheep farms were 'perfectly compatible with retaining the ancient population of the

[32] SC, Loch to Gunn, 24–2–1820, 28–3–1820; Gunn to Loch, 11–3–1820, 4–5–1820; Loch to Gordon, 1–5–1818; Suther to Lady Stafford, 14–5–1820; J. Mackay to Loch, 9–8–1822; Loch to Suther, 25–4–1821, 18–4–1821, 14–5–1822; Loch to Mackenzie, 26–5–1821, 14–5–1822; Suther to Loch, 17–4–1821, 19–5–1822, 3–7–1822; W. Mackenzie to Loch, 11–5–1822; Loch to Edwards, 29–9–1825, D593/N341/3. The *Military Register*, 24–12–1820.

country' and no man had been removed without being provided with a lot. It was somewhat ironic that in 1841 the *Inverness Journal* attributed the current destitution to the injudicious means which were taken to prevent emigration some thirty years previously. [33]

[33] Loch, *Account* (1815), 20; Barron, op. cit., II, 28–4–1841. Andrew Kennedy, together with three other families, migrated to America from Assynt in 1809. Altogether they had possessed £700. After a journey of eight weeks to New York they pressed 200 miles into the back settlements in search of land. They had met old acquaintances who had migrated thirty years earlier—'but so miserably poor as scarcely able to afford them quarters'. The inhospitable and heavily-wooded land cost $5 an acre—and in great disappointment the families 'returned to their native country in July 1810 as they had so little encouragement to them remaining in America from the destitute state of the people who had been settled there for many years'. Highlanders in America, said Kennedy, existed in a state of abject poverty 'and thousands of them would willingly come home if they could procure a passage' and were not nearly so comfortably settled as the coastal lotters in Sutherland. Accounts from abroad were wildly inconsistent. The migrant, often in desperation, cut through his attachments to his ancient homeland and departed for a land which was literally unknown. SC, Gunn to Grant, 26–4–1826.

XV

***

Capital, Labour and Prices in the New Economy

***

The economic policies pursued by James Loch and his predecessors in Sutherland generated an unpredicted degree of turbulence in the local economy. They were implemented in an atmosphere of compulsion and consequent disruption. Indeed, most of the literature concerned with the Sutherland policies has been preoccupied with the social injustices, to the total neglect of the more positive and constructive aspects. Yet the policy was purposely designed to accommodate the rising population in a more secure economic situation. In a sense, it was a regional development plan, in which the clearances were seen as imperative for the rehabilitation of the economy. It was an attempt to revolutionize the economy by way of planned diversification.

James Loch knew as well as anyone that a swift, radical transformation of the economy would create social problems and provoke hostility. It was his constant regret that the common people were unable to comprehend the ultimate wisdom and benefit of the plans. He acknowledged that hardships were experienced, but these he regarded as the temporary and inescapable costs of a better order of existence. He believed that the exceptional benevolence of the Stafford family had minimized the problems of dislocation. Obviously, Loch cannot be regarded as an impartial observer—but it seems reasonable to expect Loch's critics to suggest possible economic alternatives, given the prevailing circumstances. Equally desirable is some measure of the character, magnitude and results of the improvement plans as a whole. At present the relevant evidence is sparse and only the most tentative conclusions are possible.

220

One of the more persistent criticisms of the Sutherland regime has been that it was governed by rigid, doctrinaire notions derived from economic dicta. James Loch was steeped in the tradition of Adam Smith, but the relationship between the ideas of the 'economists' and the policy in practice is by no means clear. For the most part a more nebulous 'gospel of improvement' was followed—an *ad hoc* approach to the problems of the economy. Changing circumstances and a faith in technical innovation and self-help, rather than a new economic theory, determined the outlines of the Sutherland policies. Nevertheless, two elementary propositions were accepted—that the natural resources of the land should be exploited in the most appropriate economic manner (given changing techniques and market pressures), and that labour should be employed where the returns seemed to be greatest, thus involving specialization. Such was the rationale for the movement of sheep into the interior, and the people to the coast. The economy in total would be more viable, the people less vulnerable to famine. In addition, the growth of population would be held in check by restrictions on the subdivision of lots and by the encouragement of 'moral habits' in the new communities. Since the *per capita* levels of income and saving were extremely low, capital imports were essential, at least in the early stages. This function was performed by southern entrepreneurs, the government, and pre-eminently the landlord. And, although precise figures are not available, all the evidence points to an unprecedent influx of capital into the county in the early nineteenth century. The English connection of the House of Sutherland enabled the family to reverse the usual outflow of capital which attended most Highland landlordism.

The foundations of the new economy were planned and initiated in the decade before 1815—a period of extraordinarily high prices for the key commodities—wool, flax, kelp, cattle, fish, salt and coal. Young and, to a lesser extent, Loch appear to have laboured in the notion that the process of industrial development, so effectively demonstrated in Lancashire, could be transplanted into virtually any context—given a sufficient supply of capital, labour, initiative and effective communications.[1] Hence the dominant belief that the coastal economy could be fertilized with imported technology and skills.

But time was short. The foundations of the new regional economy

[1] They were not alone in this belief. See, for example, A. Irvine, *An Inquiry into the Causes and Effects of Emigration from the Highlands* (1802), 129–30.

were created in haste because they depended literally on the life of Lord Stafford. On Stafford's death the source of capital imports would be cut off. His health, never very robust, was a matter of high concern—and it helps to explain why the Sutherland policy was so rapidly executed. It was, in effect, an attempt to telescope the development of an export-based economy.

The fishing industry, set up largely on the east coast of Sutherland, was an essential part of the general scheme. It was not a new idea— in 1630, Sir Robert Gordon wrote that Strathnaver was better suited for pasture and fishing than the cultivation of corn. In the late eighteenth century many writers had championed fishing as a solution to the Highland problems. Sutherland waters were said to be abundant with white fish and herring. The establishment of commercial fishing in the county was accelerated by the introduction of southern entrepreneurs in 1813–14. The focal point of the east-coast industry was Helmsdale. It was planned as a model village and became an important reception area for evicted people. There, and at other fishing stations, especially Port Gower and Brora, curing yards, warehouses and piers were constructed, together with river dredging and harbour improvements. Population and employment rapidly increased so that, by 1840, 'Helmsdale was exerting all the centripetal influences of an active commerce of a port equipped for the steady marketing of fish.'[2] While other reception areas were less successful, Helmsdale does appear to have justified the hopes of the Sutherland management, at least until 1840.

Although the fishing industry was subject to violent fluctuation, it demonstrated long-term growth. In 1814, 148 people with 20 boats were employed at Helmsdale. One year later Loch reported from Helmsdale 'the most gratifying sight imaginable, 48 boats manned by Highlanders, in number 350 of whom 100 are from Kildonan'. The year 1818 was yet more encouraging; 17,000 barrels of herrings were caught by 142 boats, half of which were manned by natives of Sutherland; employment opportunities grew—each boat had 5 men, there were 72 coopers at work, and 568 women employed in the curing processes, earning an aggregate of £6,600—in addition to ancillary activities and boat and cottage construction; 82 vessels

[2] Gray, op. cit., 163. See also J. Viner, Introduction to J. Rae, *Life of Adam Smith* (1965 ed.), 88–101. T. Telford, *Survey and Reports of the Coasts and Central Highlands of Scotland in Autumn of 1802*, 15–17. J. Knox, *Observations on the Northern Fisheries* (1786), 144.

arrived with cargoes of salt, hoops, barrels and timber, and 73 cargoes of herring valued at more than £30,000 were cleared—to widely dispersed markets in Ireland, England, the West Indies, the Baltic and the Mediterranean. Loch was ecstatic; Helmsdale had been magically transformed into an idyllic scene of industry and 'it will in a short space of time become the first fishing station in the north and will be the centre of the population, the wealth, and the cultivation of this country.' Loch told Bradshaw that in one night the Helmsdale boats had caught 1,200 barrels—'that is about 24/- to each man for a night's work'. The boom continued and in 1819 Loch told Lady Stafford that 'Helmsdale as usual was delightful, so full of life and increasing wealth and industrious exertion . . . about 2,200 people hard at work tumbling over each other like ants'—the scene of construction, said Loch, 'put me in mind of the erection and progress of an American town'. Loch denied that there was over-crowding at Helmsdale and claimed that 'the more people I can fix on the coast the better'. When he heard that many removees were leaving the estate during the 1819 clearances, Loch told Suther, 'I certainly could have wished many more of them had settled as I fear the fisheries may be in want of hands'. In 1820 fishing at Helmsdale employed 1,714 people with 203 boats, and other stations on the north and west coasts were rising.

But after 1820 progress was very slow—partly due to erratic fish migration, partly due to adverse market pressures—the price of fish in 1822–4 was 50 per cent lower than in 1814–15, and exports to the West Indian and Baltic markets declined while Irish competition grew. Nevertheless, in 1825 a record 30,000 barrels of herring were exported from the east coast of Sutherland and, despite persistent difficulties, Helmsdale weathered several crises and, in 1841, employed 253 boats and 2,450 people. [3]

The organization of the fishing industry was marked by a clear division of function. The boats were manned independently by co-operating fishermen who sold their catch, at a price arranged at the beginning of the short season, to the fish curers. The landlord, in

[3] Gray, op. cit., 163. Loch, *Account* (1820), 129. SC, Suther to Loch, 6–8–1817, 17–10–1818, 29–12–1818; Young to Loch, 24–5–1814; Young to Stafford, June 1816; Loch to Stafford, 14–8–1815; Loch to Mackenzie, 25–6–1819; Mackay to Loch, 22–11–1817; Loch to Bradshaw, 21–8–1818, 24–10–1818; Grant to Loch, 14–7–1818; Loch to Lady Stafford, 16–8–1818, 8–8–1819; Loch to Suther, 27–11–1818; Simpson to Loch, 27–10–1824; Sellar to Stewart, 18–5–1826; D593/N/4/1/3, Charles Young to Loch, 7–11–1821.

addition to the construction of harbour facilities, provided some of the loan-capital for boats and equipment, employed advisers, and arranged competitions between the Helmsdale and Brora fishing communities. The larger entrepreneurial tasks were undertaken by southern merchants who often had direct connections with Dundee, Leith, Wick and Billingsgate. It was deliberate estate policy to attract curers to settle in Sutherland instead of Caithness. One of these men of 'capital and experience', Simpson, told Loch in 1820 that there were 'few men in Helmsdale not already part of a herring boat, even the greater part of those who have lately got allotments here from the parish of Kildonan are connected with the fishing, and many of them are well pleased to get near the place where they find employment.' But Simpson complained of a falling trend of prices and the lack of initiative of many of the natives. To counter the latter the Sutherland regime offered prizes of £20 to the best native fishermen; they tempted Fife and even Dutch fishermen to settle on the estate with inducements of ten years rent-free accommodation—in order to set an example to the natives; but, most of all, the landlord provided crofts so small that the inhabitants had little alternative but to take to the sea. The hazards were great—the evictees were highly inexperienced and there were appalling accidents. In January 1821 seven of the best Brora fishermen were lost in a storm, leaving behind twenty-three dependants.

The fishing industry promised to 'make a very handsome profit and circulate a great deal of money through the country'; and it was certainly an industry with strong backward and forward linkages which provided wide employment opportunities. It was a major pillar of the policy: it improved both the commercial and subsistence prospects of the economy. The major disadvantages were the seasonal and fickle character of the herring, and the fact that prices were determined in a market much larger than Sutherland. Loch hoped that fishing (herring *and* whitefish) would eventually become 'the constant source of employment for a great body of people', who would 'gradually get huddled into fishing villages leaving their crofts to be turned, in the natural course of things, into large farms'. He dreaded a 'crofting system' which would merely increase population at a lower level of income—and thus the prohibition of sub-letting and subdivision of land on the estate. [4]

[4] SC, Simpson to Loch, 5-1-1820; Suther to Loch, 27-9-1818, 27-12-1819, 16-7-1820, 20-1-1821; Loch to Simpson, 16-8-1818; Loch to Lady Stafford,

The falling prices after 1820 frustrated Loch's ideal solution. Efforts were made to open new markets for fish, in Portugal for example: the opening of the Caledonian Canal promised to reduce costs for sales in Ireland and south-east Scotland. But the state of the market generally discouraged, though it did not entirely prevent, further growth until after 1840. The industry did not collapse, nor did Helmsdale lose its position as a major fishing centre; but the initial momentum was lost; the labour-force in fishing at Helmsdale was smaller in 1827 than in 1820; rents were reduced; the Sutherland boats lost ground to the more specialized fishing fleets of the south. The herring fisheries suffered a further set-back in 1830 when government bounties were finally abolished. Loch, true to his free-trade principles, refused to petition against the abolition; he believed that the national industry had over-expanded (there had been a fourfold increase in the output of the fisheries between 1809 and 1828) and that the industry should find its 'natural' level of output by way of rationalization. [5]

The new coastal economy of Sutherland was not designed to be exclusively dependent upon fishing. The fisheries were promoted in conjunction with other industrial projects—especially at Brora where the Stafford family spent many thousands of pounds in an attempt to create an industrial base for the local economy. Although the Brora coal/salt deposits had been worked intermittently since the sixteenth century, Sutherland had continued to rely on imports— in addition to other basic materials such as bricks, tiles and lime. After 1811 attempts were made to render the economy not only self-sufficient but also an exporter of these products. [6] The operations were initiated under the confident direction of William Young who believed that a new era was about to dawn in 'this long forgotten

8–1–1819; Loch to Stafford, 21–11–1820; MacCulloch to Loch, 25–3–1820; Loch to MacCulloch, 25–3–1820; D5932/2/9, 'Report', 96 ff. *Pace* M. I. Adam, op. cit., 177–8.

[5] SC, Young to Loch, 28–4–1828; Miller to Loch, 6–3–1828, 15–3–1828; Loch to Miller, 11–3–1828; Gunn to Loch, 25–11–1826; Mackay to Loch, 7–1–1828; Simpson to Loch, 8–3–1823, 12–8–1823, 8–9–1823, 15–2–1824, 27–10–1824, 18–12–1824. See also M. Gray, 'Organization and growth in the east coast herring fishing, 1800–1885', in *Studies in Scottish Business History*, ed. P. L. Payne (1967).

[6] Fuel scarcity was a fundamental deficiency of the Highland economy. In 1790, for instance, petitioners from the West Highlands complained that 'the inhabitants almost perished from want of fuel, being compelled to burn their household furniture. The Aged, the Infirm, and the Children were confined to bed, having no alternative or refuge.' NLS, Melville Papers, MS. 642.

country'. Limestone was discovered near Golspie, and at Brora a wide range of activities was set in motion by a landlord functioning in the role of entrepreneur. By the middle of 1816 Young was able to report that two hundred tons of coal per week were being produced for use in salt making, lime burning, the manufacture of bricks and tiles, as well as domestic consumption and a potential export of 25 per cent of the output. Potter's clay had also been discovered and Young had visions of Sutherland potteries supplying the whole of the north and east of Scotland with china, and giving 'bread to hundreds of fine boys and girls who are gaping for work and as quick as any children I ever saw south or north'. Loch, however, was sceptical and told Young that they could never compete with 'the extent of capital, the style, and perfection of machinery in Staffordshire—which enables them to undersell the world. I really think the things that are to make Sutherland are your salt, your lime if sold at prime cost to the tenants—your roads and fishing villages—really without a joke I think that £10,000 expended on roads upon the Sutherland estate would be as beneficially laid out as any his Lordship could expend.' Nor did Loch believe that the coal works should be promoted as a major commercial enterprise with the primary object of reaping high profits—its main function, he believed, was to create a basis for other enterprises—by 'the means it will afford in the establishment of other branches of manufacture among the people'. Exports were unimportant, said Loch, for the coal should be reserved as 'the ground work of a vast industry rising in the Country'.[7]

At Brora a new village was created; steam engines were introduced into the coal mines from which ran a railway direct to the newly improved harbour; salt pans were erected, together with a brewery, brick and tile works. Skills had to be imported, and in 1814 Young was recruiting colliers from Glasgow, Fife, Wales, and, most importantly, from the Trentham estate in Staffordshire. They were introduced in order to train Sutherland men in the arts of mining—the colliers travelled free, they had rent-free accommodation and were expected to earn £100 a year. But all was not well. In 1815 there were reports that the Staffordshire men could not tolerate the conditions, and had written home to their wives instructing them to sell what they could to raise money to bring them home. They alleged

[7] SC, Young to Loch, 12–11–1814, 18–12–1814; Loch to Young, 3–9–1814, 28–11–1814; Loch to Grant, 1–7–1816.

that they had earned a mere 16s. for working a fortnight, 'that they lie all night in straw—that they cannot get bread for money . . . The Potteries were full of it, and no man will . . . be got to venture there on any terms', wrote the agent.[8] Loch told Young that the colliers were 'accustomed to many comforts unknown to the Highlanders and without which you cannot expect them to remain'. He made arrangements to send the colliers' wives north to Sutherland. In 1820 Loch reported that native Sutherlanders had successfully taken over as trained colliers at Brora.

Young admitted that outlays at Brora had been 'immense' but he insisted that the projects would be self-sustaining and would attract capitalists from the south: he had particular hopes of a tanning and pork curing industry. There were good prospects of salt sales in the Baltic. Coal was exported to Ross-shire distilleries and in 1818 plans were forwarded for the erection of a distilling industry on the Sutherland estate. The prohibition of the domestic whisky industry had, according to Loch, 'deprived a large class of the people of one of their most profitable sources of income'. At Clynelish a commercial, respectable, whisky industry was set up and employed fifty men and had the added advantage of providing a market for local coal and barley supplies.[9]

Expansion certainly occurred. Between 1814 and 1828, 20,000 tons of salt were produced. The villages grew and by 1818 the base of the local economy had been widened. Building construction had changed the face of the estate—there was only one black hut remaining in Golspie. In 1818 50,000 tiles and 90,000 bricks were manufactured. The expansion was evident at the newly-revived market at Brora in 1819 when about fifty merchants sold £1,500 of consumer goods in three days in exchange for cattle, cloth and money earned in the fishing industry. The merchants declared that they had 'never in the northern counties . . . brought their goods to nearly so good a market'.[10]

The rate of industrial progress was not sustained after 1820. The

[8] Loch made no reference to these difficulties in his *Account* of 1820.

[9] SC, Young to Loch, 11–9–1814, 20–2–1815, 5–2–1815; Germain to Loch, 8–1–1815; Loch to Young, 4–2–1815, 13–2–1815; Loch to Farey, 5–5–1815; Suther to Loch, 31–1–1815, 8–12–1815, 2–6–1818; Loch to Suther, 11–5–1815; Loch to Lord Stafford, 8–3–1822; Loch to Gower, 14–4–1818. D. W. Kemp (ed.), *Selections from the Sutherlandshire Magazine of 1826* (1898), 15. MacCulloch, op. cit., II, 475–7.

[10] SC, Suther to Loch, 26–11–1819, D593/L/2/1, 35–96.

salt and coal trades suffered from poor quality and the price-reducing effects of southern competition. The entire Brora industrial establishment made a loss of £4,000 between 1819 and 1821—mainly on the colliery operations. Loch thought that they could expect very little profit. Moreover, Lord Stafford, upon whom the whole enterprise depended, was unwilling to sanction the previous levels of capital investment. Retrenchment was ordered in 1821 but the works were not immediately abandoned because 'the men could find no work'. A vain attempt was made to lease the works to an independent entrepreneur, and eventually, in 1825, the coal works were closed. Loch regretted the closure, but nevertheless insisted that the mines had 'awakened new objects of activity and produced new sources of industry which will confer lasting and permanent advantages to Sutherland'. However, while disinvestment and redundancy occurred at Brora, various efforts were made to attract other industry to the coastal economy. Loch tempted textile entrepreneurs from Yorkshire, Dundee and Aberdeen to invest in Sutherland. 'The population of this estate' he told a capitalist in 1822, 'is very quiet, the people not in constant employment, sober, and when they have anything to do, industrious—they have all some little land—*labour remarkably cheap*. The population is fixed in three principal stations on the coast, and in one valley near the coast, near each of which there are powerful streams, and a ready communication with harbours.' The response was poor and Loch fell back on the long-discarded idea of domestic flax spinning—despite the assurances of the Dundee merchants that the returns to hand labour were derisory. Loch, faced with the situation of large-scale under-employment, persuaded a flax manufacturer to begin operations in 1822—there were five hundred women eager for the work. The experiment failed and the entrepreneur had to be compensated for the losses he had incurred. Indeed, the general post-war decline of prices had a constricting effect on the coastal economy and Loch was hesitant about making long-term decisions until prices had stabilized. But prices remained discouraging for many more years and this, together with the retrenchment of landlord expenditure, led to a consolidation of the Sutherland plans at a less ambitious level than had been anticipated prior to 1820.[11] In practice, the consequence was that the

[11] SC, Loch to Lady Stafford, 28-1-1822; Loch to Lord Stafford, 8-3-1822, 25-10-1822; Suther to Loch, 5-4-1822, 18-10-1822, 24-10-1822, 13-1-1823, 10-7-1823, 31-7-1823; Gower to Loch, 6-9-1822, 27-9-1823; Young to Loch,

coastal population came to rely on the subsistence produce of their meagre lots to a much greater degree than Loch had ever envisaged.

Another major pillar of the improvement policy was communications. Cheaper transport, wider markets and the easier penetration of new influences were central elements in Loch's thinking. In the early nineteenth century land-owners with substantial government aid made large efforts to push roads into and through the Highlands. The House of Sutherland built many miles of roads without parliamentary assistance. Loch told Shaftesbury that the Stafford family had spent £79,414 on roads between 1811 and 1843. This added greatly to other capital expenditure on harbours, the promotion of shipping and postal services, sheep-drains, great reclamation schemes and building construction. In 1814 most of the skilled labour work had been undertaken by Moray men; ten years later when a packet service to Leith was established, native Sutherland masons spent the summer in Edinburgh earning 27s. per week. Road construction served two purposes—it created conditions for economic progress, but it was also deliberately used to absorb part of the under-employed labour force, especially in times of famine when road-work became a service-payment in lieu of rent and relief—which signified a temporary but recurring retrogression to pre-clearance circumstances. The termination of parliamentary assistance for road construction in 1816 shifted the onus of transport improvement onto the landlord at a time when rental income was beginning to decline.[12]

The Sutherland policies were founded on two expectations—an increase of rent and a diminution of relief expenditure. In 1819 Loch told Brougham that rents from stock farmers had enabled Lord Stafford to provide relief in the previous year. William Young had promised total rents in excess of £20,000 per annum and, while wool prices were high, the promise was reasonable. In 1818 Sellar noted that 'stock farmers never had such good times' and exports of wool from Sutherland trebled between 1815 and 1820. However, after 1820, wool prices fell catastrophically; average prices were

20–9–1822; Davidson to Loch, 17–9–1822; Loch to Davidson, 15–9–1822; Loch to Fergus, 15–9–1822; Fergus to Loch, 19–9–1822; Loch to Maberly 3–9–1822; Henderson to Loch, 4–10–1822; Loch to Gower, 27–9–1822, 28–10–1822; 24–11–1822; Loch to Arbuthnot, 28–10–1822; Gunn to Loch, 21–3–1825 Loch to McHendrick, 14–2–1826; Simpson to Loch, 19–4–1826. *NSA*, XV 156–8. Cf. Ross, op. cit., 19.
[12] SC, Loch to Shaftesbury, 4–6–1853; Loch to J. Loch, 8–10–1824; Suther to Loch, 4–6–1824. J. Mitchell, op. cit., I, 35.

almost 50 per cent less in the 1820s than in the 1810s. In 1822 Sellar beseeched Loch to reduce his rent—'do not insist on the ruin of my wife and family', he cried. Rents were reduced and placed on a scale geared to prices. The position worsened—in 1828–9 prices were the lowest of the century and 'woefully depressed'. Loch noted that Inverness market dealt with three million pounds of wool more than it had fifteen years earlier. But Sellar blamed the rise of foreign competition and joined other sheep farmers in efforts to persuade the government to give them protection. They received no sympathy from Loch who was delighted when Wellington refused to countenance a wool tax—he believed that low wool prices were partially consequent upon the Corn Laws which had caused arable land in Europe to be converted into sheep-walks. Wool prices rose a little in the mid-1830s but failed to regain the wartime levels upon which the early sheep clearances were promoted.[13]

The tribulations of the new sectors of the northern economy were matched by the experience of the traditional pursuits. Income from Sutherland soldiers in the army diminished in 1815 at the end of the French wars. Domestic industries continued their inexorable decline, and the kelp trade collapsed in the face of technological progress in the English soap and glass industry, and the removal of import control on foreign supplies of alkali substitutes. Kelp prices fell from £20 per ton in 1810 to £3 in 1834. Kelp was particularly important on the west coast of Sutherland—in Assynt and Reay. The rents of small tenants on Lord Reay's estate 'were kept far higher than they could ever pay, were it not from the manufacture of kelp'— and when the latter failed, Reay was forced to sell out to Lord Stafford in 1829. The Kelp Proprietors claimed that 50,000 people were dependent on kelp, and it was certainly a savage blow at the basis of the West Highland economy. Loch tried to promote fishing on the Reay coast, and to persuade the government to reduce duties on glass and soap production. He wrote to the Board of Trade of the misery

in the very remote, poor and desolate districts where the manufacture of kelp formerly existed . . . The rent arising from kelp was made the subject of local taxation like the rent of land. It has become the subject of secur-

[13] SC, Loch to Brougham, 27–12–1819; Sellar to Loch, 19–6–1818, 14–1–1820, 29–4–1822; Loch to Suther, 23–2–1820; Gunn to Loch, 18–2–1824, 20–6–1828; Suther to Loch, 10–3–1824; Reed to Loch, 6–6–1828; Loch to Horne, 23–6–1828; Maxwell to Gunn, 1–7–1828; Loch to Lord Francis, 21–7–1828; SC, D593/N/4/4/1.

ities, of jointures and of younger children's portions. All this is gone and with it the means of supporting in these barren regions the extra population which the culture and manufacture had nurtured and produced.

But there was no relief. To add to the agony, the old staple of cattle sales also contracted. Many of the interior tenants continued to rely on cattle, but in the mid-1820s prices were half those of 1818; in 1824 they reached the lowest point for thirty years in Assynt. Many of the people were utterly unable to pay rents (or raise loans) and the landlord accepted cattle in lieu. Attempts were made to find a market in the south for the unwanted cattle—many were driven south to Trentham and a 'confidential person' was appointed to 'call at all or most of the gentlemen's seats' between Carlisle and Trentham, 'in order to get acquainted with those that are in want of such cattle'. Loch even envisaged a bilateral trade between the English and Scottish estates—he spoke of sending wood from Lilleshall to Sutherland to be made into barrels for the Sutherland fishing trade. In 1826 Lord Stafford gave encouragement to a steam boat scheme to transport goods (including cattle) to southern markets.[14]

Overall the 1820s were years of disillusionment in virtually all sectors of the Highland economy. Old and new forms of enterprise suffered alike from the secular decline in prices—they also felt the hardening edge of competition from the industrializing economy in the south. The infant developments of the war years were the most perishable: but the traditional economy was no less subject to the tragic decline in employment and income opportunities. Further structural alteration was thus imposed on a regional economy still in the throes of adjustment to the great landlord-initiated changes.

In answer to criticisms of the Sutherland policies, Loch invariably asserted that vast amounts of money had been invested by Lord Stafford on improvements. In reply to a vociferous attack in the House of Commons in 1845 Loch said 'that from 1811 to 1833 not one sixpence of rent had been received from that county, but on the contrary, there has been sent there, for the improvement and benefit of the people, a sum exceeding £60,000 in addition to the entire rental being laid out there.' In later years Loch claimed that no net

[14] SC, Petition to Grout, 18-4-1829; Gunn to Loch, 24-2-1823, 25-3-1823, 16-4-1824, 2-3-1829; Loch to Board of Trade, 31-1-1831; Auckland to Loch, 3-2-1831; Simpson to Loch, 15-2-1824, 23-3-1825; Duncan to Loch, 14-6-1823; D593/N/4/1/1.

income had been received between 1812 and 1854. A contemporary observer stated that £210,000 had been spent by 1825, although 'no return is to be expected for this vast expenditure'. Donald Macleod produced the unlikely calculation of £1,380,000 for the period 1811 to 1833. In 1819 Southey stated that more than twice the rental was expended annually.[15]

Unfortunately none of these figures can be accepted with confidence and the picture remains confused. With some certainty it can be said that the Sutherland estate yielded no net income between 1812 and 1822, and that the rental situation did not improve significantly until about 1840. Rental figures are meagre and are complicated by the changing acreage and the varying accountancy methods of the estate. Very approximate orders of magnitude may be indicated as follows: rents in 1811, £11,650; 1814, £18,181; 1819, £20,000; 1825, £17,351; 1827, £20,212; 1829, £17,493; probably above £20,000 in the early 1830s; 1842, £24,921; 1856, £35,814. An informed guess of the level of expenditure can be made if two assumptions are accepted—first, that Loch had told the truth, and second, that the average rent between 1811 and 1833 was about £19,000. Thus, taking Loch's assertion literally, total expenditure by the Stafford family before 1833 was very close to £500,000. This estimate does not include investments in land purchases in Sutherland in the same years, which totalled £554,000.[16]

One of the most galling comments that Loch endured was that, despite the history of atrocities and of unparalleled capital outlay, the improvements failed to pay—rents did not rise sufficiently, sheep farming profits were sluggish and the fishing industry was disappointing. In 1826 a correspondent remarked that 'had the Stafford family laid out the sum expended in Sutherland in a purchase in Ireland they would have received £25 or £30,000 per annum'.[17] Indeed, it seems quite clear that the family knew full well that it was not maximizing the return on its capital.

The question arises: why did the family continue to sanction this expenditure? In part, the family had no choice since it was committed to solving the economic problem of its estates and, once begun, it could not abnegate its avowed responsibilities—despite the fact

[15] Hansard, 12–6–1845. Stewart, op. cit. (1825), 168. Mackenzie, op. cit., 127. C. H. Herford, op. cit., 138.
[16] SC, D593/G/8/2/1–6, D593/G/8/3/1, D593/N/4/4/1. Sellar, *Statement*, op. cit., appendix I. Cf. Mackenzie, op. cit., 127, and Prebble, 58–62, 120, 165.
[17] SC, Loch to Gunn, 18–7–1845; Rose to Loch, 3–1–1826.

that general pressures made the solution increasingly difficult. But the commitment was more positive for, while many Highland proprietors sold off their ancient domains, the House of Sutherland consistently increased its territorial empire.

There were many unforeseen circumstances which undermined the fulfilment of the early promises of development in Sutherland. Foremost among these was the sagging level of prices after 1815. Moreover, the impact of the Sutherland clearance/improvement policy has to be measured against the changing economic structure of the entire region. The foundations of the traditional economy— cattle, kelp and domestic industries—had collapsed under the influence of the general price trends. The perennial problem of under-employment was gravely exacerbated. In Sutherland, however, landlord policy acted, at least in part, in the opposite direction. Indeed, the large, concentrated and planned capital investments of the House of Sutherland, *a priori*, must have induced substantial income- and employment-generating effects on this economy. The 'planners' made many miscalculations but they created—at least in the short run—a new range of opportunities in the coastal economy. This was made clear after the death of the 1st Duke in 1833 when capital expenditure was radically reduced. Loch was compelled to admit that the consequence was a sudden contraction of employment on the estate.[18] The flow of English capital into the economy enabled the landlord to support—by way of the local multiplier effect—a significantly higher level of economic activity than would otherwise have been possible.[19]

If, as R. H. Campbell suggests,[20] the Scottish landlord held a pressing responsibility to promote economic development, then the House of Sutherland discharged its responsibility without rival. Indeed, the very alacrity with which it took up its bounden duty brought the gravest criticism. The methods used were autocratic and the upheaval was great—being commensurate with the scale of

[18] SC, D593K/1/3/33. See also Poor Law Inquiry (Scotland) 1844, appendix, part II, 278, 286, 293.

[19] The exact consequences of the investments depended on the complicated relationships between, e.g., employment, prices, incomes, production, and the propensities to consume, import and save. Most of these statistics are, of course, either unavailable or non-existent. The positive effect of the investment has to be set against the mainly negative effect of the clearances, which is equally ill-documented.

[20] Campbell, op. cit., 4. See also the strictures of Adam Smith in 1759, quoted in *Survey of Lochtayside* (edited by M. M. McArthur, 1936), xviii.

the problem as conceived by the Sutherland planners. There was no intention to depopulate the county—the intention was to accommodate the increased population within the estate on a firmer, more viable economic foundation—in conjunction with a rising rental income to the landlord.

The plan involved the rationalization of the economy of the interior areas by the introduction of pastoral farming, and the creation of a diversified, closely settled, parallel economy on the coasts—in effect a two-sector economy was established. Both required very large outlays of capital, mainly from the landlord. It seems clear that the increment to the region's income derived from the expanded wool export industry did little to broaden the base of the regional economy as a whole—except perhaps in the ability of the landlord to sustain a relatively high level of investment. The character of the sheep farming economy created few employment opportunities, negligible ancillary activity, and the distribution of income in this sector did little to activate the rest of local economy. Conversely, capital investment and growth in the coastal sector must have brought much stronger income-generating effects—for instance, in road, harbour and building construction, and the expansion of export income from the nascent fishing industry. Income was distributed more equally in this sector and the likelihood of self-sustaining advance was much greater. But here again some proportion of the income-generating effects undoubtedly 'leaked away' from the region. Moreover, there was little interaction between the two parts of the economy—in 1819 Sellar actually demanded the construction of 'a wall of defence' to separate the sheep farms from the coastal settlements.[21] More importantly, sustained growth was frustrated by unforeseen difficulties on both demand and supply sides of the new industries. It was not the first nor the last time that plans for economic development in the Highlands have only partly succeeded.

The evidence suggests two points: first, that, on certain criteria, the landlord in Sutherland did undertake his responsibilities, and second, that some temporary mitigation of the Malthusian problem was obtained—though at very high social and financial costs.

The diverse objectives of the Sutherland management frequently came into conflict. While the strongest efforts were made to render

[21] SC, Sellar to Loch, 12–11–1819.

Sutherland a viable economy which could support its inhabitants without periodic collapse, the purpose was also to secure a future rental income commensurate with the capital outlay. More specifically, it was hoped that on the death of Lord Stafford, his wife the Countess, would be able to live exclusively from the net receipts of her northern estate. The intention was to render it self-sufficient, free of subsidy from the English estates. As high expenditure continued year after year, the patience of the family approached its limit.

In 1821 Loch told Suther that he must 'economise and methodise'; 'it is . . . decidedly Lord and Lady Stafford's wish at present to derive income from Sutherland . . . therefore confine your expenditure within the narrowest possible bounds'—especially at Helmsdale where, said Loch, 'the people must now do what is necessary for themselves. They have been rather spoiled—both they and the lotters are launched, they must now swim for themselves.' Retrenchment, reported Suther, diminished employment and provoked emigration among the younger people—who left behind 'aged parents, infirm relatives and others incapable of earning a livelihood' as a burden on the landlord. Rent-reductions became imperative and in 1825–6 expenses exceeded income by £9,000. The succession of George Gunn as factor on the death of Suther gave Loch confidence to say that the previous level of expenditure 'is at last got to an end'. He estimated that the gross rental of about £18,500 would yield a net revenue of £2,340. But he was over-sanguine. In 1831 Loch wrote dejectedly that 'according to the present state of matters [there is] no income for her [Lady Stafford] to live upon if it was her estate. Much has been done, but it must be a prelude to farther exertion to cut down expenditure, and outlay in every possible manner.' A total abstinence from all new works was ordered.[22]

The retrenchment drives in the north ran parallel to similar exertions on the English estates. In 1825 Lord Stafford's declining health and his advancing years (he was then sixty-seven) gave rise to great anxiety for the family fortunes. Loch instructed the English agents that 'Economy must be studied in every department . . . for when there is every chance of a very large portion of his Lordship's income [i.e. the Bridgewater profits] being cut off, it becomes our duty to limit every possible expense.' The impending investments

[22] SC, Loch to Suther, 24–12–1821; Loch to Stafford, 7–2–1826, 16–1–1830; Suther to Loch, 19–5–1822; Loch to Gunn, 13–2–1823; Gunn to Loch, 4–2–1826.

in canal, railway and landed properties gave retrenchment extra urgency. Loch pointed to the expense on the Trentham estate: 'It is too like our Sutherland proceedings,' he wrote, 'It must come down.'[23]

The drive for economy was accompanied by the very considerable territorial expansion of the Sutherland estate. In 1829 the Reay Estate (400,000 acres in Tongue, Edderachyllis and Durness) was purchased for £300,000. The purchase was prompted by dynastic aggrandizement, but it was also expected to pay a reasonable return. Loch declared, 'I cannot sufficiently express the satisfaction I have on this domain being added to the Ancient possessions of your family. Its capabilities are immense ... it will be a most valuable principality.' An adviser commented that as Lord Reay had obtained £8,400 per annum, 'it would in Lord Stafford's hands produce much more'—possibly £10,000. Loch ordered that the Reay Country was to be 'kept free from the more unlimited scale of expenditure which prevailed on the other side of the county'. But there were problems: as one correspondent pointed out, the price of wool and kelp had fallen, and Stafford could not expect profits until they rose again.[24]

In 1829 Loch travelled north to view the land and six thousand people of Reay. So isolated were the villages of the west coast that he had to employ 'an open boat and walk over moss and muir to get back again to the low country as the path is impracticable for a pony' —'it had to be performed by boating on the Atlantic, walking and on pony's back in the most mountainous and rugged, but the most prodigiously capable country imaginable ... it was performed with considerable fatigue and by much exertion.' Loch was evidently not overwhelmed by the physical grandeur of his new commission. 'What a field for exertion, the application of capital and the exercise of benevolence', he exulted, 'and what happiness to the individual who owns it, and he has the heart and possessing the means of giving effect to these pure and ennobling feelings.' He reported to Lord Stafford that the Reay people were generally satisfied with the change of ownership and with the knowledge that they were 'to be put on the same footing as the people of Assynt and Strathnaver—the condition of these people whom you *oppressed* and *burnt-out* being

[23] SC, Loch to Lewis, 15–1–1825.
[24] SC, Mackenzie to Loch, 3–10–1828; Loch to Gunn, 1–2–1829; Reed to Loch, 16–2–1829; D593P/18/1, Loch to Lady Stafford, 13–8–1829.

the standard of comfort and happiness to the population of this country'. The first priority, Loch concluded, was the provision of roads which would open up Reay to men of capital with the effect of 'calling into life the vast resources of this great, but hitherto, totally neglected District'. Lord Stafford is said to have spent £40,000 building roads along the Reay coast.[25]

Plans for major clearances in 1828 were shelved in favour of smaller, occasional removals over a longer period. In 1831 Loch ordered the reinstatement of people on the coast south of Scourie from which Lord Reay had previously cleared them to make way for sheep. Further fishing settlements were promoted on the newly-acquired lands of the west. Loch was also considering the reduction in the average size of the large farms; 'what was best in 1812 may not do now', he conceded. But the clearances continued; in 1831 126 people were removed from Strath Halladale to the coast—despite a petition from the people who stated that they would prefer begging in Caithness to accepting 'the said lots of ground which undoubtedly would soon put an end to our lives with starvation and famine'. The general condition of the people varied widely from one year to another and from area to area. In 1830 Gunn reported that the fishermen of the west were opulent, 'the little children . . . running about with sovereigns' and the doctors complaining of the lack of illness. The following year he told of great suffering and poverty in the same area. Emigration rose to 'a torrent' in 1830 and Loch, constantly anxious about the rapid rise of population, regarded it as an 'excellent . . . drainage of . . . overpopulation as it increases'— but he refused to allow Gunn to give direct encouragement to emigration. The Rev. Findlater of Durness declared that the young men migrated in consequence of the want of work and coastal lots. Loch pointed out that road construction employed many hands. He opposed direct charity to the indigent—'it would only be putting off the evil day' and 'would only encourage the further and more rapid increase of population'. Emigration, or a proper commitment to fishing, were the only real alternatives, Loch declared. Generally, Loch was satisfied with the progress he saw on his annual inspection of Sutherland; minor modifications might be necessary, but the foundation for the future had been established. In 1831 he wrote metaphorically, 'I consider that the landlord has executed all the

[25] SC, Loch to Currie, 17–6–1829; Loch to Lady Stafford, 13–8–1829, D593/ N/4/1/1d. G. Huxley, *Victorian Duke* (1967), 23. *NSA*, XV, 185–6.

great triangular mensuration of the country—it remains with the tenants to complete the detailed survey.'[26]

But in the wider world the Sutherland policies remained a target for public attack. John MacCulloch was vilified for giving countenance to the clearances.[27] The name of Patrick Sellar was resurrected as an object for hatred—especially by the influential pen of Major-General David Stewart of Garth in Perthshire.

After a distinguished military career, Stewart devoted a large part of his retirement to championing the cause of the Highlanders, whom he regarded as a distinct and separate race. He was a passionate advocate of the traditional values of Highland life, and in 1822 he published his *Sketches of the Character, Manners and Present State of the Highlanders of Scotland*, which has become a classic work of anti-clearance literature from which a large part of later criticism is derived. Stewart abhorred 'the gross spirit of speculation' epitomized by the clearances, which he condemned as an unmitigated disaster destroying the very essence of an honourable society. The clearances, he said, were cruel, wrong-headed, and economically absurd. He believed that large sheep farms were unnecessary since the landlord, if patient, could obtain rents equally high from the existing population in their existing situations—'the soil of the Highlands should be improved by the labours of the occupier fed and clothed and supported in all necessary expenses by the produce.' Stewart acknowledged the current poverty and rapid population increase of the Highlands, but he attributed both to the policy of landlord speculation. Before the clearances, he wrote, the ancient and respectable tenantry had 'passed the greater part of life in the enjoyment of abundance'; the new system had 'spread with fatal rapidity' and the people had been reduced to 'a species of slavery' not unlike that of the negro. Stewart singled out the case of Sutherland as the meanest example of 'the desolating system of turning out

[26] SC, Loch to Lewis, 30–8–1831; Gunn to Lady Stafford, 20–2–1830; Innes to Lady Stafford, 10–1–1831; Horsburgh to Loch, 28–1–1831, 2–3–1831, 18–3–1831, 12–5–1831, 10–6–1831; Gunn to Loch, 8–1–1831, 14–1–1831, 6–5–1831; Loch to Gunn, 23–1–1830, 21–1–1831, 10–1–1831, 10–5–1831, 1–10–1831; Loch to Young, 27–1–1831; Young to Loch, 31–1–1831; Loch to Gordon, 10–1–1831, 8–4–1831; Loch to Lady Stafford, 28–1–1831; Mackenzie to Loch, 5–8–1830, 9–8–1831; Loch to Horsburgh, 17–4–1831; Findlater to Loch, 22–9–1830; Loch to Findlater, 30–10–1830; Edderachilis Petition, 9–2–1831.
[27] J. Browne, *A Critical Examination of Dr. MacCulloch's Work on the Highlands and Western Islands of Scotland* (1825).

and extirpating a whole race'. Moreover, he claimed, 'Had Lady Stafford sent her money to the funds instead of to the encouragement of the new tenants of "Skill and Capital", and had she allowed the ancient race to remain on their farms improving them, she would have been much richer.' Stewart had neither visited Sutherland nor read Loch's *Account* before he wrote his book—when he did both his opinions were unchanged. He remarked that Sellar's acquittal 'did by no means diminish the general feeling of culpability'. Sellar, thoroughly provoked, considered prosecuting this 'ignorant, intermeddling, impertinent man'.

Stewart's book ran into several editions and the royalties gave very welcome support to his own precarious financial position. His Perthshire estates were already heavily encumbered when he inherited them in 1821. With rents of about £1,000, Stewart was faced with a debt of over £26,000. In November 1821 he told his brother-in-law, 'we must increase our rents as much as possible ... if the present tenants will not give it we must take the rent from others.' Tenants who could not pay went to America: 'I have wished to encourage voluntary emigration', he wrote, 'and that thinning of population which is absolutely necessary.' His finances deteriorated very rapidly; the estates were fully mortgaged and he tried to raise money on personal security; Stewart had high hopes of profits from his slave-plantations in Trinidad and St Vincent, but falling sugar prices and mismanagement merely added to his despair. He spent a good deal of time in London making contacts with aristocratic society—in May 1823 he rejoiced that he had sat fifth from the Duke of Clarence—'all this is very gratifying', he reported, 'and I only want money to enable me to hold my station in such society.' Eventually, after much effort, he obtained the post of Governor of St Lucia, by the salary of which he hoped to redeem his debts within ten years. But in 1829 he died of fever—and three years later the estates were sold, more than ever in debt.[28]

Contemporary opinion on the Sutherland schemes was divided. In 1829 Joseph Mitchell overflowed with praise; the latent wealth of the previously barren country had been awakened—80,000 fleeces, 20,000 sheep, several cargoes of grain, the output of 3 distilleries, many droves of cattle, 30–40,000 barrels of herring, were being

[28] *Sketches* (1822), I, 163–71, 1825 ed. *passim*. *NLS*, MS. 791. I am particularly grateful to Mr A. Irvine Robertson of Stirling for allowing me to study the collection of records relating to the Stewart family in his possession.

exported annually.[29] The very character of the people had changed—the people who were 'brought by compression to the coast' now used carts and wheels, 'the pigs and cattle are treated to a separate table; the dunghill is turned to the outside of the house; the tartan tatters have given place to the produce of Huddersfield and Manchester, Glasgow and Paisley; the Gaelic to English; and few persons are to be found who cannot both read and write.'[30] Yet at much the same time Beriah Botfield, in a strikingly ambivalent account, wrote of the 'inconsiderate benevolence' of a landlord who forcibly converted 'a pastoral and poetical people into a plodding and commercial race'.[31]

Several years earlier, in late 1821, Charles Young of Forfar toured Sutherland and wrote an unsolicited report to Loch which specifically compared the condition of the removed and the unremoved population of the estate. He examined the condition of the uncleared tenants of Strathbrora in the interior. 'Many of these creatures', he wrote, were 'in such a state as scarcely to deserve the name of human—covered with filth and cutaneous disease, living in mud hovels into which one could only enter on hands and knees'. The scene, which he insisted was typical, 'was not only shocking, but really degrading to human nature'. The people lived with their animals 'and the stench which arises from their united excrement is loathesome and must engender disease'. The condition of the coastal removees was a complete contrast—they were happy and cheerful, two thousand were employed in the fishing, and they were 'living in neat and comfortable cottages built of stone, amidst comparative luxury and affluence'.[32]

In 1832 an anonymous correspondent threatened retribution to the 'scourgers' that Lord Stafford 'employed to remove Brave Sutherland people to make room for sheep'. In the following year William Cobbett launched a characteristically biting indictment on the same policies in a debate in the Commons. The debate concerned Russian crimes in

[29] Compare with the much higher estimates given in 1831 by Patrick Sellar, *Library of Useful Knowledge*, Farm Reports, no. III, County of Sutherland (1831), 66.
[30] Quoted in Haldane, op. cit., 138–9.
[31] *Journal of a Tour Through the Highlands* (1830), xv–xvi, 110, 133, 141–52. Similarly, see Anon., *A Summer Ramble in the North Highlands* (1825), 95–105, 154–9.
[32] SC, D593/N/4/1/3, Young to Loch, 7-11–1821. See also Lord Teignmouth, *Sketches of the Coasts and Lands of Scotland and the Isle of Man* (2 vols, 1836), II, 1–18.

Poland, but Cobbett believed that monstrous injustices could be found nearer home—namely in Sutherland where 'the inhabitants of almost an entire county have had their houses burnt down, and themselves driven at the point of a bayonet from the land upon which they were born'. Soon afterwards Loch urged upon the agents the necessity of vigilance: 'any slip in your conduct, or slackness in your exertions will be eagerly caught at and severely observed on.'[33]

On the death of the 1st Duke of Sutherland in 1833, Loch ordered a sharp retrenchment. All improvements were to cease for a time, every energy to be directed to reduction—'no false shame must impede this', he told the agents, 'you are no longer representative of the richest nobleman in England'. The Duchess/Countess was now dependent on this source of income, and if expenditure did not fall the people would suffer, 'as she would have to raise rents'. Loch estimated that she would receive, at best, a net income of £11,835 out of a nominal rental of £27,140. The agents pledged their support.[34]

The Countess visited her northern realm in September 1833. She said she would live within her income, but she could not comprehend why the Dunrobin factorship yielded a mere £4,000, 'after all Lord Stafford's outlay, when before the improvements commenced, he got £3,000 and I £1,000 from the estate regularly'. The agent, Gunn, explained that thirty years previously war-prices had yielded higher rents and that the net income of the estate was reduced by interest payments on a £60,000 loan and the burden of road and other assessments. There is, of course, every indication that the return on capital in the Highlands was very much lower than in the south.[35]

Of all the contradictory descriptions of changing living standards in Sutherland during the time of the clearances that of the agent Gunn is perhaps the most interesting. Writing in 1828, Gunn was ready to concede that, before the clearances:

the people certainly enjoyed, for nine months of the year, many comforts which the present race cannot attain. From June to February they were abundantly supplied with the produce of their crops and of the dairy, they had a profusion of milk, butter and cheese, and few were so poor but they could provide sheep and goats for their winter feed. But in Spring [he

[33] SC, 'Highlander' to Stafford, 24–11–1832; Loch to Gunn, 2–3–1833, 30–3–1833. Hansard, 1–3–1833.
[34] SC, Loch to Gunn, 2–11–1833; Loch to Agents, 7–9–1833; Loch to Sutherland, 15–9–1833; Loch to Davidson, 30–12–1833.
[35] SC, Gunn to Loch, 6–9–1833.

continued] they paid dearly for these advantages, particularly if the pre-ceeding crop had been deficient—then would be seen troops of men with horses hastening to Caithness for meal ... they were obliged to make ruinous sacrifices to procure it. When the Spring turned out unfavourable and provender failed, their cattle died—they had no means of supplying their own wants, and misery and starvation frequently ensued unless relieved by the proprietor. Thus more was paid out and lost in supporting them for one season than their rents would amount to for many years.

Gunn also admitted that the clearances initially created [36]

great privations—but the scene is now altered, and from the many sources of employment and their newly-acquired habits of industry, they are afforded the steady means of support throughout the year. Their healthy appearance and dress is the best proof of this improved comfort ... During the herring fishing they earn what is sufficient to purchase meal and clothing—their lots supply them with potatoes, and they always care to lay in a store of herrings to serve them plentifully during the winter.

[36] SC, Gunn to Loch, 12–5–1828.

XVI

- -

Progress, Poverty and Criticism

- -

The Dowager Duchess/Countess, on the death of her husband, told her agents that she considered the common people of Sutherland under her special care; all their little disputes were to be listened to. They were to be treated with the greatest kindness. 'Recollect how a person in the Duchess's position is watched as to her treatment of the people', wrote Loch. None the less, further removals occurred in the years 1833–4, and, in one instance, the common people had to be threatened against being 'foolish enough to use violence'. The removees were usually given timber for their new houses, some old potato land for their immediate support and a period of rent-free occupation. But there were problems in the older reception areas— at Oldshores on the west coast there was overcrowding which Loch attributed to 'natural causes and produced by the people themselves', and he believed that the inconvenience would help 'to compel them either to depend entirely upon fishing or emigrate to the colonies'. Loch's attitude to emigration was changing—in 1833 he wrote that, 'even at the risk of our losing occasionally some of the best settlers, the advantages which are derived by the withdrawal of the surplus population are very great not only to those who go but to those who stay.'[1]

In 1835 Loch again perambulated the Sutherland estates. He submitted a lengthy report, a justification of the estate policies. He cited the particular example of Knockan and Elphin, the only remaining uncleared interior districts of Assynt, where crops were produced with the greatest difficulty—clearly demonstrating, Loch

[1] SC, Loch to Bairgie, 17–2–1834, 25–3–1834, 27–3–1834, 18–8–1834; Loch to Gunn, 2–3–1833.

243

claimed, 'the risk that the country would run, even in these days, if any large proportion of its population were to be resident in the high interior'. The miserable, wretched hovels of the old settlers contrasted with the houses and industry of the resettled people. He gave examples of the worthy change. But he did acknowledge that many people had experienced great difficulty at the beginning, particularly in the erection of their houses. It had 'greatly exhausted their means', as also had the cessation of employment on road construction and the collapse of the kelp trade. But, Loch insisted, these problems had been magnified by a minority of cottars who were congenitally given to hyperbole. Viewing the clearances as a whole, Loch confronted the perennial criticisms of the policy and answered: 'I am satisfied now more than ever . . . that the course pursued was the correct one and that it produced less suffering than a slower process would have done.' Furthermore,

Had it to be done again I should adhere as near as possible to the course that was pursued. The ancient customs of the people are not to be rashly innovated upon. They are to be shook by degrees, and their minds gradually prepared for the change. But this being done, the change must still be effected by one general, combined, determined exertion.

In conclusion, Loch wrote that the old habits had been 'broken through'. He conceded that, at the time of the clearances, he had expected too much exertion from the people—but exertion had been utterly essential. The death of the 1st Duke in 1833, and the fact that the major 'sinews of improvement' had been undertaken, implied that 'a slower progress is now not only necessary, but it is wiser to adopt it.' Loch was always ready to make a virtue of a necessity. In the hands of the Duchess, retrenchment in Sutherland was to continue, while some rents were to be raised.[2]

Paramount in Loch's thinking throughout these years was the question of population growth on the west coast of Sutherland which threatened the very foundations of his plans for economic advance. Unless the increase of economic resources and population kept in phase, disaster was inevitable. Loch's attitude was derived directly from his conventional 'Malthusian' conception of the problem. It provided the rationale of the eradication of the middleman from Sutherland society, the prohibition of subdivision, and the measures taken to prevent early marriage. 'An extreme evil arises from marry-

[2] SC, Loch's report, 26–10–1835. Cf. *NSA*, XV, esp. 176–86, 152–63, 73–81. SC, D593K/1/8/20, Sutherland Fiars Prices.

ing without adequate means of supporting a family', he wrote, 'bringing into the world a set of helpless infants—the fertile source of dissolute conduct in the parents, undutiful conduct in the child, wretchedness and ruin of all.' On another occasion he wrote that 'the advantage of doing away with subtenancy is that it is the best means of curbing an overgrowth of people to their own injury.'

Out of these attitudes grew a policy of marriage control which became notorious for its alleged inhumanity. Sub-letting was strictly forbidden; married children were not allowed to live on the land of their fathers; they could not build separate houses; only one child could succeed to a lot. In 1831, Gunn declared that without these regulations 'the population would soon become unmanageable and as dense as any part of Ireland.' But Loch's rules were extremely unpopular—many people had no land at all and were virtually forced to emigrate. [3]

The year 1836 brought catastrophic destitution to the Northern Highlands. From Assynt, the Rev. Gordon reported that the crop failure was the worst for twenty-nine years—and made more serious by the fact that many families had no land at all. Many were eating the seed reserved for the following season. Relief was a stern necessity, and Gordon suggested that road-work and credit be made available to the destitute. Many of the indigent wished to go to Canada and hoped that the government or the Countess would assist their passages. Emigration would relieve the general situation, 'and without some resource or other to provide for the redundant population, it is impossible to predict what shall become of them soon.' [4]

The immediate response of Loch and the Countess was to help migrants from Assynt. The great thing was to get people from 'this vastly over-peopled district to emigrate to Nova Scotia'. But large numbers of them wanted to leave. Many of them had no money for the passage. Horsburgh, the factor, commented, 'Privately I wish the one half of the whole population [of the Highlands] would go, it would add greatly to the interest and welfare of the remainder, and greatly to the interest of the landlord, and more especially if one could get quit of the worthless retaining the more respectable.'

[3] SC, Loch to Lorne, 10–10–1846; Loch to Lewis, 19–6–1833; Gunn to Loch, 14–1–1831; Loch to Newspapers, 25–8–1842. *Northern Ensign*, 15–1–1853. Evidence of Rev. C. Gordon, Poor Law Inquiry (Scotland) 1845, appendix, part II, 292.

[4] SC, Gordon to Loch, 15–3–1836; Gunn to Countess, 13–2–1836. *NSA*, XV, 113.

The management, however, could not entertain the prospect of a comprehensive subsidization of emigration. Only marginal assistance was deemed possible.[5]

The problem of crop failure, and therefore of emigration, assumed much larger proportions in the winter of 1836-7. In many parts there was a total failure of the potato crop, particularly on the west coast, the high interior and in the Hebrides. There had not been a dry day for nine months, said one report; there was 'a state of *prospective starvation* ... how the people will stand it out till the next crop, God only knows.' In the Reay country the position was as disastrous as it had been in 1816-17. One observer believed that the proprietors could not possibly provide more than one tenth of the assistance that the population required: 'Government alone can do it.' A Ross-shire landowner (and no great friend of the Sutherland estate) defined the problem for Loch: the population was too great; the people who had been driven to the coast by sheep farming now depended mainly on fishing; for two seasons both their crops and the fishing had failed—'they are therefore in a state bordering on absolute want ... That many will die of mere starvation is very probable and depredations have already begun on property.' In 1835 his own tenants had been kept alive by shellfish and his relief; but he could not keep 8,000 people alive. Emigration would help, but a more immediate solution was required: specifically he suggested a road-building project sponsored by government and land-owners acting together. Loch replied with sympathy and said that he was aware of the 'lamentable conditions' in Ross, and had heard 'that they can hardly make coffins fast enough, and that many lie unburied as they cannot perform the funerals quick enough'.[6]

Initially, Loch's factors reported that Sutherland was less severely afflicted than the rest of the Highlands. Some relief was sanctioned—imported oats, beans and potatoes, charity for the indigent, credit for others—which was provided on the strict understanding that it would be repaid—'for they must be aware if they fail in this', said Loch, 'they put it out of her Grace's power to relieve them in a similar manner on any future emergency.' The management pro-

[5] SC, Loch to Bairgie, 23-3-1836, 16-5-1836; Bairgie to Loch, 16-4-1836; Horsburgh to Loch, 15-4-1836.
[6] SC, Findlater to Loch, 23-12-1836; M. Mackenzie to J. H. Mackenzie, 31-12-1836; M. Mackenzie to Loch, 28-1-1837; Mackay to Loch, 3-1-1837; Clarke to Loch, 8-1-1837; Loch to M. Mackenzie, 28-1-1837. See also J. N. Macleod, *Memorials of the Rev. Norman Macleod* (1898), 128-30.

bably underestimated the severity of the destitution on the estate. In March 1837 snow storms and intense frost multiplied the hardships. In Lairg, cattle were dying. As one minister put it, 'with ourselves they [the cattle] are becoming skeletons ... Early relief for man and beast is much needed. From 30 to 50 families are in danger of Starvation if not soon supplied.' Seed was being converted into meal to prevent starvation. An agent feared that any supplies of relief meal would be seized with violence on its arrival. In Assynt, starvation threatened coastal and interior tenants alike. It was 'utterly indescribable'.[7]

Gunn, the main Sutherland factor, was compelled to defend himself against charges that he had grossly underestimated the needs of the people. He said he had kept within prudent limits in order to aid the people to 'put sound seed into the ground and enable them to subsist till the fishing commenced'. 'I never contemplated that her Grace was to import a sufficiency of meal to support in idleness for six months the population exceeding 20,000 souls.' There were no grounds for complaint, he claimed; more meal was in transit and he did not believe 'the people are reduced to the state of lawless desperation.' When the cargoes of meal arrived the people were loudly grateful. Loch instructed that it be distributed 'in the most economical', manner—'if they expect it to be a gift they will expend it with less care—who knows what will be their condition next year.' The following year, however, was not in any way comparable. In August 1837 Loch reported enthusiastically, 'I never saw the same amounts of produce on the earth in this quarter—oats is the strongest and finest crop I ever saw and a prodigious fishing.'[8]

The lessons of the destitution were not allowed to slip away. Loch said that the famine demonstrated to the world that the Highlands contained a 'super-abundant population'. He told the Colonial Office that the Countess was anxious to co-operate with any government schemes for emigration. Many Highlanders departed for the Australian colonies—there being a temporary 'dread of Canada'. The agent, Gunn, remarked that 'it gives rise to very

[7] SC, Gunn to Loch, 7–2–1837; Loch to Horsburgh, 17–2–1837; Loch to Bairgie, 10–3–1837; Tulloch to Loch, 20–2–1837; Bairgie to Loch, 29–3–1837; Reid to Davidson, 4–4–1837; Mackenzie to Loch, 29–3–1837; Reports from Rispond and Assynt, 17–3–1837, 20–3–1837.

[8] SC, Gunn to Loch, 17–4–1837, 27–4–1837; Bairgie to Loch, 8–5–1837; Loch to Horsburgh, 2–5–1837; Loch to Lewis, 20–8–1837; D593/P/20, Loch to Countess, 5–8–1836, 15–8–1836.

unpleasant and desponding feelings to see the poor, virtuous men, launch themselves voluntarily on such a distant and doubtful speculation, and being so unused to the world, to be settled amidst strangers, without being near any individual to whom they can look up to and claim protection.' But paternalism was no substitute for subsistence, and Loch told Gunn that he need have no gloomy feelings for those who went to Australia. Indeed, it seems that the 2nd Duke of Sutherland had considered buying land in South Australia to enable 'the surplus population of this estate to settle as Colonists in that country'. But this was deferred in favour of support for a Land Company applying 'the profits . . . to the object of aiding others to follow the example of the first colonists'. George Loch had heard of one South Australian grazier who required five hundred immigrants 'and particularly such as would assist in Sheep Farms'. The younger Loch had suggested, without conscious irony, that Sutherlanders would suit the purpose perfectly.[9]

Considerable criticism has frequently been voiced against the arbitrary power vested in the hands of the Sutherland factors. Such criticism is well-founded in the case of Bairgie, who was dismissed in 1836 for the gross misuse of his authority during the destitution. Half a century later James Cumming, a Free Church minister, told the Napier Commissioners that the Duke of Sutherland's agents were 'his hands, his eyes, his ears, and his feet, and in their dealing with the people they are constantly like a wall of ice between his Grace and his Grace's people.'

The power of the district factors was prodigious, and the system of management gave them almost unlimited discretion. Three factors administered an estate of above 1m. acres and a population of more than 20,000. Moreover, as Loch pointed out:

the Sutherland factors have duties to perform which none others exercise. These are in point of fact the principal gentlemen in the district—they had to discharge the duty therefore of deputy-Lieutenants, J.Ps etc.— besides the constant occupation they have among the lotters . . . a most serious, important and constant duty, but one never performed by Factors in any other country, and where done at all, is performed by the Gentry and Landlords each on his own estate.

Hence the factors were of necessity responsible and powerful men.
The decline of traditional society in the Highlands, particularly in

[9] SC, Loch to Spring-Rice, 3–3–1837; Gunn to Loch, 16–7–1838; Loch to Gunn, 20–7–1838; G. Loch to Loch, 22–8–1838. Barron, op. cit., II, *passim.*

Sutherland, had tended to erase many of the intermediary links between the land-owner and the smaller tenantry. The abolition of the tacksmen and sub-tenancy had destroyed most of the vestiges of social cohesion, and the sheep farmers, admitted Loch, washed their hands of the general population—the people had been, he said, 'dreadfully oppressed and tyrannized over' by the graziers. Loch began to favour smaller sheep farmers because it would 'keep up that gradation of ranks, so necessary in all countries, and which perhaps in Sutherland prevails too little.'[10]

During the years in which the Countess was expected to live off the rents of her northern estates, the demands for retrenchment were heavily counter-balanced by the demands for the relief of destitution. In the four years to 1837 the Sutherland estate appears to have incurred a net loss of £17,402 and the most sanguine estimate produced a net income of a mere £2,602 for the following year. The factors were implored to follow the strictest economy, but by January 1838 the Countess's deficit had increased to £29,330. The factors were called together and reminded of the 'more limited income' of the Countess. Letters heavily marked with *Retrenchment* were despatched; there was even talk of dismissing the main agent and reducing factors' salaries. The problem was intractable.[11]

During the 1830s an attempt was made to bolster the estate income by leasing the shooting rights of large stretches of the estate to sportsmen. In 1836 427,000 acres were advertised for a combined rent of £1,330. At first the sheep farmers welcomed the proposal—though Sellar made a distinction between two classes of sportsmen—the less desirable class of 'encumbered lairds, half-pay Captains, and retired subordinate civilians', and the more agreeable 'Noblemen and gentlemen of respectability' from the south who 'fish and shoot like gentlemen and leave money cheerfully behind them'. However, in practice, the shooting experiment raised difficulties: the shepherds were inclined to steal deer and the latter trespassed on sheep pasture. In 1838 a dispute developed over the compatibility of sheep and deer. Sellar protested that he, and not the deer, should possess Strathnaver.[12]

[10] SC, An Inventory of Complaints, October 1836; Loch to Young, 22–12–1836, D593/N/4/1/1. *NSA*, XV, 99. See also the rambling recollections of Bairgie's successor, Evander MacIver of Scourie, *Memoirs of a Highland Gentleman* (1905). NLS, MS. 926, Loch to Lockhart, 24–3–1827; Napier Report, 1884, Q.25259.
[11] SC, Davidson to Loch, 12–4–1837; Loch to Davidson, 24–1–1838; Loch to Mackenzie, 31–1–1838; Loch to Factors, 1–2–1838.
[12] SC, Loch to Gunn, 21–1–1834, 14–2–1834; Sellar to Horsburgh, 17–4–1836; Sellar to Loch, 8–11–1838.

Despite the depredations of the red deer, the sheep farmers experienced good times in the later 1830s. Loch observed that 'there should be a great increasing accumulation of capital among the stock farmers.' Sheep and wool prices rose after 1837 and, in the next thirty years, it is said, 'a great deal of money was made all over Scotland by sheep farmers'. Between 1838 and 1844 Sellar established himself as a laird in Argyll where he bought 21,575 acres for £29,850.[13]

The Countess died in January 1839. The Highland estates descended to her son (the 2nd Duke of Sutherland) and thus returned to the general administration of the property of the House of Sutherland. In 1839 the Duke relinquished all claim to the rent-arrears of the small tenants, and instituted construction works costing more than £4,500 in that year. By 1843 there appears to have been a substantial net income from Sutherland—which was the occasion for optimism, even high spirits, amongst the management.[14]

But, for the population at large, there was little improvement of prospects. In 1839 a recurrence of smallpox and the partial failure of the corn and potato crops as well as the fishing had produced acute distress in many areas. The Minister of Assynt reported that 'there are several families who know not in the morning, where, or how, they are to obtain the means necessary for continuing existence till the evening.' An agent thought that relief on the scale of 1837 would lessen individual exertion and produce 'a population of absolute paupers—none of whom would ever leave the country'. Another believed emigration to be the only solution since the landlord could not subsidize the people for ever.[15]

Inevitably, the conditions of 1839–40 quickened the migration of many Highlanders. Often the people were too poor to pay their passage, and there was again a general clamour for assistance. On average it cost 48s. to assist the migrant to America. But the idea of full-scale subsidization was resisted by the 2nd Duke, although he remitted all arrears of rent of prospective migrants, and directed that any coastal lot vacated by such be given to the adjoining lotter.

[13] SC, Loch to Gunn, 20–7–1836; MacIver, op. cit., 67; Gaskell, op. cit., 40–1.
[14] SC, Davidson to Loch, 4–1–1839, 10–1–1840, 2–1–1841, 24–1–1843; Gunn to Loch, 23–5–1840.
[15] SC, Gordon to Loch, 17–7–1839; Stewart to Loch, 19–7–1839; Horsburgh to Loch, 31–5–1839.

In 1841 he gave £200 to aid migrants, but with firm instructions: 'Ask no one to go, and allow none the full cost of their passage, but assist them who are desirous to go.' It was stated categorically that all manner of pressure was to be avoided. Acute distress returned in 1842 and the spirit of migration revived with 'double vigour'. On the west coast, for instance, twenty families arrived at the factor's house at Scourie demanding that the Duke pay their full passages. 'As scarcely one family had one shilling to spare for that purpose ... I see nothing but misery staring them in their faces', reported the factor who provided some assistance.[16]

Anti-clearance violence again erupted in September 1841: at Durness on the north coast. A year earlier tenants at Culrain in Ross had set a renewed precedent for resistance to removal warrants. The Durness Riots were presaged by a petition from the people against their immediate landlord, James Anderson. In 1818 Anderson had taken a lease from Lord Reay of a large stretch of the northern coast of the parish of Durness. The lease did not expire until 1846. Anderson was involved in cod-fishing in which he employed a large number of sub-tenants—his lease allowed him to contravene Loch's most basic rules against sub-letting. In 1829 Anderson had boasted of the hard battle he had fought 'to keep my tenants from going to Caithness' and he had extended his operations into Assynt where, he remarked, the uncontrolled headstrong people were backward in everything except procreation. In 1839 the fishing was in decline and Anderson decided to quit—he determined to exploit sheep farming instead of fishing, a rational switch of capital in the prevailing economic circumstances. Great distress ensued for his sub-tenants. Anderson set about their clearance. The first stage involved thirty-two families, some of whom migrated, but most of whom dispersed into the Sutherland estate. Anderson planned a second ejectment of thirty-one families in September 1841. He made no provision for their resettlement and the people turned to the Duke of Sutherland to intercede and give them 'shelter against the threatening and expected storm of tyranny'. Sutherland gave no answer.[17]

Anderson, apparently with full legal warrant, attempted to evict the people on forty-eight hours' notice. The Sheriff's party arrived

[16] SC, Horsburgh to Loch, 24–6–1842, 1–7–1842; Sinclair to Loch, 31–3–1843; Loch to Stewart, 6–4–1841.

[17] SC, Arbuthnot to Gunn, 21–1–1826; Anderson to Arbuthnot, 12–1–1826; Anderson to Stafford, 9–5–1829; Anderson to Loch, 21–9–1829; Loch to Reay, 16–8–1829. D593P/22/1/28. D593/N/4/1/1d.

at Durness only to be resisted by 'the menaces and threats of an angry mob', mainly of women—'a large body of officers were deforced, assaulted, threatened with instant death, and expelled at Midnight from the parish of Durness by a ferocious mob,' it was reported. Three attempts to serve the summonses failed and there were fears of a general mutiny to mobilize support from the Assynt and Culrain people. It was not until military intervention was threatened that a compromise was negotiated, by which the people gained a further six months' notice. The Sutherland management was highly critical of Anderson's actions—the fundamental cause was said to have been 'that wretched system of subletting' which had been abolished in every case except Anderson's. Although the Duke had the power of resuming the lease, it was felt that Anderson would demand unreasonable compensation. Loch was particularly displeased, and refused to give Anderson the right to clear any land he held on annual tenancy. He sternly upbraided Anderson and told him he was under a strong obligation to see that the evicted tenants were secure in their future livelihood—and that they should have ample warning and should be fully compensated. In no way whatsoever did Loch condone Anderson's actions.[18]

Active resistance and public criticism acted as a brake on the operation of landlord policy in Sutherland. Gunn, the factor, remarked that 'the state of public opinion is such nowadays, that a Proprietor cannot exercise his just and legal rights without being exposed to all sorts of calumny and mis-statements.' In 1843 an attempt to remove one man, John Macleod, from Balchladdich was greeted by threats to rouse 'the *whole people* of Assynt' against the Sutherland management, and the resistance was only subdued by the intervention of a large body of officers, the surrender of Macleod and the incarceration of a few prisoners.[19]

The Durness incidents coincided with a new wave of criticism of the Sutherland clearances. In a general way the agents had already detected a spirit of resistance to the authority of the management among the population; Patrick Sellar branded them as 'the most lying, psalm singing, unprincipled peasantry in the Queen's dominions'. The trouble was ascribed to the restricted level of estate expenditure

[18] SC, September, October 1841; D593/P/22/1/7. EBC, Loch to Lord Francis, 5–10–1841, 12–10–1841. On Anderson, see Teignmouth, op. cit., II, 17 ff.
[19] SC, Gunn to Loch, 14–9–1841; D593/P/22/1/7.

during the time of the Countess/Duchess. This had reduced employment opportunities and driven the young men south 'where they imbibed many of the notions, and contracted not a few of the vices of the class with whom they associated'. Such ideas, said Horsburgh, the agent, spread rapidly among unemployed people and 'they became much more inclined to question the authority of those who cannot give work to the active and deserving'.

But in 1841 there were wider criticisms. The ashes of the Sellar affair were raked up. Thomas Dudgeon returned from America and promised a most damaging exposé of the policies. Donald Macleod published a series of direct attacks on the Sutherland regime, which, said Gunn, were designed 'to instill the poison and spread its baleful effects among our virtuous and peaceable tenantry' by the means of abominable and slanderous falsehoods. Hugh Miller, referring to Sutherland, wrote that 'a singularly well conditioned and wholesome district of a country has been converted into one wide ulcer of wretchedness.'

Then, in 1843 *The Westminster Review* published the ideas of Sismondi concerning 'Celtic Tenures' in Sutherland. Sismondi, in 1837, had written a systematic denunciation of the Countess and the system of tenurial law which permitted the inhumanity of the clearances. His radical ideas, which Loch considered subversive, spread into the Scottish newspapers. Loch took precautions; he wrote to Gunn: 'From certain doctrines that have been lately promulgated, it becomes more than ever necessary that the Duke's ownership should be asserted upon every change of occupancy.' Criticisms of the Sutherland policies took on another dimension when the Duke became involved with the theological complexities of the Disruption of the Scottish Church. Apparently the Duke refused sites to the Free Church on his estate for theological reasons, and this inevitably led to allegations of cruelty.[20] One irate correspondent drew a parallel with the clearances and announced that,

[20] It seems that nine out of fifteen ministers in Sutherland defected to the Free Church at the time of the Disruption. H. Scott, *Fasti Ecclesiae Scoticanae* (1928), VIII. Differences of religion added another edge to contemporary criticisms of the House of Sutherland. This is especially striking in Sage's *Memorabilia Domestica* (1889 ed., 53), where he gives an account of the admission of Mr Walter Ross as Minister at Clyne in 1777:

His admission was opposed by the parishioners who had set their affections upon Mr Graham . . . Known to be a godly man. The then Countess of Sutherland was an enemy of God's truth, and her practice was to appoint, to every parish in

'If repentance comes not soon ... the day of righteous retribution will arrive, and ... the Cries of this suffering people will be heard by that God in whose esteem the soul of the Peasant is as precious as that of the Prince.'[21] Patrick Sellar branded the new outburst of criticism as 'part of a system adopted to stir up the unwashed part of mankind against those who shave and wear a clean shirt'.

The House of Sutherland made no public answer to the mounting criticism until 1845. Loch believed it unworthy of notice. 'We had our first days of abuse', he remarked, 'we then had our days of popularity—we have perhaps now a little abuse again, but in the long run, depend upon it, that he who acts in a straightforward, honest, manner with a determination to do right, will survive such and many other attacks.' Loch preferred to answer criticism by private communication with influential people of his acquaintance.

One criticism which has always been raised—and an extremely important criticism—is that the Highland clearances, in effect, caused the destitution of the 1830s and 1840s. Such a claim is extremely difficult to verify. Only detailed and careful comparative studies of cleared and uncleared areas can approach a solution. So far the necessary research has not been done. Loch himself had two answers —first, that the destitution affected Sutherland less than elsewhere, and, second, that unavoidable and unpredictable forces were its root causes.[22]

In 1841 Loch was asked to supply information for the *New Statistical Account*. He acknowledged that his evidence could be construed as biased, but he welcomed constructive criticism. He said that he would never accept the charge that the Sutherland 'experiment' had been undertaken recklessly: 'I was indignant at this, knowing the years of preparation which we had in the care that was taken to meet every contingency. A man must be a fool and more who

---

her gift, men who in every way brought reproach on the ministerial character. The Countess, therefore, indignantly rejected Mr Graham, and Mr Ross, whose principles were in strict accordance with those of his patron, was presented.

This account loses some of its force when the age of the Countess is taken into consideration—in 1777 she was eleven.

[21] SC, Crichton to Loch, 16–10–1843; Jackson to Loch, 2–2–1843; Mackenzie to Loch, 23–3–1842; Gunn to Loch, 21–3–1842; Sellar to Loch, 8–1–1841, 16–1–1841, 1–12–1841; Horsburgh to Loch, 20–10–1841, 3–3–1846; Loch to Gunn, 13–3–1843. S. de Sismondi, *Political Economy and the Philosophy of Government* (ed. Mignet, 1857). *Westminster Review*, XXXIX, 69–80. Allardyce, op. cit., 537, 549, 556, 560.

[22] SC, Loch to Mackenzie, 25–3–1842.

undertook to advise such a measure without feeling the deep responsibility which he incurred in dealing with the comfort, the welfare and the happiness of so many of his fellow beings.' He surveyed the results of the policies, parish by parish, and concluded: 'The experiment has succeeded to the utmost in some districts, less well in others, has failed in some.' Loch admitted that he and his advisers had seriously miscalculated the fisheries: they had misunderstood the 'migratory habits of the fish', and had overestimated the demand for fish. They had especially failed to predict the consequences of the abolition of slavery upon the West Indian market for fish. This acknowledgment was, no doubt, a bitter pill for Loch, since the success of the fishing industry was a prerequisite for the improvement of the Sutherland population. While admitting his fallibility, Loch wrote, 'my conscience tells me that in advising this great measure, I have upon the whole added to the amount of human improvement, notwithstanding the more rapid increase in population than I expected, and without calling to aid the vast benefit which the nation has obtained from the great additional supply of food and wool, the result of the change'. Such was Loch's justification. Many have reached diametrically opposed conclusions: in the same year, 1841, Hugh Miller said that the Sutherland experiment was akin to carving up a dog live for the benefit of science.[23]

The 2nd Duke was unable and probably unwilling to sanction the levels of expenditure in the north as his father had done. There is a slight but perceptible impression of disenchantment; certainly, the idea of further territorial expansion held little appeal. In 1843, instead of raising money by selling holdings in the funds, the Duke thought it preferable to dispose of his Ardross estate. He told Loch, 'I have no attachments to it—I have already more than enough in the North, I do not wish to be mixed in Ross-shire matters—as the proprietor of Ardross ought to be—I cannot lay out money to improve it—on the contrary far from having any to spare I am in want, I don't want to appear more wealthy than I am, it is extremely inconvenient to do so.' He pointed out that the prospective buyer, Matheson, was not 'a tyrannical or grasping man', was politically acceptable and would be able to improve Ardross and employ the people. The Duke said that his northern possessions were sufficient to please anyone and since his circumstances were 'very different from those of my father' it would be better to sell. His brother

[23] SC, Loch to Lockhart, 2–10–1841, 6–10–1841. Miller, op. cit.

thought it a positive advantage 'to diminish the size of the landed target at which the landless love to shoot'.

Loch however was pained by this change of land policy. The name and consequence of the House of Sutherland would diminish; it would be another serious inroad into the permanent capital. He informed the Duke, 'it is the extent of your Northern possessions more than their relative value which adds to the great station you hold.' Loch's regrets and assumptions were, for once, ignored. The Ardross Estate was sold.[24]

Loch had always feared a discussion of the clearances in parliament. An average orator would find it easy to dramatize the evictions into an example, *par excellence*, of exploitation and cruelty. It was much more difficult to defend and justify the policy without a long, and probably rather tedious, exposition of the complicated circumstances. Any defence would appear as a gloss. In any case, even if the criticisms were fully answered, the mud would stick. In public debate, to admit some error would be to admit defeat.

Moreover, Loch had always asserted that the policy would be justified by its results. But the condition of west and northern Sutherland in the 1840s was not at all an unequivocal demonstration of the benefits of the clearance system. In 1845 the Sutherland question was raised in a debate on the Scottish Poor Law Amendment Bill.[25] Loch was twice challenged to defend the policy with which he had been associated since 1812; his answer was not a balanced rationale, but rather a desperate defence in the face of a formidable personal attack.

The parliamentary proceedings were prefaced by a series of articles in *The Times* by its reporter, Foster. Loch told the northern factors to give Foster 'all civility and show him all, for if there is anything to want let it be known'. Horsburgh met Foster and reported that he was 'an agreeable and clever man . . . and not at all likely to indulge in the low abuse we have had so much of late . . . He is clear that woollen manufactures should be forthwith established and minerals wrought, on a large scale!' Gunn said that Foster had been 'quite satisfied', to which the Duke (having read *The Times*) retorted,

[24] SC, Sutherland to Loch, 15–11–1843, 20–11–1843, 22–11–1843; Loch to Sutherland, 18–11–1845, 24–5–1845; D593P/22/1/5, Lord Francis to Sutherland, 20–11–1843.

[25] See Poor Law Inquiry (Scotland), 1845, esp. appendix, parts II and IV.

'Indeed! he expresses satisfaction then in a very extraordinary style'.

Foster's reports were an indictment of the Sutherland regime, based upon a collection of specific examples of unrelieved destitution and suffering. They were designed as an exposé of a system of land-ownership which permitted the unbridled exercise of autocratic power and the culpable neglect of the welfare of the poor. Suther-land, wrote Foster, was not an exaggerated case, since the 2nd Duke was widely regarded as a liberal landlord. He dismissed any Mal-thusian justification as neither valid nor humane; he scorned 'the principles of Scotch philosophical calculation' on which the clear-ances were founded; the policy was 'narrow-minded and unwise'. His own solution was the immediate promotion of fishing and manu-factures. Foster's articles were accompanied by other contributions which spoke of iron despotism, monstrous iniquities, the extirpation of the Highland people, of Celts suffering at the hands of the Saxons, and of the transformation of the Highlands into steppes.[26] *The Times* rampant was a formidable opponent.

The Duke believed that the reports were misrepresentations characteristic of the newspaper. But, he said, parts of the report were true; Sutherland was no Arcadia; no one could deny the poverty of the people, that assistance was small, or that many habitations were wretched. Loch, however, was angered. Foster, he claimed, had been sent north to make a case against the Poor Law Bill, to promote the peculiar notions of his editor on the treatment of the poor and on the enclosure of commons, 'and lastly to chime in with the prevailing feeling of this country and to sell the paper'. Loch never failed to discredit the motives of his critics. But he ad-mitted that cases of individual suffering existed, though he asked, 'Are the English towns or agricultural districts unexempted, I fear not.' Loch was infuriated that Foster had withheld evidence that the Duke had made vast efforts to relieve poverty and hardship: 'Why does he not go to some part of the country where no alteration of the Highland system has taken place, where he will find many people, higher rents, and none got except by harsh means?'[27]

Within a few days the first debate on the Poor Law began. This was made the occasion for the attack on the Sutherland policies by

[26] *The Times*, 1845, May 24, 26, 28, June 6, 7, 11, 12, 16. See also *Punch*, VIII, 251. SC, Loch to Horsburgh, 28-5-1845; Horsburgh to Loch, 3-6-1845.

[27] SC, Sutherland to Loch, 30-5-1845; Duchess of Sutherland to Loch, 4-3-1845; Loch to Sutherland, 2-6-1845, 4-6-1845.

opponents armed with *The Times*'s reports. Loch gave his reply—which was largely a recital of statistics of relief and improvement expenditure, and a blanket denunciation of his critics. The Duchess thought Loch had spoken very well, and the Duke said it was very satisfactory. Loch was also content: *The Times* reports had been ill-received and, he said, 'the few words of explanation which I gave ... show that they gave no credence to them.'[28]

Nevertheless, the shock of this public attack caused misgivings in the noble proprietors. Loch filled many letters in an effort to assure them of the fundamental wisdom of their policies. He said that the evidence of the opposition was worthless, that the common people's conditions had always been given the deepest consideration. He stated categorically that the system that had worked well for more than thirty years could not now be abandoned. But the Duchess remained doubtful. Could it be true, she asked, that the herring fishing did not pay the people employed in it? Had Loch no misgivings about the enormous size of the sheep farms?—for it was said that Sellar had made very large profits and had been able to buy land in Argyll 'where they say he is not popular'. The Duke was also perturbed and had begun a personal investigation of poverty in Sutherland. He told Loch, 'I certainly acknowledge feeling that we have been disposed to flatter ourselves as to the improvements in Cottages, though there has been much.' He considered a public statement essential. He questioned Loch:

I don't quite know how you meet the observation that the giving up rent for such a time and adding a cost of £60,000 should not yet have a richer result—it rather agrees with my question how proprietors who cannot afford such sacrifices can live. An answer is that much of it goes to public benefit, roads, ports, inns which are not expected to repay their cost.

Loch replied that the lesser Scottish lairds lived in a very melancholy condition: 'Those who possess their estates in fee simple are obliged to sell them, those who are prevented doing so by their entails are literally beggars. The Highlands are gradually getting into the hands of English capitalists.' On the question of rents, Loch stated that the Sutherland rental had slightly increased since 1815—while in five out of seven agricultural counties in Scotland rents had fallen. Hence, he claimed, the policy had succeeded 'whether regard

[28] SC, Duchess to Loch, 12–6–1845; Sutherland to Loch, 21–6–1845; Loch to Sutherland, 13–6–1845, 1–7–1845; Loch to Mackenzie, 26–6–1845, 4–7–1845. Hansard, 12–6–1845. Cf. Grimble, op. cit., 89–93.

is paid to the improvement of the country, the real income of the landlord, or above all the temporal comfort and the moral and religious education of the people'.[29]

For the second debate on the Poor Law Bill, Loch was better prepared. He had consulted the *New Statistical Account* and had prepared a pamphlet of *Facts* to accompany his parliamentary defence. The lines of his argument are familiar. Before 1817 'the people were exposed to the most severe occasional privations ... on such occasions they were frequently reduced to the necessity of bleeding their cattle in order to mix the blood with the remnant of meal left to them for food.' Since that time there had been no such calamity. Until 1811 the landlord had received rent from his estate; since then the equivalent of all the rent plus £60,000 had been expended upon the estate; the 2nd Duke had abandoned arrears of £10,000; when the Reay Country was acquired, rents were reduced by 30 per cent. Loch affirmed that the rents of the small tenants were reduced when the sub-letting system was abolished. The policy was designed to remove poverty; it should not be judged by English prejudices but by Highland standards. As for the removals, notice had always been given, and although destitution had sometimes occurred, it was necessary to take into account the failure of the kelp trade. Loch cited many figures for the proof of improvement— ploughs, gigs, bakers, shops, blacksmiths, carpenters—'Showing that there must be a considerable surplus of capital among the people'. He claimed that the fishing industry employed 3,900 people.[30]

Loch's speech of 3 July 1845 was supported by Dundas. The Duke congratulated them both: they had distinguished themselves, he said. Loch himself reported, 'The statement I had to make was very well received and appeared to be quite satisfactory to Peel, who cheered it.' Dundas, however, warned Loch against publishing a justification of the Sutherland system. '*The Times* and the Detractors', he said, 'would rejoice as the birds of prey do, at the sight of such food.' It was expedient to remain quiet rather than stimulate the excited taste of the public. No answer, he said, could excuse the cases of destitution that had been proven; there had been 'sad neglects and oversights', and any answer would 'lead to further odium and insult'; it would reveal 'the *dark* features of the case ... without any solid

[29] SC, Duchess to Loch, 26-6-1845; Loch to Duchess, 23-6-1845, 8-7-1845; Sutherland to Loch, June 1845; Loch to Gunn, 18-7-1845.
[30] J. Loch, *Facts, passim.* SC, Sutherland to Loch, 6-6-1845.

advantages to the *bright* ones'. Nevertheless, Loch's pamphlet of *Facts* was published within a few weeks, apparently without much public attention. [31]

Throughout the public debate Loch had argued from general grounds and aggregate statistics, and had completely failed to answer the specific charges of individual destitution that Foster and the Poor Law Commissioners' Report had cited. Loch was ignorant of the cases and was embarrassed by the gaps in his defence. After the debate he instructed the local factors in Sutherland to investigate every instance quoted. Gunn reported that he had been aware of

every case of them for years back, and contributed to their support and comfort, whenever there was a demand by the Parish Ministers ... and nothing can exceed the rancorous hate and black deception of the Free Kirk Ministers, when they conceal all this, and a great deal that the Duchess/Countess and the Duke gave lavishly ... making it appear to the world that all that the Proprietor contributed to the poor was £6 in each parish.

The other agent, Horsburgh of Tongue, replied more calmly, and generally corroborated the instances of dire poverty and minimal relief that existed in Sutherland. The Duke, who had personally examined, and was deeply concerned by, the conditions on his estate, remarked that if Foster went 'a few doors from his house in London ... he will find want equally calling for his charity and gratuitous succour as in Sutherland'. At the same time, the Duke issued instructions for the provision of more fishing facilities on the west coast of his estate. [32]

The public debate left its mark on Sutherland policy. Loch became ultra-cautious in sanctioning the removal and resettlement of tenants; an agent was told, 'on no account to move them unless he can be put elsewhere'. Every action, said Loch bitterly, was to be governed by a principle: 'whether you have a case that the people of England and the Press will support you in ... the present tendency of both is to conclude that the landlord is wrong and the tenant is right.' All effort was to be expended in keeping petitions from parliament. Loch thus accepted that public opinion was the

[31] Hansard, 3–7–1845. SC, Sutherland to Loch, 6–7–1845; Loch to Sutherland, 4–7–1845; Dundas to Loch, 13–7–1845, 18–7–1845. Cf. Grimble, 93.
[32] SC, Sinclair to Loch, 27–6–1845; Loch to Gunn, 4–7–1845; Gunn to Loch, 29–7–1845; Horsburgh to Loch, 8–8–1845; Sutherland to G. Loch, 31–8–1845; Dempster to Loch, 9–6–1845; Sutherland to Loch, 20–6–1845; D593P/22/1/33, Horsburgh to Loch, 11–7–1845.

overruling consideration. It was 'owing to the change in the times', he said.

But Loch's faith in the general policy of the rearrangement of Highland estates had not weakened. In 1846 he advised the Marchioness of Lorne that a radical reform on the Sutherland pattern was the only solution to the financial problems of her family. But, he warned, 'do nothing too fast, or you fail in gaining your end, for if the people don't go along with you, they will resist in a thousand ways, besides all mankind must be allowed to a certain extent to be happy in their own way.'

Loch would admit only two mistakes in the Sutherland plan: first, that 'the great body of the people should have been settled in America and not in Sutherland', and, second, that the farms were too large— but this had been necessary to induce substantial tenants to settle in the county. The latter confession was important since it heralded a change in the leasing policy of the estate. Smaller farms, Loch now believed, would encourage the establishment of a much needed middle class of small capitalists. Commenting on the change of policy, Loch remarked, 'It is foolish not to be taught wisdom from experience, or to think oneself too old to learn, or that what one has achieved is perfect. The Rocks upon which all old men split, this I will endeavour to put off if I can avoid it.'[33]

In September 1845 the Duke of Sutherland was told that his small tenants were very fortunately placed. 'In Ireland they would pay almost as many pounds as they pay you shillings and would fight to the death for the land.' In the same month *The Times* commended the improvements of Lord George Hill in Donegal which, remarked George Loch, were remarkably similar to the Sutherland schemes— 'they were equally carried out in spite of opposition from the people.' Comparisons between Sutherland and Ireland became more ominous in the following months.[34]

[33] SC, Loch to Sutherland, 4–4–1846, 7–11–1846; Loch to Gunn, 6–4–1846, 18–5–1846; Loch to Horsburgh, 2–5–1846; D593/P/20, Sutherland to Sellar, 6–10–1847; Loch to Sellar, 8–11–1847.

[34] SC, Denison to Sutherland, 16–9–1845; G. Loch to Sutherland, 20–9–1845.

XVII

❖❖❖

Famine and the Final Years

❖❖❖

In June 1845 Loch had claimed in his own defence that there had been no calamitous famine in Sutherland since 1817. In the following November the first fears of the potato blight were reported from the Highlands. During that winter there was little panic, and the disease does not appear to have caught hold of Sutherland crops. But great care was taken to persuade the people to preserve their potato seed for the coming season.

In September 1846 the potato situation in the Highlands and Islands deteriorated rapidly—although the distress varied and was greatest on the western edge of the region. Lord Lorne reported that the population of his Mull and Tiree estates was 'absolutely threatened with total famine'. The potato disease had attacked at a much earlier stage than in the previous year. In Sutherland the factors were optimistic at first, the crop was expected to be average. But very quickly the disease seems to have taken a stronger grip of the major subsistence crop of the West Highland economy. Petitions for help were drawn up. One petition came from Knockan and Elphin, the only uncleared district of Assynt, where the tenants faced starvation and asked for meal supplies and relief employment. The Duke of Sutherland hoped for government assistance, adding morosely, 'The redundant amount of population cannot be doubted—and has been apparent for some time—but what remedy?'[1]

Loch, in contrast, was far less pessimistic. He did not believe disaster to be imminent. He told Sutherland that crops other than potatoes were good, that fishing catches were plentiful, and that

[1] SC, Lorne to Loch, 8–9–1846; Loch to Wood, 8–9–1846; MacIver to Loch, 8–9–1846, 11–9–1846; Horsburgh to Loch, 9–9–1846, 16–9–1846; Sutherland to Loch, September 1846; Barclay to Loch, 25–9–1846.

there was a good deal of work available in the south of Scotland. The people should be assured that, 'if the necessity shall arise, you are prepared to discharge your duty towards all.' But, until such emergency conditions obtained, the people ought to be compelled to look to their own resources, otherwise the Duke would 'paralyse the exertions of the industrious and encourage the less active'. Loch bluntly told the Duke that 'the difficulty of the whole country is over-population which is increased by the kindness with which they are treated.'[2]

Taking up an extreme doctrinaire position almost certainly derived from Smith's *Wealth of Nations*,[3] Loch believed that comprehensive gratuitous relief would destroy the self-reliance of the people and cast them 'back in the Scale of Civilization'. The Duke's 'extreme benevolence', argued Loch, 'would often induce him to interfere in trying to help them, to an extent that would ultimately be to their own harm . . . They are indolent like all people—they would rather beg than work—they would rather be content with little than labour hard.' Moreover, Loch insisted, if the Duke took upon himself to supply the people, he would discourage the private dealers who would always be able to organize the trade most efficiently. The normal functioning of the market guaranteed the cheapest supply: 'the regular dealer should not be interfered with so long as he serves the country at reasonable prices.' Monopoly or famine price-levels would not occur because the estate factors had contracted the dealers to supply at southern prices. The people would buy meal at the market price, and they could get work in the south or on relief employment. Only in an emergency should the Duke intervene—and Loch had already organized a reserve of emergency supplies. 'I do not think that some pressure of distress will not reach our people', Loch declared, 'I think it will and I *think it ought*, it is the only thing that will induce them to work.' The Duke had received petitions from his Helmsdale tenants for cheaper potato land. He had been inclined to grant this, and to subsidize the price of his meal imports. Loch was entirely opposed to both measures.[4]

A clear rift had developed between Loch and the Duke of Sutherland. Loch believed that the landlord could and should provide

[2] SC, Loch to MacIver, 27–9–1846; Loch to Sutherland, 10–10–1846.

[3] II, 24–8 (Everyman ed., 1910).

[4] SC, Loch to Dundas, 1–11–1846; Loch to Sutherland, 12–11–1846, 15–11–1846, 19–11–1846; Loch to MacIver, 9–10–1846.

relief-employment on the Sutherland estate without assistance from the government or relief charities. Indeed on this question Loch persuaded the doubtful Duke to decline government assistance—on the grounds that it would avoid public taunts that the Duke 'is a man rich enough to maintain his people . . . and what was intended for the relief of the poor of the needy landlord is taken for the necessities of the people of the rich one'. But the Duke disagreed with Loch's insistence that relief should be supplied only at market rates. The Duke, who was deeply moved by the harrowing destitution and had pledged his own family not to eat potatoes during the crisis, was not prepared to accept Loch's logic. He told Loch that the supply of meal could not be left entirely to the mechanism of supply and demand. There were 'exceptional cases in which the usual laws of proportion are not to be found applicable', he wrote. His own economic theory was impeccable: 'The doctrine itself regarding Demand and Supply, viz. that demand seeking the cheapest, and supply the dearest market, will occasion a proper balance to be found, is good if the premise be established, that there is a choice of market.' The Duke did not believe the premises were fulfilled in Sutherland. Action was necessary to supply the poor on more moderate terms.[5]

Certainly the situation was black, particularly on the west coast. The Scourie factorship alone required 10,000 bolls of meal. The potatoes were diseased, the seed was rotting. There was extreme suffering. The factor, Evander MacIver, saw a future of gloom and apprehension. For, although the coastal lots of the resettled population were much improved, they simply could not support the people and the west-coast fishing remained undeveloped. 'What', said MacIver, 'is to become of the people?' The landlord could not support them—'the pecuniary loss would be ruinous'—and continual amelioration would merely worsen the dilemma. Emigration, he said, was an answer, but in this the government should help: 'Surely when Government are making such enormous pecuniary sacrifices for the people of Ireland, they will do something for the Highlanders who are suffering so quietly and peaceably'. The other factor, Gunn, was less indulgent. Gunn believed that 'the young and able-bodied men and women skulk idly at home in such an emergency as the present.' If they refused the ample opportunities of

[5] SC, Sutherland to Loch, 19-10-1846; Gunn to Loch, 29-1-1847; Draft Address to Tenants of Sutherland, 12-10-1846.

employment, he declared, 'let them die of starvation . . . and the Duke will be free and absolved from the consequences of the law of God and man.' The Duke dissociated himself from Gunn's remarks.[6]

Meanwhile Loch decided to remonstrate with the government against the sale of meal in the north at prices below the rates in Liverpool and Glasgow. His critics believed him disastrously wrong in this proposal—Lorne said it was 'a stretch of political economy which is indeed extreme'—and the Duke of Sutherland counter-manded Loch's intention. The Duke was equally annoyed that the meal he had bought in Liverpool in August had been delayed so long in its despatch north. It should not be sold at the market rate—'it seems to me to be out of the question that the poor should be charged at that rate.' Moreover, since Loch had refused the offer of government meal, 'I think the people have the right to say that they have been prevented receiving the meal by our refusing the offered means of supplying it—and consequently I *must do* as Government does, having in fact engaged to do so.' The Duke explained, 'we cannot agree with you that the food in Assynt should cost as dear as in Yorkshire, Liverpool and Manchester. There is work in those places which we have not.' People were actually starving in the western Highlands he said.[7]

Loch, although overruled, continued to insist that the Sutherland management was supplying the people at rates below those of any other landlord in the country, and 'as cheap as Government meal'. In effect, the landlord was fulfilling his emergency responsibilities, and government aid was neither necessary nor welcome—and hence perfectly consistent with Loch's parliamentary defence of poor relief provision in Sutherland during the Scottish Poor Law debate of 1845. Loch's assertions appeared to be vindicated by Sir Charles Trevelyan who, in January 1847, commended the Suther-land relief measures and stated that government prices (which were

[6] SC, MacIver to Loch, 1–12–1846, 8–12–1846, 22–12–1846, 28–12–1846; Gunn to Loch, 3–12–1846, 17–12–1846; Sutherland to Loch, 20–11–1846, 25–12–1846.

[7] SC, Lorne to Loch, 30–12–1846; Sutherland to Loch, 29–12–1846, 31–12–1846. See also Letter XXIX in *Extracts from letters to the Rev. Dr. McLeod*, ed. N. Macleod (1847), in which the Minister for Assynt declared that 'I have no hesitation in saying unless something is done, and that immediately, for their relief, hundreds of my poor parishioners will, ere two months elapse, be in eternity' (December 1846).

likely to rise) were already 3*d*. a boll higher than those in Sutherland. Indeed, said Trevelyan, the government was forced 'to adhere to the market price else we shall have the whole country upon us and all private trade and exertion will end'.[8]

Undoubtedly relief had been mobilized on an unprecedented scale on the Sutherland estate. The most critical area—the Scourie factorship on the west coast—absorbed the majority of the money. MacIver, the factor, sent a ship to Norway to look for potatoes; in January 1847 meal ships arrived carrying Indian corn, wheat and potatoes, purchased by the management. The people were given work, mainly on drainage, and credit was provided where 'necessary'. Bounties were offered to those enlisting in the army or seeking work in the south. Emigrants were offered free passage to Canada. Loch wrote that 'the factors have unlimited powers to meet the exigencies of the lamentable state of matters.' He told the Duke of the financial burden: 'Large as the demands from Sutherland are ... you are fully enabled to meet the calamity with which it has pleased God to visit your people in common with many who have not the income.' But there were signs of strain. It is clear, for instance, that expenditure was being diverted from the English estates for the purpose of northern relief. Loch also applied to the Drainage Commissioners for a loan of £50,000 for Sutherland.[9]

The difficulties of food supply intensified in 1847. The price of meal continued to rise, and it became desperately important to preserve seed potatoes for the forthcoming season. MacIver was besieged— the people were in a pitiful condition—'you will see in the faces of some of them marks of hunger', wrote a factor. The famine requirements of Ireland, of course, rendered the supply of the Highlands immensely more difficult. The Duke declared, 'their millions make our thousands more difficult to provide ... all that can be bought, begged, borrowed from other parts will be wanted and sought for Ireland, an imposing competition for us.' Meanwhile potato shortages in France and Flanders forestalled Loch's plans for imports from Europe. In neighbouring Caithness the militia had been compelled to fire on people at Wick to prevent further violence. In Sutherland, by contrast the factors were ordered to shoot deer to provide soup and venison for the people. Soup kettles, barley and ship's biscuits

[8] SC, Sutherland to Loch, 1–1–1847; Trevelyan to Loch, 13–1–1847.
[9] SC, Loch to Sutherland, 21–1–1847, 8–2–1847; Loch to Smith, 5–2–1847. See also *Reports of Free Church Committee on Destitution*, 1847.

were ordered, and Loch's daughter helped distribute the soup to the destitute.[10]

Loch was infuriated by current reports that the Duke was doing nothing to assist the destitute. It was an unqualified falsehood: before the end of February 1847 he had already spent £12,000 on the purchase of supplies for his estate. A year later the Inspector-General, Elliot, of the Highland Destitution Committee, recorded that 'this benevolent nobleman, in the year of Destitution, upon a rent-roll of about £39,000 in Sutherland, expended in the entire county somewhere about £78,000.' This, of course, was not entirely a gift, though much of it was probably irrecoverable. Meal stores were set up at various points on the north and west coasts. There were stringent regulations governing the distribution of food. It was subject to the orders of the Parochial Board; it was provided free to the destitute; sold to those who had money to pay for it; others could do specified relief work for the food. Moreover, 'No young men who could work at the Railway in the South were to have work, but they were ... offered £1 each to help them south.' Employment on a railway at Aberdeen had been found for 130 men—but many of the Sutherlanders refused to go. An added difficulty was the belated limitation on loans imposed by the Drainage Act Commissioners in March 1847.

The Duke of Sutherland was ill with anxiety for the suffering in the Highlands and Ireland. As a proprietor he accepted his responsibility of providing relief for the people on his estate. Trevelyan declared that Sutherland was a fine example of the best in landlordism —for the Duke had not asked for government assistance and had pledged himself to support his people.[11]

Emigration increased during the famine years. Petitions were received for aid in transport to America, and the Duke of Sutherland began to subsidize emigration on a large scale—in 1847 he spent £2,000 in this way in the district of Scourie alone. Loch opened negotiations with the Colonial Office with a prospect of the Duke buying an estate in Cape Breton Island or South Australia, the land

[10] SC, MacIver to Loch, 29–1–1847; Sutherland to Loch, 25–2–1847, 4–3–1847; Loch to Sutherland, 25–2–1847; Loch to Mackenzie, 22–2–1847. Barron, op. cit., III, 133.
[11] SC, Gunn to Loch, 12–11–1846, 20–11–1846, 25–11–1846, 26–2–1847, 25–3–1847; Leslie to Loch, 25–11–1846; Loch to Sutherland, 25–2–1847, 12–3–1847; Sutherland to Loch, 9–3–1847. R. Elliot, *Special Report on Sutherland and the West Highlands* (1848), 10. See also Cavendish, op. cit., 80–7.

to be rented to the migrants whose passage the Duke would pay. There was, apparently, a strong feeling amongst the prospective migrants against Australia—'they would prefer being paupers at home to going there', it was reported. MacIver thought that they should be encouraged to go to Canada. 'It would be a pity', he wrote, 'to lose so very favourable an opportunity of getting so many to leave the country'. Patrick Sellar threw in his own unsolicited support. At the height of the famine he advocated the use of ships to export people instead of importing food:

> The *difference of cost* of eating Indian corn in America, besides eating at home would pay the expense of their transport, £10 millions spent in applying the remedy would be a profitable investment. But £10 millions applied, merely to pass through the Bowels of a misgoverned people is worse than throwing away. It destroys the self-reliance—makes them a mistletoe on the British oak.

Without necessarily sharing Sellar's sentiments, the Sutherland estate sponsored many migrants. In June 1847, for example, a shipment of migrants left north-west Sutherland—'397 souls have been sent at an expense equal to £4–7–11 each soul'—destined for Pictou and Montreal. They departed in despair, not in hope.[12]

Sir Edward Coffin, a man whose historical reputation has not suffered despite his association with the famine administration in Ireland, journeyed north in July 1847 to investigate the distress in the Highlands. The Sutherland factors were instructed to inform Coffin of the precise details of the relief measures, and to distinguish between gratuitous and repayable assistance. In fact, Coffin's report was highly gratifying and Loch was congratulated by Trevelyan. The report stressed that the incidence of famine was not uniform; it paid a glowing tribute to the manner and scale of the Sutherland relief, and pointed out that £18,000 had been spent 'exclusive of money payments for wages and other payments'. Eight months later Captain Elliot performed a similar investigation of Sutherland, and his report was yet more complimentary—he thought that the Duke had been excessively generous and that the people tended to be ungrateful, deceitful, indolent and often simply lacked the enterprise to provide their own subsistence by fishing.[13]

[12] SC, Loch to Sutherland, 11–2–1847; MacIver to Loch, February 1847, 26–6–1847; Sellar to Loch, 6–3–1847, 27–3–1847.

[13] SC, Loch to Factors, 7–6–1847; MacIver to Loch, 23–7–1847; Trevelyan to Loch, 23–8–1847; Loch to Sutherland, 17–5–1847; Culverwell to Loch, 20–10–1847. Elliot, op. cit., *passim*.

The relief was obviously a major financial burden on the landlord. Neither his English nor his Scottish estates produced any net income in 1847. The cost of relief can be compared with other items of expenditure at this time—for instance, the reconstruction of Dunrobin Castle had cost £41,414 by 1848. A new harbour at Leck Robie was contemplated at an estimated cost of £51,000—the major advantage of which would be sailing facilities for the Sutherland heirs, and an auspicious disembarkation point for Queen Victoria.[14]

The potato blight returned in the winter of 1847–8. Again there was considerable suffering in north-west Sutherland. Emigration continued. Letters from satisfied migrants in Canada were lithographed and circulated amongst the population. The Duke of Sutherland paid the passage money (about £4 per person), a gratuity of £2 (which was often spent on clothes and bonded stores for the voyage), and a pension to 'any old decrepit person who did not choose to follow his friends or family'. It was stipulated that the prospective migrant should ask, of his own volition, for this aid from the landlord: 'It is better on every account that the emigration should be voluntary', declared Loch. In return the migrant signed a pledge, on penalty of £50, to migrate and renounce all claims on the estate of Sutherland. In June 1848 the vessel *Scotia* left Loch Eriboll with 206 souls whose passage cost the Duke £1,133. Horsburgh, the factor, attended the embarkation and reported to the Duke as follows:[15]

The scene . . . became at the end a rather trying one, and when I dropped from the vessel into the boat, under the hearty cheers of my poor but honest friends, I admit that I felt moved in no ordinary degree. They were unquestionably right to go when so liberally provided for. God grant, my Lord, that they be just as fortunate and happy as I know your Grace sincerely wishes them to be.

The amendment of the Passenger Acts and the Canadian proposal to exact an entrance fee of 10s. per immigrant produced consternation in the Sutherland management. MacIver thought that the new Acts would amount to a prohibition of emigration. The regulations,

---

[14] SC, Neish to Loch, 28–1–1848; Loch to Sutherland, 23–7–1847, 25–1–1848, 22–1–1848; Loch to Duchess, 4–9–1847.

[15] SC, Horsburgh to Loch, 12–10–1847; MacIver to Loch, 5–11–1847, 24–1–1848; Loch to Trevelyan, 10–1–1848; Loch to Sutherland, 10–1–1848; D593P/22/1/33. See also the rather fatuous *Tour of Sutherlandshire* (1884 ed.), by Charles St John, I, 80–1.

K

he considered, were unnecessary: 'last year nearly 400 were sent to America in two ships from this district and . . . they all arrived in perfect health in America.' Conditions in Canada were not idyllic. In July 1848 400 Sutherlanders arrived at Brantford in Ontario where the inhabitants raised a subscription to relieve their destitution and help them to reach Zorra where they intended to settle. In April 1849 recent migrants to Nova Scotia petitioned the Duke of Sutherland to relieve their continuing poverty.[16]

In practice emigration from the west coast was partly associated with more clearances. A clearance in Assynt had been planned for 1849. The potato famine gave a justification for the removal: 740 people had applied for emigration assistance, many of them from coastal lots. MacIver said, 'There will be more lots vacated than will be sufficient for all the tenants of Knockan and Elphin'—the areas to be cleared. Despite the fact that rents were given up for the year prior to the clearance, and a reception area reserved, the interior people were not impressed. Petitions were sent to the Duke, and in 1848 Loch postponed the clearance, admitting that the coastal lots would be overcrowded. Nevertheless, Loch was convinced that the welfare of the coastal lotter (even in Assynt) was better than that of the uncleared population. The estate, he wrote, was still the best example for the improving Highland owner. Moreover, he re-affirmed, emigration was no substitute for improvement.[17]

Famine relief seriously interfered with Loch's hopes for retrench-ment. The greater participation of the 2nd Duke in estate affairs, together with the destitution, gave rise to some rethinking of policy—the agent Horsburgh even suggested a five-year plan. For although estate receipts amounted to about £39,000, expenditure persistently outstripped income. In September of 1848 Loch wrote, 'not only have all the rents gone, but a very large sum has been remitted from England, and nearly as large a sum will be required to complete the year. I have therefore begged of his Grace to undertake no new expenditure'. By March 1848 the Duke had spent £58,519 on meal, labour and emigration. However, the figures for relief expenditure are ambiguous since very little was given gratuitously. In 1853 Loch told Shaftesbury that £20,913 of unrecovered money had been

[16] SC, MacIver to Loch, 17–3–1848, 18–3–1848; Loch to MacIver, 9–6–1848; D593P/20, Petition from Picton; D593P/28/9, Letter to *Galt Reporter*.
[17] SC, MacIver to Loch, 23–3–1847, 24–3–1847, 1–2–1848; Loch to MacIver, 10–6–1848, 21–6–1848; Loch to Sutherland, 22–6–1848.

expended during the famine—yet almost half of this was spent on road construction. [18]

Despite the inescapable financial problems of the northern estates, Loch's optimism did not fail him. He believed that the future would bring a diminution of expenditure and the emergence of a class of independent, prosperous lotters on the coasts. Furthermore, the sheep farms were to be remodelled; as the leases fell in they were to be broken up and made 'available to men of middling capital . . . and each farm shall have the means of raising turnips sufficient to meet its own wants or nearly so'. There were to be farms of £50–£100 annual rent. Improved transport facilities would attract capital to the estate. Thus the original social and economic experiment was in the process of significant modification. The Duke of Sutherland even managed to entertain hopes of woollen manufactures in the county. [19]

The potato famine in the north and west lingered on from winter to winter. In February 1849 MacIver told of three famines in succession which had been exacerbated by the failure of the herring fishing, by stormy weather, and by the loss of 'means and stock to pay for meal'. He was pessimistic for the future of the small tenants throughout the west Highlands. The blight reappeared in the two following years, and despite the reduced price of meal, the position was desperate. The quantity of potatoes sown had been reduced, cattle prices had fallen and the west-coast fishing failed to yield sufficient returns. MacIver believed that only one conclusion was possible— the land was not capable of supporting the population: 'the surface is so rocky and rugged that to improve it at a reasonable expense is out of the question.' The Scourie factorship could not yield a net income; on the contrary, it would be a continual drain from the land-lord's purse—unless the population could be reduced. The latter could be accomplished only by a comprehensive scheme of emigration. [20]

Such extreme pessimism was echoed by the Duke of Sutherland. 'I have no income from Scotland', he grumbled in 1850, 'and . . . my expenditure [has] every year exceeded income.' He agreed that it was partly a result of his own personal extravagance, but he could not

[18] SC, Neish to Loch, 10–6–1848; Loch to Skene, 4–4–1848; Loch to Duchess, 16–9–1848; Loch to Sutherland, 25–3–1848; Loch to Shaftesbury, 25–4–1854. See also Allardyce, op. cit., 598.
[19] SC, Loch to Skene, 20–7–1848; Loch to Sutherland, 10–1–1849; Loch to Hall, 10–1–1849.
[20] SC, MacIver to Loch, 23–2–1849, 11–9–1849, 3–10–1850.

avoid having guests at Dunrobin Castle. Retrenchment, he concurred, was essential; but he saw no prospect of financial benefits.
Other proprietors, he noted, had sold off their property in Scotland.
On his own estate, the Tongue factorship was 'the only remunerative
district and not one with any charm'. He was seriously considering
the sale of Assynt, 'but having it and in such a state as the people
there were, and are, we must improve them if we don't get quit of the
concern'. Loch replied, 'that if Assynt were in the hands of the most
liberal landlord in Britain he never would spend as much money on it
as you do.'[21]

Assynt and the west coast defied every attempt to promote improvement. The people existed in conditions of abysmal poverty.
The clearances and a high rate of population growth had created
overcrowding on the coastal lots, and the fishing failed to compete
with the east-coast centres. Many of the Assynt people were tied to
the truck-system and heavily indebted to fish curers. Yet the tenants
of uncleared Elphin and Knockan in the interior were equally
impoverished and in 1850 preparations were again made to execute
their removal. The people were promised lots on the coast or a free
passage to America. But it was extremely unpopular. MacIver
believed that it should proceed despite the odium and despite the
'pecuniary sacrifice' to the landlord—it was the only solution. The
Duke disagreed with both MacIver and Loch, saying that it would
be too unpopular and that the people paid their rents well enough,
and the coastal reception areas would be overcrowded. Loch argued
that if the people stayed their periodic poverty and distress would
simply intensify as their population grew. In the upshot a removal
was attempted in 1851; the people became violent and resisted
MacIver who reported that 'not one of them would admit they
did wrong . . . and seem quite resolved to do so again.' The Duke was
annoyed and rebuked his agents for their poor advice. Loch, however, refused to believe that the troubles in any way detracted from
the basic wisdom of the policy. For instance, in 1853 he advised
Lady Stafford to pursue a clearance policy for her Cromarty estates—
which, when effected, was also attended by well-publicized violent
resistance.[22]

[21] SC, Loch to Sutherland, 5–2–1850; Sutherland to Loch, 30–1–1850.

[22] SC, MacIver to Loch, 7–2–1850, 14–4–1851; Loch to Sutherland, 24–2–1850,
11–2–1851; Sutherland to Loch, 1–4–1851, 30–4–1851; Horsburgh to Loch,
11–7–1854; Loch to Duchess of Sutherland, 12–1–1853; Loch to Melville, 1–6–
1853.

Despite occasional resistance, whole townships in the west were cleared, either for resettlement or emigration. In seven years, one sixth of the entire population of the Scourie district emigrated. 'Of these', observed the factor, 'a large proportion were compelled to go for want of food.' The cost to the Duke had been £5,610 but, wrote MacIver, the benefits exceeded the costs. The policy towards emigration, of course, had completely changed since the early years of Loch's administration. In the 1850s the people of Assynt were urged to migrate. They were told that 'the Duke of Sutherland is quite willing to pay their passages whenever they choose to go.'[23] Subsidized emigration was the antithesis of the original policy and Loch acknowledged that, so far as the west-coast settlements were concerned, his intentions had been defeated. He attributed this to the extraordinary indolence and fecundity of the people and to the capricious behaviour of the fish—both of which were beyond his control. Had the people remained in the hills, their destitution would have been yet greater. A reduced population on the coasts could subsist adequately from their crofts and the fishing—but, Loch said, they must shed their indolent habits. 'Before their eyes a Buckie crew from Banffshire comes yearly to Scourie, and catches a large supply of cod and other fish, which they cure, and carry to the southern markets', he wrote in 1850. 'The native boatmen remaining inactive sometimes purchasing a few fish caught by these more industrious strangers. A crew which gained one of the Duke's prize boats, have actually sold it.' Many of the people preferred emigration to a precarious life in the fisheries. On the discovery of gold in Australia large numbers sought to leave. Single men were not eligible for the passage and were disappointed—'a good many however undertook to marry or get sisters.'[24]

The impact of the Sutherland clearance policies on the pattern of landholding was demonstrated in a detailed estate survey for the year 1852.

The 'large tenants' were spread over 120 holdings; twenty-eight paid more than £250 per annum; seven paid more than £1,000; the rental of the Sellar lease was £2,243 per annum. Between them they

---

[23] SC, MacIver to Loch, 30-4-1852, 1-5-1854; J. Sutherland to Loch, 24-10-1851. D593K/1/8/20.
[24] SC, MacIver to Loch, 31-3-1854, 10-5-1854; D593/V/6/87. J. Loch, *A Selection of Papers . . . of the Improvements in Sutherland, passim.*

possessed 127,170 sheep. Their arable land was not inconsiderable: in the Dunrobin factorship alone they worked more than 5,500 acres. These tenants contributed £25,258 to the annual income of the estate.

There were 2,785 'small tenants'. They paid a total annual rental of £5,933. Excluding hill pasture attached to the crofts, they held a total of 11,066 acres, of which 7,775 acres were cultivated. On this land there subsisted (officially) 10,211 people. The average lot or croft was 3·97 acres, which paid £2 2s. 6d. per annum rent. The average number of people subsisting on each lot was 3·7. The small tenants owned 920 ploughs, 1,717 harrows, 1,177 carts, and 1,691 horses.

The averages disguise certain significant variations. The western district, Scourie, which suffered most acutely during the famine, was the only area to suffer a net decline of population in the 1840s. Nevertheless, the Scourie tenants generally held larger lots, cultivated more land, and owned more cattle and sheep than their counterparts in Tongue and Dunrobin. The continuing poverty of the west was the result of the narrowness of employment opportunities and the relative failure of the fishing industry.

The 1852 rental survey gave no space to a third group in the Sutherland population. These were the cottars who represented rather more than 20 per cent of the population. They lived in cottages rent free 'and though they had properly speaking, no land allotted to them, they have yet, in many cases, small bits of potato ground. They are sometimes also allowed by sufferance . . . to keep a cow and a few sheep on the common.' The cottars found employment wherever they could. The estate management actively discriminated against them when seeking labour. It is significant that the proportion of cottars to local population was greatest in the Scourie district: they were the submerged stratum of a highly vulnerable society.[25]

The final years of Loch's life, like the earlier, were darkened by criticisms. A particularly vehement attacker was Thomas Mulock, an itinerant Irish journalist. He accused the Duke of Sutherland of misusing the Charitable Destitution Fund, and of 'perpetrating enormities in Sutherlandshire'. He also condemned Loch for mis-

---

[25] SC, D593H/14/6/1–2; *Reports of Free Church Committee on Destitution*, 1847. Poor Law Inquiry (Scotland) 1844, appendix, part II, 298. See also Gray, op. cit., 261.

leading in an unscrupulous manner the novelist, Harriet Beecher Stowe, who in her volume of *Sunny Memories of Foreign Lands* had praised the ducal family in a fulsome fashion. Loch, with his usual disdain for critics, dismissed Mulock as a 'thoroughgoing quack'. In 1853 Mulock publicly apologized for his vituperative remarks. It was said that he had been bribed to do so by the Sutherland family, but this is unlikely since Mulock continued to attack Loch after the apology.[26]

Much of the unpopularity arising from the Sutherland clearances was directed at Loch himself. While canvassing the voters of Wick during an electoral contest in 1852 Loch was trailed by 'a man dressed . . . as a ground officer bearing a drawn sword, and four men carrying a board on their shoulders, on which was fixed the model of a half-burned Highland cottage'. They followed him 'all over the town, the mob imitating the baaing of sheep'. Loch lost the election.[27]

In 1855 Loch sensed 'a feeling of a very Radical tendency' in the Highlands, 'a feeling among the people that they would all resume possession of what they conceived to be the possessions of their fathers.'[28] The radical assault upon Highland landlordism after the famine was central in much of the criticism of the Sutherland family. Donald Macleod, in a renewed series of attacks, castigated the hypocrisy of Mrs Stowe and the Duchess of Sutherland, who mouthed anti-slavery sentiments while conniving at 'the extirpation of the Celtic Race from the Highlands of Scotland'.

Although he was one of the most damaging critics of the Sutherland regime, the career of Donald Macleod is somewhat obscure. An itinerant stonemason by trade, Macleod had certainly experienced the Sutherland policies at first hand, and was an eye-witness of Sellar's notorious clearance in 1814. In 1823 he settled in the parish of Farr as a sub-tenant; he had failed to obtain the tenancy of the lot of his late father-in-law. In early 1829 Macleod was charged with failing to pay a debt to a destitute carpenter on the estate. A rancorous dispute developed between Macleod and the estate administration and, in October 1830, he was evicted as an illegal sub-tenant

[26] SC, Sutherland to Loch, 5–3–1849; Loch to Sutherland, 21–10–1853, 26–9–1854; Mulock to Loch, September 1854; Loch to Mulock, 1–9–1854. See also Prebble, op. cit., 262–6.

[27] Mitchell, op. cit., 93–4. See also Catherine Sinclair, *Sketches and Stories of Scotland and the Scotch* (n.d.), 200. SC, Sutherland to Loch, 28–7–1852.

[28] SC, D593/P/22/1/23. SC, Loch to Gunn, 25–3–1847.

and 'a troublesome and turbulent character'. In 1831 and 1832 Macleod brought an action against Angus Leslie, the sub-factor, for wrongful imprisonment and defamation in 1829, and oppressive removal in 1830. In his defence Leslie denied all the charges, chronicled the quarrelsome life of Macleod, and described the action as 'the attempt of a needy adventurer to extort money'. According to another factor, when Macleod's counsel read Leslie's defence he 'saw that he was in the wrong box and went no farther'. Ejected and thoroughly embittered, Macleod left the county and, in 1840, began a prolonged tirade against the Sutherland estate.[29]

Equally trenchant denunciation came from the pen of Donald Ross, whose writings helped to consolidate the popular impression of the resolute wickedness of the Sutherland policies. Ross asked the troublesome question: 'whose is the soil, and how should it be distributed?' and predicted that 'when the problem is fully solved, the base on which the British aristocracy rest—at present secure, will be most seriously undermined.' The younger Loch assured the Sutherland family that its critics relied on 'perversions of the truth', and pointed out that 'Donald Ross ... was, when in residence in Sutherland, convicted of forgery and imprisoned in Dornoch Jail.' Nevertheless, the influence of Macleod and Ross on the public mind was irresistible; it was part of the growing literature of popular protest which prepared the way for the Napier Commission Reports of 1884.[30]

Another critic, of much greater stature, was Karl Marx. In 1853 he published an article entitled 'Sutherland and Slavery' in the *New York Herald Tribune*. This was quickly reprinted in various British newspapers. The Sutherland clearances became Marx's favourite example of the 'wholesale expropriation of the agricultural population from the soil' by landlords vested with absolute power over the native population.

Loch found one defender in the *Elgin Courier* who advised those who would stop improvement 'to remove themselves and families to

[29] SC, Mackenzie to Loch, 2–3–1832; Loch to Mackenzie, 28–2–1832; D593/ N/4/1/1d, 265. See Grimble, op. cit., 58–75. NLS, Letters of John Stuart Blackie, MS. 2644, 2634. 'Donald Macleod, Author of *Gloomy Memories*', *Celtic Magazine*, X (1885). See also Sage, op. cit., 116. It is curious that Macleod gave no evidence at the trial of Patrick Sellar, and that he withheld his denunciation of the Sutherland clearances for almost three decades.

[30] See G. Shepperson, 'Harriet Beecher Stowe and Scotland, 1852–3', *SHR*, 1953. D. Ross, op. cit., 7. SC, D59/P/22/1/25. See also T. MacLauchlan, *The Depopulation System in the Highlands* (1849).

the backwoods of America, or probably better still, to Siberia, where they would have a chance to become nobles of the Czar of all the Russias'. And in 1855 the French political economist, Lavergne, recorded, rather inaccurately, that 'all Mr Loch's hopes have been realised. Time has brought all his prognostications to pass.'[31]

Loch refused to sanction a second edition of his justificatory *Account* of 1820, nor would he allow his son to rewrite it—'you don't recollect what it was [in 1820] and you have not lived enough in it to convey the changes to others', Loch told him. 'No one knew my *motives* and *objects* but myself.'[32] But Loch did take great pains to persuade Lord Shaftesbury,[33] the informant of Mrs Stowe. Loch outlined the history of the 'improvement policy' which, he said, 'began in the southern counties soon after the union of the Crowns', and which proceeded more rapidly after 1764 when the system reached Inverness-shire. In the south 'the demand for labour in the great towns absorbed the population that had to look for other homes', but in the north the facilities for the disposal of the surplus population were less favourable and 'emigration to America became the resource.' In Ross between 1790 and 1800 the same system was imposed and 'many emigrated to America, many placed themselves in Sutherland; but the kelp manufacture came to the temporary relief of the coast-side population, though it has since fallen a sacrifice to the progress of modern science, aggravating greatly the suffering of the people in the long run.' The policy was introduced into Sutherland in 1790 by Sir Charles Ross of Balnagowan, followed by the Armadale, Reay and Bighouse estates.

Clearances on the Sutherland estate, continued Loch, began in 1806 and, because of the isolation of the district, a different course was pursued—the people were resettled within the estate in circumstances 'where by labour and industry they could maintain themselves'. The change had been implemented with the greatest humanity and expense. The people had felt strongly 'leaving their Highland abodes,' but they had greatly benefited. 'The present generation', observed Loch, 'presents a far stronger and more athletic appearance than those who preceeded them ... Nothing could exceed the prosperity of the country this last year [1853].' The fishing, he claimed, employed

[31] K. Marx, *Capital* (Moscow ed.), I, 728–33. I. Berlin, *Karl Marx* (1960), 198–9. *People's Paper*, 12–3–1853. L. de Lavergne, *The Rural Economy of England, Scotland and Ireland* (1855), 328. SC, October 1854.

[32] SC, Loch to G. Loch, 7–11–1845.

[33] SC, Loch to Shaftesbury, 4–6–1853, 26–1–1854.

3,900 people out of a population of about 22,000—which, even given the seasonality of the industry and the west-coast difficulties, was a remarkably high ratio. Loch told Shaftesbury that 'in the end the truth will prevail.'

Thus at the age of seventy-four Loch's retrospective judgment on the policy he had directed for forty years indicates a measure of satisfaction. But, he admitted, the introduction of southern capitalists had not been 'entirely successful', and conceded that 'these attempts ran before the times [i.e. 1811–20] ... and a slower progress was adopted.' It had been a mistake to make the sheep-farms so large, and this was to be remedied. [34] He emphasized that the arable acreage had increased in Sutherland—in 1807, 13,420 acres were cultivated, in 1852, 32,237 acres. [35] Loch also admitted significantly that the management of the estate was too exclusive, that the factors were autocrats. He fervently hoped that the new gentry, 'the better of the middle class in Sutherland', would take a much larger share in the administration of the country. Perhaps most significantly of all, Loch continued to couch his explanations in terms of a future improvement of conditions—thereby implicitly conceding that, after three decades, the tangible achievement had not yet produced a complete vindication of his policies. [36]

In June 1855 James Loch contracted an illness while attending the arrival of Emperor Napoleon III in London. He attempted to continue working, but he weakened. His son wrote, 'I fear we cannot flatter ourselves that there is an improvement, and it is all the more touching that (though one of the symptoms of his complaint) he fancies himself from here, and always striving to reach Tongue, as the place in which he hopes to find peace and quiet.' [37] He died on 28 June.

Joseph Mitchell was at that time travelling in Sutherland. 'Along the whole course of my journey through the county', he recollected,

---

[34] On this point compare Mitchell, op. cit., 99, and H. H. Dixon, *Field and Fern* (1865), II, 55.

[35] SC, Loch to Home, March 1854. Cf. Ross, op. cit., 7. J. MacDonald, 'On the agriculture of the County of Sutherland', *Trans. of the Highland and Agric. Society of Scotland*, 4th series, XII, 49. Napier Report, 1884, Evidence, 38230–47, 38610–17.

[36] SC, D593/V/6/87; SC, Loch to Sutherland, 23-6-1853, 3-4-1855, 4-4-1855.

[37] SC, G. Loch to Horsburgh, 22-6-1855.

'I was asked in quiet, exulting whispers, "Did you hear the news? Loch is dead!" ' [38]

George Loch succeeded his father as commissioner to the House of Sutherland.

In September 1855 an army recruiting sergeant toured Sutherland, but with little success. The conflicting interpretations of this event epitomize the controversy to which every aspect of the Sutherland experience is subject. It has been represented as the fruit of total alienation of the Sutherland people from their landlord, the direct result of the clearance atrocities. The cry went forth, 'Let —— with his sheep go and fight the Russians.' [39] On the other hand, MacIver pointed out that 'the same aversion exists all over the North and in Districts from which no removals were made.' 'The pay is . . . so small', he said, 'as not to hold any inducement to Labourers to go into the Militia.' He reported also that the men were unashamedly afraid of being killed. But George Loch insisted that the main reason was that 'the people are no longer an ill-conditioned, half-civilized, distressed population living among the hills, deriving a precarious subsistence from the cultivation of wretched patches of ground— but have become industrious well-doing people, in many cases earning large wages, and thus surrounded with every inducement to stay at home.' [40]

Shortly after the death of James Loch, a testimony was received from Lord Grey. George Loch observed to the 2nd Duke: 'What a happiness it would have been to him, had he but known it—for though he was supported by his own conviction and your approval, he felt at times in a greater degree than it deserved, the obloquy to which his views and efforts were occasionally exposed.' [41]

---

[38] Mitchell, op. cit., 94.
[39] Alexander Mackay, *Sketches of Sutherland Characters* (1889), 48.
[40] SC, G. Loch to Sutherland, 28-9-1855; D593/P/22/1/24, G. Loch to Sutherland, 14-10-1855; D593/P/22/1/7, MacIver to Sutherland, 26-1-1855. Prebble, op. cit., 320-4.
[41] SC, G. Loch to Sutherland, 4-7-1855; Earl Grey Papers, University of Durham, Sutherland to 3rd Earl Grey, 3-7-1855.

Part Four

Perspectives

XVIII

The Uses of an Aristocratic Fortune

The prodigious inherited wealth of the Sutherland family permitted a succession of dukes to live in almost unrivalled grandeur and prestige, dominating metropolitan society in Victorian Britain. The same wealth allowed them to exercise immense power over the lives of thousands of people on their great landed estates. The scale of the family's possessions meant that extended discretion had to be vested in the hands of its professional managers, led by James Loch. Loch's professionalism guaranteed a proper flow of information to his masters. They sought his advice on policy matters, great and small. Yet the reliance placed upon the managerial expertise of James Loch does not diminish the responsibility of the family. They had ample opportunity to examine at first hand the methods and consequences of the uses of their authority. They retained the ultimate control.

Unquestionably the Sutherland fortune left its mark on the economy of Britain in the first half of the nineteenth century. A combination of circumstances directed much of their accumulated capital resources into two great economic experiments of the Age of Improvement—the Highland clearances, and the expansion of the transport sector of the industrial economy. In part the use made of capital was determined by the existing disposition of the assets among the heirs, but it was also the product of deliberate choice. Referring to the purchase of an estate in Ross-shire by the 1st Duke, Lord Francis Egerton remarked, 'I never could understand my father's policy in buying it, but he was in a condition as to money and expenditure which gave him a privilege of indulging any such caprice.'[1]

[1] SC, D593P/22/1/s, Lord Francis to Sutherland, 20–11–1845.

Yet, though power and wealth were administered with arbitrary pleasure, this was subject to a conception of the role of the aristocratic magnate and his duty to his people and his descendants. By most standards this restraint was not severe—as the clearances indicate. But even these were subject to the consistent belief that tenants could not be evicted without alternative accommodation—however minimal it might appear. The Sutherland family, solidly supported by Loch, abhorred the many examples of wholesale eviction in the Highlands. These they regarded as the antithesis of their own policies.

The Sutherland family was also subject to the increasing pressure of a more sensitive and vocal body of public opinion. The curbs imposed upon aristocratic political influence were partly paralleled by informal restraints upon economic power. The changing public mood meant that actions which had been possible in 1810 became significantly less tolerable by 1850. This could not be ignored. The House of Sutherland learned to be careful about actions which might provoke a fresh outburst of criticism.

The Sutherland family always tried to avoid the rancour of public dispute. In the 1820s, for instance, it abdicated a large part of its influence in the traditional centre of the political power of the Leveson-Gowers in Staffordshire. After the traumatic electoral defeat of 1820 the family wanted no further part in the unpleasantness and 'broiling and political quarrels' of elections. No amount of persuasion could make them re-enter county politics. Similarly, the bitterness of industrial relations associated with coal mining on the Midland estates led the family to withdraw from colliery working at Trentham in 1822. The recurrent outbursts of criticism demonstrated, said Loch, 'how impossible it is for a person of Lord Stafford's rank and fortune to hold a coal work and not dissatisfy all the neighbourhood'. The roles of aristocrat and captain of industry had become incompatible, or so it would seem. In its desire to isolate itself from the popular tension of local politics and industry, the House of Sutherland abrogated part of its former role in society. The family turned inwards towards the landed, agrarian foundation of its wealth and dignity—where its traditional role seemed to be more secure and more acceptable.[2]

Nevertheless, no one knew better than James Loch that the fortune, if not the social esteem, of the Sutherland family derived pre-

[2] See Richards, op. cit., chapter 4.

eminently from its participation in the industrial development of the national economy. Lord Stafford in 1825 diverted a part of the Bridgewater income into his investment in the 'Grand British Experimental Railway', the Liverpool and Manchester. But the motives were exceedingly complex, and the family signally failed to extend its involvement in the railways after 1830—even though the railway industry became the most rapidly growing sector of the national economy. Instead, much larger amounts of capital were sunk in the improvement of the landed estates, in the construction of extravagant houses, in the Funds, and in the Highlands. This pattern of deployment of the Sutherland fortune certainly did not maximize the return on its capital; on economic grounds the decisions taken were unwise. The great flow of funds to the Highlands, especially after about 1825, had less chance of an adequate return than virtually any other investment in the British economy. There are three possible explanations for what would seem to be perverse investment in the Highland estates—that the calculation was simply wrong, that the motives were substantially non-economic, or that the expectation of profit was extremely long-term. In reality they were not mutually exclusive.

James Loch probably expended less time investigating the economic feasibility of the Sutherland clearance policy than he gave to the economics of railways and canals. The Sutherland family was already committed to the policy before Loch took up his commission in 1812. Moreover, the definition of the Highland problem, and the solution of that problem, seemed too obvious to be questioned. The Industrial Revolution had widened the possibilities of economic progress and improvement and there appeared to be no insuperable reason why the Sutherland estate should not be brought within the orbit of the expanding national economy. The removal of the archaic impediments on economic advance, it was thought, would release the energies of an under-employed population and the latent resources of a territorial empire. It was part of the internal colonization of Britain.

Loch and the Sutherland planners undoubtedly placed too much reliance on fishing: they underestimated the chronic degree of uncertainty inherent in fishing as a source of income, employment and subsistence. Equally, they miscalculated the severity and duration of the secular decline of prices which followed the Napoleonic Wars. Insufficient regard was given to the competition of industrialism in the south, and to the impact of free-trade policies which Loch himself consistently supported. Continuing population growth, especially on the west coast of Sutherland, outstripped the creation of new employment opportunities. Moreover, the House of Sutherland bought further trouble by extending its empire in the county. The tragic result of the Sutherland development policy was the dependence of a substantial part of the Sutherland population on minute coastal crofts with little chance of additional employment. It was the precise outcome which Loch had striven to avoid. His policies had produced perverse results. For instance, it was on Loch's fiat that the resettlement lots were deliberately made too small to provide an adequate subsistence by agriculture alone—the people were to be compelled to fish.[3] But fishing failed to meet the expectations of the *annus mirabilis* 1818. Similarly Loch's stringent rules prohibiting the subdivision of land in order to control marriage-rates created grave difficulties since many people, in consequence, had no land at all.

Clearly, the Sutherland policies were imposed upon an unwilling population. There was no consultation between the landlord and the people—the very idea is anachronistic. The clearances provoked a series of ugly incidents which, though often exaggerated, were not figments of the imagination of a deluded people. The policies were executed too rapidly. They were frequently mismanaged. The choice of district factors was poor—in 1833 Loch appointed Bairgie, even though he knew him to have a reputation as 'uppish, opinionative . . . and harsh to those under him'. Loch knew also of Gunn's 'love of exclusive power and his keeping at a distance whoever differs in opinion from him'.[4] Loch was not anti-Celt, but he abhorred sloth and indolence wherever he found it. His attitude to the common people, while not unfeeling, was one of rather distant condescension.[5] Although he found some influential support, Loch was unable to convince the world at large that the policies he had implemented were either necessary or humane. Increasingly, the existence of a hostile population in Sutherland and an unsympathetic public in the south began to check the unrestricted exercise of wealth and power in the north.

[3] Cf. M. M. Leigh, 'The crofting problem, 1780–1883', *Scottish Journal of Agriculture*, XI, 270–1.
[4] SC, Loch to Gunn, 15-2-1832; Loch to Sutherland, 4-4-1855.
[5] For example, see SC, D593/N/4/3/1, Loch to Fleming, 10-8-1849.

The final verdict on the economic consequences of the Sutherland clearances must rest on a conjectural comparison between the actual situation in 1855 and the situation that would have developed had the clearances not been executed. The task is exceedingly difficult—particularly since the *status quo ante* the clearances is open to dispute. The descendants of the cleared population understandably exaggerated 'the golden age' of their forebears—particularly regarding the extent of arable land in the pre-clearance straths. Had they remained they would have been victims of the same economic trends which undermined Loch's policies. A growing population in the interior parts would have become progressively more vulnerable to famine.[6] Further subdivision of the land and more reliance on potato crops could not have been avoided. Sources of cash-income—the means of payment for meal imports—had dried up in the traditional economy. Emigration would have continued. The fishing industry and the ancilliary activities would not have developed (despite all the difficulties, there were 364 boats operating from Helmsdale in 1864).[7] Moreover, without the introduction of capitalistic sheep farming, the Sutherland rental would have been smaller. Thus, while it is very likely that the burden of recurrent famine would have increased, the financial capacity of the landlord to provide relief would have been substantially reduced. In reality, no other landlord spent so

[6] The interior townships of Knockan and Elphin remained uncleared throughout the period. Located on relatively good limestone country in Assynt, they were said to be the 'best interior Towns on the Estate'. According to Loch in 1829, they were 'remarkable for containing a fine, handsome, industrious and moral set of people ... who have ... done much to their land though little compared with what has been done on the Coast-side lots.' In 1835 he found the lateness of their crops 'clearly proving the risk that the country would run, even in these days, if any large proportion of its population were to be resident in the high interior'. In 1841 Loch wrote that 'Their present state is miserable and must yearly become more so.' Gunn agreed: it resulted 'from causes which no human power could foresee or prevent—the seasons have proved unfavourable for a series of years, and their crops were rendered useless by frost and mildew—the fine old class of men have died away, and they are succeeded by their widows and sons, and some way or other, they are quite a degenerate race in comparison with the former stock.' In September 1846 the tenants of Knockan and Elphin petitioned the Duke of Sutherland for relief. They declared that they had 'lost their crops of Potatoes, being the almost only source of subsistence they have had ... there is no prospect before them if not supplied in time but next to Starvation.' D593/N/4/1/1d; SC, Report ... on Sutherland and Reay, 26–10–1835; Loch to Gunn, 29–9–1841; Gunn to Loch, 14–9–1841; MacIver to Loch, 11–9–1846. N. Macleod, op. cit., Letter XXIX.
[7] Napier Commission Report, Q.2458. See also E. Burritt, *A Walk from London to John O'Groats* (1864), 396.

287

much capital in the Highlands as the Dukes of Sutherland. It is difficult to avoid the conclusion that employment and even subsistence opportunities would have been even smaller had the Sutherland policies not been implemented.

The foundations of the Sutherland fortune were formidable. In 1766 James Brindley wrote to the Duke of Bridgewater, 'I hope, my Lord Duke, to see your Navigation finished, and to bring you annual treasures, such as few peers can boast of.'[8] In the outcome it was the Leveson-Gowers who gained the treasures of the Bridgewater enterprises. During the time of the 2nd Marquis of Stafford (1803–1833), R. H. Bradshaw paid over £2m. to the family. In 1831 the capital gain on the investment of £155,000 in the Liverpool and Manchester Railway was calculated as £148,000. In the year 1833 holdings of government stock alone yielded an annual income in the region of £34,000—a net income, in that year, which was probably greater than the net yield of all the landed estates combined. Such resources provided an exceptional range within which the family could plan its investments and expenditure. In this light, moreover, Loch's insistent and repeated demands for retrenchment cannot be taken as signals of impending bankruptcy. In reality, Loch's warnings referred to a relative weakening of that financial strength to the perpetuation of which he had devoted his life.

Despite the preponderant commercial and industrial sources of the family fortune, Loch never ceased to believe that the future social standing and economic resilience of the family rested on primarily territorial foundations. The concerted effort to render the landed estates viable in financial terms was the keystone, and perhaps the millstone, of his thinking. The diversion of the resources of the family towards the landed estates represents a central paradox in the affairs of the House of Sutherland. In addition to other motives, it is possible that the influence of contemporary economic doctrine may have been at play. Ricardian economics seemed to imply that, in a situation of rising population and increasing output, the landowners would do well—in the long run. The criterion of the Sutherland land purchases was explicitly long-run, and Loch was thoroughly acquainted with current doctrine.

In 1817 Loch was told that Lord Stafford was 'perfectly willing to purchase in Sutherland *wherever* he can get a reasonable bargain . . .

[8] Anon. [J. Brindley], *The History of Inland Navigators* (2nd ed., 1769), Preface.

his declaration against purchasing in the North was only with regard to other counties ... he is very willing (particularly now) to make a good purchase in Sutherland, or in Staffordshire, or ... in Shropshire.' A stream of land purchases followed. Loch was enthusiastic and frequently advised sales from the funds in order to buy land. In 1817 he told Stafford that he could 'add most considerably to the amount of your capital by selling from the funds and purchasing land where it can be got at no great distance from your Lordship's other property'. The funds yielded 3·14 per cent and Loch said that land would yield about 4 per cent. But the economic return was not the only consideration—a purchase of land at Lichfield in 1818 was a political investment while at Lane End land was bought partly to prevent urban development in the proximity of Trentham Hall.[9]

The criteria for investment were sometimes shaped by general political and social circumstances. For instance, during the disruptive radicalism of 1819, Loch dreaded 'a shock to public credit'. The temper of the times produced an anxiety and disquietude which depressed trade and industry, and the funds. 'In these times', wrote Loch, 'it appears to me that land is far the best security to possess ... I firmly believe that the great landed proprietors will suffer least whatever happens to the funds.' In 1820 he reiterated his faith: 'either land or good mortgage or heritable security is the best and most certain way of investing money, and of these land is the best, for in this country whatever may happen that will be safe, and at present it can be had on advantageous terms.'[10]

The question of investment generally concerned the switching of capital between the funds, and land and mortgages. However, in 1825, there followed a rush of investments in a wider range of projects. The Duke of York was provided with a loan of £60,000 for the construction of York House. In June Stafford arranged to spend £58,000 on the Bridgewater Canal, and a further sum on the Liverpool and Birmingham Junction Canal. In September a mortgaged loan of £100,000 was arranged for Lord Reay. In December of the same year Stafford bought his way into the Liverpool and Manchester Railway at a price of £100,000.

Taken together, these transactions represented an outflow of capital of about £350,000. There were short-term problems in raising the sums. Bradshaw found some difficulty in making his

---

[9] SC, Lady Stafford to Loch, 19–7–1817; Loch to Stafford, 19–12–1817.
[10] SC, Loch to Stafford, 9–11–1819, 16–12–1820.

annual remittances, and advised: 'I should certainly borrow from my Bankers, in preference to selling Stock, at this time, although I have no good reason for thinking that the Funds will improve much ... it is all a chance. I will give what aid I can ... but I am poorer than usual this year, my expenses are heavy, and the railroad fight cost me, altogether, little short of £10,000.' A sale of houses at Newcastle-under-Lyme was arranged, and this yielded about £54,000. More importantly, the Lichfield political influence was sold to Lord Anson for £120,000.[11]

The transactions negotiated with Lords Anson and Reay, and the Duke of York, served to emphasize the contrast between the financial strength of Stafford, and the insecurity of some of his aristocratic contemporaries. York died in 1827 surrounded by debts, and Anson was in serious financial difficulties by 1832. Lord Reay was a Highland proprietor fallen on hard times. His 400,000-acre estate in Sutherland was 'a wild, hilly, rocky district, with rivers and valleys and some good hill pasture'. It seems that a sale had been contemplated for some time, but the reluctance of Lord Stafford and certain legal difficulties had prevented a settlement. In July 1825 Reay accepted a mortgaged loan of £100,000 at $3\frac{1}{2}$ per cent from Stafford. Loch's account of the negotiation exposed the motive: 'As I have throughout considered there was an ulterious object in view, I have acted with more coyness than I should have thought necessary in another case ... it is sure in my opinion to lead to the further result'—i.e. the eventual acquisition of the Reay estate. In the upshot Loch was correct. Reay resolved, in 1828, to sell his ancient domain —after protracted negotiations the parties eventually agreed on a price of £300,000. Loch suggested that the reason for the purchase was to keep the land out of the hands of a third party—and the family regarded its northern purchases as a process of the reunification of the ancient Sutherland properties which had been dispersed in previous centuries.[12]

Once again the Bridgewater profits were tapped to effect the investment. Bradshaw paid in £65,000 and reported that 'I have continued by means of Sweeping the Till, squeezing both the Debtors and Creditors a little, and running our Bankers harder than I like, to scrape together another £10,000.' Lord Reay suffered an unhappy

---

[11] SC, Loch to Bradshaw, 25-9-1825, 1-10-1825; Bradshaw to Loch, 27-9-1825.
[12] SC, Mackenzie to Loch, 6-12-1829; Loch to Stafford, 20-7-1825.

fate—apparently he lent some of the money on West Indian property and lost it, and finally died a bankrupt. There were also doubts concerning the wisdom of Stafford's purchase. One correspondent pointed out that the price of wool and kelp had fallen and that 'till these raise again Lord Stafford must be content with a loss per centage for his money'. In fact, the Reay estate became a further burden on the Sutherland exchequer, particularly during the famine.[13]

In 1828, despite Loch's repeated protestations that land 'must always bear the first value in every country', Lord Stafford expressed 'a determined dislike to invest his money in any way but in the funds'. Nevertheless, in 1830, most of the remaining tracts of Sutherland were bought up. Loch set forth the arguments: Stafford could not allow the land to get into the hands of a third party; he had 'surplus money' to invest; the funds offered little chance of profit and considerable risk. Land was not subject to legacy or probate duty. Between 1830 and 1833 almost £200,000 was spent on land in the north—indeed Loch had to advise against the acquisition of the entire county of Sutherland because it would constitute too obvious a monopoly of political influence.[14]

Over and above the extraordinary investment outflow were the normal expenditures of an aristocratic family—for example, election accounts, living expenses and estate improvements. Lord Stafford's two daughters received marriage settlements amounting to £50,000 while his son, Gower, received the Lilleshall rental of about £20,000 per annum when he married in 1823. Notwithstanding the continuously high levels of expenditure, the stockholdings of the family were greater in 1833 than they had been a decade earlier. On his death the 1st Duke of Sutherland possessed stock to the value of £1·1m. His property in the province of Canterbury alone exceeded the limit upon which probate duty was chargeable.[15]

The investment policy of the House of Sutherland between 1803 and 1833 clearly rested upon long-run considerations—the long run in which the 1st Duke of Sutherland would be dead. Lord Francis was provided for by the Bridgewater Will. Investment had been channelled into the landed property in England and Scotland to

[13] SC, Bradshaw to Loch, 16–1–1829, 12–2–1829, 22–12–1829; Reed to Loch, 16–2–1829. See also MacIver, op. cit., 66.
[14] SC, Loch to Stafford, 2–1–1831, 26–1–1828; D593/N/4/1/1d; D593/P/18/1, Loch to Stafford, 4–7–1832.
[15] SC, Loch to Drummonds, 7–10–1833.

secure the financial viability of the estates of the direct descendants—
this was the territorial foundation of the family's status at the fore-
front of the aristocracy. The railway investment served to balance
the loss of the Bridgewater income for Lord Gower. Similarly the
purchase of York House balanced the loss of Cleveland House. In
Sutherlandshire the widowed Countess/Duchess was also provided
for. In essence, the policy signified the aggrandizement of the direct
line of the House of Sutherland.

The story of the familial fortunes under the 2nd Duke from 1833
to 1861 is one of relative decline. Income had fallen, expenditure
fell rather less. There were many signs of economic retreat, gradual
though it was.

For twenty-two years Loch wrestled with the growing difficulties.
He defined the problem in 1834; it was a matter of restraining
expenditure so as not to encroach upon the 2nd Duke's capital.
Already, it had become necessary to sell £100,000 of stock to help
pay for legacies and the purchase of the Ardross estate. At the end
of the first year of the new era, Loch made a detailed appraisal of the
family finances. He found that the Duke received a gross annual
income of £113,000. He estimated that this figure, with all 'ordinary
expenses' deducted, yielded a mere £16,000 'to meet all the extraordinary and increasing and in some degree unestimated expenditure
going on'. Total expenditure he estimated at £133,983, and he
emphasized that income was likely to diminish as a result of the
falling price of wheat.

Expenditure was particularly large on the current improvements to
Stafford House and Lilleshall and Trentham Halls which, Loch told
the Duke, were costing £105,000 'of which £22,000 has been paid . . .
it is a sum that will take about 6 years of your free income as stated
above to pay off'. Loch was particularly critical of the architect
Barry: 'let me beg you to keep your architects in order', Loch
advised Sutherland; 'I am quite sure . . . that they do not think it
[keeping within estimates] a matter of much importance.' Agitated
by the results of his enquiry, Loch implored the Duke to consider
'the propriety, I should say the necessity, of no new works being
ordered'—otherwise a diminution of capital was inevitable. The
estate factors were told 'that by an exertion now, we *sink* or *swim*'.[16]

Yet, each time Loch investigated the finances, they appeared less

[16] SC, Loch to Sutherland, 27–2–1835, 21–8–1835; Loch to Davidson, 29–3–
1837.

favourable; in late 1835 he told the Duke that a further sale of capital would be necessary; he was apologetically pessimistic, but stated the two main reasons: 'You have four large houses to keep up, with a regular establishment at each, which no other nobleman has', and 'your income will be diminished . . . from the Corn Rents.' Again, in 1836–7, it was found necessary to borrow money at 5 per cent, and to sell consols, in order to purchase new railway shares. Concurrently, the Sutherland property failed to yield the Countess/ Duchess a sufficient income and she too had to borrow money—a position exacerbated by the destitution of 1837–8. Loch was 'surprised as well as disturbed', and again sounded the retrenchment alarm.

Encroachments upon capital continued into the 1840s. In 1843 Sutherland sanctioned the disposal of the Ardross property in order to avoid 'selling out of funds'—despite Loch's warning that 'your name and consequence and that of your family would receive a considerable blow.' Of all Loch's accounting problems, the high level of consumption by the family proved the most difficult. The construction of Stafford House and its sumptuous decoration had cost more than £$\frac{1}{4}$m. by 1841; living expenses were equally intractable: continental travel and graceful life in London were increasingly expensive. In 1840 Loch was told that 'if the past is to be the rule for the future, £40,000 is the very least that can be set down' for family expenditure in London. Loch complained of the rising cost, pointing out that the landed estates, 'which would pay interest', were being starved of finance for that very reason.[17]

The outcome was well typified in the year 1842 when Sutherland's income was £109,189 while his expenditure was £150,908—the deficiency being made good by land sales. When the Duke contemplated these figures he found himself 'very deaf and stormy in the head'. Loch told the Duchess that Sutherland continued 'to encroach upon his capital and how long it will continue I cannot say'. His estimates showed 'a bare possibility of reducing the expenditure within the income'—but the likelihood was small since the architects' outlays 'continued to be extreme'. The diminution of the funded property was striking. In 1834 it had stood at £1·1 million, yielding an annual income of £34,000. In 1845 the figure was £648,894, yielding £20,000. It was a measure of the decline. Loch calculated

[17] SC, Loch to Duncannon, 6–5–1841; Loch to Sutherland, 26–2–1844.

that in twelve years the Duke had spent £175,000 above and beyond any form of investment.[18]

Each year was a separate crisis. In 1847, for instance, Loch observed that 'the depreciation of all funded property and of railway shares has diminished the value of the Duke's property greatly.' Work at Trentham could not be financed *except out of capital*, and since the market was low it would be preferable to postpone all work 'until the Money Market improves and the pressures arising from the exertions required to feed the people has passed over'. Once more expenditure exceeded income and Loch's demands for retrenchment became more insistent. Despite Loch's alarm, the Duke himself was nonchalant. He thought the accounts were approximately as comprehensible as algebra, and he told Loch, 'you may be sure that I shall be extravagant when I get to Scotland—as I cannot afford *time* to delay paying money for what I wish to have done for me to *see*. I could give you a list of extras, which may occasion my leaving a bit of debt for posterity, but I trust not thrown away.'[19]

The reconstruction of Dunrobin Castle had begun, and by 1848 the cost was £41,414. Loch begged the Duke to undertake no new outlays. Further sales of stock were necessary to meet current expenses. When the heir, Lord Stafford, decided to marry in 1849, it was thought that he should have the Lilleshall estate—as his father had in 1823. Loch advised against it: 'I think that he [the Duke] could not afford to give up so large a portion of his income'—a comment symptomatic of the change that had been wrought in the family finances.[20]

Loch became steadily gloomier. He could see little chance of a net income accruing to the family. He monotonously repeated 'how large a proportion the Household expenditure bears to the English and Scottish estate expenditure and improvements'. Railway dividends fell, rental income was disappointing. Moreover, Loch pointed out, unproductive purchases had been made—in this category he included the purchase of Cliveden in 1849 for about £50,000—which, Loch noted, had reduced Sutherland's income by a further £2,370 per annum. The net effect, Loch warned, was that the income of the heir 'will necessarily be from £10,000 to £12,000 less than his father's'.

---

[18] SC, Sutherland to Loch, 6–1–1844; Loch to Sutherland, 5–1–1844, 16–4–1844, 25–12–1845, 3–3–1846; Loch to Duchess, 9–1–1844, 19–2–1844.
[19] SC, Loch to Duchess, 30–4–1847, 4–9–1847; Sutherland to Loch, 24–2–1848.
[20] SC, Neish to Loch, 28–1–1848; Loch to Duchess, 19–11–1848.

The Duchess gave Loch a much more receptive ear, and he intimated to her that the object of his remonstrances 'is the one you have so much at heart, to stop further diminution of the Duke's capital'. 'I assure you', he told her, 'the inroads on the Duke's capital are serious and rapid and will be extremely harassing if retrenchments are not made to meet this expenditure over income.' Large savings, he insisted, were the only answer.[21]

The Duke of Sutherland agreed to forgo granite chimney pieces at Dunrobin Castle. He was not optimistic about the effects of personal abstinence. He thought the situation ironic—after all, he possessed 'a vast income for food and all enjoyment! ! only requiring some reduction'. He agreed that he had received no income from Scotland and that his expenditure in every year had outstripped his income—'consequently I have been extravagant.' But he lamented, 'How can we avoid having as many guests at Dunrobin as last year, when all the world will bring the Queen there . . . the Duchess must of course have guests with her numerous family and society in London. I really avoid I think as much as possible anyway—I have no wish to go to London again.' He thought that parts of the Scottish property could be sacrificed since they yielded no income. He added two rueful comments: he wished he could throw the responsibility on his son, Stafford: and he wished Stafford House had been burned down instead of Cliveden (which caught fire in November 1849)—it would have been a great saving.[22]

Loch's thankless exertions achieved a limited measure of success in the early 1850s. He estimated income for 1851 at £125,000, expenditure at £110,000; and in June of that year he was 'very much pleased' with the results of the retrenchment. But he demanded continued restraint—'it has been with difficulty that this system of control has been established.'

The years of constant vigil had not prevented the diminution of the family's resources. Even while retrenchment disciplined the excesses of family expenditure, it remained extremely difficult to raise a sizeable net income. The depletion of the family's funded wealth continued to the end of Loch's life—so that in 1853 the Duke of Sutherland possessed consols to the value of £534,964, American stock of $188,842, and railway shares to the value of £245,330.[23]

[21] SC, Loch to Sutherland, 17–5–1849, 21–1–1850.
[22] SC, Sutherland to Loch, 21–2–1850, 30–1–1850.
[23] SC, Loch to Sutherland, 14–3–1851, 3–1–1853.

In return for the efflux of income since 1812, the House of Sutherland had created an enviable position in London society; it had extended its unremunerative territorial empire in the Highlands; it had reconstructed and refurbished its houses in London, Trentham, Lilleshall and Dunrobin, and had acquired Cliveden; it had improved its English estates to the approval of the noted agriculturalist James Caird; and it had consolidated its stake in the transport sector of the economy by its investment in railways. It had also obtained a dukedom. It is clear that, despite Loch's perennial strictures, the prodigious resources of the House of Sutherland were not deployed to maximize income—Loch categorized a very large proportion of the 2nd Duke's investment as 'unproductive'.

There is nothing mysterious about the failure of the House of Sutherland to consolidate its economic position after 1833. The 2nd Duke inherited a diminished income, but he also inherited a standard of living which tended to increase rather than to diminish. His financial responsibilities in the north of Scotland became increasingly onerous. The return on the investment made prior to 1833 failed to honour the sanguine expectations of Loch and the 1st Duke —notably in the case of the landed estates. Furthermore, by diverting so much of his income into conventional aristocratic consumption, the 2nd Duke severely limited any possibility of a progressive growth of his fortune. The bias towards investment in land precluded any emulation of his illustrious predecessor, the Duke of Bridgewater. In the 1840s even the railway shares were disappointing. The two pressures, rising expenditure and a fallen income, produced a dwindling surplus for new investment.

The problem did not expire with James Loch. The pattern of expenditure recurred in the following generations. In 1883 the Sutherland estate factors told the Napier Commission that the family had spent £1,285,122 in the Highlands during the previous thirty years, which was almost £$\frac{1}{4}$m. beyond its rental income. Nor had attitudes changed very much. Replying to 'a certain class of Land League agitators' in 1887 R. M. Brereton, the commissioner of the Sutherland estates, declared that 'No government, no corporation, and no association of capitalists would have done so much for Sutherland as has been done during the past twenty-five years by the present Duke.'[24]

[24] Napier, Report, Q. 39343–5. R. M. Brereton, *A Word on the Duke of Sutherland's Management* (1887). *John O'Groats Journal*, 7-3-1861.

The working career of James Loch spanned the years during which Britain emerged as the first recognizably modern economy. He entered this world as an Edinburgh intellectual schooled in the philosophy of rationality and improvement. He believed in progress and stability. To him the great aristocratic estate was an indispensable groundwork of social and political stability. It also offered the most ample opportunity for the improvement of the nation.

Over a period of four decades Loch wrestled with two great problems which constantly recur in the history of economic development. The first was that of the assimilation of technical innovation; the second was that of regional imbalance during rapid economic change. Loch's work in railways demonstrated, in the initial stages, the capacity of an old technology to temper the impact of the new by various forms of collective action. In the Highlands the Sutherland policies demonstrated how difficult it was to establish the conditions of economic progress, and how regions on the periphery could suffer as well as benefit from expansion at the centre of the industrializing economy. Economic expansion in Sutherland was largely frustrated by objective environmental conditions which were mostly created outside the region.

In this wider perspective Loch's failure to discover acceptable solutions has to be seen in relation to our own imperfect understanding of the causes and consequences of economic revolution.

Bibliography

Manuscript sources

Blair Adam Papers, private, Blair Adam, Kinross.
Brougham Papers, University College, London.
Constable Letter Books, NLS, Edinburgh.
Earl Grey Papers, University of Durham.
Ellesmere-Brackley Collection, Northampton CRO.
Home Office (Scotland) Correspondence, Register House, Edinburgh.
Huskisson Papers, BM.
Irvine-Robertson Papers, Register House, Edinburgh.
Letters to John Stuart Blackie, NLS.
Letters of James Loch, NLS.
Letters to Sir Walter Scott, NLS.
Letters of George Stephenson, Liverpool Public Library.
Letters to and from William Huskisson, Liverpool Public Library.
Liverpool and Manchester Railway Correspondence and Circulars, Liverpool Public Library.
Melville Papers, NLS.
'Particulars of Stockton and Darlington Railway', Birmingham Public Library.
Picton Autographs, Picton Library, Liverpool.
Selkirk Papers, Public Archives of Canada, Ottawa.
Stewart of Garth Papers, private, Stirling.
Sutherland Papers, Shrewsbury CRO, Stafford CRO.
Twenlow Papers, Stafford CRO.

Newspapers and periodicals

Annual Register
Celtic Magazine
Edinburgh Advertiser
Edinburgh Review
Elgin Courier
Herapath's Railway Magazine
Inverness Journal
John O'Groats Journal
Military Register
Northern Ensign
People's Paper
Punch
Quarterly Review
Scots Magazine
Scotsman
Shrewsbury Chronicle
Staffordshire Advertiser
The Times
Westminster Review

Unpublished theses

CARLSON, R. E., 'The Liverpool and Manchester Railway Project, 1821–1831', University of Pittsburgh, Ph.D., 1955.

DONAGHY, L., 'An Operational History of the Liverpool and Manchester Railway, 1831–1845', University of Pittsburgh, Ph.D., 1960.

MCARTHUR, MARGARET M., 'The Sutherland Clearances', University of London, Ph.D., 1940.

RICHARDS, E. S., 'James Loch and the House of Sutherland, 1812–1855', University of Nottingham, Ph.D., 1967.

Books, articles, pamphlets etc.

'A HIGHLANDER', *The Present Conduct of the Chieftains in the Highlands of Scotland*, 1773.

ADAM, M. I., 'The Highland emigration of 1770', *SHR*, 1919.

ADAM, M. I., 'Causes of the Highland emigration, 1783–1803', *SHR*, 1920.

ADAM, M. I., 'The eighteenth-century Highland landlords and the poverty problem', *SHR*, 1922.

ADAM, R. J. (ed.), *John Homes's Survey of Assynt*, 1960.

ALISTER, R., *Barriers to the National Prosperity of Scotland*, 1853.

ALLARDYCE, A. (ed.), *Letters from and to Charles Kirkpatrick Sharpe*, 1888.

ANON. [Joseph Parkes], *A Statement of the Claim of the Subscribers to the Birmingham and Liverpool Railroad to an Act of Parliament*, 1824.

ANON., *A Summer Ramble in the North Highlands*, 1825.

ARGYLL, DOWAGER DUCHESS OF (ed.), *George Douglas, 8th Duke of Argyll, Autobiography and Memoirs*, 1906.

ASPINALL, A., *Later Correspondence of George III*, 1962.

ASPINALL, A., *Politics and the Press, 1780–1850*, 1949.

ATKINSON, R. H. M. BUDDLE, and JACKSON, G. A., *Brougham and his Early Friends, Letters to James Loch, 1798–1809*, 3 vols, 1908.

BAINES, T., *History of the Commerce and Town of Liverpool*, 1852.

BAKEWELL, T., *Remarks on a Publication of James Loch, Esq.*, 1820.

BARRON, J., *The Northern Highlands in the Nineteenth Century*, 3 vols, 1903–1913.

BASNETT, I., 'The first public railway in Lancashire: the history of the Bolton and Leigh Railway, based on the Hulton Papers (1824–8)', *Transactions of the Lancashire and Cheshire Antiquarian Society*, LXII, 1950–1.

BATEMAN, J., *Great Landowners of Great Britain*, 1883.

BAYNE, P., *Life and Letters of Hugh Miller*, 2 vols, 1871.

BICKLEY, F. (ed.), *The Diaries of Sylvester Douglas*, 2 vols, 1928.

BISHTON, J., *General View of the Agriculture of Shropshire*, 1794.

BLACK, R. D. COLLISTON, *Economic Thought and the Irish Question, 1817–1870*, 1960.

BLACKIE, J. S., *The Scottish Highlands and the Land Laws*, 1885.

BOOTH, H., *An Account of the Liverpool and Manchester Railway*, 1830.

BOTFIELD, B., *Journal of a Tour Through the Highlands*, published anonymously, 1830.

BRADY, A., *William Huskisson and Liberal Reform*, 1928.
BREMNER, D., *The Industries of Scotland*, 1869.
BRERETON, R. M., *A Word on the Duke of Sutherland's Management*, 1887.
BROADBRIDGE, S. A., 'The early capital market: The Lancashire and Yorkshire Railway', *EcHR*, 1955.
BROWNE, J., *A Critical Examination of Dr. MacCulloch's Work on the Highlands and Western Islands of Scotland*, 1825.
BROWNE, JAMES, *A History of the Highlands and the Highland Clans*, 4 vols, 1838.
BROWNING, O., *Despatches of Lord Gower, 1790–1792*, 1885.
BRUCE, J., *Destitution in the Highlands*, 1847.
BUCKLEY, J. K., *Joseph Parkes of Birmingham*, 1926.
BURRITT, E., *A Walk from London to John O'Groats*, 1864.
BURT, E., *Letters from a Gentleman in the North of Scotland*, 2 vols, 1759.
CAIRD, J., *English Agriculture in 1850–51*, 1851.
CAMPBELL, LORD COLIN, *The Crofter in History*, 1880.
CAMPBELL, H. F., 'Notes on the county of Sutherland in the eighteenth century', *TGSI*, XXVI, 1907.
CAMPBELL, R. H., *Scotland since 1707*, 1965.
CAMPBELL, R. H., 'The Highland Economy, 1750–1850', *SJPE*, 1959.
CARSWELL, J., *The South Sea Bubble*, 1960.
CASTALIA, COUNTESS GRANVILLE (ed.), *Lord Granville Leveson-Gower, Private Correspondence, 1781–1821*, 1917.
Catalogue of Dunrobin muniments, typescript at Register House, Edinburgh.
CAVENDISH, A. E. J., *An Reisineid Chataich. The 93rd Sutherland Highlanders*, 1928.
CHALONER, W. H., 'The Canal Duke', *History Today*, 1951.
CHAMBERS, J. D., *Workshop of the World*, 1961.
CHECKLAND, S. G., 'Economic Attitudes in Liverpool, 1793–1897', *EcHR*, 1952.
CHRISTIE, I. R., *The End of North's Ministry*, 1958.
CHRISTIE, O. F., *The Transition from Aristocracy*, 1927.
CLAPHAM, J. H., *An Economic History of Modern Britain*, 3 vols, 1926–38.
CLAPP, B. W., *John Owens, Manchester Merchant*, 1965.
CLEVELAND-STEVENS, E., *English Railways. Their Development and their Relation to the State*, 1915.
CLIVE, J., *Scotch Reviewers*, 1957.
COBBETT, W., *Rural Rides*, 1930 ed.
COLLIER, A., *The Crofting Problem*, 1953.
CONYBEARE, F. A., *Dingle Bank, A Sketch*, 1925.
COOTNER, P. H., 'The role of railroads in United States economic growth', *JEH*, 1963.
COWAN, H. I., *British Emigration to British North America*, 1961 ed.
CRAUFURD, J. R. H., *Extracts from MS. Correspondence at Craufurdland Castle*, Archaeological and Historical Collections relating to the Counties of Ayr and Wigton, vol. II.
CREGEEN, E. R. (ed.), *Argyll Estate Instructions*, 1964.

DARLING, F. F. (ed.), *West Highland Survey*, 1955.

DAWSON, J. H., *The Abridged Statistical History of the Scottish Counties*, 1862.

DAY, J. P., *Public Administration in the Highlands*, 1918.

DIXON, H. H., *Field and Fern*, 1865.

DONALDSON, G., *The Scots Overseas*, 1966.

Edinburgh University Matriculation Rolls, Arts, Law, Divinity, 1623–1858, Edinburgh University Library.

ELLESMERE, EARL OF, *Essays on History, Biography, Geography, Engineering etc.*, 1858.

ELLIOT, R., *Special Report on Sutherland and the West Highlands*, 1848.

E.M.P.S., *The Two James's and the Two Stephensons*, ed. L. T. C. Rolt, 1961.

ESPINASSE, F., *Lancashire Worthies*, 1874.

FAIRBAIRN, H. A., *A Treatise on the Political Economy of Railroads*, 1836.

FAIRHURST, H., 'The surveys for the Sutherland clearances, 1813–1820', *Scottish Studies*, VIII, 1964.

FAIRHURST, H., 'Scottish Clachans', *Scottish Geographical Magazine*, LXXVI, 1960.

FAIRHURST, H. and PETRIE, G., 'Scottish Clachans II: Lix and Rosal', *Scottish Geographical Magazine*, LXXX, 1964.

FALK, B., *The Bridgewater Millions*, 1942.

FAY, C. R., *Huskisson and his Age*, 1951.

FEILING, K. G., *The Second Tory Party, 1714–1832*, 1959.

FERGUSSON, J., *Letters of George Dempster to Sir Adam Fergusson, 1756–1813*, 1934.

FETTER, F. W. (ed.), *The Writings of Francis Horner*, 1957.

FISHLOW, A., *Railroads and the Transformation of the Ante-Bellum Economy*, 1965.

FITZMAURICE, E., *The Life of Lord Granville*, 1905.

FOGEL, R. W., *Railroads and American Economic Growth: Essays in Econometric History*, 1964.

FRANCIS, J., *A History of the English Railway*, 2 vols, 1851.

FRASER, W., *The Sutherland Book*, 3 vols, 1892.

GAILEY, R. A., 'Mobility of tenants on an Highland estate in the early nineteenth century', *SHR*, 1961.

GAILEY, R. A., 'Agrarian improvement and the development of enclosure in the south-west Highlands of Scotland', *SHR*, 1963.

GASKELL, P., *Morvern Transformed*, 1968.

GAYER, A. D., ROSTOW, W. W. and SCHWARTZ, A., *The Growth and Fluctuation of the British Economy, 1790-1850*, 2 vols, 1953.

GIBB, A., *The Story of Telford*, 1935.

GILL, C., *History of Birmingham*, I, 1952.

GILLANDERS, F., 'The West Highland economy', *TGSI*, XLIII, 1964.

GINTER, D. E., 'The financing of the Whig party organization 1783–1793', *American Historical Review*, LXXI, 1965–6.

GOWER, R., *My Reminiscences*, 1883.

GOWER, R. (ed.), *Stafford House Letters*, 1891.

GRAHAM, H. G., *The Social Life of Scotland in the Eighteenth Century*, 1928.

GRAHAM, I. C. C., *Colonists from Scotland, 1956.*

GRAY, M., 'Settlement in the Highlands 1750–1950: the documentary and the written record', *Scottish Studies*, VI, 1962.

GRAY, M., *The Highland Economy, 1750–1850*, 1957.

GRAY, M., 'Organization and growth in the east coast herring fishing 1880—1885', in *Studies in Scottish Business History*, ed. P. L. Payne, 1967.

GRAY, W. FORBES, *An Edinburgh Miscellany*, 1925.

GRIEG, J. (ed.), *The Farington Diaries*, 1923.

GRIMBLE, I., *The Trial of Patrick Sellar,* 1962.

GRIMBLE, I., 'Emigration in the time of Rob Dunn, 1714–1778', *Scottish Studies*, VII, 1963.

GRIMBLE, I., 'Gael and Saxon in Scotland', *Yale Review*, LII, 1962.

GUNN, D., *History of Manitoba*, 1880.

HALDANE, A. R. B., *The Drove Roads of Scotland*, 1952.

HAMILTON, H., *The Industrial Revolution in Scotland*, 1932.

HANDLEY, J. E., *The Agricultural Revolution in Scotland*, 1963.

HARDING, W., 'Facts bearing on the progress of the railway system', *Journal of the Statistical Society of London*, XI, 1848.

HARDY, S. M. and BAILY, R. C., 'The downfall of the Gower interest, 1800–1830', *Historical Collections of Staffordshire*, 1950–1.

HARRIS, J. R. (ed.), *Liverpool and Merseyside*, 1969.

HARRISON, W., *History of the Manchester Railways*, 1882, reprinted 1967.

HAWES, F., *Henry Brougham: A Nineteenth-century Portrait*, 1957.

HENDERSON, J., *General View of the Agriculture of the County of Sutherland*, 1812.

HERFORD, C. H. (ed.), *Robert Southey's Journal of a Tour of Scotland*, 1929.

HOBSBAWM, E. J., *Industry and Empire*, 1968.

HOBSBAWM, E. J., *The Age of Revolution, 1789–1848*, 1964.

HOLT, G. O., *A Short History of the Liverpool and Manchester Railway,* 1965.

HORNER, L. (ed.), *Memoirs and Correspondence of Francis Horner*, 1843.

HUGHES, J., *Liverpool Banks and Bankers*, 1906.

HUSKISSON, W., *The Speeches of the Right Honorable William Huskisson,* 3 vols, 1831.

HUXLEY, G., *Victorian Duke*, 1967.

HUXLEY, G., *Lady Elizabeth and the Grosvenors,* 1965.

HYDE, F. G., *Mr. Gladstone at the Board of Trade*, 1934.

ILCHESTER, EARL OF (ed.), *Lady Holland and her Son*, 1946.

JACKMAN, W. T., *The Development of Transportation in Modern England,* 2nd ed., 1962.

JEAFFRESON, J. C., *The Life of Robert Stephenson*, 1884.

JENKS, L. J., 'Railroads as an economic force in American development', *JEH*, 1944.

JOHNSON, S., *Journey to the Western Islands of Scotland in 1773*, 1930 ed.

KELLAS, J. G., 'Highland migration to Glasgow and the origin of the Scottish labour movement', *Society for the Study of Labour History Bulletin*, no. 12, spring 1966.

KEMP, D. W., *The Sutherland Democracy*, 1890.

KEMP, D. W. (ed.), *The Tour of Dr. Richard Pococke . . . Through Sutherland and Caithness in 1760*, 1888.

KEMP, D. W. (ed.), *Selections from the Sutherlandshire Magazine of 1826*, 1898.

KENWOOD, A. G., 'Railway investment in Britain, 1825–1875', *Economica*, 1965.

KNIGHT, C., *Passages from a Working Life*, 1864.

KNOX, J., *Observations on the Northern Fisheries with a Discourse on the Expediency of Establishing Fishing Stations or Small Towns in the Highlands of Scotland*, 1786.

KNOX, J., *A Tour through the Highlands of Scotland and the Hebride Isles in 1786*, 1787.

KYD, J. G. (ed.), *Scottish Population Statistics*, 1952.

LAVERGNE, L. DE, *The Rural Economy of England, Scotland and Ireland*, 1885.

LECONFIELD, LADY and GORE, J. (eds.), *Three Howard Sisters*, 1955.

LEECH, SIR BOSDIN, *History of the Manchester Ship Canal*, 2 vols, 1907.

LEIGH, M. M., 'The crofting problem 1780–1883', *Scottish Journal of Agriculture*, XI, 1928.

LEIGHTON, R. (ed.), *Correspondence of Charlotte Grenville, Lady Williams Wynn*, 1920.

LESLIE, W., *General View of the Agriculture of the Counties of Nairn and Moray*, 1813.

LEVESON-GOWER, F. (ed.), *Letters of Harriet, Countess Granville, 1810–1845*, 2 vols, 1894.

LEWIN, H. G., *Early British Railways: A Short History of Their Origin and Development*, 1925.

LOCH, C. S., 'Poor relief in Scotland: its statistics and development, 1791 to 1891', *Journal of the Royal Statistical Society*, LXI, 1898.

LOCH, G., *The Family of Loch*, 1934.

LOCH, J., *Account of the Improvements on the Estates of the Marquess of Stafford*, 1815 (anonymously) and 1820.

LOCH, J., 'Memoir of George Granville, late Duke of Sutherland', not published, 1834.

LOCH, J., *Facts as to the Past and Present State of the Estate of Sutherland*, published anonymously, 1845.

LOCH, J., 'Dates and Documents relating to the Family and Property of Sutherland', not published, 1859.

LOCH, J., *A Selection of Papers of the Improvements in Sutherland*, n.d.

LOCH, J. and LAWS, CAPTAIN, *Correspondence between James Loch, Esq., M.P., and Captain Laws, R.N.*, 1842.

MCARTHUR, M. M. (ed.), *Survey of Lochtayside*, 1936.

MACCULLOCH, JOHN, *The Highlands and Western Isles of Scotland*, 4 vols., 1824.

MCCULLOCH, J. R., *Commercial Dictionary*, 1859.

MACDONALD, D. F., *Scotland's Shifting Population, 1770–1850*, 1937.

MACDONALD, J., 'On the agriculture of the country of Sutherland', *Transactions of the Highland and Agricultural Society of Scotland*, 4th series, XII.

MCGREGOR, O. R., 'Research possibilities for family study', *British Journal of Sociology*, 1961.

MACIVER, E., *Memoirs of a Highland Gentleman*, 1905.

MACKAY, A., *Sketches of Sutherland Characters*, 1889.

MACKAY, D. J. and BUXTON, N. K., 'The north of Scotland—a case for redevelopment?', *SJPE*, 1965.

MACKENZIE, A. (ed.), *The Trial of Patrick Sellar*, 1883.

MACKENZIE, A., *History of the Highland Clearances*, 1883, revised ed. 1914.

MACKENZIE, SIR GEORGE, *Letter to the Proprietors of Land in Ross-shire*, 1803.

MACLAUCHLAN, T., *The Depopulation System in the Highlands*, 1849.

MACLEOD, D., *History of the Destitution of Sutherlandshire*, 1841.

MACLEOD, D., *The Sutherlandshire Clearances*, 1856.

MACLEOD, D., *Gloomy Memories in the Highlands of Scotland*, 1857.

MACLEOD, J. N., *Memorials of the Rev. Norman Macleod*, 1898.

MACLEOD, N., *Extracts from Letters to the Rev. Dr. McLeod, Glasgow, regarding the Famine and Destitution in the Highlands and Islands of Scotland*, 1847.

MACMILLAN, D. S., *Scotland and Australia, 1788–1850*, 1967.

MALET, H., *The Canal Duke*, 1961.

MARSHALL, C. F. D., *Centenary History of the Liverpool and Manchester Railway, 1930*.

MARSHALL, D., *The Rise of George Canning*, 1938.

MARTIN, C., *Lord Selkirk's Work in Canada*, 1916.

MARX, KARL, 'Sutherland and slavery or the duchess at Home', the *People's Paper*, 12–3–1853.

MARX, KARL, *Capital,* Moscow ed., n.d.

MASON, J., 'Conditions in the Highlands after the "Forty-Five"', *SHR*, 1947.

MATHER, F. C., 'The Duke of Bridgewater's trustees and the coming of the railways', *TRHS*, 1964.

MATHER, F. C., *After the Canal Duke. A Study of the Industrial Estates Administered by the Trustees of the Third Duke of Bridgewater in the Age of Railway Building, 1825–1872*, 1970.

MATTHEWS, R. C. O., *A Study in Trade Cycle History*, 1954.

MAXWELL, H. (ed.), *The Creevey Papers*, 1904.

MAXWELL, J. H., 'Report of the inquiry into the agricultural statistics of the counties of Roxburgh, Haddington and Sutherland', *Transactions of the Highland and Agricultural Society of Scotland*, new series, 1853–4.

MAZLISH, B. (ed.), *The Railroad and the Space Program*, 1965.

MECHIE, S., *The Church and Scottish Social Development, 1700–1870*, 1960.

MELVILLE, L. (ed.), *The Huskisson Papers*, 1931.

MEYER, D., *The Highland Scots of North Carolina, 1732–1776*, 1957.

MILLER, H., *Sutherland as it was and is, or, How a Country may be Ruined* 1843.

MILLER, R., 'Land use by summer sheilings', *Scottish Studies*, 1967.

MITCHELL, B. R., 'The coming of the railways and U.K. economic growth', *JEH*, 1964.

MITCHELL, J., *Reminiscences of My Life in the Highlands*, 1883.

MITCHISON, R., *Agricultural Sir John*, 1962.

MITCHISON, R., 'The movement of Scottish corn prices in the seventeenth and eighteenth centuries', *EcHR*, 1965.

MORTON, CHESTER, *Lord Selkirk's Work in Canada*, 1916.

MULLINEUX, F., *The Duke of Bridgewater's Canal*, 1959.

MULOCK, T., *The Western Highlands and Islands of Scotland Socially Considered with Reference to Proprietors and People*, 1850.

NAMIER, L. and BROOKE, J., *History of Parliament: The House of Commons, 1754–1790*, 1964.

New Statistical Account of Scotland, 1835–45.

NICHOLS, SIR GEORGE, *A History of the Scotch Poor Laws*, 1856.

NICHOLSON, N., *Lord of the Isles*, 1960.

Old Statistical Account of Scotland, 21 vols, 1790–8.

OTTLEY, G., *A Bibliography of British Railway History*, 1965.

PARRIS, H., *Government and the Railways in Nineteenth-Century Britain*, 1965.

PENNANT, T., *Tour in Scotland and Voyage to the Hebrides*, 1774.

PITT, W., *History of Staffordshire*, 1817.

PLYMLEY, J., *General View of the Agriculture of Shropshire*, 1803.

POLLINS, H., 'The finances of the Liverpool and Manchester Railway', *EcHR*, 1952.

POLLINS, H., 'The marketing of railway shares in the first half of the nineteenth century', *EcHR*, 1954.

POOLE, B., 'The economy of railways', *Minutes of Proceedings of the Institution of Civil Engineers*, XI, 1852.

PP Report of the Select Committee on the Survey of the Central Highlands of Scotland, 1802–3.

PP Proceedings of the Committee of the House of Commons on the Liverpool and Manchester Railroad Bill, 1825.

PP Report of the Select Committee on Scotch Entails, 1828.

PP First Report from the Select Committee appointed to look into the Ltate of Agriculture, 1836.

PP Report on the Applicability of Emigration to relieve Distress in the Highlands, 1841.

PP Report from Her Majesty's Commissioners for Inquiry into the Administration and Practical Operation of the Poor Laws of Scotland, 1844, xxi–xxiv.

PP Report on the State of the Harbours of Scotland, 1846.

PP Report of the Commissioners of Inquiry into the Condition of the Crofters and Cotters in the Highlands and Islands of Scotland (Napier Report), 1884.

PRATT, E. A., *A History of Inland Transport and Communication in England*, 1912.

PREBBLE, J., *The Highland Clearances*, 1963.

PRITCHETT, J. P., *The Red River Valley, 1811–1849, A Regional Study*, 1942.

RAE, J., *Life of Adam Smith*, ed. J. Viner, 1965.

REED, M. C. (ed.), *Railways in the Victorian Economy*, 1969.

REEVE, H. (ed.), *The Greville Memoirs*, 1888.

Reports of Free Church Committee on Destitution, 1847.

ROBSON, R. (ed.), *Ideas and Institutions of Victorian Britain*, 1967.

ROLLO, P. J. V., *George Canning*, 1965.

ROLT, L. T. C., *Thomas Telford*, 1958.

ROLT, L. T. C., *George and Robert Stephenson*, 1960.

ROMILLY, S. H., *Letters to 'Ivy' from the 1st Earl of Dudley*, 1906.

ROSS, D., *The Scottish Highlanders; their Present Sufferings and Future Prospects*, 1852.

ROSS, D., *Real Scottish Grievances*, 1854.

SAGE, D., *Memorabilia Domestica*, 1889.

ST JOHN, C., *Tour of Sutherlandshire*, 1884.

SANDARS, J., *A Letter on the Subject of the Projected Railroad between Liverpool and Manchester*, 1824.

SANFORD, J. L. and TOWNSEND, M., *The Great Governing Families of England*, 1865.

SCHUMPETER, J. A., *Capitalism, Socialism, and Democracy*, 1950.

SELKIRK, EARL OF, *On Emigration and the State of the Highlands*, 1806.

SELLAR, E. M., *Recollections and Impressions*, 1907.

SELLAR, P., *Statement by Patrick Sellar*, 1826.

SELLAR, P., *Library of Useful Knowledge*, Farm Reports, or Accounts of the Management of Select Farms, no. III, County of Sutherland, 1831.

SELLAR, T., *The Sutherland Evictions of 1814*, 1883.

SHEPPERSON, G., 'Harriet Beecher Stowe and Scotland, 1852–3', *SHR*, 1953.

SIMMONS, J., *The Railways of Britain*, 1961.

SIMMONS, J., 'For and against the locomotive', *Journal of Transport History*, II, 1955–6.

SINCLAIR, C., *Sketches and Stories of Scotland and the Scotch*, n.d.

SINCLAIR, D. M., 'Highland emigration to Nova Scotia', *Dalhousie Review*, 1963.

SINCLAIR, SIR JOHN, *General View of the Agriculture of the Northern Counties*, 1795.

SINGER, W., 'On the introduction of sheep farming into the Highlands', *Transactions of the Highland Society of Scotland*, III, 1807.

SISMONDI, S. DE, *Political Economy and the Philosophy of Government*, 1857.

SMILES, R., *Memoir of the Late Henry Booth*, 1869.

SMITH, A., *The Wealth of Nations*, Everyman ed., 1910.

SMITH, F. T., *The Land of Britain . . . Sutherland*, 1939.

SMITH, N. L. (ed.), *Letters of Sydney Smith*, 1952.

SMOUT, T. C., 'Scottish landowners and economic growth, 1650–1850', *SJPE*, 1964.

SMOUT, T. C. and FENTON, A., 'Scottish agriculture before the improvers', *Agricultural History Review*, XIII.

SPRING, D., *The English Landed Estate in the Nineteenth Century*, 1963.

SPRING, D., 'English landed society in the eighteenth and nineteenth centuries', *EcHR*, 1964.

STEEL, W. L., *The History of the London and North Western Railway*, 1914.

STEWART, D., *Sketches of the Character, Manners and Present State of the Highlanders of Scotland*, 2 vols, 1822, 1825.

STOWE, H. B., *Sunny Memories of Foreign Lands*, 1854.

SUTHERLAND, DUKE OF, *The Story of Stafford House*, 1935.

SYMON, J. A., *Scottish Farming, Past and Present*, 1959.

TELFORD, T., *Life* written by himself, ed. by J. Rickman, 1838.

THOMPSON, F. M. L., *English Landed Society in the Nineteenth Century*, 1963.

THOMSON, J., *The Value and Importance of the Scottish Fisheries*, 1849.

T.M.T., *Distinguished Men of the County, or Biographical Annals of Kinross-shire*, 1932.

TURNBULL, G. L., 'The railway revolution and carriers' response: Messrs. Pickford & Company, 1830–50', *Transport History*, II, no. 1, 1969.

VEITCH, G. S., *Huskisson and Liverpool*, 1929.

VEITCH, G. S., *The Struggle for the Liverpool and Manchester Railway*, 1930.

VIGNOLES, O. J., *Life of Charles Blacker Vignoles*, 1889.

WALKER, JOHN, *An Economical History of the Hebrides and Highlands of Scotland*, 2 vols, 1808.

WALKER, J. S., *An Accurate Description of the Liverpool and Manchester Railway*, 1830, reprinted 1968.

WALLING, R. A. J., *The Diaries of John Bright*, 1930.

WARD, J. T., *Sir James Graham*, 1967.

WARDEN, A. J., *The Linen Trade, Ancient and Modern*, 1864.

WATSON, J. A. S., 'The rise and development of the sheep industry in the Highlands and north of Scotland', *Transactions of the Highland and Agricultural Society of Scotland*, 5th series, XLIV, 1932.

WATSON, W., *The History of the Speculative Society, 1764–1904*, 1905.

WHEELER, J., *Manchester, Its Political, Social and Commercial History*, 1836.

WHEELER, P. T., 'Landownership and the crofting system in Sutherland since 1800', *Agricultural History Review*, XIV, 1966.

WOOD, J. P., *The Ancient and Modern State of the Parish of Cramond*, 1794.

YOUNG, R., *The Parish of Spynie*, 1871.

YOUNG, R., *Annals of the Parish and Burgh of Elgin*, 1879.

Index

Aberdeen, 228, 267
Achavandra (Sutherland), 173–4, 176
Achness (Sutherland), 214–16
Adam, R. J., 162
Adam, William, 20, 24, 25, 186, 195
Addington, Henry, 8
Alva, Lady, 10
American colonies, 7, 161–2, 164, 170, 174, 217, 219n
Anderson, James, 251
Anne, Queen, 6
Annual Register, 189
Anson, Lord, 108, 290
Antoinette, Marie, 8
Ardross Estate, 255–6, 292–3
Argyll, 250, 258
Argyll, Dukes of, xvi
aristocracy, survival of, 3
Armadale (Sutherland), 179–80, 277
Assynt (Sutherland), 162–3, 170, 177, 182, 203, 214, 218, 219n, 230–1, 236, 243, 245, 247, 250, 252, 262, 265, 270, 272
Athol, Duke of, 59
Australia, 247–8, 268, 273; *see also* individual colonies

Badinloch (Sutherland), 205
Bairgrie, R., 248, 286
Bakewell, Thomas, 33
Balchladdich (Sutherland), 252
Baltic, 223, 227
Banffshire, 273
Bathurst, Lord, 217

Beaumont, Lady, 141
Bedford, Duke of, 4, 6–7
Benson, Robert, 121
Bighouse (Sutherland), 203, 277
Billingsgate, 224
Birley, Hugh, 60–1
Birmingham, xi, xii, xiii, 41, 51–3, 56, 87, 89–90, 95, 98–9, 100, 102, 111
Birmingham Canal Company, 53, 88
Birmingham and Liverpool Junction Canal, xiii, 65, 68, 73, 75, 78, 90–3, 96, 100–1, 106–8, 122–3, 131, 289
Birmingham and Liverpool Railroad, projected, 52–3, 67, 111
Blair Adam (Kinross), 20, 22
Bolton, 50
Bolton and Leigh Railway, 79
Booth, Henry, 78, 126, 129, 135, 137, 140
Botfield, Beriah, 240
Bradshaw, Captain James, 74–5, 77, 87–8, 115; suicide, 116–17
Bradshaw, R. H., xi, xiii, 42–4, 45n, 47–9, 54n, 55–6, 58, 61, 63–70, 82, 87, 90–2, 96, 99–100, 114, 116, 120, 132, 288–90; contracts for railway work, 76; on costs of opposition to railway, 67; on Lord Stafford, 80; meets Moss, 79–80; modifies canal rates, 64, 112, 115; on railway expansion, 102; relations with James Loch, 69, 79, 91–3, 114–15; resignation, 116–17; on Telford, 91
Brantford (Canada), 270
Brereton, R. M., 296

309

Bridgewater, Duke of, 6–7, 14, 42, 48, 142, 288; will, 11n, 41–3, 117, 291, 296

Bridgewater Canal, xi, xiii, 14, 41, 42–43, 44, 46–9, 54–5, 58, 60, 64–6, 67–71, 75, 79–80, 88, 90–2, 96, 99, 112, 115, 118–21, 124, 131–2, 135, 141–3, 145–7, 287, 289; agreements, 119–120, 131–4, 135–7; rates, 119–20; tonnages, 119–20

Bright, John, 18

Brindley, James, 42, 288

Brora (Sutherland), xv, 173, 176–7, 184, 195, 205, 207, 222, 224, 226–7

Brougham, Henry, ix, 20–3, 30, 46, 61, 64, 89, 203, 209, 212, 229

Buckie (Banffshire), 273

Burghead (Moray), 178

Burn, John, 190

Buxton, N. K., 250

Byron, George Gordon, Lord, 10

Caird, James, 296

Caithness, 162, 165–6, 190, 207–8, 215, 217, 224, 242, 251, 266

Caledonian Canal, 225

Campbell, R. H., 157, 233

Canada, 181, 245, 247, 266, 268–70

Cape Breton Island, 267

Cape of Good Hope, 216

Carlisle, Earls of, 6, 10, 12, 29, 66, 77

Chalmers, Thomas, 30

Chandos, Marquis of, 59

Chat Moss (Lancashire), 76–7, 82

Chisholm, William, 187

Clapham, J. H., 119, 123

Clarence, Duke of, 239

Cleveland House (later Bridgewater House), 14, 192, 292

Clive, Lord, 73–4, 89, 96, 98, 103, 108, 115, 132

Cliveden House (Bucks.), 16, 294–5

Clunes, Major, 198

Clyne (Sutherland), 177, 214, 253

Clynelish (Sutherland), 227

Cobbett, William, 150, 240–1

Cockburn, Henry, 20

Coffin, Sir Edward, 268

Cootner, P. H., 120

Cork, Lady, 66

Coventry, 100

Cranstoun, Thomas, 179, 182–3, 185, 189

Creevey, Thomas, 8, 10, 15, 62–3

Criech (Sutherland), 163–4

Cromarty Estate, 272

Cromford Railway, 57

Cropper, James, 60, 82, 109, 130

Cubbit, William, 122

Culgower (Sutherland), 173

Culmailly (Sutherland), 171, 176, 187

Culrain (Ross), 213, 251–2

Cumming, James, 248

Currie, William Wallace, Mayor of Liverpool, 67, 81, 83–4, 86, 95–6, 99, 110, 112, 120, 125, 128

Dale, David, 167

Darling, F. F., 183

Dempster, George, 166–8, 170, 196

Derby, Lord, 55, 61, 63–4, 102

Devonshire, Duke of, 4

Dictionary of National Biography, 32

Disraeli, Benjamin, 16

Disruption of the Church, 253

Dornoch (Sutherland), 167, 173, 177, 180

Douglas, Sylvester, 10

Drainage Act Commissioners, 266–7

Drylaw, 19

Dudgeon, Thomas, of Fearn, 210–12, 214–15, 217, 253

Dudley, Lord, 28, 29

Dunbartonshire, 156

Dundas, Sir David, MP, 196, 259–60

Dundee, 224, 228

Dunrobin Castle (Sutherland), 10, 12, 14, 15, 16, 147, 162n, 166, 174, 241, 269, 272, 273, 294–5

Durness (Sutherland), 163, 251–2

Edderachyllis (Sutherland), 164, 169

Edinburgh, 51, 77, 153, 191, 209

Edinburgh Evening Courant, 161

Edinburgh Review, ix, 20–3

Edinburgh, University of, ix, 10, 178

Egerton, Lady Louisa, 7

Egerton, Lord Francis (formerly Leveson-Gower), 1st Earl of Ellesmere, 9, 10, 11n, 29, 42–4, 47–8, 52, 55, 69, 71, 91, 96, 99, 116, 120, 124, 142, 145; on Bradshaw, 44, 117; on canals, 116, 143; income, 118, 291; on land, 255–6, 283; on railways, 63, 73; on Sothern, 117, 131

Elgin, 173

Elgin Courier, 276
Elliot, Captain R., 267–8
Ellis, Lister, 60
Elphin (Sutherland), 243, 262, 270, 272, 287n
Escott, E. S., 34
Evelix (Sutherland), 205
Exchequer Loan Office, 75–8, 80–2, 126

Falconer, Cosmo, 173–5, 198
famine, potato, in Sutherland, 13
Farr (Sutherland), 163, 275
Fellner, W., 45n
Fife, 224, 226
Findlater, Rev., 237
Fisheries, British, 225; *see also* Sutherland Estate
Florida, 210
Fort George (Inverness-shire), 180, 215
Franklin, Benjamin, 174
Fraser, W., 150

Galloway, Earl of, 6
Garibaldi, 17–18
Gaskell, Philip, 155
Gilbert, the brothers, 42
Gladstone, John, 81–2
Glasgow, 124, 207, 222, 240, 265
Goldsmith, Oliver, 159
Golspie (Sutherland), 163, 171, 173, 177, 227
Gordon, Elizabeth, Countess of Sutherland (frequently referred to as Lady Stafford, and, after 1833, Duchess/Countess of Sutherland), 5, 8, 24, 31, 55, 147, 161, 166–8, 170, 186, 188, 193, 212, 214, 241, 244, 246, 249, 253, 293; admirers, 10; childhood, 9; descriptions of, 10; education, 10; on Highland improvement, 177, 200, 203, 206, 243; and Huskisson, 69–70
Gordon, Joseph, 218
Gordon, Robert, 188, 205
Gordon, Sir Robert, 150, 222
Gordon, William, 17th Earl of Sutherland, 9
Gower, Earl, Viscount Trentham, 6
Gower, Lord Ronald, 15
Gower, Thomas, 5
Graham, Thomas, 66

Grampound, 27
Grand Junction Canal, 45–6
Grand Junction Railway, xiii, 111, 113, 121–2, 124, 133, 140, 144
Grant, Charles, 20
Grant, MacPherson, 197
Gray, Malcolm, 150, 153, 222
Grenville, Lord, 24
Greville, Charles, 12, 17
Grey, Lord, 24, 30, 279
Grimble, Ian, 32, 155
Grocers Company, 86
Grubmore (Sutherland), 203
Gruids (Sutherland), 214–15
Gunn, George, 203, 237, 241–2, 244, 247, 253, 260, 264, 286
Gunn, John of Knockfin, 187
Gurney, Goldsworthy, 89

Hebrides, 246
Helmsdale (Sutherland), 173, 177, 191–2, 201, 205, 207, 212, 222, 287
Henderson, John, 165, 176
Hetton, 57
Highland Destitution Committee, 267
Highlands: agriculture, 153; archaeological evidence, 160; clearances, 150–1, 155–8, 177n; emigration, 157; exports, 153; fuel, 225n; Highland problem, 150, 297; industries, 156, 167; introduction of commercial sheep farming, 156, 167; landlords, 153, 158; landownership, 153; land reform, 275–6, 296; population, 153–6; potatoes, 155, 157, 246, 262, 265; prices, 156, 158, 196, 224–5, 228–31, 250; racial aspect, 153n, 178, 239, 257, 275, 286; statistical evidence, 160; villages for, 167–8, 170
Hill, Lord George, 261
Hobsbawm, E. J., 123
Hopeman (Moray), 171
Horner, Francis, 20–1, 31, 157n
Horsburgh, Robert, 245, 253, 256, 260, 269
Huddersfield, 240
Huskisson, William, xii, 10, 28, 30, 96–8, 99, 110; death, 101–2; influence on Stafford interest, 69–72; on railways, 59, 60, 63–4, 74, 79, 81, 127

India, 23, 218
Inverness, 183–4, 192–3, 230
Inverness Journal, 219
Inverugie (Moray), 172
Ireland, 58, 87, 132, 223, 232, 244, 261, 264, 266, 268

Jackman, W. T., 44, 111
James, William, 50–1
Jessop, 57, 76

Keith, Viscount, 29
Kennedy, Andrew, 219
Kenworthy Company, 86
Kildonan (Sutherland), xvi, 179–83, 193, 198, 205, 222, 224
Killingworth, 57
Kintradwell (Sutherland), 173
Kirkby Moss (Lancashire), 60
Knight, Charles, 34
Knockan (Sutherland), 243, 262, 270, 272, 286n
Knockglass (Sutherland), 173
Knox, John, 161, 165

Labouchere, Henry, President of the Board of Trade, 137
Lairg (Sutherland), 170, 247
Lancashire, 44, 49, 52, 76, 87, 95, 151, 167, 221
Lane End (Staffordshire), 289
Lavergne, L. de, 33, 277
Leck Robie, 269
Lee, Thomas Eyre, 51–2, 62, 73, 88–9, 98, 100–1, 107, 122
Leith, 224
Lerwick (Shetland), 162n
Leslie, Angus, 276
Leveson, Sir John, 5
Leveson-Gower, George Granville, 2nd Marquis of Stafford, 1st Duke of Sutherland (1758–1833), 39, 42, 51, 53, 55, 57, 62, 64, 107, 172–6, 180, 189, 201–2, 215, 236; canal investments, 64–5, 88, 100, 116, 289; death, 241, 243, 291; diplomatic career, 8; education, 8; family origins, 5; health, 8, 48, 104, 235; Highland expenditures, 170, 182–3, 197, 203, 206, 209, 216, 226–9, 231–233, 237; 'Leviathan of Wealth', phrase used, 4, 12, 18; marriage, 5, 166; marriage settlements, 291;

political views, 8; railway investment, 67–73, 84, 89, 94, 100, 104, 111; wealth, 4, 13, 43, 80, 118, 166, 169, 222, 288
Leveson-Gower, George Granville, 2nd Duke of Sutherland (1786–1861), (referred to as Lord Gower until 1833), 58, 70, 73, 91, 93, 212, 248, 251, 261; canal investments, 122, 296; character, 12; deafness, 13; death, 13; expenditures in Sutherland, 146, 255, 258–9, 269; on his finances, 271–2, 293–5; on Highland affairs, 255, 257–61, 262, 266; inheritance, 11, 47, 55, 71, 118, 292; marriage, 12, 291; railway investments, 128–9, 139–40, 145, 147, 294, 296; wealth, 17, 118, 128, 292–6
Leveson-Gower, George Granville William, 3rd Duke of Sutherland (1828–92), 13, 296
Leveson-Gower, Granville, 2nd Earl Gower, 1st Marquis of Stafford (1721–1803): created Marquis, 7; family connections, 6–7; 'Gower Party', 7; as industrialist, 42; marriages, 7; political background, 6
Leveson-Gower, Harriet, 2nd Duchess of Sutherland (daughter of Earl of Carlisle) (1806–68), 12, 17, 258, 275, 293–4
Leveson-Gower, Sir John, Baron Gower, 6
Leveson-Gower, Sir William, 5
Lichfield, 289
Lilleshall (Shropshire), 6, 14, 15, 16, 197, 291, 294
Liverpool, xi, xii, 41, 44, 46, 47, 49, 51, 59–60, 65, 77, 87, 95, 265
Liverpool Advertiser, 54
Liverpool and Birmingham Junction Canal, *see* Birmingham and Liverpool Junction Canal
Liverpool and Birmingham Railway, proposals for, 101, 102, 103, 104
Liverpool Corn Exchange, 49
Liverpool and Manchester Railway, 47, 151; agreements with canals, 112, 131–3, 135; amalgamation ideas, 113, 121–2, 133, 144–5; attitude to Stafford's investment, 95, 98, 103, 113, 128–9, 139; carriers' offers, 85–86; construction, 75–7; costs of

Liverpool & Man. Railway—*continued*
pioneering, 59–60, 95n, 106, 110, 124, 129; described as Liverpool Railway Company, 55; efficiency, 111n, 128–9, 136; extension, 90, 95, 98–9, 103, 111, 139; formation, xii, 49–51, 54, 91; Liverpool and Manchester interest, 60–1; Lord Stafford's investment, 67, 75, 92, 94, 103, 147, 288–9; opening, 102; parliamentary battle, 56–9, 61–4, 66–74; profits, 119, 124–6, 145; railway competition, 109, 111, 113–114, 120–1, 123–5, 127–30, 138, 144; raising capital for, 67, 75, 78–82, 110–11, 124–8, 140; rates, 74, 79, 137; shareholdings in, 61n, 66n, 67, 92; share prices, 102, 112, 118, 125, 128, 140, 145; Telford's examination, 81–2; ten per cent clause, 60–1, 74, 79–81, 86, 109, 124–9; traffic on, 109, 112, 119, 132, 141, 143

Loch, George (father of James), 19–20

Loch, George (son of James), 124n, 128, 134, 136, 143, 248, 261, 279

Loch, George (family historian), 32

Loch, James: his *Account*, 159, 189–90, 196, 209, 227n, 239, 277; on architects, 292; on aristocracy, xvii, 26–8, 30, 256, 297; on Bradshaw, 100, 114–15; on canal capital, 96–7, 122, 144; on chartism, 30; critics, 32–3, 118, 139, 275; on critics, 33, 275–6; on crofting, 205–6, 224, 271; death, 278–9; dreams, xviii, 142, 278; education, ix, 20–1; on education, 27; on emigration, 216–218, 243, 261; on engines, 77; on estate management, 25–6, 31–2; on famine, x, 262–73; on free trade, 28, 30, 59, 225, 230; on Highlanders, x, xv, xvi, xviii, 151, 198, 204–5, 208, 210, 212–13, 227, 228, 230–1, 244, 261, 277; on improvement, 22, 23, 47, 188–9, 191, 206, 215–16, 272; on India, 23; on James Anderson, 252; on land, x, xvii, 256, 288–9, 291; legal training, 22–4; on locomotives, 52, 57, 83; Lord Grey's testimonial, 279; Moss on, 127; on old age, 261; opinions on, 29; parents,

19–20; in parliament, 258–9; parliamentary career, 29; on political economy, 31, 221, 263–4; political views, x, 27–8, 30; on population, xi, 31, 263; on posterity, 34; on railway costs, 77–8, 89; on relief provision, 202, 262–73; on rent, 26, 29; responsibilities, 105, 158, 178, 195–7, 283; salary, 25; on Sellar, 192, 195, 200, 206, 209; on steampower, 84; strategy on railway/canal affairs, 41, 42, 53, 56–7, 64–5, 68–72, 75, 86, 88–93, 94–5, 100–1, 103, 113–15, 118–19, 124–5, 131, 135–6, 141–3, 146, 297; on Sutherland development, 220–2, 237–8, 254–5, 273, 277–8, 284, 286, 297; on Sutherland scenery, 136, 236; on Telford, 108, 122; on transport economics, xii, 46, 57, 65, 68, 134, 226, 229

Lochinver (Sutherland), 183

London, xi, 12, 14, 47, 51, 89, 91, 153, 180, 209, 260

London and North-Western Railway, xiv

Lorne, Marchioness of, 261, 265

Loth (Sutherland), 153n, 164, 177

Macclesfield Canal, 81

MacCulloch, Dr John, 159, 213, 238

McCulloch, J. R., 112, 210

MacDonald, 180–1

MacIver, Evander, 249n, 264, 269, 271, 279

Mackay, D. J., 150

Mackay, Captain Kenneth, 207–8, 211

Mackenzie, Alexander, 150, 177

Mackenzie, Rev. David, 189, 204–5

Mackid, Robert, 171, 179, 181–3, 185–195

Macleod, Donald, of Rossal, 34, 159, 177, 185, 190, 193, 232, 253, 275–6

Macleod, John, 252

Malthus, Thomas, 31

Manchester, xi, 41, 44, 46, 47, 49, 51, 61, 77, 79, 87, 107, 124–5, 130, 144, 240

Manchester Ship Canal, 119, 140

Marwade, Edris, 66

Marx, Karl, 34, 193, 276

Mather, F. C., 43n, 45n, 68n, 71, 119, 143, 147n

Mediterranean, 223
Meikle Ferry (Sutherland), 210
Mersey and Irwell Navigation Company, 45–6, 60, 74, 112, 120, 131, 135–9, 140–3
Military Register, 148, 160, 185, 189, 193, 194n
Miller, Hugh, 159, 165, 193, 253, 255
Mills, James, 81–2
Mitchell, Joseph, 159, 166, 239, 278
Montreal, 268
Moray, 171, 178, 229
Moray, Lord, 209
Morning Chronicle, 55
Morning Star, 180, 209
Morrison, James, M.P., 125
Moss, John, 50, 70n, 78–80, 81, 84, 87–90, 95, 100, 112–13, 114, 117, 121, 124, 126–8, 133, 136–7
Mull, 262
Mulock, Thomas, 31, 34, 274
Munro, William, 188
Munro of Novar, 213
Murray, John, 20

Napier Commission, 159, 248, 276, 296
Naworth Castle, 66
New Quay Company, 85–7
New South Wales, 216
New Statistical Account, 254, 259
New York, 219
Newcastle-under-Lyme, 290
Newfoundland, 170
Newport (Shropshire), 109
Newton (Lancashire), 111
Norbury Park (Staffordshire), 108
Norfolk Militia, 183
Northumberland, 57
Northumberland, Duke of, 4
Norway, 266
Nova Scotia, 216, 245

Old Quay Company, *see* Mersey and Irwell Navigation Company
Old Statistical Account, 162–3
Oldshores (Sutherland), 243

Paisley, 240
Peel, Sir Robert, 30, 84, 97, 99, 125
Pennant, Thomas, 155, 161
Perthshire, 156
Petty, Lord Henry, 20
Pickfords, 86

Pictou (Canada), 218, 268
Pitt, William, 7, 8, 10
Police Gazette, 189
Pollins, H., 111, 126, 140
Poole, Braithwaite, 39
Port Gower (Sutherland), 222
Portland, Duke of, 6
Portugal, 225
Prebble, John, 32
Pritt, 75–6, 81–3, 95, 100, 110

Quakers, 60, 130
Quarterly Review, 37, 51, 143

Railways: employment in Scotland, 267; as industrial organization, 134; related to the economy, xiv, 39–41, 123; and the state, 106, 109–10, 114, 124–5, 129, 134
Rainhill (Lancashire), trials at, 83, 85, 89, 96
Rastrick, John, 76, 83, 111
Rathbone, Theodore, 126–7, 130
Reay Estate, 164, 236–7, 246, 259, 277
Reay, Lord, 169, 206, 230, 237, 251, 289–91
Rennie, John, 76
Rhives (Sutherland), 180
Ricardo, David, x, 31, 288
rioting, 76, 179–83, 196, 207, 213–16, 251–2
Rogart (Sutherland), 164, 177
Rolt, L. T. C., 108
Ross, Sir Charles, of Balnagowan, 277
Ross, Donald, 157, 276
Ross, Gordon, 215
Ross, Walter, 253
Ross-shire, 200, 212, 246, 255, 277, 283
Roy, 187, 191–2, 203
Runcorn Gap, 99
Russell, Lord John, 27
Russell of Westfield, 178
Rutland, Duke of, 6

Sage, Alexander, 212
Sage, Donald, 159, 212
Sandars, Joseph, 50, 54, 61–2, 87, 102, 123, 129
Sandon, Lord, 125
Sanford, J. L. and Townsend, M., 13
Schumpeter, Joseph, 48
Scotia, 269
Scotsman, 209

Scott, Walter, 10, 11, 177

Scourie (Sutherland), 251, 264, 267, 271, 274

Sefton, Lord, 55, 61

Selkirk, Earl of, 167, 181, 184

Sellar, Patrick: attacked in print, 238; described, 178, 185–6, 191, 193–5, 199; early life, 178; on disruption, 254; on emigration, 201, 208, 216, 268; on famine, 177; on Highlanders, 184; as landowner, 250; and Mackid, 181–2, 186–94; on rents, 203; on rioting, 180, 252; as sheep farmer, 176, 178, 183, 199–200, 273–4; on sheep farming, 178, 206; on sportsmen, 249; plans, 171–5, 176; sacked, 194; the Sellar case, 183–96; trial, 192–4, 276n

Seymour, Lord, 134

Shaftesbury, Lord, 17, 229, 271, 277–8

Sharpe, C. K., 12, 146

Shelmore (Staffordshire), 107–8, 122

Shropshire, xi, 42, 46, 65, 105, 109, 195, 197, 289

Sidmouth, Lord, 179, 181

Sinclair, Sir John, 28, 156, 166, 196, 209

Sismondi, S. de, 29, 33

Skelbo (Sutherland), 173, 186

Skibo (Sutherland), 209

Smith, Adam, 31, 159, 163, 221, 233n, 263

Smith, Richard, 131

Smith, Sydney, 20

Sothern, James, 74, 81; resignation, 131; succeeds Bradshaw, 117, 120

South America, 24

South Australia, 248, 267

South Sea Bubble, 6

Southey, Robert, 33

Speculative Society, 20–1

Spence, Thomas, 29

Spinningdale (Sutherland), 167

Spitalfields, 17

Spring, David, 32

Stafford House, 4, 13, 14, 16, 17, 289, 292–3, 295

Staffordshire, 5, 8, 12, 15, 27, 33, 51, 105, 166, 195, 197, 226, 284, 289

Stephenson, George, 46–7, 51, 54–5, 58, 76–7, 82; Loch's opinion of, 82n, 83, 85, 109, 122, 130

Stewart, David of Garth, 34, 193; estates, 239; on Highland clearances, 238; publication by, 238; on Sellar, 239; slave plantations, 239; on slavery, 238

Stewart, Dugald, 21

Stittenham (Yorkshire), 5, 6

Stockton and Darlington Railway, 51, 77

Stoke, 15

Stowe, Harriet Beecher, 16, 34, 275, 277

Strath Halladale (Sutherland), 237

Strathbrora (Sunderland), 206–7, 215, 240

Strathnaver (Sutherland), 160–1, 165, 170, 178, 183–90, 193, 199, 203–4, 222, 236, 249

Strathy Estate (Sutherland), 169, 179, 204

Suther, Francis, 195, 203, 205–19

Sutherland, Alexander, 189

Sutherland Estate: capital imports, 221, 232–4, 241, 285, 296; cattle, 162–5, 180, 201, 203, 217, 227, 231, 239, 247; clearances, xv, xvi, 158–160, 169, 173, 178–83, 197, 203–5, 212–17, 243, 251, 256, 270, 272, 286–7; cottars, 274; emigration, 161, 174, 181, 205, 207–8, 216–19, 243, 246–8, 251–2, 264, 266–70; extent, 161; famine, 165, 173, 177, 182, 200–3, 219, 241–2, 245–6, 250–251, 262–73; fishing, xv, 164, 173, 176, 184, 201–2, 204, 207, 212, 222–225, 230, 237, 239–40, 251, 255, 259, 271, 274, 277–8, 285, 287; flax, 172–4; improvement plans, xv; industry, 171, 174, 176–7, 184, 191, 221, 225–9, 259, 271; interpretation of policies, 160, 238, 253–5, 279; introduction of sheep, 164, 169, 217, 277; land purchases, 177, 179; military service, 170n, 217, 230, 279; population, 162–4, 191, 201, 216n, 244–5; pre-clearances, 160–8, 287; relief, 202–4, 262–73; rents, 11, 162, 164, 166, 169, 172, 175–6, 184, 203–204, 217, 229–33, 235, 240, 249, 258–60, 270, 273, 287–8; resettlement zones, 169, 174, 182–3, 198, 203–4, 207, 223, 270; rioting, 179–183, 207, 213–16, 251–2; roads, 165–7, 229, 236; role of factors,

Sutherland Estate—*continued*
202; sheep farmers, 170, 176, 177n, 191, 198–9, 229–30, 250; size of farms, 237, 258, 261, 271, 273, 274; smallpox, 163, 251; squatters, 200; tacksmen, 161–2, 248–9; use of fire, 160, 185, 187–8, 206–9, 212; village system, 167–8, 172, 224f; whisky, 181, 183, 203–4, 227, 239
Sutherland, House of: aristocratic connections, 12; art collection, 14; attacked on religious grounds, 253; conspicuous consumption, 4, 16, 18, 145, 283, 285, 293–5; decline, 13, 296; dynastic difficulties, 41, 47, 71, 91–2, 105, 116, 118, 121, 147n, 148; English estates, xiv; expenditure, ix, 14, 296; Highland emigration, 217–219; Highland investments, xvi, 13, 37, 171, 181, 225, 231–4; in Industrial Revolution, 37, 283, 285; political role, 284, 290; railway investment, xii, 13, 37, 41, 285; Sellar's trial, 192; territories, xiv, 13
Sutherland Transatlantic Friendly Society, 210–13
Syre (Sutherland), 203

Telford, Thomas, xiii, 56, 65, 67, 76, 78, 81, 88, 91–2, 98, 103, 107–9, 122, 178
Thompson, E. P., 159
Thomson, Poulett, President of Board of Trade, 125, 127
Thurso (Caithness), 187
Tierney, George, 23
Times, The, xvi, 50, 256–7
Tiree, 262
Tongue (Sutherland), 34, 163, 272, 274
trade conditions, 75–6, 87, 116, 122, 129, 135–6, 138
Tremadoc (North Wales), 177

Trent and Mersey Canal, 123, 138
Trentham (Staffordshire), 5, 6, 14, 15, 16, 197, 226, 231, 284, 289, 292, 294
Trevelyan, Sir Charles, 265–8

Unapool (Sutherland), 214

Van Diemen's Land, 216
Victoria, Queen, 17, 269, 295

Walker, 83, 111n
Warrington, 111
Warrington and Newton Railroad, 121
Webster, Alexander, 162
Wellington, Duke of, 99, 231
West Indies, 223, 239, 255
Wester Garty (Sutherland), 173
Westminster Review, 253
Wharncliffe, Lord, 29
Wick Burghs, 28, 30, 224, 266, 275
Wilberforce, W., 210
Winter, Gilbert, 115
Worsley (Lancashire), 112
Wrottesley, Sir John, 122
Wynn, Lady Williams, 165, 170–1

York, Archbishop of, 62, 70
York, Duke of, 16, 289–90
Yorkshire, 76, 79, 228, 265
Young, Charles, 240
Young, William, 177, 225; appointed agent, 171; criticized and sacked, 194–5; defends clearances, 182–3; described, 178; on Highlanders, 171–5, 179, 184; on improvements, 184, 187, 221; plans, 171–5, 229; threatens to resign, 191; to Wales, 176

Zorra (Canada), 270

STUDIES IN SOCIAL HISTORY

Editor: HAROLD PERKIN

Professor of Social History, University of Lancaster

Assistant Editor: ERIC J. EVANS

Lecturer in History, University of Lancaster

ANCIENT CRETE: A Social History from Early Times until the Roman Occupation — R. F. Willetts

CHILDREN IN ENGLISH SOCIETY, VOL. I: From Tudor Times to the Eighteenth Century — I. Pinchbeck & M. Hewitt

CHILDREN IN ENGLISH SOCIETY, VOL. II: From the Eighteenth Century to the Children Act 1948 — I. Pinchbeck & M. Hewitt

CHURCHES AND THE WORKING CLASSES IN VICTORIAN ENGLAND — K. S. Inglis

EDUCATION IN RENAISSANCE ENGLAND — Kenneth Charlton

ENGLISH LANDED SOCIETY in the Eighteenth Century — G. E. Mingay

ENGLISH LANDED SOCIETY in the Nineteenth Century — F. M. L. Thompson

ENGLISH PARISH CLERGY ON THE EVE OF THE REFORMATION — P. Heath

FROM CHARITY TO SOCIAL WORK in England and the United States — Kathleen Woodroofe

HEAVENS BELOW: Utopian Experiments in England, 1560–1960 — W. H. G. Armytage

A HISTORY OF SHOPPING — Dorothy Davis

THE IMPACT OF RAILWAYS ON VICTORIAN CITIES — J. R. Kellett

THE ORIGINS OF MODERN ENGLISH SOCIETY, 1780–1880 — H. Perkin